CITIZEN
EXTRAORDINAIRE

Affectionately yours

1912

CITIZEN EXTRAORDINAIRE

The Diplomatic Diaries of
VANCE McCORMICK
in London and Paris, 1917–1919
With Other Documents from a High-Minded American Life

EDITED BY MICHAEL BARTON
with Cherie Fieser, Susan Meehan, and Teresa Weisser

STACKPOLE
BOOKS

Published by
STACKPOLE BOOKS
5067 Ritter Road
Mechanicsburg, PA 17055
www.stackpolebooks.com

Printed in the United States of America.

10 9 8 7 6 5 4 3 2 1

FIRST EDITION

♾ The paper used in this publication meets the minimum requirements of the American National Standard for Information Sciences—Permanence of Paper for Printed Library Materials, ANSI Z39.48-1984.

Frontispiece: Vance McCormick in 1916. The picture, signed "Affectionately yours," may have been one of several he intended for colleagues in Woodrow Wilson's re-election campaign, which he managed successfully. HISTORICAL SOCIETY OF DAUPHIN COUNTY

Library of Congress Cataloging-in-Publication Data

McCormick, Vance Criswell, 1872–1946.
    Citizen extraordinaire : the diplomatic diaries of Vance McCormick in London and Paris, 1917–1919, with other documents from a high-minded American life / edited by Michael Barton . . . [et al.].— 1st ed.
        p.   cm.
    Includes bibliographical references and index.
    ISBN 0-8117-0121-2
    1. McCormick, Vance Criswell, 1872–1946—Diaries.   2. McCormick, Vance Criswell, 1872–1946—Archives.   3. Diplomats—United States—Diaries.   4. Diplomats—England—London—Diaries.   5. Diplomats—France—Paris—Diaries.   6. World War, 1914–1918—Diplomatic history—Sources.   7. United States—Foreign relations—1913–1921—Sources.   8. Politicians—Pennsylvania—Archives.   9. Pennsylvania—Politics and government—1865–1950—Sources.   10. Harrisburg (Pa.)—Biography.   I. Barton, Michael.   II. Title.
E748.M1463A3   2004
940.3'2273'092—dc22

                                                                        2004004929

CONTENTS

The McCormick Family Papers Project

Michael Barton

This volume on the life of Vance McCormick is part of the McCormick Family Papers Project, co-sponsored by the Historical Society of Dauphin County, the Center for Pennsylvania Culture Studies at the Pennsylvania State University at Harrisburg, and the McCormick Family Foundation. The story behind this achievement, sketched here, shows how serendipity and generosity, as well as curiosity and energy, surely figure in historical research.

I had been associated with the Historical Society since the early 1980s, first as a neighbor, then as a member, and eventually as trustee and president. When a book I wrote (*Life by the Moving Road: An Illustrated History of Greater Harrisburg*) featured my research in the society's archives, it occurred to Prof. Simon Bronner, coordinator of the American Studies program at Penn State Harrisburg, that our graduate students should make use of those archives. Working there would give them experience in dealing with original documents: handling them, transcribing them, editing them, and using them as evidence in scholarly essays and theses. It would also integrate local history with our interdisciplinary American Studies program. So in 1991, I began ushering students to the society's headquarters in the John Harris/Simon Cameron Mansion in Harrisburg, in conjunction with my graduate seminar in Nineteenth-Century American Civilization. This arrangement depended on the kindness of the society, because my seminar met in the evening, and we needed a staff member, working overtime, to assist us.

One of the collections made available to us was the McCormick Family Papers, consisting of nine boxes of letters, diaries, photographs, official documents, newspaper clippings, and other similar materials. The Historical Society had begun receiving artifacts and documents from family members, such as Anne and Vance McCormick, before 1938, which was when the Historical Records Survey, directed by the New Deal's Works Progress Administration, sent Mrs. Clive H. Smith to begin the cataloguing of the McCormick Collection, as it was then called. In 1993, shortly after my graduate students began working there, Peter Seibert, executive director of the Historical Society (and a graduate of our American Studies master's program), pointed out to me that a new trove of McCormick materials had recently been donated to the society by Louisa Finney France, the daughter of Eliza McCormick Finney. Her generosity prompted me to have the students immediately concentrate their editorial labors on the McCormick papers.

The McCormicks were one of the leading families of south-central Pennsylvania for two hundred years. Thomas McCormick (1702–62) was the first of the lineage to emigrate from Ireland, arriving on the west shore of the Susquehanna River in Cumberland County, Pennsylvania, about 1745. He farmed there, as did his son James (1729–1802) and James's son William (1766–1805). Of the Scots-Irish immigrants in general, the genealogist Leander McCormick wrote that "the most prominent feature in their general character was the intensity of their religious feeling. They seem to have united the impulsive ardor of the Irish with the keen and cool intellectual perception and shrewdness of the Scotch," an ethnic caricature that might be censored today. A descendant also named James McCormick (1832–1917), writing to his son Donald (1868–1945) at Yale, simply called his ancestors Thomas, James, and William "plain good farmers."

It was the fourth generation, led by William's son James McCormick (1801–70), that took the family into Harrisburg and its commerce. A graduate of Princeton, he was admitted to the bar in 1823 and became a successful attorney. By 1840, he was president of Dauphin Deposit Bank, and by the 1850s, he was also president of the Harrisburg Bridge Company and the Harrisburg Cotton Company, and owner of the Paxton Iron

Works and the West Fairview Nail Works. Luther Reily Kelker reports, in his *History of Dauphin County,* that on his retirement, James "devoted his attention to the management of a large estate, consisting of furnaces, grist mills, rolling mills, and farms. All of these interests were successfully controlled by him in a most masterly and systematic manner," despite his blindness. He was also a trustee of Pine Street Presbyterian Church in Harrisburg, associating the family with that institution for the rest of their lives.

Subsequent generations capitalized on James's successes and distributed them among family members. His son Henry (1831–1900) continued as president of the bank, iron works, and nail works, and was trustee of the McCormick Trust. Usually referred to as Colonel, Henry was a graduate of Yale (the McCormicks had come to consider Princeton too parochial) and a veteran of the Civil War. Henry's brother James (1832–1917) was also president of Dauphin Deposit Bank and a trustee of the McCormick Trust. The McCormicks also became linked to another prominent Harrisburg family when Henry's sister Mary (1834–74) married J. Donald Cameron (1833–1918), a banker and railroad president who served as U.S. senator from 1877 to 1897. J. Donald was the son of Simon Cameron, a U.S. senator before and after the Civil War, the secretary of war, and ambassador to Russia. The Camerons, like the McCormicks, were deeply involved in the management of local banking, ironmaking, and railroading.

The sixth American generation of McCormicks consisted of the children of James and Henry. James had four sons: Donald (1868–1945), still another James (1863–1943), Henry Jr. (1862–1939), and Robert (1878–1925). Those four sons had interests in Dauphin Deposit Bank, the Harrisburg Bridge Company, Paxton Flour Mills, McCormick Farms, and Paxton Iron and Steel Company, and as well as ties to Yale University and Pine Street Presbyterian Church. Col. Henry McCormick's children included sons Henry B. (1869–1941) and Vance (1872–1946), and daughter Anne (1879–1964); three other offspring died in their infancy or youth.

The Colonel had tried his hand at politics, but it was his son Vance who tried and won. After graduating from Yale in 1893, Vance helped manage the family's interests, becoming a director of the Central Iron and Steel Works in south Harrisburg. When the opportunity came to run for city council, he took it and won, and then ran as the Democratic candidate for mayor in 1902, in a now famous reform campaign. He stepped away from management of Central Iron and Steel temporarily but went into newspaper publishing permanently, purchasing the Harrisburg *Patriot* a decent interval after the mayoral election, and founding the Harrisburg *Evening News* some years later. He came to be highly regarded as a candidate for governor of Pennsylvania in 1914, chairman of the Democratic National Committee in 1916, manager of President Woodrow Wilson's reelection campaign in 1916, director of the War Trade Board coordinating the blockade of Germany in World War I, a member of the 1917 House Mission to Europe to plan war strategy, and Wilson's advisor at the Paris Peace Conference in 1919.

By 1995, as the students' editorial work on the McCormick family's documents began to accumulate, Professor Bronner and I began to imagine that their research projects might someday be brought together in a book. We believed publication would give our students the chance to show their work, give scholars the opportunity to learn about the McCormick papers, and give greater recognition at large to the roles that members of this distinguished and accomplished family played in local, national, and international history.

In 2000, Prof. William Mahar, then director of Penn State Harrisburg's School of Humanities, knowing much about our work, began discussions with representatives of the McCormick Family Foundation. It was his thought that they might be willing to offer their financial support to the project and a subvention for an eventual publication. Led by Larry Hartman of the former Dauphin Deposit Bank, now M & T Bank, the McCormick Family Foundation subsequently approved our formal proposal and awarded a grant to the McCormick Family Papers Project. Their generosity has made it possible for Stackpole Books to publish this volume, which Stackpole's staff and I believed should feature the personal papers of Vance McCormick, the most historically significant member of the family.

The foundation's financial support has also made possible the construction and maintenance of an Internet website where McCormick family documents that could not be included in the book are now available to the public. This was another inspiration of Professor Bronner. The website includes myriad materials, such as the diaries of Col. Henry McCormick, Vance's father; letters of Eliza Buehler McCormick, his grandmother; letters of William McCormick, his cousin; and letters of James McCormick, his uncle. Photographs of family members also appear there. The website was developed by MaryAlice Bitts, a Penn State Harrisburg graduate student and professional webmaster. Its address is www.hbg.psu.edu/hum/McCormick/index2.htm.

From 1991 to 2000, forty American Studies graduate students worked on the McCormick Family Papers and McCormick-related documents while enrolled in my research seminar. They were, in chronological order: LeRoy Toddes, John Denniston, Scott Briell, Craig Cassel, Anne Marie Ickes, Claire Messimer, Kenneth Patrick, Jeffrey Seiler, Willis Shirk, Cathay Snyder, Casimer Sowa, Gary Tuma, Margaret DeAngelis, Christine Swisher, William J. Switala Jr., Robert Vassian, Jeffrey Waring, David Weyl, Joyce White, Beth Bisbano, Karen Horner, S. Luke Kempski, Leta Maloney, Eric Mark, Bob McCullough, Daryl Umberger, Anita Paynter, Richter Voight, Eugenia Lohss, Joanne Beaver, Richard Berrier Jr., Thomas Clark, Brian Moore, Mike Smith, Art Titzel, Sara Good, Mary Keat, Susan Eyster Meehan, Teresa Weisser, and Jason Wilson. The results of their labors are in this book, on the McCormick website, at the Historical Society, or in other publications of their own.

Three of these seminar students wrote articles that were published in scholarly journals: LeRoy W. Toddes, "Vance McCormick's Relationship with Woodrow Wilson: A View through Their Correspondence"; and Margaret DeAngelis, "William McCormick, Friend of Youth." Another publication outlet for student work begun in my seminar was the inaugural issue of *Susquehanna Heritage: A Journal of the Historical Society of Dauphin County,* launched in the summer of 2003 with support from the McCormick Foundations and the Center for Pennsylvania Culture Studies at Penn State–Harrisburg. That issue, of which I was guest editor, focused on "The McCormicks of Harrisburg" and featured three articles by former seminar students: the master's project of Thomas Clark, "Cleaning Up Harrisburg: The Good Government Reforms of Mayor Vance C. McCormick, 1902–1903"; the master's project of Art Titzel, "The Ablest Navigator: The Rise of Vance McCormick in the Wilson Years"; and the seminar paper of Gary Tuma, "William McCormick's Work with Working Boys." The fourth article in the journal, by Emily Murphy, "'I am Raising Boys . . . Not Grass': The McCormick Homes in Central Pennsylvania," was completed in another course taught by Prof. Irwin Richman, then senior member of our American Studies program and still an authority on Pennsylvania's arts and architecture.

The grant from the McCormick Foundations in 2000 made it possible to employ the following eleven American Studies graduate students, who worked energetically on the McCormick papers outside my graduate seminar: Emily Murphy, Angela Minner, Gino Pasi, Amy Miller, Amy Fox, Leann Fawver, Hattie Charley, Melissa Fisher, Kathryn Kingsbury, Karen Tickner, and Stephanie Patterson Gilbert. In addition to transcribing more McCormick manuscripts, they did all that was required to adapt the seminar students' work for inclusion either in this volume or on the McCormick website.

The editorial methodology for the transcription of the McCormick Papers and the guidelines for the preparation of the final draft of the book manuscript were expertly developed by Cherie Fieser for the students.

Three American Studies graduate students played particulary valuable roles in the McCormick project, and I have decided they deserve to be listed as coeditors of this volume because their contributions during their course work and afterward have been extensive and crucial. Cherie Fieser did independent studies with the McCormick papers and has worked alongside me since the early 1990s. She located, organized, and edited McCormick documents from the Historical Society and around the country. She is now Assistant to the Director of the Murray Library at Messiah College and a freelance editor. Susan Meehan, a seminar student, did extra duty, producing in-depth studies and annotations on Vance McCormick's diaries, and discovering supplemental materials in U.S. government archives. She is now an independent historical researcher and the author of the recently published book *The New Way: Greeks Come to Carlisle, Pennsylvania*. Teresa Weisser, another seminar student, also did extra duty, researching and annotating Vance McCormick's diaries, using all her bibliographical skills. She is now a librarian at Millersville University. The three of them were model students; indeed, they were much more than students.

That makes fifty-two students, in sum, who can be certified as having worked on the McCormick Family Papers Project from 1991 to 2004 (some creative accounting could probably put the number higher). I told them at the end of each semester how grateful I was for their work, and how I hoped that doing their research had made them better historians. I also promised to list them in the book when it was finally published. Their end of the bargain was much more demanding than mine.

At the Historical Society of Dauphin County, staff members provided indispensable assistance. In particular, we want to thank Gary Smith, executive director, for his cooperation and guidance; Robert D. Hill, Director of Collections (and an American Studies master's graduate of Penn State

Harrisburg), for his continuing assistance and expertise; Warren Wirebach, society librarian, for his help throughout the project, especially during the evenings when students were working on their assignments; Mary Parry, volunteer archivist, now Mrs. Louis Joseph Jackubowski, for her initial work cataloging the collection; and Louise Owen, current archivist of the McCormick Family Papers (and also supported by the McCormick Foundations), for sharing with us her expert knowledge of the manuscript collection and her crucial advice. The trustees of the society, in addition to allowing us to work both day and night in the archives, have granted us permission to publish the papers and the many photographs in this volume. Without their cooperation and their service to the society, this project could not even have been conceived.

In Harrisburg, Spencer G. Nauman Jr., eminent attorney and stepgrandson of Vance McCormick, provided us with vital information and materials as the project neared conclusion. Lewis Lehrman, formerly of Harrisburg and now Greenwich, Connecticut, was once a student of Vance McCormick's career and now, through the Gilder Lehrman Institute, is a distinguished supporter of the work of other historians. He generously contributed to our project as soon as he heard about it.

At the Yale University Library, Danelle Moon, staff member in manuscripts and archives, gave us perfectly professional service when we did research there and when we consulted her afterward.

Our editor at Stackpole Books, Kyle R. Weaver (also an alumnus of Penn State Harrisburg's American Studies graduate program), was supportive from the beginning. Judith M. Schnell, Stackpole's editorial director, made the beginning with them possible. Our copyeditor, Joyce Bond, was eagle-eyed and caught all our mistakes.

Finally, there is our essential obligation to the McCormicks themselves, and their kin, who began literally creating this heritage two hundred years ago, and then opened their lives to us by contributing their papers to the society. Owing so much to so many, past and present, is a great debt, but also an honor.

About This Book

Without including any notes or commentary, McCormick had a limited number of copies of his 1917 and 1919 diaries privately printed and distributed to his associates in late 1919 or the early 1920s. The title of that first edition is *Diaries of Vance C. McCormick, Member of the American War Mission to Inter-Allied Conference in London and Paris: and Adviser to President Wilson and the Peace Conference in Paris, in 1919.* The 1917 diary is found on pages 3–24, and the 1919 diary, pages 27–121. McCormick's purpose in keeping the diaries appears on the first page:

> These diaries were kept for the purpose of giving my Mother and members of my Family a connected narrative of my activities and observations during the stirring days of this period of the World War and of the Peace Conference, which would have been difficult to do in correspondence. It is preserved in this form for whatever value it may possess and is lovingly dedicated to my Mother.

Today a few research libraries hold these printed copies, including the Library of Congress and the Yale University Library, which is the repository of Vance McCormick's official papers. One may assume there were original handwritten and typescript copies of the diary, but they have never been documented or located. Our edition follows, verbatim, a printed copy of the diary owned by the Historical Society of Dauphin County in Harrisburg, Pennsylvania, where the McCormick Family Papers are kept. We have made a few changes in punctuation and, more important, added introductions, notes, and glossaries that identify significant persons and places mentioned in the diaries.

The editorial work on the 1917 diary was a team effort. Susan Meehan transcribed the diary, wrote the notes, helped with the introduction, and found illustrations. Teresa Weisser authored the bulk of the introduction and researched and wrote the glossary of names and places. Gino Pasi also provided material for the glossary. All three contributors, Meehan, Weisser, and Pasi, were graduate students in the American Studies Program at Penn State Harrisburg when they did this work as part of the McCormick Family Papers Project. Professor Barton was editor of the final draft of the 1917 diary.

Susan Meehan took the lead in annotating the 1919 diary and preparing the glossary of names and places mentioned in it. Other students contributing to the glossary were Joanne Beaver, Arthur Titzel, Thomas Clark, Mike Smith, and Karen Tickner. Cherie Fieser researched documents relating to the 1919 diary and McCormick's contributions to the peace conference. Professor Barton was responsible for the introduction to, and the final editing of, the 1919 diary.

The final documents that follow the two diaries were edited over the course of the project by Professor Barton and Cherie Fieser. Their contents and contexts are explained in the headnotes. They feature observations of McCormick made by his contemporaries, particularly journalists, throughout his life.

For God, for Country, for Yale, and for Harrisburg
The Loyalties of Vance McCormick

Michael Barton

When introducing a well-known subject to readers who may already be well informed about it, the author's challenge is to say something fresh. Such is the case here with writing about Vance Criswell McCormick. Journalist-historian Paul B. Beers has written a fact-filled essay, "Vance McCormick . . . The All-American," which is a chapter in his *Profiles from the Susquehanna Valley*. The inaugural issue of *Susquehanna Heritage: A Journal of the Historical Society of Dauphin County,* published in the summer of 2003, contains two essays about McCormick, by Thomas Clark and Art Titzel. And Prof. Gerald G. Eggert's *Harrisburg Industrializes: The Coming of Factories to an American Community,* the unrivaled account of the McCormick family's economic influence on Harrisburg, contains much detail on Vance's interests. Furthermore, we are including in this volume some campaign biographies of McCormick, as well as the authoritative obituary published in the *Patriot* in June 1946. All of these sources make it unnecessary to retell here the main facts of McCormick's life.

The previously published research deals mainly with his political and diplomatic achievements. Our goal here is to create a better understanding of Vance McCormick as a Yale man, a social patrician, and an American moralist, for we believe those were his distinctive loyalties, alongside his commitment to his family and his nation. To that end, we give a more

1

detailed review of his football career, taking into account its cultural context; we discuss his social life, including his activities both inside and outside Harrisburg; and finally, we consider the ethical positions he took throughout his career, especially as those positions would seem to have complicated that career. We are bold to say, this perspective is one McCormick himself might have agreed to.

A Man for the Fall Season

When Vance McCormick campaigned for political office in the early 1900s, the newspapers, looking for an angle, headlined him as a former football player. Said the Harrisburg *Star-Independent*: At Yale, "they still talk of him . . . with glistening eyes," remembering that "the Sunday supplements printed his picture in a dozen different positions." The *New York Times* noted that the "stalwart figure" had "not let his sturdy body lose a particle of its vim and strength." In a line good enough for a song, their reporter wrote, "He looks a whole lot like a man." McCormick, in fact, had been a famous footballer at Yale in the 1890s, and he continued to play on those experiences during his later public life. Even his obituaries dwelled on his athletic prowess.

He was nicknamed "Little Vance," even though at 5 feet, 6 inches tall and 165 pounds, he was not much smaller than his teammates. "Pudge" Heffelfinger, the country's first true football star, playing just before McCormick, was 6 feet, 3 inches and 205 pounds, but Frank Hinkey, known as the "disembodied spirit" during McCormick's years, weighed just 150 pounds. Protected only by slight pads and a thin leather helmet during the sometimes fatal "flying wedge" era, Little Vance blocked for keeps, played defense to perfection, and booted winning field goals. He was called "one of the greatest goal kickers Yale ever had," once defeating Princeton with a forty-yard dropkick between the uprights.

During his senior year, McCormick was captain of the team. Yale's first game that season was with Wesleyan on October 5, 1892. McCormick played quarterback on offense and behind the line on defense. His first act to gain the *Yale Daily News* reporter's attention was his recovery of Wesleyan's fumble on its second possession. Subsequently, he was mentioned twice for his blocking ("running interference"). In the second half, he was replaced at quarterback by G. T. Adee, and C. D. Bliss scored Yale's only touchdown near the end of game when his teammates shoved him over the goal line, a common tactic before the rules disallowed it. They had expected a better victory than 6–0, and the reporter complained of a "lack of teamwork."

Their second game, on October 8, was against Crescent in front of three thousand fans. Yale won, 28–0. "The strong points of Yale's play," said the *Yale Daily News,* were McCormick's offense, but again he was a force on defense: "The Crescents at one time came within one yard of scoring but lost the ball to Yale, McCormick breaking through and getting it."

Against Williams four days later, on October 12, McCormick was hurt and replaced by Adee. The Eli won again, 32–0, maintaining their perfect defense against scoring.

Against the Manhattan Athletic Club three days later, on October 15, McCormick was again saluted for his tackling: He "broke through" once to stop the MAC runner for no gain, and later stopped a punt. McCormick "retired in favor of Adee" in the second half. Yale 22, MAC 0.

Amherst was the opponent on October 19. McCormick was cited in the paper for breaking through their arms-linked linemen and stopping the V-shaped flying wedge on the first play of the game. Adee again relieved McCormick in the second half, and again Yale won, 29–0.

Yale defeated the Orange Athletic Club on October 22 by a score of 58–0. McCormick played the entire game at quarterback, but his press notices were for his tackling—once for a loss of five yards, another time for stopping the wedge—and blocking, running interference for Yale's first touchdown.

McCormick didn't play against the Springfield YMCA on October 26. Yale won a "very uninteresting game," 50–0. Neither did he play against Tufts on October 29, which Yale defeated 44–0, nor against Wesleyan when they played a second time on November 5, Yale winning 72–0. He may have been recovering from injuries, as the reporter mentioned that against Tufts, Yale was "weakened by the absence of some of its best players." The fourth game in a row that McCormick missed—or perhaps he wasn't needed—was against the New York Athletic Club on November 8, which Yale won 48–0. Despite winning four games by 214–0, the team was heavily criticized by the *Yale Daily News:* "The word poor hardly expresses the way in which the team played," scolded its reporter after the NYAC game.

But against the University of Pennsylvania on November 12, McCormick's presence was decisive again, as he led Yale to a 28–0 victory. He "excelled in tackling and interfering," said the *Yale Daily News,* by throwing Penn's runners for losses and springing Yale's halfbacks for touch-

downs. In one of his own runs, he got out from behind the wedge for fifteen yards, although the play was called back. Near the end of the game,
Penn ran the wedge seven times in succession and took the ball to Yale's
five-yard line, but McCormick broke through and grabbed the ball,
"undoubtedly preventing a touch-down." Thus Yale's perfect defense
continued.

On November 14, the college newspaper began the buildup to the Harvard and Princeton games, which would determine the winner of the
Championship Series (the teams were not called the Ivy League officially
until the 1950s). A lengthy editorial condemned the "very undesirable
practice of speculating" in football tickets. The November 17 issue provided a table of comparative records, showing that Williams had not
scored on either Yale or Harvard, and Wesleyan was scoreless against both
Yale and Princeton.

On Saturday, November 19, the day of the game, "The day was perfect
for foot-ball," reported the *Yale Daily News*. Eighteen thousand spectators watched a game "won strictly on its merits." Yale was congratulated
for "excellent team work and grand defensive play." As for their captain:
"Behind the line McCormick excelled, the able manner in which he handled his team and his superb tackling being one of the strongest points."
The first play showed McCormick on offense—he went behind the wedge
for twenty yards. But Harvard held, then Yale held, and so on, and the
game was scoreless at halftime. At this point, reported the *New York
Times*, the Excelsior Club of Brooklyn, a singing group of Yale graduates,
broke into song. It "not only proved a mascot," wrote the *Times*, "but put
marrow in the Yale boy's bones." They sang:

> McCormick is a dandy,
> And Laurie Bliss and Pop,
> While Stillman in the center,
> Would make a cyclone stop.
> With Hinkey on the left end,
> And Greenway on the right,
> We'll prove that poor old Harvard
> Was never in the fight.

Well into the second half, Yale's C. D. Bliss finally scored behind the
wedge for four points, and F. S. Butterworth kicked the goal for two points,
making it Yale 6, Harvard 0. And that would be the final score. The *Yale*

Daily News called the game "one of the closest and most exciting that has been played in years." But now they had to prepare for the game with Princeton the following Thursday, November 24, mindful that "over-confidence against any team, however poor, is an inexcusable fault."

The last game of the 1892 season, with Princeton, was played in Manhattan, making for a crowd of thirty-five thousand. Yale scored early, and then the contest settled down to a defensive struggle, like the battle with Harvard. In the second half, a blocked punt recovered by Yale in Princeton's end zone, followed by another successful goal kick, gave the Eli a 12–0 lead, which turned out to be the final score. Although Vance didn't cross the goal line, the *Yale Daily News* concluded: "Captain McCormick, at quarter-back, is beyond comment, his clever handling of his team together with his own grand individual work, were the chief causes of Yale's fine showing."

The next day, November 25, the *New York Times* reported that "for Yale, Butterworth, C. D. Bliss, McCormick, Wallis, and Winter were conspicuous, although it would be hard telling which man played the best, as all the Yale players played scientific football."

In a final report on the football season, published November 25, the *Yale Daily News* said, "Captain McCormick deserves the greatest praise for his untiring efforts in the developing of his team," noting that "the outlook at the beginning of the season was not a cheerful one for him, as many of the strongest of last year's players had left." The newspaper was referring to the All-Americans William Heffelfinger and Lee McClung, heroes of the 1891 squad, which their coach considered his best team ever. The next day, the paper published the individual records of all the Harvard, Yale, and Princeton players. Total points scored were Yale 435, opponents 0. But McCormick had not tallied a single touchdown.

Therefore, it must have been his leadership and defensive play that earned McCormick a place on Walter Camp's All-America team in 1892. Camp, the "father of modern American football," had been, like McCormick, Yale's quarterback and captain; furthermore, he was Yale's coach in 1892, so one might suspect him of favoritism in picking the nation's star players. But that year he chose more Harvard than Yale players for his All-America team, so his choice of McCormick does not seem unwarranted. Undefeated Yale was declared national champion in 1892, as they had been seven out of the previous ten years. Camp retired as coach that year with a record of 67–2.

Let's now consider the cultural meanings that could be attached to his playmaking, especially the parallel between McCormick's character and the qualities of certain ficticious American athletes. That those imaginary warriors wore Yale's colors is not surprising, for the Bulldogs were considered the quintessential college football team in the sport's early days. No doubt exaggerating, Notre Dame's fabled coach Knute Rockne once said that all the important developments in college football came from Yale. As testimony to the degree of its dominance of the game, the record book shows that Yale is still near the top in total number of victories and All-Americans. What other team can boast that undergrad Cole Porter wrote its fight songs?

Was Vance McCormick the model for Frank Merriwell, Yale's fictional hero at the turn of the century? The similarities are close enough that one can imagine the public reading of Merriwell and thinking of McCormick, or vice versa. Gilbert Patten, under the pen name of Burt L. Standish, wrote *Frank Merriwell at Yale* in 1897, four years after McCormick graduated. Merriwell was certainly the literary incarnation of Walter Camp's principles of sportsmanship. Like McCormick, he was captain of the team and later a coach; and like McCormick, he was praised for being honest and fair. *Frank Merriwell at Yale Again; or, Battling for the Blue,* published in 1899, says on the cover, "Frank did not hesitate to tackle the giant of the gridiron," which sounds exactly like McCormick against Harvard and Princeton his senior year. One commentator wrote that Merriwell had "a body like Tarzan's and a head like Einstein's . . . the perfect union of brain and brawn"; in political biographies, McCormick was described somewhat similarly: "He has broad shoulders, as befits a fullback, and a nicely squared jaw," said one. Merriwell's adventures, two hundred of them published in *Tip Top Weekly,* sold up to two hundred thousand copies a week, making him the most popular dime-novel hero between the years 1896 and 1916, which was almost exactly the period of McCormick's political fame.

Associating him with Merriwell would be enough to make the point, but still another contemporary icon can be connected with McCormick's persona and career. Owen Johnson graduated from Yale in 1900, and his sports novel *Stover at Yale,* was published in 1911. Like Frank Merriwell, the fictional Dink Stover played heroic football "four glorious years" and embodied Yale's values. He "held up an honest standard" and "played hard but square." Dink filled the Yale Bowl with tens of thousands of fans in raccoon coats and straw hats waving pennants. The novel was victorious in the marketplace, and references to Stover became commonplace in popular culture. In 1950, Metro-Goldwyn-Mayer made a Dink Stover movie, *The Happy Years*. Collier Books republished *Stover at Yale* in 1968, with an introduction by Kingman Brewster Jr., Yale's esteemed president. In 1997, Yale republished *Stover* again to celebrate the opening of the Yale Bookstore. Most recently, in February 2003, the *Yale Alumni Magazine* carried a story about Stover, Merriwell, and other fictive classmates, titled "The Ten Greatest Yalies Who Never Were."

McCormick was a match for Stover on the field, but in one respect he was not his equal on the Yale campus. In Owen Johnson's book, Dink Stover made it into Skull and Bones, Yale's prestigious secret society. Vance McCormick's father, Henry, was Skull and Bones in 1852. Several of Vance's football teammates in the 1892 season—Henry Graves, Frank Hinkey, Frank Butterworth, and Leland Stillman—were "Bonesmen." But their team captain and class president, Vance McCormick, was never tapped for the honor. Perhaps he turned it down, or instead was affiliated with one of the other secret societies, such as Scroll and Key, Berzelivs, Book and Snake, Wolf's Head, or St. Anthony Hall. But the exact reason remains a mystery, like Skull and Bones itself.

What McCormick's press clippings and Merriwell's and Stover's stories show us is how the interplay of imagery among football players, politicians, and military heroes was developing at the turn of the century. Politicians throughout history have been associated with warriors, and likewise, warriors associated with politicians. Now the football hero could be part of the mix: He could be described in warrior terms, if he showed those virtues, and the politician could be described in football terms, if he had the statistics. It is not unreasonable to assume that McCormick would have been successful in politics even without his athletic record. It is also reasonable to believe his football experience helped him appreciably. McCormick used the sport when he explained himself to others, and reporters used it when they explained him to their readers. A contemporary and friend of McCormick's, Theodore Roosevelt, showed the same interplay of imagery. Roosevelt's political reputation was tied to both his warrior experiences and his athletic transformation of himself, and reporters could refer to his cowboy life as well.

The strength of such relationships continues in modern politics. We can quickly think of recent presidents who were warriors, football players, baseball players, lifeguards, or at the least, golfers, because we are provided that information, and apparently we want to receive it. Most recently, we have a state governor who is the world's most popular body builder and action hero. Vance McCormick was present at the creation of these games.

McCormick's Social World

A defining characteristic of Vance McCormick's life was his membership in the upper class. The most obvious sign of that membership, and his social status, was his club memberships. In New York City, he was a member of the University, Yale, Manhattan, and St. Anthony Clubs; in New Haven, the Graduates Club; in Philadelphia, the Philadelphia Club; in Washington, the Metropolitan and National Press Clubs; in South Carolina, the Oakland in St. Stephens and Yeomen's Hall in Charleston; in State College, Pennsylvania, the University Club; in Charlottesville, Virginia, the Farmington Club; and in Harrisburg, the University Club, Harrisburg Club, and Country Club of Harrisburg. We know something about the last two.

The Harrisburg Club, organized on November 6, 1884, was the "in place" for the upper class. Its founders, many of them attorneys, did not include any of the McCormicks, but they joined soon after its start. Colonel Henry was admitted almost immediately, in 1884, and was a member of its governing committee in 1889–90. Then three scions in the family's next generation joined: Henry B. in 1893, Vance in 1894, and Donald in 1896, when they were in their twenties. Harrisburg's other prominent families were on the membership roster: Alricks, Bailey, Bergner, Boas, Boyd, Buehler, Calder, Cameron, Detweiler, Dull, Eby, Fleming, Fox, Gilbert, Gorgas, Gross, Haldeman, Hamilton, Herr, Kunkel, Lamberton, McCreath, Snodgrass, and the like. The entrance fee was $50, and annual dues were $40. There were 110 resident members in 1894, 137 resident and 53 nonresident members in 1898, and 178 total members in 1910, a slight decline, when the club was old enough to list its 44 deceased members in the back of its handbook.

The first Club House opened on February 28, 1885, at 213 Walnut Street. Said the Harrisburg *Patriot,* in a news story that day about the event, "This city has never contained what might be called a very tony club, and the idea of organizing one finally dawned upon the minds of some of the representatives of the elite of this city." Members moved to a new, more regal building on the northeast corner of Front and Market Streets on April 1, 1897. The *Patriot* covered the club's opening with headlines on the front page: "Club in its New Home . . . Prominent Men Present." The Harrisburg *Telegraph* headlined it too. According to Mary O. Bradley in her "Cornerstone" column (Harrisburg *Patriot,* September 29, 1998), the new facility was a four-story, Italianate brownstone. The first story had round-arched windows and doors, with Palladian-style windows and an exterior balcony over the main entrance. The interior was formal and comfortable, like the members themselves. The first-floor walls were oak paneled, and a grand stairway went to a surrounding balcony. An immense oriental carpet covered the main hall floor, and leather-covered chairs faced a fireplace. Apartments for resident and nonresident members occupied the upper floors. The servants wore livery with blue and gold braid.

The club's rules reflected the upper-class sense of propriety: no loud talking in the library, no card playing in bedrooms, no games on Sunday, no tipping, no cash, and no gambling ever. No women were allowed unless they were the immediate family of members, and those were permitted only between 9:30 A.M. and 3:30 P.M. They had to enter through the lesser Front Street entrance, not the main entrance on Market Street, and be escorted to the ladies' reception room and private dining room on the second floor.

Vance McCormick likely used the downtown club for business lunches and other social affairs; he easily could have walked there from his home at 301 North Front Street. His cousin Donald lived even closer, in the family's original mansion at 101 North Front Street. Many other members had residential or business addresses only a few blocks from the club, as Front Street at the time was the domain of Harrisburg's upper class. According to Gerald Eggert in *Harrisburg Industrializes* (Penn State, 1993), his very thorough book about the urban elite and their businesses, they were called the "Front Street Set." But as the nation and the city changed, so did Front Street and the club. In 1935, it fell on hard times and was moved out of its central location by the sheriff. That event was featured in the *Patriot* too: "Sheriff Locks Doors of Harrisburg Club . . . Prominent Members of Fifty-Year-Old Organization Denied Admittance." Between then and 1946, its downtown address changed three times. It was no longer listed in the city directory after 1946. McCormick had died, and urban elites had begun moving out of town. The ornate building itself was torn down in 1963 to make way for a larger office-hotel-apartment complex that never came to pass.

If the downtown club itself was gone, Bradley writes, its legend could be found in John O'Hara's 1949 novel, *A Rage to Live,* where Harrisburg was called Fort Penn, and the Harrisburg Club, naturally, the Fort Penn Club. O'Hara suggests the centrality of the club in Harrisburg society at the turn of the century:

> The Fort Penn Club was beginning to catch on; men from Pittsburgh and Philadelphia and Scranton and Wilkes-Barre and Reading and Allentown were at the club every day while the Legislature was in session, and William and Isaac agreed that it seemed a pity not to meet those fellows and exchange views. . . . They made many valuable friend-ships by establishing the new lunch custom, and without intending to do so, they effected a revolutionary change in the social life of Fort Penn: when other men saw Isaac and Will lunching downtown, they too took up the custom.

The Country Club of Harrisburg, also mentioned in *A Rage to Live,* was McCormick's suburban social equivalent of the downtown Harrisburg Club. Construction on its original Tudor-style building, located on North Front Street in Susquehanna Township, was completed in 1897, the same year the downtown club moved into its new building. The memberships were largely the same, too, reports Mary O. Bradley in the first of her "Cornerstone" columns for the *Patriot* (January 21, 1997):

> From its inception, the life of the Country Club of Harrisburg has revolved around Front Street, for it was along the scenic river frontage that the creme de la creme of society lived. The names of the founders and early members are a veritable Who's Who of Harrisburg: Cameron, Calder, Forster, Kunkel, Fleming, Boyd, Reily, McCormick, McCreath and Haldeman.

Marlin E. Olmsted, Harrisburg's "most prominent citizen," was president of the Harrisburg Club in 1893, president of the Country Club in 1896, and member of the U.S. House of Representatives from 1897 to 1913.

The original clubhouse burned down in 1915, and a new one was built farther north, off Fishing Creek Valley Road, in 1917. Now the Country Club had one hundred acres instead of six, and room for more tennis and an eighteen-hole rather than a nine-hole golf course. Nestled between Blue Mountain and Second Mountain, it overlooked the Susquehanna River. In 1919, however, this new clubhouse burned down, and members had to build again. The Country Club recovered and thrived until, like the Harrisburg Club, it fell on hard times. After World War II, traffic congestion hampered access, offspring did not take their parents' places, and the very exclusiveness that had once made such clubs attractive now made them less appealing. Eventually the Country Club realized, unlike the downtown club, that it needed to be managed like a business instead of a private clique, so it reinvented itself, concentrating on family activities rather than the "staid social affairs of a bygone era"—which were probably just what Vance McCormick enjoyed.

Besides his clubs in Harrisburg, McCormick had an active social life in Maine, where he spent his summers from July 4 until early September, as was the custom of the upper class. His first press notice appeared on August 14, 1898, in the *New York Times,* under the heading, "The Week At Bar Harbor," and showed what a social whirl there could be among the "summer colony" singles:

> The first event of importance this week was of course the Malvern ball and dinner parties Monday night. Nine dinner parties were given before the dance. . . . Miss Clarke had as guests Mr. and Mrs. Rieman Duval, Miss Coles, Vance McCormick, Miss Anne Thomson, and Dennie M. Bare.

But a story published thirty-six years later, on August 22, 1934, may have been the one that made him proudest, as the *Times* noted the results of a yacht race at Northeast Harbor. In a seventeen-knot southwest breeze, "Vance C. McCormick's Mecoh II took first place from Wharton Sinkler's Last Chance by nearly two minutes." McCormick's time was 2:26:47. Rev. Malcolm Peabody's *Daffydill* was third; Eugene duPont's *Salcee* took just over two and half hours and placed fifth.

When Vance McCormick married Gertrude Howard Olmsted, the widow of Congressman Marlin E. Olmsted, in 1925, he brought her to his social world, and she brought him to hers. On May 13, 1928, the *New York Times* reported that Miss Jane Olmsted, daughter of Mrs. Vance McCormick, had recently been presented before the king and queen of England at Buckingham Palace. Miss Olmsted had "for years been identified with the social life of New York." When Mr. and Mrs. McCormick and their two daughters returned from England aboard the *Mauretania,* the *Times* noted that too.

From that point on, Mrs. McCormick by herself was a subject for the *Times'* social coverage. When President and Mrs. Herbert Hoover had a luncheon and musicale in the White House East Room on April 20, 1929, her attendance, and that of Vance's sister Anne, was listed in the newspaper. She would be having their Harrisburg friend J. Horace McFarland speak on "Adventures in Rose Gardening" to the Garden Club in Northeast Harbor, Maine, reported the *Times* on August 11, 1929. And on February 9, 1931, the *Times* reported that Mrs. McCormick's son Marlin died of a heart attack as he was about to exercise his polo ponies.

The most impressive *Times* story on McCormick activities in Maine appeared on July 30, 1934, when the paper reported that five hundred guests gathered at Westward Way, the McCormick's grand summer home at Northeast Harbor. The occasion was a reception, "arranged in the interests of world fellowship," for dignitaries of the YWCA, one of Mrs. Olmsted's favorite charities (another favorite was the Girl Scouts, for which she served as first vice president). In the summers of 1938 through 1941, Gertrude McCormick was mentioned in the *Times* as a patron for a fancy dress ball at the Bar Harbor Club, as hostess for a tea at Westward Way for the Mount Desert Island Hospital committee, as a guest at a Bar Harbor luncheon that included Mrs. John D. Rockefeller, and as hostess for a luncheon honoring Sir John and Lady Reith. The McCormicks' last recorded mention on the *New York Times* society page appeared on November 14, 1941, in the simple sentence "Mr. and Mrs. Vance McCormick of Harrisburg, Pa., are at the Plaza." There must have been no reason to say why.

Another element of McCormick's social life was his ongoing fellowship with Yale and Yale men. His classmates elected him their president and called him "the Ablest Navigator." After playing fullback in the 1891 season and quarterback in 1892, he helped coach the Bulldog football team; he helped again twenty-three years later, when he chaired a search committee looking for a new head coach. His Yale teammates kept in touch and came to Harrisburg to help with his political campaigns. For his "civic righteousness" Yale awarded him an honorary master's degree in 1907. He was elected a fellow of the Yale Corporation in 1913; "of the 3,365 votes cast, you received 1,574, your nearest competitor having 985," said his letter of notification. He was to fill the vacancy caused by the resignation of William Howard Taft, who had other duties as president of the United States. His diplomatic diaries are studded with the names of Eli alumni he happily encountered overseas. A highlight of his stay in Paris in 1917 was attending a dinner for 150 Yale men who were in the city at the time, either in uniform or otherwise serving their country. In a 1935 letter he wrote to the *Yale Alumni Weekly*, Vance proudly noted of his grandfather: "although a Princeton man, [he] sent my father and his brother to Yale, in the Classes of '52 and '53." One could even say that Vance McCormick was literally part of Yale, for in the gateway leading to the Hadley entryway to the Quadrangle at the college, the likeness of his head was carved in honor of his chairmanship of the Yale Corporation's committee on architectural planning. He was dutiful to his alma mater to the end of his life, leaving Yale $250,000 in his will, the largest of any of the bequests that were listed in his obituary. "He attended most of Yale's football games until recent years," said his obituary. His devotion to that institution, and all it stood for, Yale must have thought ideal.

High-Minded McCormick

Vance McCormick held high-minded views. He learned these, no doubt, from his family and his church. He carried them to Yale, where he was deacon of his class, vice president of the college YMCA, and later in life, a member of the Yale Foreign Missionary Society and the university's Council on Religious Life. In his political campaigns, he announced that it was his purpose to work for good government, which he defined not simply as more efficient government, but as moral government. His approach epitomized what was called progressivism in the early twentieth century. At the same time, he embodied what was called "muscular Christianity" by preachers who wanted traditional faith to be competitive in modern culture.

A sampling of the rhetoric from his political career shows his moralism. In the mayor's race of 1902, his campaign literature stated that his election would be a victory of "men of honesty and unselfishness over petty politicians and scheming spoils-men." In 1910, the *Star-Independent,* a newspaper he didn't own, said "McCormick retired from the office with the 'well-done-good-and-faithful-servant' from all classes of people," and that he was still "fighting what he believes is wrong and battling for the right." J. Horace McFarland, a progressive ally in the "City Beautiful" movement, said that McCormick had cleaned up Harrisburg "morally and physically." In the gubernatorial race of 1914, campaign literature said he had closed up the capital city's "gambling houses, speakeasies, and disorderly houses" and put his party's affairs "in the hands of clean, unselfish, progressive Democrats."

That rhetoric, one can say with confidence, was not part of an insincere pose to win public approval. In the McCormick Family Papers is private correspondence from his coprogressives congratulating him on the moral manner in which he conducted Woodrow Wilson's reelection campaign of 1916. William McAdoo telegraphed him that his practices were in "sharp contrast with the unscrupulous and sinister methods of the opposition." Newton Baker complimented McCormick on "the fine man's kind of campaign you conducted," saying he had "preserved our self-respect as a party and as a people." Finally, President Wilson himself wrote McCormick from the White House on November 13, 1916: "The first letter I write from my desk here must be to you. . . . The whole country has seen and appreciated your quality. . . .You were throughout the moving and guiding spirit. . . . [You have] won this admiration by an unselfish service of the first magnitude."

Even as he stepped back from active electoral politics, McCormick did not forget that his loyalty was to moral politics. A pivotal act was his refusal to support Al Smith, the Democratic nominee for the presidency in 1928, on account of Smith's opposition to prohibition. Then, in July 1930, McCormick's "dry" convictions led him to reject the Democratic nominee for governor of Pennsylvania and endorse instead another dry Republican, Gifford Pinchot. On August 3, the *New York Times* reported that the Democrats of Harrisburg and Dauphin County "by an overwhelming vote . . . repudiated the leadership of Vance McCormick" and elected instead an entire slate of "wet" candidates. "Opponents of Mr. McCormick declared after the meeting that the action marked a definite end of the McCormick influence in Harrisburg and Dauphin County," said the *Times*. His defection from the Democrats in 1940, when he supported Republican Wendell Wilkie over Franklin Roosevelt, running for an unprecedented third term, was not surprising. McCormick's *Patriot* editorialized, on July 20, that Roosevelt's nomination "breaks the . . . hearts of millions of Democrats who had hoped the dangerous and uneconomic policies of the New Deal would be repudiated and the party rededicated to its fundamental principles." Declared the newspaper, Wilkie more closely followed "the course of the genuine believer in Jeffersonian democracy," a theory of virtuous government.

McCormick's moralism appeared even in his attitude toward changes that were taking place in college football. He joined in the plea to give the game "Back to Boys Who Play It," as headlined the *New York Times* on April 30, 1941. "What we have in our games today," bemoaned McCormick, "are two highly paid coaches sitting on opposite sides of the field, directing the play. If this is not professionalism, what is it?" What was needed, he said, was that the "strategy and direction of the game should be turned over to the captain and his teammates" on game day.

In retrospect, while McCormick was a man born of an upper-class family, who attended an upper-class college and inhabited an upper-class social world, the irony is that his values were profoundly middle-class.

One doubts he would have disagreed one iota with the list of bourgeois virtues that Benjamin Franklin had first recommended to Americans in his *Autobiography*—temperance, silence, order, resolution, frugality, industry, sincerity, justice, moderation, cleanliness, tranquility, chastity, and humility—although the virtue of frugality was violated when McCormick purchased a custom-made Phantom II Rolls-Royce during the Great Depression, paying $18,885, when a Cadillac would have sold for about $600. But then, even Franklin grew fond of fine wine.

McCormick's Influence on Harrisburg

Vance Criswell McCormick met the three duties of his alma mater's famous directive: to be for God, for country, and for Yale. To those he added one more loyalty—to serve Harrisburg—and the city became a better place because McCormick was, directly and indirectly, a dutiful patrician. Evidence of his and his family's continuing influence is in the benefactions of the McCormick Family Foundation, the establishment of the McCormick Library at the Harrisburg Area Community College, and the naming of the McCormick Public Services Center at the Martin Luther King Jr. City Government Center.

Near the northern city limits, McCormicks Island lies beneath the George Wade/Interstate 81 bridge over the Susquehanna River. McCormick Drive is near Rosegarden, the family's former country estate, and McCormick Road winds around what were the family's farms near Bowmansdale and alongside the Yellow Breeches Creek. Two handsome columns standing at the Harrisburg end of the Market Street Bridge, retrieved from the burned wreckage of the old state capitol building, were placed there with funds provided in 1904 by the McCormick Estate. At the northeast corner of Front and Walnut Streets, facing the river, still stands the stately McCormick mansion, where the family lived and Vance grew up in the presence of their fellow citizens.

Today Harrisburg is more progressive and democratic than Vance McCormick could possibly have imagined, or perhaps accepted. But with all the advances, and with due respect for the most recent reformers, there has been a loss—the loss of his kind.

Diplomatic Diaries

From the Ritz to Verdun

Vance McCormick's Diary
of the House Mission, 1917

Edited by Susan Meehan
and Teresa Weisser

O n October 5, 1917, Woodrow Wilson signed an executive order creating the War Trade Board, an agency designed to wage economic warfare against the Central Powers. Less than a month later, Vance McCormick, the director of the board, left Harrisburg to travel to London and Paris as a member of the American delegation charged with coordinating America's war effort with those of the Allies. The House Mission, as the delegation came to be known, was led by Wilson's close friend and advisor, Col. Edward House, and consisted of civilian and military officials involved with the military, financial, and economic prosecution of the war.

The trip began on a note of great secrecy, with McCormick knowing only that he would be met in New York by a particular "tall man with big bay window and carrying a New York Evening Post," who would convey him to the appropriate departure point for his voyage to Europe. From New York, the members of the delegation traveled by train to Halifax, Nova Scotia, where they boarded ships for London. Although the voyage was uneventful, the danger of a German submarine attack was very real, and the ships carrying the delegates traveled with a convoy of destroyers.

On arriving in London, the members of the House Mission began a series of meetings with British and other Allied officials charged with responsibility in their particular areas of expertise. As a representative of the War Trade Board, McCormick worked closely with Allied officials involved in administering the blockade of Germany and with those grappling with the complicated problem of securing additional shipping capacity to replace the tonnage lost to German submarines. During the two weeks McCormick spent in London, he participated in negotiations regarding trade and financial relations with the neutral nations of Norway, Denmark, Sweden, and Holland. He also was heavily involved in conferences regarding the lack of adequate shipping capacity and the consequent difficulties in transporting troops to the battlefields and supplies to the military and to the European home front.

As members of a high-level American delegation, McCormick and his companions were entertained by the social and political leaders of Great Britain, including the prime minister, the foreign minister, members of the House of Commons, and the king and queen. The trip also afforded him the opportunity to visit friends and fellow Yale graduates in the London area, and to become acquainted with new people, most notably Leander McCormick-Goodhart, a distant cousin whom he had never met.

Throughout his stay in London, McCormick was impressed with British dedication to the war effort. He comments favorably on the cooperative attitude and leadership qualities of the men he met and notes the significant war work done by British women. He describes London as a city where the war can be felt in the darkness of the streets and the apparent rationing of food and other necessities.

On November 22, the House Mission left Britain for the short trip across the English Channel to France. As in London, McCormick represented the United States in discussions regarding relations between the Allies and neutral nations, in this case Switzerland and Spain. At first these discussions were conducted with representatives of the French Ministry of Blockade, but as delegates from other nations gathered for the Inter-Allied Conference, which began on November 29, negotiations expanded to include them as well. At the conference, McCormick was assigned to the Blockade and Tonnage Committees. As part of the Blockade Committee, he was involved in negotiating an agreement with the Swiss; his principal contribution to the Tonnage Committee was a proposal for the creation of an Inter-Allied Shipping Board.

The entertainment that the members of the House Mission were treated to in Paris was even more lavish than it had been in London. After dinners at the homes of the French president Poincare and foreign minister Pichon, McCormick comments on the quality of the food and notes the apparent lack of food rationing in Paris. On his free evenings, McCormick frequently dined with other members of the House Mission or with American friends stationed in Paris as a result of the war effort. One gathering he particularly enjoyed was a dinner attended by 150 Yale alumni at the Café Cardinal.

The longest single entries in McCormick's diary concern his trip to the battlefront on December 2 and 3. Leaving Paris late on the first, McCormick and a small group of American officials traveled first to the field headquarters of the American Expeditionary Force in Chaumont. After meeting the military commanders, the party visited American troops near Neufchateau, then moved on to the American training grounds at Gondrecourt. Late in the day on December 2, they reached Bar-le-Duc, the terminus of the only open road leading to Verdun. Early the next morning, the group drove to Verdun, stopping to visit the French commander in his headquarters at Souilly before moving on to the impressive Verdun Citadel. After touring the citadel and the devastated city, the Americans drove to the trenches, arriving in time to witness an artillery battle. At the end of the day, they returned to the citadel and began their journey back to Paris. Throughout the second day of the trip, McCormick notes the tremendous destruction that was evident for miles around Verdun.

After arriving back in Paris on December 3, McCormick concluded the remaining business of the trip in meetings with American officials and journalists and with the Inter-Allied Conference Committee on Blockade. The House Mission's departure from Paris was as mysterious as McCormick's trip to New York had been. Members of the mission were driven separately to a Paris train station, all by different routes. Only after their train had left the station were they told that they would sail from the French port of Brest. The return voyage, like the trip to Europe, was ultimately uneventful, but the ship operated under tight security precautions and was accompanied by a convoy of destroyers for the first several days at sea. On December 15, the party landed in New York. McCormick wasted no time in catching the next train back to Harrisburg, arriving home at 9:30 P.M. on the same day.

McCormick's diary shows the establishment of working relationships among American, British, and French officials that would go deeper than the usual exchange of diplomatic memos and official documents. These relationships later facilitated the difficult work that had to be done at the Paris Peace Conference. In a letter written on May 16, 1919, for example, Andre Tardieu informed McCormick that he was to be named, on Tardieu's recommendation, a commander of the French Legion of Honor; this award was in recognition of McCormick's leadership on the blockade. Closing his letter to McCormick, Tardieu wrote, "With affectionate felicitations, I am sending you, dear friend, my cordial remembrances." McCormick replied to Tardieu from the Hotel Crillon in Paris on May 18: "I again desire to express to you my sincerest thanks for this greatest of honors, and with my most cordial felicitations and gratitude to yourself personally, I am, my dear Mr. Tardieu,

Faithfully yours." Those expressions show a friendship that seems to have gone beyond the usual diplomatic niceties.

McCormick's social observations, his scrutiny of wartime conditions in London and Paris, and his account of the trip to the battlefield trenches near Verdun help make up for the lack of detail about the actual inner workings of the House Commission, which he kept confidential.

OCTOBER 28, 1917 (SUNDAY)—

Left Harrisburg at 6:53 P.M., en route to New York under greatest secrecy, with instructions that I would be met at the Pennsylvania Railroad station[1] by a tall man with a big bay window and carrying a *New York Evening Post*. Met him in accordance with instructions at 1 A.M., and was placed by my large friend in a private car standing in the Pennsylvania Railroad station, in a state room with Gordon Auchincloss.

OCTOBER 29 (MONDAY)—

When I appeared in the morning I found I was on a special train somewhere in Massachusetts, en route to Halifax, with Col. House and wife; Miss Denton, Private Secretary to Col. House; Gordon Auchincloss; Admiral Benson, and his aide, Lieut. Commander Carter; General Bliss and his aide, Major Wallace; Assistant Secretary of the Treasury Crosby and Mr. Cravath, an international lawyer and advisor to Mr. Crosby; Bainbridge Colby, of the Shipping Board; Mr. Perkins, representing the War Industries Board, and a former Harvard crew captain of about my time in college; Dr. Taylor, of the War Trade Board, and representing the Food Administrator; Milton L. Young, my Secretary; and a number of stenographers, a marine engineer, Mr. Day, and a statistician, Mr. Burgess. We were forbidden to leave the car for fear we might be recognized, and the railroad officials were told the train was a theatrical special.

OCTOBER 30 (TUESDAY)—

We arrived at Halifax at 9 A.M., and we were taken at once from the train to the dock and the party was divided between the two armoured cruisers

1. The Pennsylvania Railroad was the official governmental and military transport between Washington and New York.

awaiting us in the harbor. Col. and Mrs. House, Miss Denton, Gordon Auchincloss, and myself, with our secretaries, Admiral Benson and General Bliss, with their aides, sailing on the cruiser "Huntingdon" [*sic*], formerly the battleship "West Virginia," with a maximum speed of 20 knots. The rest of the party went aboard the cruiser "St. Louis," a slightly smaller vessel, with a speed of 17 knots. We pulled out about noon—good weather—with an attractive view of the harbor and Nova Scotia. We were particularly interested in the camouflage on the vessels in the harbor.

Col. House and family occupied the Admiral's quarters, messing in their own rooms. Admiral Benson, General Bliss, and I, had the Captain and Executive Officers' quarters—the Captain messing with us. The rest of the party were in the ward-room mess. The quarters were most comfortable, considering we were on a war vessel. We were escorted from Halifax by the torpedo boat destroyer "Balch."

OCTOBER 31 (WEDNESDAY) NOVEMBER 1–2–3
(THURSDAY, FRIDAY AND SATURDAY)—

Nothing eventful. Weather cloudy, with the sea comfortable, and the vessel steady. Crews constantly drilling—gun drill, and abandon ship drill. In the latter we were all assigned to our places with our life preservers on. Also smoke bomb practice.

I had many interesting conversations with the Admiral, and the General, at mess, also walks with Col. House.

The "St. Louis" always maintained her position about 500 yards in the rear. The destroyer was constantly scouting about from 500 to 1500 yards distant from us. To save coal for the rush for the last 1500 miles we made only about 250 miles per day.

We aimed for a rendezvous in the middle of the ocean where a large oil tanker was stationed to supply destroyers acting as convoys with an additional supply of fuel, where we expected to replenish the destroyer "Balch." Another reason for reducing speed is to wait until the moon wanes, as moonlight is exceedingly dangerous for submarine attacks. After tomorrow, Sunday morning, we will drive ahead at full speed and make a mad rush on a zigzag course for Liverpool.[2]

---

2. McCormick's ship followed the route used by U.S. troop convoys to Europe in 1917. As the German resumption of unrestricted submarine warfare was the immediate cause of American entry into World War I, one can appreciate the passengers' and crews' anxiety during the voyage.

NOVEMBER 4 (SUNDAY)—

On account of severe cloudy weather, which necessitated dead reckoning we did not pick up the oil tanker, "Arathusa," [sic] until 8 A.M., instead of 5 A.M. We were also delayed in waiting for the "St. Louis" during the night. In the meantime we hailed the cruiser "Seattle" by wireless, and had taken from her another destroyer, the "Downs." We had to fill up both destroyers from the oil tanker, with a considerable sea on, which was an interesting and thrilling operation to watch, as it was necessary to pass a hose from the destroyer to the tanker and have both proceed side by side at about 7 knots per hour until the destroyers were filled. This took until 3:30 P.M., when with rain still falling, we started on our last lap of 1500 miles at full speed. The two destroyers speeding along ahead of the "Huntingdon," and the "St. Louis" about 500 yards astern. I was out on the bridge most of the day, enjoying the oiling operation, and the handling of the "Huntingdon" [sic]. Everything is now cleared for action, and life preservers on all the crew and passengers: the latter are ordered on "Abandon Ship" signal to report on the quarter-deck and take to the small boats. While at dinner the Captain was handed two radiograms, warning of submarines located off the coast of France.

The Admiral, the General, Col. House and I had discussion concerning military and naval problems connected with the War Trade Board's negotiations with the Northern Neutrals.[3]

NOVEMBER 5 (MONDAY)—

Still cloudy and raining, but the wind has changed to the northwest, and afternoon clear. Nearing danger zone and everyone ordered to keep on his life preserver, and keep it on night and day, from the Captain down. I can see that the Admiral does not like this regulation, as he thinks it weakens the morale of the men, but it is an order of the Navy Department.

Signalled by radio three times from the four destroyers en route to meet us to act as our convoy. They wanted to know of our position, and later advised us of change of course we were to take after meeting them at the rendezvous at 6:30 tomorrow morning.

I can see that the Admiral and the Captain did not like so much radioing.

---

3. According to Colonel House's account on November 10, 1917, the United States and Great Britain were considering commandeering all neutral shipping in the world.

Unfortunately at this writing, 12 P.M., the waning moon is shining quite brilliantly. We wished for dark nights. Expect to pick up the convoy tomorrow morning.

NOVEMBER 6 (TUESDAY)—

Arrived at rendezvous at 8 A.M., two hours late, on account of delay of the "St. Louis," which held us back, she having trouble in keeping up with our speed. We picked up our convoy of four destroyers, the "Cushing," the flagship; the "Wilkes," the "Davis," and another. They signalled us that owing to the rough conditions of the sea, and the speed we were maintaining it would not be necessary for us to zigzag, and we could take the straight course. They darted back and forth all around us, doing scout duty all day, at a speed of about 30 knots per hour. We saw nothing all day. The sun came out and we had a pleasant day overhead, but rough sea with strong northwest winds. Signalled by the "Cushing" that we were to make for Davenport, near Plymouth, which course takes up the Channel for a short distance.

Last night and this night we all slept with our clothes on and with life preservers, and the crew were not allowed to sleep in their hammocks, but slept on the decks, as they were not permitted to swing their hammocks, as all passages must be clear. The gun crews were on duty continuously, standing by their guns. Large depth bombs were placed on the quarter-deck, which we thought was very dangerous, as we slept directly under them and if a torpedo had struck that part of our ship nothing would have been left of us.

I disobeyed orders by undressing last night, and had a good night.

The Captain has worked out tonight that at the speed of 18 knots, which we are now making, we will land at Davenport at about 5 P.M., if all goes well. At 12 P.M. it is rolling a good deal, the furniture in the dining cabin being turned over, but this roughness is bad for the submarines, so it satisfies us. We are told that at 6 o'clock tomorrow morning, just at dawn, will be the very worst time, and the beginning of the dangerous portion of the submarine zone.

NOVEMBER 7 (WEDNESDAY)—

Had a good night. Slept without life preserver and clothes. Thought I could dress quickly enough if need be. Up at 7, everything going well. Nearly everyone on board was up all night. We were making good time, with sun out, squalls and strong wind; typical Channel weather. We were excited in the morning, as in this very dangerous ground the "St. Louis" stopped dead, with engine and valve trouble, expecting a torpedo any minute. The destroyers and "Huntingdon" scattered and circled around the "St. Louis" until she was repaired, which took about 40 minutes. We reached Eddystone lighthouse at 4:30 P.M. We were met there by a British destroyer and British airplane, which escorted us into Plymouth, where we arrived at 5:30 P.M. Here we dropped our four scouts, and steamed slowly up to Davenport, where the British have their great naval yards, arriving there at 6 P.M., and docked.

Here we were met by Admiral Jellicoe and head of the British Navy; Gen. Caldwell, Sir Wm. Wiseman, Mr. Balfour's Secretary, and Mr. Irwin Laughlin, Counselor of our Legation, and were put on a special train which left for London at 7 P.M.

We arrived in London at midnight, and were met at the station by Mr. Balfour, Ambassador Page, and other officials.

Col. and Mrs. House went to Chesterfield House, the home of the Duke of Roxbury, and the rest of the party went to Claridges Hotel, where we found comfortable quarters waiting for us. The management seemed glad to have me back again.

NOVEMBER 8 (THURSDAY)—

The mission called formally upon Ambassador Page at the Embassy, and there made plans and appointments for our conference with our opposites.[4]

Lunched at the Embassy, and had my first conference in the morning with Lord Robert Cecil, who is the youngest son of Lord Salsbury, and Minister of Blockade. Also under-Secretary of State. Was most favorably impressed. Generally discussed the pending negotiations, and met there Sir Joseph Maclay, the Shipping Minister.

Spent the afternoon at the Embassy, discussing matters pertaining to the work of our Board with Mr. Gunther, First Secretary, Lew Sheldon, Lieut. Frothingham, Morgan Bale, and Pennoyer, all connected with the blockade work. Sheldon being Hoover's Food Representative. While there M. Charpentier, the French representative on the Blockade Conference, called for an interview with us.

---

4. The American mission conducted business on two separate fronts: the organizational, technical meetings for the various experts, such as McCormick; and the diplomatic meetings among House, Lloyd George and their diplomatic and military advisors.

Dr. Taylor and I dined together, and went to the theater (The Boy). Taxis very scarce, and the city very dark—street lights all shaded—not a light in the windows. We passed a large hole in the Picadilly Circus, the result of a recent air raid not yet repaired. Night here has a most depressing effect; theaters crowded, mostly with soldiers. Practically no dressing—very few dress suits.

NOVEMBER 9 (FRIDAY)—

Early morning ordered some clothes.[5] At noon held our first round-table conference with Lord Robert Cecil and his staff of experts. Made progress in Norway and negotiations. Planned for another conference tomorrow. Mission lunched at Chesterfield House with Col. House to meet Ambassador Page. Picture was taken in front of the house after lunch.

Conference at the Embassy in the afternoon.

Glad to find Madge Clark Butter staying in the hotel with her husband and child. Getting house ready at Wimbledon for the winter. Had note from Leander McCormick-Goodhart, claiming relationship, and desires to entertain me.

Dined with Lew Sheldon at the old Garrick Club, an interesting place. Dr. Taylor and I had an interesting conference in the afternoon with Lord Rhondda, the Food Controller of England.

Find the heartiest co-operation everywhere, and find big men with a broad vision heading the departments.

NOVEMBER 10 (SATURDAY)—

Worked at the Embassy in the morning.

Lunched with the Butters and Sir Malcom Murray, who is connected with the Duke of Connaught. Conference with Breckenridge, naval attaché on Scandinavian countries. Conference with Lord Robert Cecil and French representatives on Northern Neutrals.

Called with Madge Butter upon her mother at the hospital. Met George there, who was off for a day from the Isle of Wight, where he is stationed with his artillery regiment. Dined at Mr. Gunther's house with Lord Robert, Sir Eyre Crowe, of the Foreign Office, Sir ——— of the Shipping Ministry, and Dr. Taylor. Talked shop all evening, making considerable progress.

---

5. Even the war did not stop men of a certain economic and social class from seeing their London tailors for custom-made clothing.

NOVEMBER 11 (SUNDAY)—

Went to St. George's Church, Hanover Square. Lunched with Lord Robert and Lady Cecil. Major Darwin, son of the Darwin of Evolution fame, was there and a most interesting man. He is a great political economist, and lectured at Harvard University. Walked in the afternoon to the Zoological Garden. Had tea with Ambassador Page. Dinner with Rowley and Mable Leigh, and Peggy, who is quite grown up.

NOVEMBER 12 (MONDAY)—

Worked in my room most of the morning preparing cables. Lunched with Charles R. Crane, just back from Russia. He was not surprised at the recent developments there, but considered the problem almost as great as the war itself. Speaks well of Ambassador Francis.

Held conference with Lord Robert, and French and Italian delegates. Mr. Crosby, Financial Representative of our Mission, was present, to discuss the financial embargo against Northern Neutrals.

Dined with Ambassador Page, met Sir Joseph Asquith, Sir Leverton-Harris, and others.

NOVEMBER 13 (TUESDAY)—

At 10 A.M. we started in my rooms the daily meetings of our Mission to better co-ordinate our work. At 11 A.M. attended a conference at Lord Milner's office with Lord Milner, Lord Robert Cecil, the French and Italian representatives, Mr. Colby and myself to discuss tonnage. Arranged later a conference in the afternoon at Lord Robert's office. Both conferences discussed shipping, particularly in the question of ways and means to secure neutral tonnage. It is fast becoming very evident that the Allies' tonnage situation was a most serious one. Lunched with Lady Birbeck at her club. Dined with the Butters and Lady Burrell and Col. Hutchinson. Conference in the afternoon with M. Charpentier and the new French delegate, Serruys, upon neutral negotiations.

NOVEMBER 14 (WEDNESDAY)—

Meeting of members of the Mission at my room at 10 A.M., with Col. House present. Conference later in the morning at Lord Robert's office, with Colby and Allied representatives to discuss pooling of neutral and other tonnage, and increase shipping facilities. Lunched in the Harcourt room at the House of Commons with the Commercial Committee of the

House of Commons, given by them in honor of Ambassador Page.[6] Mr. Balfour and Ambassador Page spoke, the latter made an especially good speech. Photo taken after lunch on terrace.

Conference at 3 P.M., with our naval attaché to the Scandinavian countries, and Capt. Concert, Representative of the British Admiralty on blockade of Northern Neutrals. Present at the conference were Zantzinger, Robinette, Frothingham, Dr. Taylor and Gunther. I met for the first time my distant cousin, Leander McCormick-Goodhart. He is in the British Admiralty, an attractive fellow, most hospitable and gracious. Dined at small informal dinner with Mr. Balfour at his home. A delightful time. Mr. Asquith, former Prime Minister; Sir Eric Geddes, head of the Admiralty; and Lord Robert Cecil were the outside guests. I sat between Mr. Balfour and Lord Robert, and had a long talk with Mr. Asquith after dinner, and thoroughly enjoyed myself. Mr. Balfour is a charming host, and his guests are most agreeable.

NOVEMBER 15 (THURSDAY)—

Members of the mission met in the morning as usual. I worked in my room balance of the morning. Lunched with Lady Ward, formerly Jean Reid, at Dudley House, with several others. Ward seemed like a good fellow.

Conference in the afternoon with Consul General Skinner on War Trade matters. Tea at the home of the Speaker of the House of Commons, Sir Joseph Gilbert, with Mr. Crane, his house guest. Met his delightful wife and daughters, also Lord Brice, Mr. Fisher, Minister of Education, a number of young M.P.'s. Particularly impressed with Philip Kerr, Lloyd George's Secretary, and Mr. White, a member of Parliament, from Edinburg. Dined with entire Mission at House of Commons, with Mr. Balfour. Dinner given in our honor. Met many distinguished men. Sat between Lord Reading and Sir Alfred Mond.

NOVEMBER 16 (FRIDAY)—

Conference with Lord Robert Cecil at his office in the morning. At 12:45, the Mission met at Chesterfield House, with Col. House and Ambassador Page, to be called for by Royal coaches from Buckingham

---

6. See the seating chart for this event.

Palace to take us to lunch at the Palace with the King and Queen. Lloyd George and Balfour, and Sir Wm. Wiseman, were the only other guests, outside the members of the household, which included Lady Dougadill and Lady Fortiscue. We were all presented to the King and Queen, Princess Mary and Prince Albert, in the reception room outside the dining room. We then went in to lunch. The King sat at the middle of the long table with Admiral Benson, and Gen. Bliss, on each side of him. The Queen sat opposite between Ambassador Page and Col. House. I sat between Lloyd George and Viscount Valencia, one of the King's gentlemen in waiting. The lunch was delightful and most informal, and after lunch we adjourned to the adjoining room for smoking and coffee, and then each of us were taken up in turn for a talk with the King and Queen respectively, and we all noted the King's evident training on topics of conversation, because he spoke to each member of the Mission upon the subject in which he was personally interested. He had evidently been well coached. He spoke to me about President Wilson, knowing of my connection with his campaign, and discussed other matters also, apparently with a full grasp of the subjects under discussion. The Queen was also most gracious, and apparently carefully trained as to our individual interests, and connections. Young Princess Mary was particularly attractive and simple, and Prince Albert, an agreeable young man. In fact, the entire family gave the impression of being desirous of pleasing, and were most hospitable. None of us had looked forward to the experience with much pleasure, and were agreeably surprised at finding that we really enjoyed ourselves.

In the afternoon I met by appointment, Sir Leverton-Harris, and studied with him the machinery of the blockade and war intelligence. Had tea with Lady Waldorf Astor. Conferences in my room at 6 o'clock, with Col. Breckenridge and Zantzinger, who is here en route to Sweden, as Special Agent for the State Department.

Dined quietly with Madge and Charlie Butter, and was glad to have a quiet evening. Worked in my room until 1 o'clock, a not unusual occurrence these days.

NOVEMBER 17 (SATURDAY)—

Conference of the Mission at 10 o'clock as usual. Called upon the French Ambassador, M. Cambon, at the French Embassy, and talked through interpreter charge d'affaires Flerieu. Lunched with Dr. Taylor, Sheldon, and Monet, French Food Representative in London. Conference in Colby's room with Mr. Lewis, the Ship Controller, on tonnage matters.

Tea alone with Ambassador Page for confidential talk over situation in London and Washington. Dined with Crosby. Went to the theater in the evening with Commander Carter, and Major Wallace to see "The Saving Grace."[7] Not much impressed. From cables received from Washington, it is apparent there is some misunderstanding there, and our negotiations are being delayed.

NOVEMBER 18 (SUNDAY)—

Called upon Col. House in the morning to explain the neutral negotiations, and discussed plan for clearing up situation in Washington. I went to Swindon on the 1 o'clock train, and drove ten miles to visit Lady Birbeck at Russley Hall, Blaydon Wilts, where she is superintendent of the remount station, run by the Government.[8] The entire establishment is run by girls. They clean the stables, care for the horses, nearly 100 in number, and are running a model station. I was more impressed than ever with the wonderful work the women of England are performing.

NOVEMBER 19 (MONDAY)—

After spending the night at Russley Hall I got up at 6 A.M., drove over the Downs at dawn, enjoying thoroughly a most beautiful drive to Lambdon, a quaint little village, where I took the train to London, arriving at 10 A.M. The Downs that I drove over had been used for years for the training of race horses, and are famous.[9] I drove by Lady Cravin's home, where she now lives, and is still hunting with the hounds, although I believe she is over 70 years old. Arrived at Claridges in time for the morning conference. Called upon Lord Robert for a confidential talk concerning our difficulty at Washington.

---

7. The play was running at the Garrick Theater, and the male lead was Noel Coward, just becoming known, in the role of Ripley Guildford.

8. Gen. Sir W. H. Birbeck headed the remount department for the British Army. Tens of thousands of horses were needed by the British alone, and lacking the necessary numbers in Britain, horse buyers sought stock in Canada and other countries. The horses were shipped to England and given several weeks at a remount station to regain "land legs," eat, and rest before embarking for the battlefront. The stations were located within a practical distance of the seaports so that the horses would have as little stress as possible. (During the war, a Blue Cross agency was established for the care of the horses.) McCormick visited a remount station run by women under the direction of Birbeck's wife. It was considered one of the best. All the women wore khaki uniforms, and the entire operation was organized in military fashion.

9. The Downs was an area of open, rolling hills in southern England.

Lunched with George Clark and his wife, Charles and Madge Butter, at the Berkley.

Conference in my room all afternoon.

Went to the Gaiety in the evening.

NOVEMBER 20 (TUESDAY)—

Conference in the morning in my room as usual.

At 11:30 the entire Mission went to Downing Street for the meeting of the Mission with the War Cabinet. The meeting was held in the same room where war was declared against the Colonies in 1776, and the same room where peace was later made.[10] Lloyd George presided—the entire War Cabinet was present—also Lord Reading, Lord Northcliffe, Lord Robert Cecil, Gen. Robertson, Gen. Smuts, Admiral Jellicoe, and others.

We discussed the important questions to be considered, which finally developed into the question of tonnage. Lloyd George suggested that he appoint a sub-committee to deal specifically with this matter to bring about a closer co-operation between Great Britain and ourselves. Lloyd George appointed Colby and myself to meet with Lord Curzon, Lord Milner and Lord Robert Cecil, and to arrange a conference later in the afternoon. This conference was held at the War Cabinet office, Whitehall Gardens. Lord Curzon presided. I was most unfavorably impressed by his egotistical and pompous manner. We made some progress, but not as much as I had hoped.

Lunched with Lord Robert and Dr. Taylor at Claridges.

Dined with Grasty of the *New York Times*.

NOVEMBER 21 (WEDNESDAY)—

Conference of the Mission in my rooms at 10 A.M., after I had returned from a breakfast alone with Lord Reading in his home, where we had a confidential talk. We had a typical English breakfast, helping ourselves from the sideboard with oatmeal, etc., and the room very cold. Conference at Lord Robert's office at 11:30 A.M., to discuss Norwegian agreement with the French and Italian representatives. At 1:30 the Mission lunched

---

10. This joint conference between the "technical" members of the American mission and the British war cabinet was held without Colonel House; Admiral Benson was the official spokesman for the Americans. Charles Seymour, *The Intimate Papers of Colonel House* (Boston: Houghton Mifflin Company, 1926), 3:243. The Cabinet Room continues to be used today for the weekly cabinet meetings of the British government, as it has for two hundred years.

with Prime Minister Lloyd George at his home, 10 Downing Street, where all the Prime Ministers have lived for years, and where the War Cabinet meets. I sat between Lord Curzon and Gen. Robertson and had a most interesting conversation with the former, concerning President Wilson's attitude before and after the war. Much to my surprise he thoroughly approved of the President, and with the latter I had a very frank discussion as to the military needs; the importance of getting our men into France at the earliest possible time, and his own opinion that the campaigns outside of the western front were of no particular value, and rather a detriment to the general situation.

Held a conference with Ambassador Page and his blockade staff at 3 P.M., at his office. Later went with Ensign Frothingham to visit Simpkins, who is really the head of all the intelligence matters connected with the operation of the blockade machine. We discussed the best methods of cooperation between the United States and Great Britain, and he offered us the use of all their accumulated data of the three years' war.[11]

Conference in my room at 5:30 P.M., with Crespi, the Food Administrator of Italy, and Dr. Taylor. Italy is begging for more wheat, and claims to be in a serious condition on account of lack of tonnage. The same old story, everything reverts back to ships. Dined with Sheldon, Taylor and Crosby. Worked in my room until midnight getting off cables.

NOVEMBER 22 (THURSDAY)—
[Mission crosses channel and arrives in Paris]

Packed for Paris in the morning. Left Charing Cross at 11 A.M. for Dover on a special train. Ambassador Page and the entire Embassy staff were down to see us off. Also, Mr. Balfour, Lord Reading, Lord Cunliffe, the head of the Bank of England, Sir Wm. Wiseman and others. Fast trip to Dover. There met by a British Admiral and Capt. Evans, famous for sinking three German destroyers, one by ramming it.[12] Delightful to hear him discuss his victories. He told of many gallant things happening in the navy, which never get into print. I think this is a pity, as the people back home should hear of the brave exploits of their fellow countrymen to keep up the enthusiasm and patriotism of the country. We crossed the

---

11. The facilitators in the technical group were able to agree and set goals, but the House-Lloyd meetings continued to be unresolved, with House pushing for a joint announcement of war aims and for unified military leadership.

12. See entry for June 18 in the 1919 diary.

Channel, which was like a mill pond, on a British destroyer in about one hour. There, were met by a special train for Paris. We were met at Calais by ——— Casenave, and several other Frenchmen with the newspaper correspondents of the American Press, *New York World* and *New York Sun*.

We arrived at Paris at 8 o'clock, and as Cravath and I did not have dinner on the train, we went to dine with Col. Logan of Pershing's staff, a great friend of Frank McCoy, and Jim Perkins, brother of Nelson Perkins of our party, and also Casenave, to the Hotel Castillion. Stopping in at the Café Voisin. On our way to the hotel, we ran across John Jay, dining alone, looking very fat and hearty. Paris full of Americans in uniform. Found upon arrival note from Gertrude Ely, asking me to dine with Martha McCook and herself; also found note from Elizabeth Hudson. Everyone feels more cheerful on account of the Cambrai victory, but the last two weeks over here have been a nightmare—the low point of the war.[13] We are comfortably housed at the Hotel Crillon, but not as good quarters as we had at Claridges in London. Col. House has his headquarters in the hotel with us.

NOVEMBER 23 (FRIDAY)—

The Mission met in Col. House's room at 10 A.M., and together went to Ambassador Sharp to present our credentials, and to get in touch with our opposites.[14] Mine being M. Jonnart, the Minister of the Blockade, who was unfortunately ill, but designated an alternate. Colby and I lunched at Mr. Belder's apartment, an American volunteer assisting Naval Attache, Sayles, in embargo work. Commander Sayles was present at the lunch with Lieut. Maas of New York, who is assisting him. We had an interesting discussion upon the Swiss embargo matters.

3 P.M. Attended the first conference upon the blockade, at the Blockade Ministry, which was held in the beautiful residence of a former German, taken over for the Blockade Ministry. The house was full of tapestry, and other rich furnishings. Our meetings were held in the dining room, which made an excellent board room. M. Delavaud presided in the absence of M.

---

13. The battle of Cambrai, which began on November 20, 1917, marked the first occasion on which a large number of tanks were used in combat. As McCormick's diary entry of November 22 indicates, the battle was initially considered a great victory for the British, who had launched the attack, but a German counteroffensive on November 29 succeeded in regaining much of the territory lost during the first phase of the encounter.

14. The technical advisors went right to work coordinating economic matters with French counterparts as they had in London with the British.

Jonnart. Dr. Taylor and I called upon Ambassador Willard of Spain to discuss embargo matters with him. Met Miss Helen Cameron in front of the hotel with Miss Willard. Find that she is staying at the Crillon. Dined at the Café de Paris with Sheldon and Taylor. We all regret the behavior of some of our officers in the cafes of Paris—it is causing much unfavorable comment.

NOVEMBER 24 (SATURDAY)—

Mission had photograph taken in Col. House's room. At 12:30 went to luncheon with the President and Madame Poincare, and all the French dignitaries from Clemenceau down, including Gen. Petain, and other famous generals and statesmen. Viviani, Tardieu, Pichon and others. I sat between Marshal Joffre and Foreign Minister Pichon. The latter speaks some English, the Marshal not a word, but Cravath, on the other side, acted as interpreter, and I had an interesting time. It was a wonderful lunch, beautifully appointed. Delicious food, and, according to the party, marvelous wines.[15] Certainly no indication of a food rationing in Paris.

4 P.M. Conference with Ambassador Willard and Col. Dawes in charge of purchasing for Pershing's army, Crosby, Perkins, Taylor, Cravath and Sheldon, on the Spanish situation, due to embargo on lumber, etc., needed by the army, and also financial matters.

7:30 Dinner of Yale Alumni at the Café Cardinal. About 150 Yale men sat down to the table. It was gotten up by George Nettleton, who is running the University Union of Paris, the headquarters for all college men. Andy Graves, Harry Graves, Lew Sheldon, Geo. Nettledon, of my time, were present. Mr. Bennat presided. Nettledon, Atterbury, and Douglas, 1914, spoke. The dinner was a great success. We were more impressed that evening with the fact that Paris doesn't seem to feel the war as keenly as London. Not as close rationing, streets were brilliantly lighted, more to eat, plenty of hot water in the hotels, if you pay for good rooms. Met John Wickersham of Lancaster at the dinner. John Greenway called, but I missed him. He was on his way to the front.

NOVEMBER 25 (SUNDAY)—

Met with Col. House Sunday morning, and several other members of the Mission to place a wreath on the tomb of Lafayette at Picpus Ceme-

---

15. McCormick abstained from alcohol, as did most of his family.

tery.[16] In the yard of the nunnery and church, nuns were strolling about the ground in pure white costumes; most of them seemed old. Very fat priests were also hovering about. On the way home we stopped at Notre Dame Cathedral, and I was more impressed than ever with the beauty of Paris. Lunched with Mrs. Whitelaw Reid to meet Gen. Pershing. Young Teddy R. and wife, Lady ————, Miss Alexander, French and Belgium officers and others present.

Conference in the afternoon with Col. Dawes and Gen. Pershing at their offices. Called upon Elizabeth Hudson, but found her in the country for Sunday.

Dined with Mrs. House to meet Martha McCook, Gertrude Ely, and Lady Paget. The girls living together at the Hotel de Choiseul. They are working in the Y.W.C.A. organization, having charge of the girls sent to the front to work in the huts. Both considerably exercised over the behavior of many of our officers, and the bad example set the men.

NOVEMBER 26 (MONDAY)—

Conference at office of new Minister of Blockade, M. Lebrun, who has just been appointed to succeed M. Jonnart, who resigned on account of ill health. Present—M. Charpentier, M. Seydeaux, Taylor and Sheldon, to discuss Switzerland and Spain. Returning to the hotel Sheldon took me to a most interesting wholesale pearl merchant to buy some studs. We went into the old quarter of the town, through dark and narrow alleys, and then into a dirty courtyard, and up two flights of stairs into an old building. We landed into the rooms of the merchant, where the situation changed, and I was dazed with the wonderful jewels which he brought out of his old safes. I purchased a modest set of studs, to replace the ones stolen at the Shoreham Hotel.

Lunch with Col. Logan at the Café Voison, and later conferred with him and Perkins in my room, discussing the difficulties of army supplies. Took a walk with Perkins on the banks of the Seine. Had a talk with Frederick Palmer, Pershing's publicity man, who called to discuss publicity. Hugh Bayne called to take Nettleton, Cravath, and Capt. ———— to call

---

16. Since 1830, an American flag has flown over Lafayette's grave. It is the custom for official American visits to include a trip to this grave. On July 4, 1917, elements of the U.S. Army paraded in Paris and at an American-sponsored annual wreath-laying ceremony. The American military leaders were present, including General Pershing, but it was Colonel Stanton who said the legendary words "Lafayette, we are here!"

upon Madame DeBilly. She was most attractive, and speaks English fluently. Her husband was in America with Tardieu's mission.

Dined at the Hotel Meurice with Charpentier, M. Jairut and wife, the latter very attractive—the best type of French woman, and is really playing her part in the war, studying and practicing rationing, which she discussed most intelligently with Dr. Taylor. Her husband is one of the best known political newspaper writers of France. At present on the *Echo d'Paris*. Had an interesting talk regarding French newspapers and French politics. Went to a real French play later in the evening. Very short dress rations apparent here. More and more impressed with the lack of economy about hotels and restaurants, and among better classes. The French Government must impose a stricter rationing system.

NOVEMBER 27 (TUESDAY)—
[*British representatives arrive in Paris*]

Worked in my room on correspondence. Frederick Allen called, also Robert Ronsay, the General Director of the S.S.S., and Col. DuReyniar, Director of the Paris Bureau, to discuss Swiss negotiations. Hayward, Attache at the Hague, and Edwards, Commercial Attache, arrived from Holland after ten days' trip. They were compelled to remain six days on a small boat in Holland waiting for convoy. Slept on benches, and two of their escorts were torpedoed on the way across the Channel. Mr. Dresel, connected with the Legation at Berne, arrived from Switzerland with startling news. Many of the Swiss fear that Germany will pass through Switzerland to invade Italy. We lunched together at the Ritz. Conference in the afternoon with Minister Lebrun, and all the blockade representatives of the Allies. Great deal of talk without accomplishing much. Appointed some committees for tomorrow. Swiss Minister called upon us at the Crillon. At our request he cabled to his Government to send representatives to continue Swiss negotiations here with Dr. Taylor and me.

Dined with Elizabeth Hudson and Miss Stillman.

NOVEMBER 28 (WEDNESDAY)—

Conference with the Minister of the Blockade Lebrun, Crosby, Cravath, and the representative of the French Finance Ministry, Col. Dawes of Pershing's staff, and others, to discuss Spanish exports to France. Lunched with Taylor and Sheldon.

Conference with the Blockade Rationing Committee from 2:30 to 5:30 preparing for Swiss agreement. Mr. Jairut called. Col. Potter called to make arrangements about our trip to the front, and said he had made arrangements for Pete Gross to report to me in Paris.

Dined with Miss McCook and Gertrude Ely at hotel. Henrietta [Ely] was up from her canteen with the French army at Epernay, and Miss Sergeant of the *New Republic,* Dr. Taylor and Col. Thorton, who married Virginia Blair, with another English officer, were present. I returned to my room and worked on reports until time for bed. Conferences are most wearing on account of my lack of French, it being particularly hard to keep track of the proceedings through interpreters.

NOVEMBER 29 (THURSDAY)—

At 9:35 A.M., entire Mission met with Col. House to proceed to the meeting of the Inter-Allied Conference, which was to be held in the Salon de l'Horloge, of the Ministry of Foreign Affairs. A Historic meeting; 18 nations represented in the International Conference.[17] Clemenceau presided at the head table with the entire French Cabinet, and at other tables sat the other delegates, Lloyd George, Balfour, Gen. Robertson, Jellicoe, et. al., representing Great Britain; Cordonna, etc., for Italy; Venizelos for Greece. Clemenceau opened with a few remarks, followed by Pichon, the Foreign Minister. They both dwelt upon the fact that the conference was here for work, and at once we were divided into five conference committees: Finance, Tonnage, Munitions, Food and Blockade.[18] I was appointed to represent the American Mission of the Blockade and Tonnage Committees. Met with the Blockade Committee at 3 P.M., and the Tonnage Committee at 5 P.M. Gen. Bliss asked me to meet in his room with Gen. Robertson, Gen. Foch and Gen. Pershing, to get from these men direct their opinion on the tonnage situation, and the necessity of our full military strength being brought over to France. They frankly discussed the situation, and each in turn gave me his views regarding the situation. I was in hearty accord with the views as recommended.

---

17. This first meeting was composed of representatives of all the Allies. It was held in the same room that later held the plenary sessions of the 1919 Peace Conference.

18. The idea, promoted by France's Pichon, was to keep general discussion (and dissension) to a minimum by breaking the conference into committees. Unaddressed here is the parallel conference of the Supreme War Council, with representatives of France, Great Britain, Italy, and the United States. Discussions were held, beginning December 1, to determine the leadership of the council. Lloyd George worked for political leadership with military advisors, whereas House and Bliss were in favor of military leadership of the council. The Lloyd George arrangement prevailed.

Lunched at the American Club Thanksgiving Day. Tardieu, Viviani, Page and Colby spoke. Joffre was present, and there was, as usual, much enthusiasm whenever his name was mentioned. Again impressed me with the extravagance in food matters. Absolutely no rationing. Apparently more economy in America than here. Took my Thanksgiving dinner at the Ritz with Mrs. Reid. Present: Balfour, Jellicoe, Gen. Robertson, Gen. Pershing, Gen. Bliss, Admiral Benson, August Belmont and wife, Lady Hatfield, Miss McCook, Mr. Bliss and wife, of the Embassy, the latter a friend of Brooks, Edith Taylor's sister, Miss Bishop and brother, Miss Alexander and others. Had a conference at 6:30 P.M., with Edwards and Hayward on Holland.

NOVEMBER 30 (FRIDAY)—

Conference at 9:30 at the Ministry of Blockade with delegates of the Allies, at which the Swiss agreement was unanimously approved. Lunched with M. Clementel, Minister of Commerce, at the Ministry, a beautiful house with attractive gardens. I sat next to M. Clementel, and the Italian Food Administrator. Madame Clementel, the only woman present, was most attractive, but could not speak English.

Conference at 3 P.M. at the Ministry of Commerce on tonnage. Colby, Day and I represented America. Detained so long I missed the Swiss delegates in my room at the hotel, where Taylor and I had an appointment with them. Taylor was present, however, and started the negotiations. Held a conference at my room with Snoucks, of Holland, representing the Foreign Minister Louden, along with Edwards and Hayward. Dined at Cafe Laferruce with Jim Hutchinson, Jim Perkins, Chadwick, Col. Logan and Taylor, and Nelson Perkins. After dinner at 10 o'clock met the Swiss delegates to discuss with them further the Swiss negotiations. After they left worked until 1 o'clock on cables, and ended one of the busiest days of the trip.

DECEMBER 1 (SATURDAY)—

At 10 A.M. attended joint meeting at the palace of the Foreign Minister of the tonnage and food section. Clementel, Minister of Commerce, presiding. All the 18 nations were represented. Each nation was called upon to speak, and I spoke for America briefly. At noon I saw Prof. Rappard, of Switzerland, who accompanied the Swiss delegates, also Snoucks of Holland, telling him of our change of plans by transferring negotiations with Holland to London, and that Dr. Taylor and I hoped to go there on

Wednesday. I lunched with Foreign Minister Pichon and his wife at the Foreign Ministry, beautiful lunch and attractive house, with another lovely French garden. Too much food everywhere for the period of the war. Noticed this everywhere I went, but am afraid the poor do not fare as well. Nearly all the delegates, about 100, were present at the lunch, and sat at one long table in the dining room. After lunch I had an interesting talk with Sir Joseph Maclay on the tonnage question, and apparently made an impression, because soon after my return to the hotel he called at my room with his assistants, Anderson and another expert, and also Mr. Monnet, the Secretary to Clementel, to discuss my proposition for a central Inter-Allied Shipping Board.

Attended a meeting of the Blockade delegates at 3:30, and at 5 P.M. attended a tonnage conference at the office of the Minister of Commerce. M. Clementel presiding. I arrived late, and much to my surprise was called upon by M. Clementel to state my views before the conference in regard to the Inter-Allied tonnage organization, as he understood I had strong views upon this subject. I made my proposal and was glad to have M. Tardieu and Lord Reading and M. Clementel strongly approve it. At about 6:30 I called upon Gen. Pershing at his request at his house and found he wanted to explain fully the military situation, and the great need of tonnage. I explained to him that I appreciated the situation, and was in perfect accord with his views, and would do all I could to impress the seriousness of the situation upon the authorities in Washington.

Took a hurried dinner in my room while packing, and caught the 8:30 P.M. train for Chaumont, with Col. Logan, Taylor and Sheldon to visit the front. We expect to arrive at 2:40 A.M. Not much accommodation for sleeping, but I was better off than Taylor and Sheldon, who missed their dinner.

DECEMBER 2 (SUNDAY)—

Arrived at Chaumont at 2:40 A.M. on time. We were compelled to have our passes[19] vized [sic] by the French and United States guards at the station.

Went to a small chateau where Frank McCoy and Logan live with Major Bowditch and Capt. Eustic, interpreter, and Col. Chambrun, the French liaison officer, who married Nick Longworth's sister. Got up for breakfast at 9 A.M., as it was Sunday. Spent the morning at the United States general headquarters, which are in the French turned over to our

---

19. See the illustration of a pass.

troops. There met Gen. Harbord, Chief of Staff, and all the members of the staff, and Jack Greenway, who had just arrived for assignment there. Went over with the heads of the bureaus their work and was impressed with the whole layout. Everything seemed businesslike and thorough, and they apparently realize what they are up against.

After 12 o'clock lunch we started for our own troops near Neuf Chateau. Met there Gen. Edwards, and saw how the division was billeted in small villages. Then proceeded to Gondrecour, where we called upon General Seibert. This place is only a few miles from the main division where Pete Gross will probably be stationed, and I had the opportunity of seeing the character of the surroundings. I had, by the way, a funny experience about Pete. Supposing he was in France, I arranged with Logan to have him assigned to me at Paris for my stay here. One day I was told Lieut. Gross was outside my room, and when I went out to see him I found a Lieut. Henry Grose, of another Machine Gun Company of the 42nd Division. I was, of course, greatly disappointed and disgusted at the mistake that had been made. That night in reading a letter from Mother I discovered that Henry had not yet left New York, his ship being compelled to return on account of some trouble.

The officers' families will be glad to know that when at the front, except when they are in the trenches, the officers are billeted in the houses of the small villages, and the men in the stables, lofts, and any old thing that has a roof over it. This is the same system used by the French army. At Neuf Chateau, I saw an interesting site of hundreds of French and American soldiers grouped together around a statue of Joan of Arc in a small public square of the town, listening to a concert by a famous French band of Huzzers [sic]. This band had one of the greatest mortality records of the war. The villagers apparently liked our soldiers, and our men seemed to fraternize with the poilus.[20] About dark we proceeded on to Bar-le-Duc, where we spent the night at the Hotel Metz et Commerce. While at Gondrecour I received a telegram from Auchincloss telling me that I would have to return to Washington at once and give up London. Not knowing the reason I was very anxious until I got him on the telephone, and I found that it was nothing more serious than my presence was needed in Washington on account of the work of our Board, and Taylor was to go alone to London.

---

20. *Poilus* was the wartime term for French soldiers, especially frontline infantry troops. The singular is *poily*. It means "hairy one," but the usage is linked to prewar French slang, when the term was applied to a tough, brave individual.

DECEMBER 3 (MONDAY)—

We were awakened early in the morning by the tramping of thousands of soldiers, horses, gun carriages, etc., passing our hotel. We made an early start in our two cars, with the party which had come from Chaumont, which consisted of Frank McCoy, Dr. Taylor, Sheldon, and Commander Hue, our French guide, for Verdun, and were at once in the midst of real warfare, as the roads were crowded with men, guns, trucks, supplies, trainloads of them, going to and from the front about 40 miles away.

Every kind of equipment passed us. I was struck with the good condition of the horses, showing plenty of food. The roads were excellent, but very slippery with snow and ice, as this was an extremely cold morning. Gangs of men, principally Chinamen, were working on the roads constantly.

At S[o]uilly we stopped at the general headquarters of the Verdun Army about 12 miles from Verdun, and there called upon General Guillaumat, who has been in command of the fighting around Verdun for more than a year, succeeding Gen. Petain. We then pushed on to the Verdun Citadel, where we were met by Col. Dehay, who is in command of that important fortification, and who has complete charge of all the movements about Verdun. He took us through the abandoned and desolate city. I have never seen such complete devastation. Not a building that is not destroyed. It was a sad and lonely sight. The Bishop's palace and great Cathedral on the hill are complete wrecks.[21] In the museum of the palace the paintings and statuary are still hanging on the walls and standing about in the rooms. Some of them are unharmed, but apparently, not worth moving. The Citadel is a wonderful underground garrison, having seven kilometers [four miles] of passageways, in which thousands of troops live, and from where the supplies are forwarded to the trenches. It is under constant bombardment, particularly at night, because all roads center in Verdun, and there are thousands of troops passing to and from the rear to the trenches. We saw the devastation done by bombs during the night of our arrival, which had broken off corners of the masonry of the Citadel.

We had a very good lunch with the Commander in his quarters 70 feet underground. You would think you were being served in a private dining

21. In February 21, 1916, the first shot of the battle of Verdun was launched from a huge German naval gun, "Big Bertha," fifteen miles distant. The shot landed in the courtyard of the bishop's palace, damaging the cathedral at the same time. This courtyard is now the site of the World Centre of Peace, opened in 1914 as a museum and conference center with support from the United Nations.

room in some chateau. Immediately after our early lunch we started for the batteries and trenches at the front. Just before we left the Citadel the Commander was called to the telephone, and told us that we could not get out as far as Duamont, because there was a heavy bombardment on, and the shells were dropping all around it. We started, however, for the next nearest fort, Souilly, and passed over the ground between the Citadel and Fort Souilly through the old city that had been fought over many times in hand to hand fights between the German and the French during the last February campaign. As far as the eye could see, the land that had once been covered with forests was as bare as a floor, and apparently not a foot of ground that had not been blown up by a shell fire, or broken up by shovel and pick for trenches.

We left our car under the brow of a hill and climbed up, which was on one of the high points of the salient.[22] Fort Duamont [*sic*] was just ahead of us about a mile on the left of another hill, and it was from these hills that the French last summer drove back the Germans on to the plains beyond, and have since that time been able to hold. When we got to Fort Souilly it seems as though an exhibition had been arranged for us, because on both sides of the hill our batteries were constantly firing, and the German batteries from a great distance on the plain were trying to locate them, and the shells were bursting all around us. At the same time, the French flying machines were sailing over the German lines, and being followed by a continual bombarding of shrapnel, which seemed to completely surround the machines, but apparently none of them were touched.

We were not permitted to get our heads above the trenches for fear of being located by the Germans. On account of the bombardment we were not able to get into the front line of trenches, which were about 2400 feet ahead of us. Toward sunset we started down the hill, and soon after we got into the car, and were riding along the road a shell exploded about 200 yards from the road, which was too close for comfort. There was not a whole house standing in any of the small villages about Verdun. The Germans have destroyed every house which might inhabit a man.

We returned to the Citadel; said farewell to our hospitable host and started back with one of the secret service men who had been sent out with us by the staff for Chalons, 60 miles away where we expected to make the train. It had been a wonderful experience, and we were most

---

22. In this context, salient refers to part of a fortification, line of defense, or trench system that thrusts outward at an angle.

fortunate in having a perfect day, as from our high point at Fort Souilly we could see the hills of Metz, and in a country where there is so much rain and cloudy weather, we were certainly to be congratulated.

Our road now lay practically parallel to the trenches, but some distance south towards Chalons on the old Berlin to Paris route. As it was dark, we could see the explosions of the light bombs and shells of the bombardment which was still going on practically the entire distance of our ride. The representative of the French General Staff, who was now acting as our guide, was a most interesting man, having been wounded seven times. He was cited in the General Army Orders three times, once by his division, and once by his regiment. He was an author and started as a private, but by his daring and bravery was soon promoted. His work was to head small commands of troops to raid the trenches to capture German prisoners for purposes of getting information, and some of his stories were most thrilling. The road we were traveling had been fought over since the days of the Huns and Gauls, and made a most interesting route. We passed by the Claremont woods and the Argonne forests with no mishaps, except auto trouble. We were on the lookout for German flying machines, because they said they were frequently attracted by the auto lights at night and attacked the cars with machine guns. We arrived in Chaumont just in time to catch the train for Paris. Had a good dinner on the car, arriving in Paris at 10 o'clock, where we left our gallant French friend, with much regret. We had dropped Frank McCoy and Commander Hue on the road, they having a blowout, and we could not wait as we had to catch the train. Frank was as attractive as ever, and I thoroughly enjoyed my two days with him.

DECEMBER 4 (TUESDAY)—

I attended a meeting of the Inter-Allied Conference Committee on Blockade with the Swiss delegates at 10 A.M., and Taylor and I were determined to close the agreement at this sitting, much against the protest of our French and Italian friends, whom we kept hard at work until 2 P.M., with the result that they missed their dejeuner, which was a great hardship, but we finished the agreement for typing, so that it could be executed the following day. Dr. Taylor and I called on M. Sedeaux of the Blockade, and then with Sheldon went to tea with Miss Hudson and Miss Stillman. Sheldon and I dined at the Café Henry, a delightful little French café. Auchincloss and I talked until 1 A.M., on the work of the Mission.

He and the Colonel seemed greatly pleased with the favorable comments they have heard from the English and French delegates upon the work of the Mission.

DECEMBER 5 (WEDNESDAY)—

Conference in the morning with Colby and Cravath about Spain and Switzerland. By appointment took Miss Roelof and fellow workers of the Y.W.C.A. to call upon Ambassador Sharp, so that they might have a friend in court if need should arise. 11 A.M., meeting in my room with the Secretary of the Foreign Minister on the question of substituting our timber for the French wood being used for our Army. 12:45, lunched with Dick Strong, an old classmate of mine, and his wife, and now famous for his work in Serbia. Present: Mrs. Hill, Dr. Alex. Lambert. 3 P.M., final conference of the Blockade delegates of the Inter-Allied Conference to witness the signing of the agreement with the Swiss. Farewell speeches were made by the French chairman of the conference, the Swiss delegates and myself. Signatures were affixed to the agreement, and the first neutral agreement was at last a reality, and I believe at this particular time a most important event, due to the strenuous propaganda being carried on in Switzerland to turn that country against the Allies.

Returned to my room to pack heavy luggage, which was to be called for tonight. Had a long interview with Gale, Consul General at Copenhagen, about conditions in Denmark. Interviewed John Bass of the *Chicago News* on publicity matters, and got him to agree to send me his recommendations in writing.

Interviewed Harry Graves concerning wood agreement with France. Dined with Hugh Bayne and Madame DeBilly at the Café Voison—delightful evening, the Madame was most enthusiastic about Americans, and is doing liaison work for her government.

DECEMBER 6 (THURSDAY)—

Breakfast, which I had every morning in my sitting room at 8:30 A.M. Talked with Crosby about my negotiations for the army materials from Switzerland and Spain, and the financial blockade of the neutrals. Concerning the latter he said that Bonar Law desired first an attempt be made to make loans with the neutrals for the Allies before any pressure is exerted.

Met Eyre of the *New York World* at 10 o'clock, and at 11 I called to see M. Clementel, Minister of Commerce, by request, at the Ministry. Clementel wanted to tell me of his appreciation of the stand I had taken at the Inter-Allied meeting on tonnage for a greater unity, and wanted to discuss with me the details of organization. He stated that Clemenceau had just appointed him as France's minister on the joint committee, and hoped our Government would appoint one of our committee to remain over and serve on the Board, so the work could be started at once. I explained why this could not be done without conference at home, which he understood. But I was strongly in favor of the suggested action proposed by Clementel.

Had another talk with Gale about Denmark and blockade matters, and organization for operating same.

Lunched with Ambassador Sharp, his two daughters and son, and Col. Dawes. At 3 o'clock had another interview with Eyre of the *New York World*. Called to say goodbye to Gertrude Ely and Miss McCook, Y.W.C.A. headquarters. Only saw Miss McCook. Met Rev. Lusk, who showed me the way to their office building. Took a long walk, and then stopped in for tea with Madame DeBilly. She thought the French people were greatly disappointed that the conference did not agree upon one Commander-in-Chief of all the armies. I believe myself that if the tide does not turn soon we will be forced into such an organization, as the present system is not effective.

Dined with Perkins and a Frenchman, and then hung around my room as we were mysteriously ordered to remain there after 8:30 P.M., and would be called for; our heavy luggage having gone the previous night to somewhere, all labeled to different parts of France as a camouflage. At 9 P.M. Ensign Richmond Fearing, a former famous Harvard athlete in my college days, called, and said that he was to take charge of Young and myself. So off we started, not knowing where.[23] We landed at a great freight depot in the center of Paris, and there found our special train, and sleeping cars with dining car, and after the arrival of our party one by one, having been driven all over Paris in different directions, we were closeted in our state-rooms and not permitted to go out. We left Paris at 10 P.M., and the party was then informed that we were on the way to Brest, via a roundabout route, so that even the railroad people did not know from which port we would sail. Admiral Benson had told me the plans several days before, as I had not expected to return with the party, but return via London.

---

23. Only two persons knew where the group was going and the exact time of departure: Colonel House and the naval commander in charge, Andrew F. Carter. Seymour, *Intimate Papers*, 3:292.

DECEMBER 7 (FRIDAY)—

When we awoke, we were north of St. Nazarre. Had a beautiful ride through Brittany to Brest, where we arrived at 12:45 P.M., and were met by Admiral Benson, a French Admiral, Admiral Sims, and a number of other naval officers, and at once took the launch for the "Mt. Vernon," our transport, formerly the "Kronprincessin Cecille," which I had crossed on the last time I went to Europe in 1913, with Jim Neale and Jim Clark. She is one of the most comfortable and fastest of the transports, and on her trip over carried 3500 troops. Anchored nearby us in the Brest harbor is the cruiser "San Diego," which was formerly the battleship "California," which is to be our escort for the entire distance across, as well as six destroyers, which are to convoy us the first part of the journey.

We pulled up anchor at 3:30 P.M. in order to get through the Channel before dark at 4:30.[24] As we steamed slowly out, the mine sweepers were just returning, having swept the Channel clear, and a big balloon was being hauled in from the sea by its tug, and the airplane was returning from its search for submarines. In addition to all these precautions Providence favored us, because it began to rain and became very misty, so we had what we had hoped for, a dark night, to run through the most dangerous part of the zone.

At 5 P.M. we were called to dinner, because all lights were out at 5:30. There is absolutely not a light in the stateroom, or anywhere else, except in the passageways about one foot above the floor where there is shaded blue light, and one blue light in a single center room used as a smoking room in which the air is unbearable. Not a porthole permitted open under penalty of arrest and guardhouse. I have a most luxurious stateroom—a big sitting room with bedroom and private bath room. It was so roomy I took Gordon Auchincloss in with me, and we are both most comfortable. Admiral Benson, General Bliss, and Col. and Mrs. House and I are at one table. We miss Crosby and Cravath, who stayed in Paris, and Taylor, who went to London, to try to advance the neutral negotiations before returning this week.

---

24. Colonel House recorded that as they steamed away from France, Bainbridge Colby said, "We have been so used to potentates and kings that the first thing we should do upon arrival in the United States is to take a week's course at Child's Restaurant, sitting on a stool, and getting down again to our own level." Ibid.

DECEMBER 8 (SATURDAY)—

Beautiful morning—no submarines sighted. We passed three empty life boats upturned. The Captain reported many S.O.S. calls during the night. After breakfast read old newspapers in my stateroom. Lunched at 12 o'clock. Worked on papers after lunch. Exercised with Perkins with medicine ball[25] and had the first perspiration for days. Took a bath and r—— for dinner at 5 o'clock. The evenings were long, sitting in absolute darkness until we turned in at 9 o'clock. Nearly all the party slept with their clothes on with life preservers nearby. Our Captain seems to be very strong for darkness, but life preserver regulations more lenient than on the "Huntingdon."

We had our first abandon ship drill this morning, and at the call of the bugle everyone grabbed his life preserver and hurried to his station to which he has been assigned to take his life boat or raft. Our life boat is No. 11, on the starboard side midship. It was carried out orderly, but I can well imagine the confusion with 3500 troops on board.

DECEMBER 9 (SUNDAY)—

At 8 o'clock we had 2550 miles to Hampton Roads, where we expect to land. There is a great guessing as to the time of our arrival. I backing [sic] 10 A.M. Saturday, the 15th. The Colonel thinks Friday night, but I am afraid he is wrong and too optimistic. Had quiet day going over papers and getting a little exercise. Our party is becoming restless at having all the lights out at 5:30, nothing to do in the dark, so the Captain consented to put a few lights in the big smoking room, and now in the evening the officers and party gather in one room, and with the paymaster at the piano, as well as an electrically operated piano, with singing, and card playing, the evenings seem shorter, although the lights are not yet brilliant enough to read by.

DECEMBER 10 (MONDAY)—

Became quite rough during the night and remained so most of the day. Some of the party were ill, and with the heavy seas on we only made between 12 and 13 knots—the schedule is supposed to be 18. As we found we were going to be late in arriving at Hampton Roads we asked the Admiral to change to New York, which he has agreed to do. We now hope to arrive Sunday morning at the latest. We are all anxious to drop

---

25. A medicine ball is a leather-covered, stuffed ball used for conditioning exercises.

our escort which is the cause of our delay, because without her we could make 23 knots, and could get in by Friday evening. It became calmer toward sundown, and it looks like a comfortable night.

DECEMBER 11 (TUESDAY)—

A beautiful morning, after a warm night, and it is now very evident that we are in the Gulf Stream. It is very hard to realize that it is the middle of December, because it is like a summer day, and reminds me of the days on the houseboat "Roxanna" in Florida. We really could wear flannels, and we have been on the deck all day without overcoats.

To make it appear more strange, we have just received wireless reports from New York and Pittsburgh telling of great blizzards and zero weather. I do not think that the ladies in the party know that we are carrying home, on the deck behind the screen, the corpse of a poor sailor, who died on the way out with tuberculosis. We are now cheered by the hope that we may get in with this kind of weather by Saturday morning, so we are all looking forward to a Sunday at home before our work begins on Monday. It is all dependent upon the weather, because our escort can only make good time in good weather. The regulations as to the lights are now becoming easier, and tonight, for the first time, we can have the lights in our stateroom. An entertainment was given by the crew in the large mess hall, which was thoroughly enjoyed—moving pictures, boxing matches, quartettes, solos, etc. A good show. Our meal hours are still—breakfast at 8, lunch at 12, and dinner at 5. Col. House called us into conference at 6:30 to give us instructions about our reports. It feels like another warm night. As this boat was fitted out at Boston most of the crew and reserve officers are from Massachusetts. There are a number of Harvard men among the officers—Bob Emmons, who was on the Harvard football team when I played, and Charles Cummings, who rowed on the Harvard crew with Perkins.

DECEMBER 12 (WEDNESDAY)—

Today was another good day, but somewhat cooler. Most of the Mission were busy working in their rooms upon their reports, appearing only for a bit of fresh air and a little exercise. We made 430 miles, which now looks like Saturday noon. The evenings are not now so long on account of lights being permitted in the stateroom, where we can work and read. They are even having side lights on both our boat and the "San Diego," which shows that they no longer have any fear of submarines.

DECEMBER 13 (THURSDAY)—

A stiff wind has been blowing all day, and the sky was overcast. The boat had considerable motion which made me feel uncomfortable working in my stateroom practically all day, and was not conducive to the preparation of an intelligible report. Blowing hard tonight, which may delay our arrival, but the gossip is that the cruiser will leave us tomorrow for Hampton Roads, in which case we can forge ahead at full speed, and get in by noon on Saturday.

DECEMBER 14 (FRIDAY)—

Sea was quite rough, and a great fall in the temperature. Nothing eventful.

DECEMBER 15 (SATURDAY)—

We were taking soundings to get our bearing, as we had not seen the sun for a long time. We expected to pick up the Fire Island light at 12 o'clock, and were only about a half hour late. Just before we reached the Ambrose light we passed the "Vaterland" steaming eastward, apparently on a trial trip. We stopped to pick up a pilot near the Ambrose light, and then steamed through the channel up to quarantine, which we reached at 4 o'clock, and were met by a police patrol boat with Bill Nye, who took us on board in order to avoid the delays in the docking of the big boat. We landed at the 34th St. pier at 4:30 P.M., and I was able to catch the 5 o'clock train for Harrisburg. I was glad to meet Elsie Ely on the train and hear some home news.

Arrived at Harrisburg at 9:30 P.M.

FINIS.

A Glossary of Names and Places

Albert, Prince (November 16)
Second son of King George V and Queen Mary, Prince Albert (1895–1952) served with both the Royal Navy and the Royal Air Force during the war. On the abdication of his brother, Edward VIII, in 1936, he ascended the throne as King George VI.

Allen, Frederick (November 27)
Possibly Frederick Hobbes Allen, a lawyer and diplomat who represented the United States and foreign governments in negotiations involving financial and commercial matters. When the United States

entered the war, Allen was commissioned a lieutenant commander in the U.S. naval reserve flying corps. In that capacity, he became an aide to the officer who commanded the U.S. naval aviation forces in England, France, and Italy.

Ambrose light (December 15)

Lighthouse on the Ambrose channel, in southeastern New York at the entrance to New York Harbor.

American Club (November 29)

The oldest nondiplomatic, organized American presence in France. It remains a viable private organization today, providing a social connection for expatriate Americans and French members who wish to maintain American business and social contacts.

American Press (November 22)

This seems to be a reference to the press in general, not a specific paper.

Anderson (December 1)

During the war, a number of Andersons were associated with the British Admiralty or Shipping Ministry in one capacity or another. Alan Anderson, an official with the shipping firm of Anderson, Anderson and Co. before the war, seems most likely to be the expert to whom McCormick refers. As Sir Eric Geddes's successor as controller of the navy, Anderson was responsible for meeting the shipbuilding needs of the Ministry of Shipping, the Admiralty, and the War Office.

"Arathusa" (November 4) Arathusa, p.4

A merchant ship built in England in 1893, the USS *Arethusa* (1898–1927) was purchased by the U.S. Navy in August 1898 and converted for use as a water tanker; around 1910, she was modified to become the navy's first oil tanker. She was decommissioned in 1922 and sold in 1927.

Argonne Forest (December 3)

A wooded ridge in northern France that forms a natural barrier between the Lorraine and Champagne regions. Although apparently peaceful when McCormick passed through its southern regions, the Argonne Forest was a battleground at various times during World War I.

Asquith, Mr. (November 14)

As leader of Britain's Liberal Party, Henry Herbert Asquith (1852–1928) had served as prime minister from 1908 through 1916. In December 1916, liberal and conservative politicians concerned with Asquith's prosecution of the war formed a coalition to replace him with fellow liberal David Lloyd George, a political rival.

Astor, Lady Waldorf (November 16)

Lady Astor, formerly Nancy Langhorne (1879–1964) of Virginia, was the wife of Waldorf Astor, a conservative member of Parliament. In 1919, Astor inherited his father's title and seat in the House of Lords, and Nancy was elected to represent her husband's district in the House of Commons, becoming the first woman to serve in that body. She was painted in 1909 by John Singer Sargent.

Atterbury (November 24)

Almost certainly William Wallace Atterbury (1866–1935), a Yale graduate who was by 1916 vice president for operations of the Pennsylvania Railroad and president of the American Railway Association. Named director general of transportation for the American Expeditionary Force soon after the United States entered the war, Atterbury oversaw the portion of the French railway system that supplied American troops. After the war, he returned to the Pennsylvania Railroad, serving as president of the company from 1925 until his retirement in 1934.

Auchincloss, Gordon (October 28, 29, 30; December 2, 4, 7)

The son-in-law of Edward House, Auchincloss (1886–1943) was a lawyer specializing in corporate law. He served the Wilson administration, primarily as secretary of the mission to the Inter-Allied Conference that McCormick attended and as his father-in-law's secretary during the Paris Peace Conference. Auchincloss, Gordon, pp. 3, 17, 19, 21.

"Balch" (October 30)

The destroyer USS *Balch* (1912–35) was built in Philadelphia and served in the Atlantic Fleet. She was part of the Neutrality Patrol prior to the U.S. entrance in the war; following that, she served as convoy escort. She was in service through 1922.

Balfour, Mr. (November 7, 14, 15, 16, 22, 29)

Appointed British foreign secretary in the cabinet reorganization that followed Lloyd George's replacement of Asquith as prime minister, Arthur James Balfour (1848–1930) had himself served as British prime minister from 1902 to 1905 and had led the opposition in the years leading up to the war. (Balfour was the nephew of the English conservative Lord Salisbury; together they were known as the "Cecil Dynasty.") As foreign secretary, he participated in the 1919 Peace Conference at Versailles and promulgated the Balfour Declaration of 1917, which supported the creation of a Jewish state in Palestine.

Bar-le-Duc (December 2)

A town in northeastern France on the Marne-Rhine Canal, Bar-le-Duc was the terminus of the only open road to Verdun. This road was designated a supply route for the trucks that were collected to supply French front lines with men and materiel during the battle of Verdun. It was known as the *Voie Sacrée.*

Bass, John (December 5)

An experienced war correspondent, John Foster Bass (1866–1931) had reported from battlefronts around the world for the *New York Times* and the *Chicago Daily News.* In addition to World War I, he covered the Spanish-American War in the Philippines, the Boxer Rebellion in China, the Russo-Japanese War of 1904, and a host of more minor conflicts.

Bayne, Hugh (November 26; December 5)

An 1892 graduate of Yale, Bayne (1870–1954) was a lawyer who served as a judge advocate for the U.S. Army in France and as counsel for the 1918 Prisoners of War Mission.

Belmont, August, (November 29)

A New York banker who arranged the financing for the construction of the West Side subway line, Belmont (1853–1924) also bred and raced Thoroughbreds. In 1905, he was appointed treasurer of the Democratic National Committee. In 1917, he received a commission in the U.S. Army, serving primarily in Spain, where he purchased and exported supplies to the U.S. military in France.

Belmont, Mrs. (November 29)

Elizabeth Robson Belmont (1879–1979) had been an actress before becoming August Belmont's second wife in 1910. During the war she was active in the Red Cross in Europe.

Benson, Admiral (October 29, 30; November 16, 29; December 6, 7)

After a slow rise through the Navy's ranks, William Shepherd Benson (1855–1932) was appointed the first chief of naval operations in 1915. In that capacity, he was instrumental in preparing the U.S. fleet for participation in the European war and in introducing antisubmarine warfare measures that helped break Germany's submarine blockade around Britain. After the war, he advised President Wilson on naval issues during the Paris Peace Conference and chaired the U.S. Shipping Board.

Bishop's Palace, (December 3)

Built in 1723 by architect Robert de Cotte for Louis XV. From 1920 to 1932, Monseigneur Ginisty, then bishop of Verdun, led the drive to create and finance the ossuary and mausoleum that now stands on the Verdun battleground.

Blaydon Wilts, (November 18)

Town in England.

Bliss, General, (October 29, 30; November 16, 29; December 7)

Named U.S. Army Chief of Staff in September 1917, Tasker Bliss (1853–1930) improved relations between General Pershing, the commander of the American Expeditionary Force in France, and the military leadership in Washington. As Woodrow Wilson's representative on the Allies' Supreme War Council, he supported Pershing's decision to keep the American forces in France together while also backing the concept of a unified Allied military command under Marshal Foch. Although the diary makes no reference to a previous acquaintance, McCormick may have known Bliss from the latter's years as president of the Army War College.

Bliss, Mr. (November 29)

Most likely Robert Woods Bliss (1875–1962), counselor at the Paris embassy between 1916 and 1920. A career Foreign Service officer, Bliss dealt primarily with alien relief matters during his posting in Paris. After the war, Bliss continued working for the State Department, becoming U.S. ambassador to Argentina in 1927.

Bliss, Mrs. (November 29)

Robert Woods Bliss married Mildred Barnes in 1908 (1879–1969). She was active in war relief work. She and her husband Robert were prominent philanthropists, art collectors, and founds of Dumbarton Oaks, a center for Byzantine Studies.

Bonar Law (December 6)

Andrew Bonar Law (1858–1923) became leader of the British Conservative Party in 1911. Dissatisfied with Asquith's conduct of the war by late 1916, he switched his support to David Lloyd George, allowing the latter to become prime minister. Under Lloyd George, Bonar Law served as chancellor of the exchequer and as a member of the war cabinet. When Lloyd George's government fell in 1922, Bonar Law became prime minister.

Bowditch, Major (December 2)

Probably Edward Bowditch (1881–?), an All-American end on Harvard's 1902 football team. Bowditch served as an aide to General Pershing during the war. After the war, he became an insurance broker.

"The Boy" (November 8)

A musical version of the 1885 Pinero farce, *The Magistrate, The Boy* opened at the Adelphi Theatre in London in mid-September, 1917.

Brest (December 6, 7)

A port on the Atlantic coast in northwest France, three hundred miles west of Paris.

Brice, Lord (November 15)

Likely a reference to Lord James Bryce (1838–1922) a British historian, statesman, and diplomat who served as ambassador to the United States from 1906 to 1913. He took up the Armenian cause after traveling there, published a book about Turkish atrocities against Armenians, and became a dedicated supporter of the League of Nations.

Brittany (December 7)

A region in northwest France.

Burgess, Mr. (October 29)

Warren Randolph Burgess (1889–1978) was a statistician with the War Industries Board when he traveled to England and France with McCormick and the other members of the House Mission. In 1918 and 1919, he served with the statistics branch of the U.S. Army general staff. Upon returning to civilian life in 1920, he began a career as a banker, first with the Federal Reserve Bank of New York and subsequently with National City Bank.

Calais (November 22)

A seaport in northwest France on the Pas de Calais (Straits of Dover). The English Channel is narrowest at the Straits of Dover, providing the shortest crossing from England to France.

"California" (December 7)

ACR 6 was an armed cruiser that began service in 1902. The ship was commissioned by the navy in 1906 as the USS *California.* The name was changed to USS *San Diego* in 1914 when Congress declared that state names would be used only for battleships. The ship was sunk off Fire Island (eight miles off Long Island's south shore) in July 1918 after it struck a mine left by a German U-boat. This was the only major warship lost by the United States in World War I.

Cambon, M. (November 17)

France's ambassador to Great Britain from 1898 to 1920, Paul Cambon (1843–1924) was instrumental in arranging the Entente Cordiale of 1904, which resolved a number of differences between France and Britain and improved relations between the two countries.

Cambrai victory (November 22)

The British massed about three hundred tanks and sent them against the Germans en masse with twelve infantry division following. This was the first such action, and it marked a revolution in modern warfare, with a huge gain of ground. The German forces rallied, however, and forced the tanks to withdraw, but the tank victory was a morale booster for Allied forces.

Carter, Lieutenant Colonel/Commander (October 29; November 17)

Cdr. A. P. Carter was Admiral Benson's aide.

Casenave (November 22)

De Casenave was head of the Press Bureau at France's Foreign Office.

Cathedral (December 3)

The Cathedral Notre Dame, on which construction began in A.D. 990.

Cecil, Lord Robert (November 12, 13, 14, 16, 19, 20, 21)

A conservative member of Parliament at the outbreak of the war, Cecil (1864–1958) was quickly appointed to a position in the Foreign Office, and in that capacity, he served as minister of blockade from 1916 to 1918. His experiences during the war led him to become a vocal advocate of disarmament and a strong supporter of the League of Nations, both within the British government and in the international arena. The Nobel Committee recognized his efforts on behalf of world peace by awarding him the Nobel Peace Prize in 1937.

Chalons (December 3)

A small town on the Marne River west of Verdun, France, the location of the famous battle of Attila the Hun in A.D. 451, considered one of the fifteen most decisive battles in western history. It was this battle that laid the deep foundation for the French antagonism against Germany.

Chambrun, Colonel (December 2)

A descendant of the Marquis de Lafayette, Col. Jacques Aldebert de Chambrun was married to Clara Longworth, the sister of prominent Republican congressman Nicholas Longworth. De Chambrun served on General Pershing's staff during the war and later lectured at the Army War College.

Charing Cross (November 22)

A railway station in central London.

Charpentier (November 26)

Raymond Charpentier was the French representative to the British blockade committee.

Chaumont (December 1, 2, 3)

A town in northeastern France located on a height overlooking the Marne River and the Marne-Saone Canal. The field headquarters for the American Expeditionary Force was located in Chaumont.

Chesterfield House (November 7, 9, 16)

Located on South Audley Street in London, Chesterfield House was an impressive mansion built by the fourth earl of Chesterfield in the middle of the eighteenth century.

Choiseul de Hotel (November 25)

Possibly the hotel of that name still found today in Paris, at 1 Rue Daunou in the Opera area.

Claridges Hotel (November 7, 19, 20)

Claridges is located on Brook Street in London. Built in 1812, it was modernized in 1898, with a major addition in 1909 following the opening of the rival Ritz in 1906. It is renowned for its quiet elegance and plush accommodations.

Clemenceau (November 24, 29; December 6)

After a long career in French politics and one previous stint as prime minister (1906–09), Georges Clemenceau (1841–1929) had again become prime minister just days before McCormick's party arrived in France. Long a critic of the French government's failure to prosecute the war successfully, Clemenceau pursued a policy of more aggressive engagement with the German forces, leading to Germany's request for an armistice in 1918. At the Paris Peace Conference, Clemenceau was one of the council of four involved in making crucial decisions regarding the peace settlement, the others being Wilson of the United States, Lloyd George of Britain, and Orlando of Italy.

Clementel (November 30; December 1, 6)

As minister of trade during the war years, Etienne Clementel (1864–1936) was responsible for coordinating the economic aspects of the war effort. During these years, the purview of the French Trade Ministry was expanded to include industry, army supplies, mail and telecommunications, transportation, agriculture, and labor.

Colby, Bainbridge (October 29; November 13, 14, 17, 20, 23, 29, 30; December 5)

A political supporter of Woodrow Wilson, Colby (1869–1950) was appointed to the Shipping Board after the United States entered World War I and, in that capacity, traveled to Europe with the mission on which McCormick also served. Despite his comparative lack of experience in international affairs, he became Wilson's secretary of state upon the resignation of Robert Lansing in early 1920.

Connaught, Duke of (November 10)

The third son of Queen Victoria and Prince Albert, Prince Arthur, duke of Connaught (1850–1942), had been a soldier and military commander at posts throughout the British Empire. From 1911 to 1916, he served as governor general of Canada.

Cordonna (November 29)

Since published reports of the Inter-Allied Conference do not mention an Italian representative named Cordonna, McCormick is probably referring to Luigi Cadorna (1850–1928), an Italian general and former chief of the Italian general staff. Named chief of staff in July 1914, Cadorna was replaced after the Italians suffered a serious defeat in the battle of Caporetto.

Crane, Charles R. (November 12, 15)

Initially a supporter of Theodore Roosevelt and William Howard Taft, Crane (1858–1939) switched his political allegiance to the Democratic Party under Woodrow Wilson. In 1917, Wilson sent Crane on a special mission to Russia.

Cravath, Mr. (Oct. 29; Nov. 22, 24, 26, 28; Dec. 5, 7)

Known primarily for his work as a corporate lawyer and for the system of law firm organization that he developed, Paul Drennan Cravath (1861–1940) served as counsel to various U.S. missions involved in financing the Allied war effort.

Cravin, Lady (November 19)

Crespi (November 21)

Named Italy's minister of food and transportation during the war, Dr. Silvio Crespi (1866–1944) was an economist who subsequently served as an Italian signatory to the Versailles Peace Treaty. In 1920, he joined the Italian Senate.

Crillon Hotel (November 22, 23, 27)

The Hotel de Crillon is still in business on the Place de la Concorde and has lost little of its eighteenth-century splendor; it was designed by Jacques-Ange Gabriel for Louis XV in 1758. In 1919, it was the headquarters for the American Commission to Negotiate Peace during the Paris Peace Conference.

Crosby, Assistant Secretary of the Treasury (October 29; November 12, 17, 24, 28; December 6, 7)

An electrical engineer with West Point training, Oscar T. Crosby (1861–1947) had spent much of his career in building and managing electric railway and power companies. He joined the Treasury Department only after the United States entered the war, becoming an assistant secretary of the treasury with responsibility for loans to the Allies. When McCormick and other members of the mission returned to the United States, Crosby remained in Europe to serve on the Inter-Allied Council for War Purchases and Finance, the agency responsible for coordinating purchases by the Allies, arranging funding, and developing loan policies.

Crowe, Sir Eyre (November 10)

A career diplomat, Sir Eyre Crowe (1864–1925) was, by 1917, assistant undersecretary of state for foreign affairs in Britain's Foreign Office.

Cummings, Charles (December 11)

Cunliffe, Lord (November 22)

Walter Cunliffe (1855–1920) was a merchant banker and governor of the Bank of England throughout the war years.

Curzon, Lord (November 20, 21)

George Nathaniel Curzon (1859–1925) had been a conservative member of Parliament and viceroy of India in the early years of the twentieth century. During the War, he was a member of both Asquith's and Lloyd George's war cabinets, becoming Foreign Secretary upon Balfour's resignation in 1919.

"Cushing" (November 6)

The U.S.S. *Cushing* was a 116-ton torpedo boat. She was built in Bristol, Rhode Island, and commissioned in April 1890, at which time she was the navy's only modern torpedo boat. Her main service was off Cuba in support of the Spanish-American War naval efforts. She served on a reserve basis after that and was ultimately used by the navy as a target in September 1920.

Darwin, Major (November 11)

Although Charles Darwin's biographies list his oldest son as a banker, rather than a political economist, William Erasmus Darwin was the only one of Darwin's sons to build a career outside the sciences or engineering.

Davenport (November 6, 7)

Possibly Devonport, one of the three towns that make up the city of Plymouth, England. Devonport is the site of an engineering college and naval barracks.

"Davis" (November 6)

DD 65, the USS *Davis*, was a Sampson-class destroyer, the first class to mount an antiaircraft gun. She was built in 1915 and utilized as a con-

voy escort until 1919, when she became idle until loaned to the Coast
Guard from 1926 to 1933. She was scrapped in 1934.

Dawes, Colonel (November 24, 25, 28; December 6)

A prominent Republican who served as the general purchasing agent
for Pershing's army, Charles Gates Dawes (1865–1951) went on to fill
a number of positions in successive Republican administrations, most
notably those of vice president of the United States under Calvin
Coolidge and U.S. ambassador to Great Britain under Herbert Hoover.
He joined the army as a major in 1917 and left twenty-six months later
as a brigadier general. He received the Nobel Peace Prize in 1925,
mainly for his 1924 report on German reparations, known as "The
Dawes Plan."

Day, Mr. (Oct. 29)

Charles Day (1879–1931) was a Philadelphia-born engineer and partner in Dodge and Day, a firm that designed and managed industrial
plants and public utilities. During the war, he conducted an investiga-
tion of American shipbuilding facilities on behalf of the secretary of
war and traveled to Europe with McCormick as both a special representative of the U.S. Shipping Board and the engineering advisor to the
House Mission.

DeBilly, Madame (November 26; December 5, 6)

Madame DeBilly donated use of her large private residence, 28 Quai
Debilly in Paris, by the American Committee for Training Maimed
Soldiers in Suitable Trades. One hundred maimed soldiers were fed,
housed, and trained in this residence.

Denton, Miss (October 29)

Frances B. Denton was Colonel House's private secretary.

Dover (November 22)

A seaport in southeastern England. The English Channel is narrowest
at this point, providing the shortest crossing to France.

Downing Street (November 20, 21)

In the context in which it appears in the diary, Downing Street refers
not to the street itself, but to Number 10 Downing Street, the official
residence of Britain's prime ministers.

Downs (November 19)

The Downs are chalk hill ranges in the south of England, primarily
located in Dorset and Hampshire, but extending into Surrey, Kent, and
East and West Sussex.

Dresel, Mr. (November 27)

As attaché at the American Embassy in Berlin, Ellis Loring Dresel (1865–1925) handled relations between British prisoners of war and the German government in the years before the United States entered the war. After the American declaration of war, he moved from a brief posting at the American Embassy in Vienna to Switzerland where he assisted the Red Cross in its efforts to provide aid to American prisoners of war.

Duamont (December 4)

Fort Douaumont, the most hotly contested section of the Verdun battlefield. The fort was five miles northeast of the city, the northeastern-most and largest of the ring of nineteen forts that extended in a circle around Verdun. Thought to be impregnable, the fort was captured by the Germans on February 25, 1916. An underground explosion at the fort on May 8 killed hundreds of Germans. Damage was so great that the area was sealed off as a mass grave. The fort was regained by the French in October 1916.

Dudley House (November 15)

Built in 1824, Dudley House was located on Park Lane in London.

Echo d'Paris (November 26)

Founded in 1884, *l'Echo de Paris* was one of the leading daily newspapers in Paris.

Ely, Elsie (December 15)

Elsie Ely and her husband, Carl, were McCormick's neighbors on Front Street in Harrisburg.

Ely, Gertrude (November 22, 25, 28)

A YMCA worker from Bryn Mawr, Pennsylvania, Gertrude Ely ran canteens for American soldiers in France. Assigned to the U.S. Army's 1st Division, she was the first American woman to cross the Rhine into Germany after the armistice.

Ely, Henrietta (November 28)

Henrietta was possibly the wife of Richard Ely, an American expert on economics associated with the War Trade Board.

Epernay (November 28)

A town in northern France on the left bank of the Marne River.

Eyre (December 6)

Lincoln Eyre had served as a correspondent for the *New York World* in both Belgium and Paris. In October 1917, he was accredited to the

American Expeditionary Force and, as such, was one of the first American war correspondents to enter Germany. He later covered the Paris Peace Conference, also for the *World*.

Fearing, Richmond (December 6)

George Richmond Fearing, Harvard graduate of 1893, is listed in the Harvard Athletic Hall of Fame for track and field. A portrait of his father was painted by John Singer Sargent.

Fire Island (December 15)

A narrow island off the southern shore of Long Island.

Fisher, Mr. (November 15)

From 1916 to 1922, British historian Herbert Albert Laurens Fisher (1865–1940) was president of the Board of Education in the government of David Lloyd George. The Fisher Act, his major contribution to British education, provided state grants for higher education and greatly improved the salaries and pensions of Britain's elementary and secondary schoolteachers.

Flerieu (November 16)

Probably Aime de Fleuriau, an official of the French Embassy in London.

Foch, General (November 29)

Chief aide to Marshal Joffre in the early years of the war, Ferdinand Foch (1851–1929) had fallen out of favor when Joffre was removed from command after the losses at Verdun in 1916. With the establishment of the Allies' Supreme War Council in 1918, however, Foch returned to power as the supreme commander of all Allied forces in the West. In this capacity, he planned and directed the battles waged between April 1918 and the capitulation of Germany and her allies in November of that year.

Fort Souilly (December 3)

During the Verdun battles, French military headquarters were in Souilly, a town eleven miles southwest of Verdun.

Fortiscue, Lady (November 16)

Francis, Ambassador (November 12)

David Rowland Francis (1850–1927) had been a successful businessman, governor of Missouri, and secretary of the interior under Grover Cleveland. Appointed ambassador to Russia in 1916, he remained in that country until late 1918, even though normal diplomatic relations between the United States and Russia ended after the Bolshevik Revolution in 1917.

Frothingham, Lieutenant (November 8, 14, 21)

Although no first name appears in the diary, this is likely Lt. Donald Frothingham, who served as an American representative to the Supreme Blockade Council which McCormick chaired after the war.

Gaiety (November 19)

Probably a reference to the Gaiety Theatre at Strand and Catherine Streets in London. At various periods in its history, the Gaiety operated as a music hall and as a theater offering farces, burlesques, and light comedies.

Gale, William H. (December 5)

A Yale graduate of the class of 1885, William Holt Gale (1864–1932) was a career diplomat who had served as the American consul at various posts in Central America and Europe. During the war, he was consul general at the American Embassy in Copenhagen.

Garrick Club (November 9)

Founded in 1831, Britain's Garrick Club is composed of actors, directors, theatrical producers, and drama patrons. The club's headquarters is located on Garrick Street in London.

Geddes, Sir Eric (November 14)

A railroad administrator before the war, Geddes (1875–1937) served the British military in a number of administrative capacities involving transportation and munitions supply. In May 1917, he was named controller at the Admiralty, advancing within a few months to the position of first lord of the Admiralty.

Gilbert, Sir Joseph (November 15)

Speaker of the House of Commons.

Gondrecour (December 2)

Probably Gondrecourt, a village in northeastern France. The area functioned as a training ground for U.S. troops.

Grasty (November 20)

During his long career in journalism, Charles H. Grasty (1863–1924) was a newspaper reporter, editor, publisher, and owner. As publisher of the *Baltimore Sun*, he campaigned to have the Democratic National Convention of 1912 take place within the city. Upon accomplishing that goal, he played a role in the nomination of Woodrow Wilson. After leaving the *Sun*, he worked as a war correspondent for the Associated Press, served a brief stint as treasurer of the *New York Times*, then returned to Europe with General Pershing as a special editorial correspondent for the *Times*.

Graves, Andy (November 24)

Probably Andrew Barbay Graves, a Yale graduate of the class of 1895 and eventually a member of the New York Stock Exchange. Graves's *New York Times* obituary lists him as the owner of Handsome Dan, the first Yale bulldog mascot.

Graves, Henry (November 24; December 5)

The diary refers to both a Henry and a Harry Graves. It seems likely that these were the same person. Henry Solon Graves (1871–1951) began a long career as a forester after graduating from Yale in 1892. A few months after the United States entered the war, he was commissioned a major in the Engineers Reserve Corps and sent to France to plan for the arrival of the forest engineers. As he did not return to the United States until 1918, he is probably both the Harry Graves who attended the Yale dinner and the Henry Graves with whom McCormick consulted about the wood agreement.

Greenway, John (November 24; December 3)

Probably John Campbell Greenway, a star athlete and an 1896 graduate of Yale. Known primarily as a mining engineer, Greenway had managed mining operations for U.S. Steel and the Calumet and Arizona Mining Company. In 1917, he went to France as a major in the Engineers Reserve Corps.

Gross, Henry ("Pete") (November 28; December 2)

Henry McCormick Gross was Vance McCormick's first cousin, the son of his mother's sister Nancy Criswell Gross and her husband, E. Z. Gross. He succeeded McCormick as mayor of Harrisburg. Trained and initially employed as a civil engineer, Gross was assistant engineer for the Harrisburg Board of Public Works from 1910 to 1914. After working in private industry for two years, he joined first the Pennsylvania National Guard, then the U.S. military. He was sent to France in early December 1917 as part of the 149th Machine Gun Battalion of the 42nd Division. In the last year of the war, he served as a machine gun instructor with the 92nd division, and finally as an aide to General Hay. Upon discharge, he returned to Harrisburg, initially resuming his career as a civil engineer but eventually becoming an investment banker.

Guillaumat, General (December 3)

At the outbreak of the war, Marie Louis Adolphe Guillaumat (1863–1940), a veteran of a number of colonial campaigns, was one of France's most experienced generals. He commanded French troops in the Marne, the Argonne, and the Somme before being named to direct the fighting around Verdun in December 1916. Shortly after McCormick met him, he became commander of the Armies of the East at Salonika, and subsequently commanded the 5th Army.

Gunther, Mr. (November 8)

First secretary at the American Embassy in London from 1914 to 1917, Franklin Mott Gunther (1885–1941) was a career diplomat who served at American embassies in Asia, South America, and Europe. His final posting was as U.S. minister to Rumania in the years just before the United States entered World War II.

Halifax (October 20)

A seaport city and the capital of Nova Scotia, Halifax was used as a naval base, convoy terminal, and point of embarkation during the war.

Hampton Roads (December 9, 10)

The point at which the James, Nansemond, and Elizabeth Rivers enter the Chesapeake Bay, Hampton Roads, in southeastern Virginia, is a natural harbor and the site of an important naval base.

Harbord, General (December 2)

Having become acquainted with Pershing during a tour of duty in the Philippines, James G. Harboard (1886–1947) was selected as the general's chief of staff in May 1917. In the last months of the war, he was given a battlefield command, only to be recalled to headquarters within two months to assume responsibility for the critical Service of Supply. After the war, he served as president and later chairman of the board of the Radio Corporation of America (RCA).

Harcourt Room (November 14)

A reception room at the lords' end of the House of Commons, used for meal service.

House, Colonel (October 29, 30, 31; November 4, 7, 9, 14, 16, 18, 22, 23, 24, 25, 29; December 7, 11)

Although he never held an official position in the government, Edward M. House (1858–1938) was Woodrow Wilson's friend and closest advisor from the beginning of Wilson's term until the president lost confidence in him during the peace negotiations at Versailles. In the years before the United States entered the war, as well as during the war years, House served as Wilson's chief foreign policy advisor, traveling to Europe on a number of occasions to serve as Wilson's spokesman in negotiations with European leaders.

House, Mrs. (October 29, 30; Nov. 7, 25; December 7)

Loulie Hunter married Edward House on August 4, 1880.

Hudson, Elizabeth (November 22, 25, 27; December 4)
Possibly the Elizabeth Hudson (?-1973) who became known as a book and art collector. When she died in 1973, an obituary published in the *Keats-Shelley Journal* noted that she had served as a volunteer nurse in France during World War I.

"Huntington," (October 30, November 4, 7; December 8)
An armed cruiser, the *Huntington* (ACR-5) began service in 1903 as the *West Virginia* and was renamed in November 1916. The first Medal of Honor for World War I was awarded to a member of her crew who saved a downed balloonist from the Atlantic in September 1917.

Hutchinson, Jim (November 30)
Possibly James Pemberton Hutchinson, a former football player and 1890 graduate of Harvard. Hutchinson was a member of a prominent Philadelphia family and a physician. In 1915, he went to France as part of the Pennsylvania Unit of the American Hospital. When the United States entered the war two years later, Hutchinson was commissioned a major in the U.S. Army and given command of the army hospital at Neuilly. After the war, he served as director of Penn Mutual Life Insurance.

Inter-Allied Conference (November 29; December 4, 5)
Held from October 28 through December 15, 1917 in Paris, France. Vance McCormick was a participant, and his observations are recorded in this diary.

Jairut, M, and wife (November 26, 28)
Jairut was a newspaperman, writing for *l'Echo de Paris*.

Jay, John (November 22)
Probably John Clarkson Jay (1880–1940), a former apprentice at the Pennsylvania Steel plant in Steelton who had worked his way up through the sales department to become vice president of the company. By 1917, Jay had left Pennsylvania Steel for a position with a civil engineering firm. Jay's wife was the former Marguerite Montgomery of Harrisburg.

Jellicoe, Admiral (November 7, 20, 29)
Commander of the British Grand Fleet at the battle of Jutland in 1916, Sir John R. Jellicoe (1859–1935) had been named first sea lord, essentially commander-in-chief of the British Navy, later that year. Soon after McCormick and his party left London, Jellicoe was removed from his position as a result of his failure to accept convoys as a solution to the problem of German submarine attacks on British shipping.

Joan of Arc (December 2)

Joan of Arc (c. 1412–31) led French forces into battle against the British at Orleans in 1429. Captured a year later, she was convicted of heresy and burned at the stake. She later became the patron saint of France.

Joffre, Marshal (November 24, 29)

Joseph Joffre (1852–1931) was the first French commander-in-chief during World War I. Although he managed to stop the German offensive at the battle of the Marne in 1914, he lost his position two years later, when Germany attacked Verdun after Joffre had ordered most of his troops and armaments out of the area to support battles elsewhere. By late 1917, he had no significant involvement in the conduct of the war.

Jonnart, Charles-Celestin (November 23, 26)

Charles-Celestin Jonnart had been high commissioner to Greece during the early years of the war. When Clemenceau came to power in November 1917, Jonnart was appointed minister of blockade and invaded regions in the new French cabinet. As McCormick notes, he resigned a few days later because of ill health.

Kerr, Philip (November 15)

Philip Kerr (1882–1940), a journalist and civil servant with experience primarily in South Africa, became David Lloyd George's secretary in December 1916. During and after the war, he was closely involved in maintaining Britain's relations with the dominions and with foreign governments, particularly the United States. After a brief period outside the government, he served as undersecretary of State for India and finally as Britain's ambassador to the United States.

King (November 16)

George V (1865–1936), king of Great Britain during the war years, had ascended the throne on the death of his father, King Edward VII, in 1910. A former sailor in the Royal Navy, the king provided symbolic leadership during the war through visits to British troops in France and to casualties recovering in hospitals.

"Kronprincessin Cecille," (December 7)

Launched in Germany in 1906, the *Kronprincessin Cecille* was confiscated at sea by the United States in July 1914. (McCormick had sailed on the ship while it was still a German commercial ocean liner.) The ship was carrying more than $14 million in gold and silver, destined to pay American industrial borrowing from British and French banks, along with 1,216 passengers, who disembarked at Bar Harbor, Maine. The ship was refitted for troop transport and renamed the *Mt. Vernon*. She was torpedoed by a German submarine in September 1918 but survived to sail again. Her last voyage was to rescue refugees and troops from Vladivostok in the fall of 1919. She was scrapped in 1940.

Lafayette (November 25)

Hero of the American and French revolutions, the Marquis de Lafayette (1757–1834) served with Washington's army during the former and created and commanded the French National Guard during a portion of the latter. As a member of the French Representative Assembly, he advocated reforms in class relationships and human rights policies.

Lambert, Dr. Alexander (December 5)

Dr. Lambert (1861–1939), a professor on the staff of Cornell University's medical school and an attending physician at Bellevue Hospital, was medical director of the American Red Cross in France during the war. During this period, the Red Cross assisted the army's own medical staff in caring for casualties.

Laughlin, Mr. Irwin (November 7)

A graduate of Yale the same year as McCormick, Laughlin (1871–1941) served as the secretary of U.S. embassies in Japan, Thailand, China, Russia, and France. From 1912 to 1919, he held various posts at the U.S. Embassy in London, including stints as secretary of the embassy, charge d'affaires, and counselor of the embassy. After the war, he served as U.S. ambassador to Greece and finally to Spain.

Lebrun, M. (November 26, 27)

A member of the National Assembly and former minister of colonies, Albert François Lebrun (1871–1950) was appointed minister of blockade while McCormick was in Paris. In the years after the war, he rose through the political ranks to become president of the French Republic in 1932. Unable to cope with the economic crisis of the Great Depression and the rise of the Nazis in Germany, Lebrun was forced from office when France was defeated in June of 1940.

Leigh, Mabel (November 11)

Mabel was the daughter of Gen. W. W. Gordon of Savannah, Georgia, and wife of Rowland Leigh.

Leigh, Rowley (November 11)

Probably Rowland Charles Frederick Leigh, a member of the bar of London's Inner Temple. Leigh's wife was an American.

Leverton-Harris (November 12, 16)

A conservative member of Parliament and an art collector, Frederick Leverton Harris (1864–1926) was one of the British officials responsible for creating and directing the Allies' blockade of Germany. From June 1916 through the end of the war, he served in various positions within the Foreign Office, most notably as the undersecretary to the Ministry of Blockade.

Liverpool (October 31)

A seaport in northwestern England about 180 miles northwest of London.

Lloyd George (November 15, 16, 20, 21, 29)

Prime minister of Great Britain from late 1916 to 1922, David Lloyd George (1863–1945) had reached this position after serving as minister of munitions and secretary of war. Through his aggressive prosecution of the war and his support for a unified Allied military command under Marshal Foch, he was instrumental in bringing the war to its conclusion. At the Paris Peace Conference, he was one of the leaders involved in shaping the Treaty of Versailles.

Logan, Colonel (November 22, 26, 30; December 1, 2)

At the outbreak of the war in 1914, James Addison Logan (1879–1930), a career military officer, was sent to France as chief of the American Military Mission to Paris. When the United States entered the war, he became involved in planning for the arrival of the American Expeditionary Force, becoming assistant chief of staff when the troops arrived in France. After the war, he worked with the Reparations Committee and was involved in administering relief efforts.

Longworth, Nick (December 2)

Nicholas Longworth (1869–1931) was a member of the U.S. House of Representatives and the son-in-law of Theodore Roosevelt. In the 1920s, Longworth, a Republican, served first as majority floor leader and subsequently as speaker of the house.

Louden, Foreign Minister (November 30)

John Louden was the Dutch foreign minister.

Maas, Lieutenant (November 23)

Possibly Charles O. Maas, a New York attorney and Republican politician who served as a naval attaché in Paris during the war.

Maclay, Sir Joseph (November 8; December 1)

Appointed shipping controller and head of the Ministry of Shipping by David Lloyd George, Joseph Maclay (1857–1951), a Scottish shipowner, was responsible for coordinating British shipping in aid of the war effort. Before his appointment, German submarine warfare had greatly reduced the amount of shipping available to the military and to industry. Maclay was charged with reorganizing British shipping to take best advantage of available resources. He also coordinated Britain's shipping efforts with those of the Allies.

Mary, Princess (November 16)

The third child and only daughter of King George V and Queen Mary.

McCook, Martha (November 22, 25, 28, 29; December 6)

Sent to France to set up YMCA canteens in September 1917, Martha McCook later headed the Women's Bureau at the Y's Paris headquarters.

McCormick-Goodhart, Leander (November 9, 14)

Leander McCormick-Goodhart was a grandson of Cyrus McCormick and the son of Leander J. McCormick, manager of McCormick Harvester Works.

McCoy, Frank (November 22; December 2, 3)

Born in Lewistown, Pennsylvania, Frank McCoy (1874–1954) was a soldier and diplomat. During the war, he was initially secretary of the general staff at Pershing's headquarters in France and later a battlefield commander, first of a regiment and then of a brigade. After the war, he served as an aide to the governor general of the Philippines, held a succession of senior military commands, and served as an American representative on various international commissions.

Metz (December 3)

Due east of Verdun, Metz is a city 175 miles from Paris, on the Moselle River. It was annexed to Germany as part of Alsace-Lorraine in 1871. Throughout World War I, the city was behind German lines.

Meurice Hotel (November 26)

The hotel is situated at 228 Rue de Rivoli, Between the Place de la Concorde and the Louvre, opposite the Tuileries Garden.

Milner, Lord (November 13, 20)

Known primarily for his service as a colonial administrator, Alfred Lord Milner (1854–1925) had been high commissioner for South Africa during the Boer War. Appointed to the war cabinet by David Lloyd George, Milner's responsibilities included apportioning shipping tonnage among government departments and developing a program for reducing imports in order to deal with the loss of available shipping.

Mond, Sir Alfred (November 15)

A British industrialist and chairman of Imperial Chemical Industries Limited, Mond (1868–1930), was also a member of Parliament and commissioner of works in Lloyd George's cabinet from 1916 to 1921.

Monet/Monnet (November 17, December 1)

Possibly Jean-Marie Monnet (1888–1979), a French financier and economic official who was responsible for France's economic planning after World War II. In 1950, Monnet developed the plan that created the European Coal and Steel Community, Europe's first common market. Although Monnet's biographies are silent about his exact position at the Ministry of Commerce during World War I, it is possible that he served as Clementel's secretary.

"Mt. Vernon" (December 7)

See "Kronprincessin Cecille"

Neale, Jim (December 7)

James Brown Neale, a coal mine operator from Minersville, Pennsylvania, who served as a member of the U.S. Fuel Administration. He graduated from Yale in 1897 (Skull and Bones) and had traveled to Europe with McCormick in 1913.

Nettleton, George (November 24)

An 1896 graduate of Yale, George H. Nettleton (1874–1959) spent most of his career as a professor of English at the university. During the war, he took a leave of absence from his position, serving first as the director of the Yale Bureau in Paris and later as director of the American University Union. He wrote the book *Yale in the World War* in 1925.

Neuf Chateau (December 2)

Probably Neufchateau, a town in eastern France located on the Meuse River.

New Republic (November 28)

New Republic: A Journal of Opinion was a weekly magazine first published in 1914. It had a wartime circulation of thirty thousand and was considered "the White House spokesman" because of its close association with Wilsonian opinion and politics. Walter Lippman was an associate editor from 1914 to 1917 and he was a member of the Inquiry, a group of noted academics who advised the American delegates at the Paris Peace Conference in 1919.

New York Evening Post (October 28)

Founded in 1801, the paper was owned for a period by Oswald Garrison Villard, whose pacifism caused the paper to lose sales. It was purchased by banker Thomas Lamont, who owned it during the war period, selling it during the 1920s.

New York Sun (November 22)

America's first "penny paper," the *Sun* (1833–1950) was at first an advocate of sensationalism, but by World War I, it was respected for its high journalistic and literary standards. The editorial policy supported advocacy of reform in government and the exposure of corruption. On March 19, 2002, a new newspaper bearing this name was launched in New York City.

New York Times (November 20)

Established in 1851, the *Times* received a 1918 Pulitzer Prize for the publication of full-text wartime documents. Although editorially conservative, the paper supported Wilson, and its wartime circulation was 320,000.

New York World (November 22; December 6)

Established in 1860, the *World* was known for its concentration on human interest stories and sensationalism. It was purchased by Joseph Pulitzer in 1883, and in 1919, it was run by his son.

Northcliffe, Lord (November 20)

As owner of both the *Daily Mail* (London) and the *Times* (London), Alfred Harmsworth, Lord Northcliffe (1865–1922), was one of Britain's most important newspaper publishers. By 1917, his press campaigns in support of the war effort had translated into an appointment as head of the British War Mission to the United States. In the last year of the war, he served as director of propaganda for enemy countries.

Northern Neutrals (November 4, 10)

The Scandinavian countries and Holland, which remained neutral throughout the war.

Page, Ambassador (November 7, 8, 9, 11, 12, 14, 16, 17, 21, 22)

Walter Hines Page (1855–1918), a newspaper and magazine reporter and editor, was appointed U.S. ambassador to Great Britain by Woodrow Wilson, at least partly as a result of Page's assistance with Wilson's political career. Once in London, Page became a vocal advocate for Britain with the president and the State Department, urging as early as 1915 that the United States enter the war on the side of the Allies.

Paget, Lady (November 26)

Lady Paget was an American woman active in war relief work in Paris.

Palmer, Frederick (November 26)

A war correspondent and freelance journalist, Palmer (1873–1958) had covered wars, rebellions, and revolutions throughout the world since the late 1890s. From 1914 until the United States entered the war, he accompanied the British military in France as the American Press Association's sole correspondent. When Pershing was selected to head the American Expeditionary Force, Palmer, who had met the general while covering the Russo-Japanese War, was commissioned as a major in the Army Signal Corps, becoming head of the press division of Pershing's staff.

Pennoyer (November 8)

Probably Richard Pennoyer, a graduate of the University of California and member of the diplomatic corps who was serving as secretary to Walter Page, the American ambassador in London.

Pennsylvania Railroad station (October 28)

Built between 1906 and 1910 in New York City, the station was designed by the architectural firm McKim, Mead and White. The imposing building was constructed of pink granite. It was torn down in 1963.

Perkins, Jim (November 22, 30)

In 1917, banker James Handasyd Perkins (1876–1940), brother of Nelson Perkins, went to France as a member of the first commission of the American Red Cross to that country. Before resigning to join the American Expeditionary Force in September 1918, he served as the American Red Cross's chief commissioner in Europe. After the war, he returned to his banking career, rising to become president of New York's National City Bank (a forerunner of Citibank).

Perkins, Nelson or Mr. (October 29; November 22, 24, 26, 30; December 6, 8, 11)

A lawyer with the firm of Ropes, Gray, Boyden and Perkins, Thomas Nelson Perkins (1870–1937) served as a legal advisor to the government, as well as to organizations and individuals. During World War I, his positions included chief counsel of the War Industries Board, assistant director of munitions, and assistant to the secretary of the war. In the years after the war, he was a member of the Reparations Commission and of the Arbitral Tribunal of Interpretation.

Pershing, General (November 22, 24, 25, 26, 28, 29; December 1)

John J. Pershing (1860–1948) was the commander of the American Expeditionary Force in Europe throughout the period of U.S. involvement in the war. (Pershing's father-in-law, Sen. Francis Warren, was chairman of the Senate Military Affairs Committee during this period.) Although American troops arrived in France less than two years before the end of the war, they participated in several major battles and were instrumental in capturing the Argonne Forest for the Allies. After the war, Pershing served as army chief of staff.

Petain, General (November 24; December 3)

Not even a full general at the outbreak of World War I, Henri Philippe Petain (1856–1951) rose quickly within the French military by advocating the then unorthodox view that machine weapons had fundamentally changed the nature of warfare. Brought in to command the fighting around Verdun in 1916, he succeeded in holding back the German Army and improving conditions at the front. After a near mutiny in the spring of 1917, Petain was named commander of the French Army, a position he held until 1931. When France was invaded by Germany in 1940, Petain became the premier of Vichy France. After the war, he was sentenced to death as a war criminal, but his sentence was commuted because of his services to the nation during World War I.

Piccadilly Circus (November 8)

The "Times Square" of London. Five major roads converge at this famous roundabout, which has a tall fountain-monument in the center created by Sir Alfred Gilbert in 1893. The figure at the top of the column was constructed of aluminum, considered quite modern at the time.

Pichon, Foreign Minister (November 24, 29; December 1)

Stephen Pichon (1857–1933) served as France's foreign secretary in the cabinets of Georges Clemenceau. Pichon had been a senator and a journalist and was an authority on international politics and law.

Picpus Cemetery (November 25)

Cemetery in Paris (12th District) where Lafayette is buried, along with many victims of the French Revolution.

Plymouth (November 6, 7)

A city in southern England consisting of the towns of Plymouth, Stonehouse and Devonport. Located on Plymouth Sound, the city is an important British port and naval center.

Poincare, President (November 24)

Raymond Poincare (1860–1934) was president of the French Republic throughout World War I. As the only major French politician to remain in power throughout the war without changing positions, he wielded considerable influence both in foreign policy and in French politics. Just before McCormick arrived in Paris, Poincare had selected Georges Clemenceau, a political rival, to be the nation's new premier. After his term as president ended in 1920, Poincare was elected to the French Senate and served as premier twice during the 1920s.

Queen (November 16)

Princess Victoria Mary of Teck (1867–1953) married the future George V of England in 1893. When he ascended the throne in 1910, she became known as Queen Mary. Their children included future kings Edward VIII and George VI.

R., Mrs. (November 25)

Eleanor Alexander Roosevelt (1889–1960) married Theodore Roosevelt Jr. in 1910. Three weeks before the United States forbade spouses of military personnel to travel to Europe, she sailed to France. During the war, Mrs. Roosevelt worked with the YMCA in Paris, operating a canteen on Avenue Montaigne and designing the Y women's uniforms.

R., Teddy (November 25)

Son of the former president, Theodore Roosevelt Jr. (1887–1944) commanded the 1st Battalion, 26th Infantry, of the 1st Division of the American Expeditionary Force. After the war, he was involved in founding the American Legion, served two terms in the New York Assembly, and unsuccessfully opposed Alfred Smith in the 1924 New York gubernatorial election. He returned to active duty in the U.S. Army in 1941, serving in Sicily and as deputy commander of the 4th Division during the D-Day invasion.

Rappard, Professor (December 1)

William E. Rappard (1883–1958) was an American-born Swiss economist and was professor of economic history at the University of Geneva from 1913 to the 1950s, specializing in the study of international labor. In addition to his academic pursuits, he represented Switzerland on a number of diplomatic missions during World War I and served on such international commissions as the International Labor Organization Committee of Experts.

Reading, Lord (November 15, 20, 21, 22; December 1)

Lord chief justice of England at the outbreak of the war, Sir Rufus Isaacs, Lord Reading (1860–1935), had been a barrister with a practice in commercial law as well as a liberal member of Parliament. During the first three years of the war, Reading advised the British war cabinet on financial matters, representing the government during two trips to the United States for financial negotiations. In January 1918, he was appointed British ambassador to Washington, and from 1921 to 1926, he served as viceroy of India.

Reid, Mrs. Whitelaw (November 15, 25)

An American philanthropist and socialite, Elisabeth Mills Reid (1858–1931) was the widow of Whitelaw Reid, the principal owner of the

New York Tribune and an 1892 candidate for vice president. From 1905 through the war years, Mrs. Reid was an active supporter of the American Red Cross, serving as the organization's London chairperson during the war. Her Red Cross activities also took her to France, where she was involved in organizing hospitals.

Rhondda, Lord (November 10)

David Alfred Thomas, Lord Rhondda (1856–1918), was a Welsh coal mine operator and liberal member of Parliament when the war broke out in 1914. In 1915, David Lloyd George, then minister of munitions, dispatched Thomas to North America to arrange for a supply of munitions from the United States and Canada. Two years later, Thomas, by then Lord Rhondda, was appointed British food minister. Among his responsibilities was the management of the nation's food-rationing program.

Ritz Hotel (November 27, 29)

Also known as simply "the Ritz," arguably the most famous and elegant hotel in Paris, located on the Place Vendôme. Its name became a synonym for ultimate luxury. Founded by Cesar Ritz, the hotel was barely twenty years old at the time of McCormick's visit.

Robertson, General (November 20, 21, 29)

The only British general during World War I to have begun his career as an enlisted man, William R. Robertson (1860–1933) had worked his way up through the ranks of the British military. First quartermaster, then chief of staff of the British Expeditionary Force in France, Robertson was recalled to London in late 1915 in order to become chief of the Imperial General Staff. When Lloyd George replaced Asquith as prime minister in late 1916, Robertson's influence began to wane and he was forced to leave his position in February 1918.

Robinette (November 14)

Probably Edward Burton Robinette (1879–1936), a Philadelphia banker who served in the U.S. Navy during the war. Robinette was initially assigned to Admiral Sims's headquarters in London, later becoming naval attaché to Sweden.

Roelof, Miss (December 5)

Henrietta Roelof worked with the YWCA in wartime France, assisting the French government with social work among women munitions workers. After the war, she continued to serve with the Y in the United States, ultimately becoming executive secretary of the YWCA Public Affairs Committee.

Ronsay, Robert (November 27)

Ronsay was the general director of the SSS, who would have had responsibilities similar to McCormick's.

Salon de l'Horloge (November 29)

This translates as "Clock Hall" and is a room in the French Ministry of Foreign Affairs, the Quai d'Orsay.

"San Diego," (December 7, 12)

See "California."

"The Saving Grace," (November 17)

The Saving Grace was a new comedy by Haddon Chambers that had premiered just over a month before McCormick saw it. Noel Coward, a virtual unknown at the time, was a member of the cast.

"Seattle," (November 4)

AC 11 began service as the USS *Washington* in 1905. She was renamed *Seattle* in 1916 and became the flagship of the U.S. destroyer fleet. In World War I she was flagship for the first American convoy to European waters, which was involved in an unsuccessful submarine attack. (The USS *Wilkes* was also part of this encounter.) After long years of service, she was scrapped in 1946.

Sedeaux, M. (December 4)

See Seydeaux.

Seine (November 26)

The river that bisects Paris, whose banks are both picturesque and commercial.

Sergeant, Miss (November 28)

Possibly Elizabeth Shepley Sergeant, an American writer who lived in Paris for many years. Sergeant was known primarily as a biographer of literary figures and an essayist.

Serruys (November 13)

Possibly Daniel Serruys, a French economist and counselor to French delegations to the League of Nations. Serruys's obituary in the *New York Times* makes no mention of his activities during World War I, but it is possible that he was the "new French delegate" to whom McCormick refers.

Seydeaux, M. (November 26)

Although McCormick spells the name as Sedeaux and Seydeaux (he did not speak French), both spellings almost certainly refer to Jacques Seydoux, one of the French directors of the Allied blockade of Germany during and after the war.

Sharp, Ambassador (November 23; December 5, 6)

William Graves Sharp (1859–1922) was a lawyer, wealthy business-man, and Democratic member of Congress when Woodrow Wilson appointed him American ambassador to France in June 1914. Since policy decisions regarding American-French relations were made in Washington, he played a limited role in setting U.S. policy toward France, but he served as American ambassador throughout the war and was actively involved with the Red Cross and YMCA in Paris. He returned to the United States in 1919. Mrs. Sharp was president of the Women's War Relief Corps in Paris, which worked closely with the Red Cross.

Sheldon, Lew (November 8, 9, 17, 21, 23, 24, 26, 28; December 1, 3, 4)

A Yale graduate and affiliate of a London banking house, Louis P. Sheldon represented the American Food Administration in the United Kingdom. In that capacity, he worked with Lord Rhondda, the British food minister, to coordinate British and American food efforts. During 1918–19, Sheldon was stationed in London as the War Trade Board representative of the Bureau of Foreign Agents and Reports. He dined often with McCormick.

Shipping Board (December 1)

When the United States entered the war, the American merchant fleet was small and ill equipped for the challenge of transporting American troops and supplies to Europe. In order to provide sufficient shipping for the United States and for America's Allies, who had suffered significant shipping losses as a result of German submarine attacks, the Shipping Board was charged with the responsibility of building and managing America's merchant fleet.

Shoreham Hotel (November 26)

A luxury hotel in Washington, D.C., at 2500 Calvert Street, N.W., in Rock Creek Park.

Sims, Admiral (December 7)

A maverick naval officer and frequent critic of both the navy bureaucracy and its conventional wisdom, William Sims (1858–1936) had become president of the Naval War College in early 1917. When the United States entered the war, he was given command of U.S. naval forces operating in Europe. In that capacity, he was involved in developing plans for the protection of Allied shipping through the convoy system and other antisubmarine measures. After the war, he was again named president of the War College.

Skinner, Consul General (November 15)

Robert Skinner (1866–1960) was a career diplomat, having served as U.S. consul general at Marseilles, Hamburg, and Berlin before assuming the same position in London in 1914. After leaving London in 1924, he held a number of positions at other U.S. embassies and was appointed ambassador to Turkey in 1933.

Smuts, General (November 20)

As a South African Boer, Jan C. Smuts (1870–1950) had led guerrilla troops against the British during the Boer War at the beginning of the century. In World War I, he fought with his former opponents, leading an offensive that drove the Germans out of South-West Africa and commanding British troops in East Africa. By late 1917, he had been called to London to serve as a member of Britain's war cabinet. Smuts continued to play a leadership role in South Africa throughout much of the first half of the twentieth century, becoming the nation's premier in August 1919.

Souilly (December 3)

A village in northeastern France about ten miles from Verdun. During the battle for Verdun, the French commanders had their headquarters at Souilly, and after September 1918, the town hall housed the American 1st Army headquarters during the Meuse-Argonne Offensive.

S.S.S. (November 27)

The Societe Suisse de Surveillance Economique, an Allied-approved Swiss trust to which products imported from the Allies were consigned for distribution to industrial syndicates within Switzerland. The SSS was designed to allow continued trade between the Allies and neutral Switzerland, while preventing Allied goods from falling into the hands of the Central Powers.

St. George's Church, Hanover Square (November 11)

A fashionable London church located on George Street in Hanover Square.

"St. Louis," (October 30, 31; November 4, 6, 7)

Built in Philadelphia, the 9,700-ton cruiser USS *St. Louis* (1906–30) served as a training and submarine support ship in the Pacific. She was transferred to the Atlantic in 1917 as a transport and to escort convoys. At the end of World War I, she served as a troop transport to return U.S. troops from Europe. She was decommissioned in March 1922 and sold in August 1930.

St. Nazarre (December 5)

Probably Saint-Nazaire, a seaport located in western France at the mouth of the Loire River.

Strong, Dick (December 5)

Like McCormick, Richard P. Strong (1872–1948) graduated from Yale in the class of 1893. After continuing his education at Johns Hopkins University's medical school, he built a career as a medical researcher and tropical disease specialist. By 1917, he was professor of tropical medicine at Harvard and a member of the medical corps at Harvey Cushing's Base Hospital No. 5. The British, French, and American governments recognized him for his role in discovering the cause of trench fever.

Swindon (November 17)

A borough in northeastern Wiltshire, England, about thirty miles from Bath.

Tardieu (November 24, 26, 29; December 1)

A French civil servant and journalist before his election to the Chamber of Deputies in 1914, Andre Tardieu (1876–1945) became high commissioner to the United States in 1917, with responsibility for managing French military procurement in America. During the last months of the war, his responsibilities expanded to include both French procurement in America and American procurement in France. After the war, he was one of France's negotiators at the Paris Peace Conference, later becoming a government minister and premier of France.

Taylor, Dr. (October 29; November 8, 9, 10, 14, 17, 20, 21, 23, 24, 26, 27, 28, 30; December 1, 2, 3, 4, 7)

Dr. Alonzo Taylor was a medical doctor and professor of physiological chemistry when he was appointed to the War Trade Board. He later served in Herbert Hoover's Food Administration, directed Stanford University's Food Research Institute, and served as director of research for General Mills. He was a frequent compatriot of McCormick.

Thornton, Colonel (November 28)

Henry Thornton (1871–1933) was an American-born railroad manager who had gone to England in 1914 to undertake the management of the Great Eastern Railway. Throughout the war, he was involved in overseeing Britain's transportation system. Active primarily in England during the early years of the war, he later went to France to oversee railway transportation for the British military in that country.

University Union (November 24)

"The headquarters for all college men" in Paris, according to McCormick.

Valencia, Viscount (November 16)

Arthur Annesley, eleventh viscount of Valentia (d. 1927), was a member of Parliament from Oxfordshire, the commanding officer in the queen's own Oxfordshire Hussars (1894–1904), and a personal friend of the king. He lost a son in World War I.

"Vaterland," (December 15)

An impounded German ship that was renamed *Imperator.* It had German-designed, technologically advanced, and unproved engines. Twenty-five German mechanics were brought from Scapa Flow to work on the ship under guard, because it was feared they might try to sink her. The *Vaterland* had been confiscated in April 1917 while docked in Hoboken, New Jersey. She was claimed by the U.S. Navy, renamed the USS *Leviathan,* repaired, and sent into transport service.

Venizelos (November 29)

Greek politician Eleftherios Venizelos (1864–1936) was serving the third of his six terms as Greek prime minister when he represented the nation at the Inter-Allied Conference in 1917. Unlike the Greek king, Constantine, Venizelos strongly supported the Allied war effort, and when the king was forced to resign in 1917, Greece entered the war on the side of the Allies. Although defeated in the nation's 1920 elections, Venizelos returned to power for brief periods in 1924 and 1933 and for an extended term from 1928 to 1932.

Verdun (December 3)

A town in northeastern France on the Meuse River thirty-six miles west of Metz, Verdun was the site of the longest and bloodiest battle of World War I, from February to December 1916. Death tolls were estimated to be 500,000 French and 430,000 German. The German strategy was to destroy this "sacred" city of France, once burned by Attila the Hun and also the site where the heirs of Charlemagne had divided the Frankish empire, thereby crushing the French psychologically.

Verdun Citadel (December 3)

After France lost Alsace-Lorraine in the Franco-Prussian War, French military engineers constructed an underground citadel at Verdun. Capable of supporting a garrison of six thousand men and storing supplies, the citadel was an important logistics center during the Battle of Verdun in 1916. The citadel was selected in 1920 as the site for the French Tomb of the Unknown Soldier.

Viviani (November 24, 29)

Prime minister of France at the outbreak of the war in 1914, Rene Viviani (1863–1925) lost both his position and most of his political influence as a result of a series of military disasters during the early years of the war. He remained a member of the cabinet and represented France on various diplomatic missions but played no further significant role in French politics.

Wallace, Major (October 29; November 17)

Possibly William Kay Wallace, a 1908 graduate of Yale and a member of the American diplomatic corps before the war. Although biographical sketches do not identify him as an aide to General Bliss, he did serve with the American general staff, preparing briefing materials and press releases related to the progress of the war. Like Bliss, Wallace traveled to Europe in 1918 as part of the American Mission to Negotiate Peace. It is possible that he went to London and Paris with the House Mission as well.

War Cabinet (November 20, 21)

The British political entity, headed by the prime minister, that directed the war effort.

Ward, Lord and Lady (November 15)

The daughter of Whitelaw and Elisabeth Mills Reid, Jean Reid had married Sir John Hubert Ward, equerry to England's Queen Alexandra (the mother of King George V).

War Industries Board (October 29)

Created to coordinate wartime production efforts in the United States, the War Industries Board established production priorities, assigned resources and raw materials, set prices, and acted as a purchasing agent for America's Allies.

War Trade Board (October 29; November 4)

McCormick traveled to London and Paris as the director of the U.S. War Trade Board. In essence, the War Trade Board waged economic warfare against the Central Powers by forbidding American firms to deal with specific foreign corporations and by attempting to control the businesses of foreign companies operating in neutral countries. Its official function, described by the government, was as follows: "Licensed exports and imports, rationed supplies to neutrals, and conserved commodities and shipping facilities for American and Allied use. Sought to keep strategic goods out of enemy hands and prohibit the use of enemy credit and financial holdings in the United States." The agency was housed in a large temporary building (Temp #2) at 20th Street and Virginia Avenue, N.W., Washington, D.C.

"West Virginia," (October 30)

See "Huntington"

Whitehall Gardens (November 20)

Once the site of the gardens attached to the king's palace at Whitehall in London, the Privy Garden had been renamed Whitehall Gardens and a row of large houses had been constructed there.

Wickersham, John (November 24)

A 1901 Yale graduate and a structural engineer, John Wickersham was commissioned a captain of engineers in June 1917. Throughout the remainder of 1917, he was stationed in Paris as requisitioning officer for engineer supplies.

Wight, Isle of (November 10)

Island in the English Channel just off the coast of southern England.

"Wilkes," (November 6)

USS *Wilkes* (Destroyer No. 67) unsuccessfully attacked a German submarine while sailing with the USS *Seattle* on the first official U.S. convoy in June 1917.

Willard, Ambassador (November 23, 24)

Appointed U.S. minister to Spain in July 1913, Joseph E. Willard (1865–1924) was a wealthy lawyer who had served in the Virginia House of Delegates and as that state's lieutenant governor. Elevated to the position of ambassador when the U.S. legation in Spain became an embassy, Willard conducted negotiations with the Spanish government on various subjects of mutual concern both before and after the United States entered the war.

Wilson, President (November 16, 21)

President of the United States from 1913 to 1921, Woodrow Wilson (1856–1924) was a Democrat with strong ties to the Progressive movement. McCormick supported Wilson in his first campaign for the White House in 1912 and served as chairman of the Democratic National Committee during Wilson's reelection campaign in 1916, which McCormick also managed.

Wimbledon (November 9)

A residential district that is now part of Greater London and well known as the site of international tennis tournaments.

Wiseman, Sir William (November 7, 16, 22)

Sir William Wiseman (1885–1962) was an international banker working at Herndon's in London before World War I. During the war he served in the infantry as a lieutenant colonel, then in military intelligence. He also acted as liaison between the British government and Wilson, and as advisor at the Paris Peace Conference. He was a confidential friend of Colonel House.

Young, Milton L. (October 29)

Young was McCormick's secretary.

Y.W.C.A. (November 25; December 5, 6)

The Young Women's Christian Association provided Hostess Houses for women serving with the American Expeditionary Force, as well as for female visitors to American soldiers. Although McCormick refers exclusively to the YWCA in his diary, some of the women he identifies as YWCA workers were, in fact, employed by the Young Men's Christian Association (YMCA).

Zantzinger (November 14, 16)

Born in Philadelphia, Clarence Clark Zantzinger (1872–1954) graduated from Yale in 1892, one year before McCormick. Zantzinger returned to Philadelphia, earned a degree in architecture, and became known for the design of such buildings as the Philadelphia Museum of Art and the Department of Justice building in Washington. During the war, he was sent to Sweden as a special representative of McCormick's U.S. War Trade Board.

Zoological Garden (November 11)

Located in London's Regent's Park, the Zoological Gardens were founded in the late 1820s, and then as now housed animals from around the world.

Called to Join the President
The Diary of Vance McCormick at the Paris Peace Conference, 1919

Edited by Susan Meehan
and Cherie Fieser

Vance McCormick's diary of the Paris Peace Conference ending World War I covers the period January 1 to July 8, 1919, from the day he left for New York City to the day he returned to Harrisburg. Like his 1917 diary of the House Mission to London and Paris, this journal records the memories of an observer rather than the reflections of an advisor. Although its format loads the reader down with detail—McCormick even tells when he wakes up late—the diary is actually a drama. It has an observant narrator, vivid characters, plot, conflict, and growing tension. Will the Allies resolve their differences? Indeed, will the American delegates resolve their differences? What should the enemy be charged with? Will the Germans agree to the treaty? And what if they don't? Can Wilson escape with his health? Are the Bolsheviks coming? And at the end, there remains the unanswered question: How did Vance McCormick survive six months in Paris without speaking French or drinking wine?

Diplomatic historians have used McCormick's diary to corroborate or flesh out the comments of other participants. Arthur Walworth has used it most extensively—twenty-seven citations—for his book Wilson and His Peacemakers. *He sees McCormick as a domestic political advisor in Paris as much as a formal consultant on international economics. Walworth notes McCormick's confrontations with Herbert Hoover over blockade policy,[1] and quotes McCormick as saying that he thought Hoover a "very exaggerated* talker."[2] He also quotes from the diary on deteriorating conditions in Germany after the armistice as "living on top of a volcano,"[3] and on Wilson's angry reaction to a French proposal that the United States pay one-third of the cost of the war.[4] Walworth repeats Bernard Baruch's remark that McCormick "almost punched" fellow advisor Gordon Auchincloss when the latter called President Wilson "Woody" and appeared to mock his competence at the peace conference.[5] McCormick and his diary also appear in the Paris portions of Mr. Baruch, Margaret L. Coit's biography of the famed financier and presidential advisor. Coit shows how the northern WASP McCormick and the southern Jewish "Bernie" were shipmates on the voyage over and compatriots in diplomacy.[6] She quotes from McCormick's 1919 diary his thought that imperialism and militarism were rife at the peace conference.[7] But in the voluminous literature on World War I diplomacy, a more typical reference to McCormick is Frederick Palmer's unadorned mention of him in his biography of General Tasker Bliss as one of the members of the American delegation.[8] The difficulty in finding evidence of McCormick's influence in the higher councils of government is that he was not prone to talk or write about it. His influence came through his relationships.

His relationship to Woodrow Wilson and others was first about friendship and respect, not utility and influence. Edith Bolling Wilson, writing in her memoir of her husband's relationship with McCormick, recounts, "We both became so fond [of him]" and he "proved so able and so true a friend.[9] After winning reelection, the president himself had sent a telegram to McCormick on November 13, 1916, closing with the following encomium:

> May I not say for myself how entirely I have had my trust in you confirmed, and how throughout these trying months my genuine affection for you has grown and strengthened?
>
> My own sense of obligation and gratitude to you is immeasurable.[10]

---

1. Arthur Walworth, *Wilson and His Peacemakers: American Diplomacy at the Paris Peace Conference, 1919* (New York: W. W. Norton, 1986), 89, n. 28.

2. Ibid., 522, n. 62.

3. Ibid., 156.

4. Ibid., 165.

5. Ibid., 297, n. 100.

6. Margaret L. Coit, *Mr. Baruch* (Boston: Houghton Mifflin, 1957), 173.

7. Ibid., 254.

8. Frederick Palmer, *Bliss, Peacemaker: The Life and Letters of General Tasker Howard Bliss* (New York: Dodd, Mead, 1934), 184, 187.

9. Edith Bolling Wilson, *My Memoir* (Indianapolis: Bobbs-Merrill, 1938), 102.

When Vance's mother, Annie Criswell McCormick, died, the president wrote to him personally on March 31, 1922, closing with repeated emphasis on their affectionate friendship:

I hope the memory of her wonderful life will serve in some small part to console you and compensate you for the great loneliness you must be feeling, and trust that the affectionate sympathy of friends like ourselves will also help. I feel that it was a privilege to know her and that her death deprives us of a friend whom we could value with deep and reverent affection. Mrs. Wilson and I join in the most affectionate messages to you and I am as always,

Your affectionate friend,
[signed] Woodrow Wilson[11]

Josephus Daniels, Wilson's secretary of the navy, wrote in his account of the administration that McCormick's "judgement and affection were an abiding rock" for the president; likewise, said Daniels, "admiration of Wilson was a passion" for McCormick. "True and tried and generous and steadfast to the end . . . they were affectionate and loyal friends."[12] When Wilson died on February 3, 1924, McCormick was named an honorary pallbearer. In sum, if Wilson accepted McCormick's advice, it was because he accepted his friendship.

McCormick's specific assignment at the Paris conference was to the Reparations Committee, where he was seated with Bernard Baruch and Norman H. Davis. He was the sole American member of the committee's Subcommission on Evaluation of Damage, which added up the costs of the war damage that the treaty required Germany to repay. In his essay on reparations included in Colonel House's book What Really Happened at Paris, *Thomas Lamont writes that in determining what should be included in the bill of costs given to Germany, "Mr. Vance McCormick gave the most painstaking and intelligent attention."[13] In other words, McCormick can be called one of the chief accountants for one of the most contentious issues at the peace con-*

---

10. Telegram, Woodrow Wilson to Vance McCormick, November 13, 1916, McCormick Family Papers, Historical Society of Dauphin County. See also LeRoy W. Toddes, "Vance McCormick's Relationship with Woodrow Wilson: A View through Their Correspondence," *Cumberland County History* 9 (Winter 1992): 69–91.

11. Letter of Woodrow Wilson to Vance McCormick, March 31, 1922, McCormick Family Papers, Historical Society of Dauphin County. See also Toddes, "McCormick's Relationship."

12. Josephus Daniels, *The Wilson Era: Years of War and After, 1917–1923* (Chapel Hill: University of North Carolina Press, 1946), 217, 360.

13. Thomas William Lamont, "Reparations," in *What Really Happened at Paris: The Story of the Peace Conference, 1918–1919*, ed. Edward Mandell House and Charles Seymour (New York: Charles Scribner's Sons, 1921), 275.

ference and afterward. The British economist John Maynard Keynes came to fame by condemning reparations and predicting that they would lead to economic chaos and another war. The latest research on war reparations and their effects, however, concludes that Germany's debt was not so onerous. This is Margaret MacMillan's position in her prize-winning book, Paris 1919: Six Months That Changed the World,[14] reiterated in Ronald Steel's review of recent World War I scholarship.[15]

The diary has its inevitable minutiae, McCormick recording where and when he ate, and with whom, and other quotidian details, but there also are telling particulars:

- He got his old football coach, Walter Camp, onto the ship, and Camp led calisthenics daily on deck for all the men. (January 2)

- Of his suite at the famed Paris Ritz, he said "I tremble at the cost." (January 11)

- Harrisburg newspapers were supplied to him on a regular basis. (January 24)

- He mentions that "Henry Loomes, my new valet, is doing nicely." (February 7)

- He frequently takes notice of "good looking" women. (February 27, e.g.)

- "Henry tells me Queen of Roumania is occupying suite next door. Things are certainly doing tonight." (March 4) The next day, when she asked to use his sitting room for several days, he writes, "We have to give way to Royalty, notwithstanding we hear so much of 'Bolshevism.'"

- He often refers to Germans as "Huns." (March 6, e.g.)

- He notes that Dr. Goodrich, pastor at the American Church in Paris, was "Yale '86." (March 23)

- He and Bernie Baruch often played tennis indoors. (March 25, e.g.)

---

14. Margaret MacMillan, Paris 1919: Six Months That Changed the World (New York: Random House, 2001), esp. chapters 13–16, 30.

15. Ronald Steel, "The Missionary," New York Review of Books (November 20, 2003): 26–28, 35.

- *"Lunched at Mrs. Linda Thomas' lovely apartment, who by the way is very good looking." (April 7)*

- *Complains of a poor dinner at the Majestic Hotel, which had "English cooking instead of French." (April 8)*

- *Easter Sunday at the American Episcopal Church, crowded with soldiers: "I am more impressed than ever with our troops; fine, manly looking lot of fellows and well behaved." (April 20)*

- *On the first real spring day: "Watched the children play and the United States soldiers playing ball. I was crazy to get into it." That night, he went to a vaudeville show. (May 5)*

- *On a trip to Verdun, which he had first visited in 1917, French soldiers "pointed out in the distance where the Germans in their hasty flight left many of their soldiers unburied and now the smell is so great that he says they cannot send the Hun prisoners to bury their own dead." (May 26)*

- *"Went to Baron Rothschild's house to dance. Wonderful place, but guests a poor lot. The kind that make Bolshevists." (May 27)*

- *On a trip outside Paris: "The country we passed through was the typical battle front, a frightful scene of desolation and destruction, not a house standing, villages completely effaced, no trees left and ground literally covered with shell holes." When they were in Brussels: A "large military band played 'The Star Spangled Banner' and 'Marseillaise.' This was followed with music by two large men's choral societies, several hundred voices and I never heard anything more inspiring. The whole sight was thrilling and made me fill up and I found I was not the only one because I saw as President Wilson walked off the Balcony into the room his eyes were filled with tears." (June 18)*

- *At a dinner to say good-bye to his French friends: "It was the first time I had worn my button as Commander of the Legion of Honor and much to my surprise when I went into the room Major Grempel kissed me in his delight." (June 26)*

McCormick was ordinarily businesslike in his dealings with other participants in the proceedings, not telling what he thought of their habits or attitudes, but occasionally his diary reveals a personal opinion:

- *McCormick thought Colonel House was the most active member of the delegation, but Wilson was the real leader, even though Hoover tried to dominate everything. (January 13)*

- *He was "amused" at Colonel House's anxiety when Robert Lansing, secretary of state, sat next to President Wilson at meetings. (January 29)*

- *French military leader Marshal Foch "is just like a child and must be humored or his feelings are hurt." (March 22)*

- *Lansing was disturbed with House because he thought House was "trying to 'hog' it." (March 23)*

- *Frank Cobb had "evidently discovered new traits in House which have apparently been developing rapidly this trip, of most interesting nature. This entire history of the inside conference will make interesting reading some day." McCormick's prediction came true. (May 6)*

- *McCormick was "always impressed with the cordiality and harmonious workings of the Four [Wilson, Clemenceau, Orlando, and Lloyd George], even with Orlando present. They are apparently frank with each other, differing frequently and earnestly but always in a most friendly spirit. Three big men trying to do the big thing in the proper spirit." (May 14)*

- *But the next day, McCormick notes Wilson's remark that the Four were "mad men." "He says he has great pity for them. They have such fear of the Germans and such great self pity." (May 15)*

The diary contains provocative information pertinent to the diplomacy surrounding the treaty, or its specific provisions:

- *For all the formal meetings, McCormick believed the most important decisions were being made during the informal meetings among the Allies. (January 14)*

- *He and Baruch did not want to see an American chairing the Reparations Commission, as it was "bound to disappoint everyone as to amount obtained from Germans." (January 30)*

- *McCormick thought the French "really hinder whenever possible." (March 5)*

- *If some thought his role in reparations was laudable, he could be more cynical: "Went to sub-committee Reparations. More hot air on cate-*

gories, getting nowhere. Marking time until the big fellows can agree on figures." (*March 24*)

- The American delegation "all agreed to the Lloyd George proposal which established a commission to determine the amount Germany can pay and the amount of claims before 1921 which will relieve Great Britain and France from the troubles of making public the small amount they are to get from reparations because both Prime Ministers believe their government will be overthrown if the facts are known. I am afraid this camouflage will not work, but it may, as the people forget so easily." (*April 1*)

- On the treaty being delivered to the Germans: "I believe the Huns will sign after a few more bluffs. Allied armies are mobilizing and we have blockade machinery ready to spring which I hope will not be necessary." (*May 23*)

- McCormick heard that "anti-Bolshevists are gaining ground every minute and it is expected Petrograd and Moscow will soon fall and the Bolshevists retreat toward the Ukraine and food." The rumors were wrong, to say the least. (*May 24*)

Even though all the treaty negotiations were done in Paris, the signing ceremony took place on June 28 at Versailles, by which the document ending World War I has since been known. McCormick was duly impressed with the facilities there, as the French kings had intended. "At the front of the Chateau in the court extending out the main avenues as far as you could see were lines of soldiers, French chasseurs with their lances, and with the setting of the Chateau in the background it made a most magnificent sight." As for the signing itself, "the whole impression was more that of a religious ceremony than anything else. . . . It was a solemn moment when the two lone German delegates walked in. You could have heard a pin drop." What disappointed McCormick? "I must say I was sorry to see some of the mothers and wives of certain minor secretaries present when many a brave general and soldier, who offered their lives for their country could not get in."

His work done with the treaty signed, McCormick boarded the George Washington with Wilson and his fellow delegates and headed back to America. On landing in New York, he skipped the reception for the president in Carnegie Hall so that, ever the good son, he could get home to his mother, Annie, to whom he dedicated the diary.

JANUARY 1, 1919 (WEDNESDAY)—

Having been called by President Wilson to join him in Paris as one of his advisers at the Peace Conference, I went to New York New Year's Day, expecting to sail on the "Leviathan."[16] When I arrived in New York, I was advised that she was disabled and that we were to be transferred to the "George Washington," which had just returned from taking President Wilson to France.

JANUARY 2 (THURSDAY)—

Sailed on "S.S. George Washington" for Brest 7:00 A.M. Arrived at Brest January 10. Uneventful trip. Most comfortable with the President's full equipment, including two Government bands, movies, sailors' vaudeville show and music. Captain McCaulay delightful host. Assistant Secretary of the Navy Roosevelt aboard, with Attorney Spellacy and wife, of Hartford, and Commander Hancock, crossing for work connected with Navy Department, also en route to Peace Conference, Chinese Mission and Mexican Mission. Other passengers were: Charles Schwab, most entertaining, with great magnetism and enthusiasm and very free talker, not apparently over-accurate, and Baruch, who was my mate, also going as President's adviser, and was sick most of the way over. Howard Heinz, of "57 Varieties," and several of Hoover's food men were aboard with other Peace experts from Shipping Board, etc.[17] Walter Camp, whom I helped get permission to cross on the steamer, was going abroad on business, and gave calisthenics daily on the deck to all the men of the party and reduced many waist measures.

At Brest, Bernie Baruch and I were officially welcomed by Gillet, representative of the French High Commissioner, and by a representative for the U.S. Army and Navy, and were well cared for with a private car to Paris, furnished by the French Government. Met Commander Todd, of Navy, in Brest, who took us to Officers's Club, an attractive house he had bought and loaned to the Club during the war and proposed giving it to

---

16. McCormick was one of many advisors who went to Paris to assist the president's handpicked American Peace Commission. President Wilson had announced the membership of the commission on November 29, 1918; it consisted of the president, Secretary of State Robert Lansing, Col. Edward House, Gen. Tasker H. Bliss, and Henry White. The only Republican in the group was White, which caused a political stir in Washington.

17. Herbert Hoover had been authorized by world leaders, after the November 1918 armistice, to head relief efforts in Europe to end the postwar food shortage. This effort was funded primarily with American dollars. Hoover had been active in food relief work in Europe since early in the war.

the United States Government for Consul's residence. Had refreshing cup of tea with him before trip to Paris.

Soldiers at Brest wild to return home. Sick of rain every day. Say camp, on account of continual rain and mud, is in frightful condition.

JANUARY 11 (SATURDAY)—
[*Supreme Council for Supply and Relief met for first time, with Herbert Hoover as chair*]

Arrived at Paris 7:30 A.M. Met at station by Stetson, of the War Trade Board,[18] who had my car there for me and took me direct to Ritz, where I have, I think, the royal suite—(I tremble at the cost)—most comfortable sitting room, bedroom, bath and dressing room. Auchincloss, Baruch, Hurley and Sheldon also at Ritz.

After breakfast I went to Crillon to look over my offices. As member of the Commission I was offered sleeping quarters there also, but preferred sleeping away from my office. Called on members of the Commission and lunched with Lansings. Met the staff of War Trade Board in the afternoon. Stetson in charge of office. Dined with Hoover, Baruch, Davis and Sheldon at Meurice Hotel. Saw many Americans there as everywhere in center of city. Hoover apparently having difficulty getting Great Britain to help him unload his surplus. His pushing his Director-Generalship and his desire to unload U.S. food surplus may cause trouble. Certainly will not help Allied co-operation at Peace Table. Auchincloss says situation almost reached point of open break, blaming Reading.

JANUARY 12 (SUNDAY)—
[*Opening session of peace conference*]

Slept very late, as was very tired. Lunched [at] Ritz with my foreign representatives of War Trade Board: Sheldon, London; Owen, Scandinavia; Stuart, Rome; Stetson, Paris; Dresel, Bernie, and Dulles, my assistant. Saw Henrietta Ely, just back from the German occupied territory and just off for a rest to Cannes; first for many months; looked very well. Called on Lord Robert Cecil. Tea with Marquise Polignac and Baruch. Stetson gave me dinner at his apartment to meet all War Trade Board representatives and Robert Bliss, Charge at Embassy, and General Secretary of Commission Grew.

---

18. The War Trade Board was created in the fall of 1917 to oversee control of U.S. international trade during the period of the war. Vance McCormick was chairman of the board.

JANUARY 13 (MONDAY)—

Began our morning conferences with War Trade Board representatives at headquarters at Crillon at 10:00 A.M. Laid out plan of operation and delegated work. Lunched at Crillon with Mrs. House and Auchincloss in their apartment. Colonel House quite ill. I think family worried. Colonel active man of Peace delegation, overlooking practically all political and economic work. Lansing legal. President real leader, however, and making tremendous impression. Fear trouble later over relationship of House and Lansing. Hoover still attempting to dominate everything. Think making enemies. Hurley very sore. Conference in afternoon with Navy and Army representatives on removal of censorship. Dined at Hotel Murat with President and Mrs. Wilson. House beautiful and regal. Many lackeys and good dinner and sociable time with just members of Peace Conference and Hoover, Hurley, Baruch, including wives, and myself. Came home with Hurley and he took me to his room to pour into my ears his trouble with Hoover and Shipping Department. I was much amused as he now claims to be the great harmonizer with the British, he all during the war having taken the other position with the President.

JANUARY 14 (TUESDAY)—

Lew Sheldon and I breakfasted together and went to the Crillon to the War Trade Conference. We called on Lord Reading and discussed Blockade matters.[19] Lord Reading did not seem quite sure of his status at Conference, and told me he may have to go back to America with the President and leave America in a proper and graceful manner, as he left before rather unceremoniously. I think we will have a new Ambassador soon. Reading will probably return home.

Baruch and I lunched with Tardieu, Gillet, Gann and Loucheur at the Café Voisin. Had helpful talk over reconstruction problems in France. French seem disorganized and very slow getting started. Called upon Sedoux, head of French blockade in foreign office, an old friend of visit of 1917. Discussed Swiss agreement, general blockade politics connected with the peace problems as great pressure is being brought from many

---

19. The British blockade, never formally declared but implemented in 1914, successfully impaired the flow of goods and munitions to Germany, but also limited access to shipping commerce for all countries, including neutrals such as the United States, thus becoming a major diplomatic sore point between Great Britain and the United States. The War Trade Board was the American agency most involved with maintaining trade on open seas.

directions, principally the United States, to release blockade on Germany. Agreed to * * * [*sic*] but opposed raw materials, etc. as most forceful weapon to make Germany sign Peace Treaty. French and British anxious to hold blockade in order to prevent Germans getting raw materials to compete against them in markets of the world with their manufactured articles. Allies cannot get indemnity paid unless Germany can produce.

Dined with Lord Robert Cecil at Hotel Majestic. Present Lord Eustace Percy, Sir Connip Guthrie, Sir Hubert Smith and Baruch. Delightful evening. Discussed informally peace problems. In my opinion, most important decisions of conference being formulated at informal conferences going on continually among various Allied representatives.

A few days after my arrival in Paris I had an interview with President Wilson and Colonel House, by appointment, in Colonel House's room at Crillon to discuss my resignation as Chairman of the Democratic National Committee which I had proposed to President Wilson by cable before I left America and he requested that I withhold definite action until I could talk the matter over with him before giving his approval. After stating my reasons for resigning, I finally secured the President's consent although he said he had hoped that I might continue on for the present.

During the discussion the President asked me who were the prospective candidates for President. I said there was no announced candidate as yet but McAdoo's friends seem to have the most active organization. House suggested Hoover as a possibility for the Democratic nomination and Pershing for Republican. The President then said that he would not consider being a candidate again unless there was some great catastrophe involving the world's affairs as well as our own which might make him the issue, in which event he might be compelled to run.

He asked me who I would suggest as my successor and I suggested Homer Cummings, the present vice-chairman, which he approved and told me to wire Tumulty of his preference which he could use if the President's advice was sought by the National Committee. I at once sent a cable to Hollister, secretary of the National Committee, to release my written resignation which I had left in his hand in America and I also notified Tumulty as directed by the Presedent.

JANUARY 15 (WEDNESDAY)—

Overslept, and late at War Trade Board conference. Lunched with Sam Fleming, eager to hear from home. Much impressed by modest and manly way he spoke of his experiences and enthusiasm over our fighting men in ranks. Said courage and spirit of his men wonderful and they were principally from the "East Side" districts of cities and of all nationalities. Said amusing to see fraternization of Germans with regiments in which there were Pennsylvania Dutch. A few hours after they were trying to kill each other, when the Armistice was declared, they were exchanging souvenirs.

Ambassador Bakhmeteff of Russia called to see me. Went to Mrs. Wilson's reception, principally Americans invited. Returned to office and was called upon by Musgrove of Alabama with Bishop Cannon, of Richmond, Methodist, and Dr. [blank], a Y.M.C.A. worker from Nashville. Wanted to present some social problems to Peace Conference.

Dined at Ritz with Monet, Secretary to Clementel, French Minister of Commerce. One of the best informed men in Paris. Picked up much valuable information.

JANUARY 16 (THURSDAY)—

Conference at headquarters. Dr. Taylor there just back from Austria-Hungary and Balkans. Tremendously impressed with distress in those countries. Blockade had done its work. Absolutely nothing left. Every clock in Prague gone, melted for the metals. Everything gone accordingly—no food, transportation broken down, relief absolutely necessary but food cannot be delivered unless supplies sent are to build up transportation. Says Germany in same condition, not so bad however. His Allied Commission in accord.

Lunched with Lord Reading to discuss organization plans of economic work for conference. Worked at office. Sent for by Minister Clementel to discuss organization plan prepared by him which he wanted me to show the President. Told me how much Clemenceau and Wilson were in accord and growing closer ever day. Clementel able man and very close to Clemenceau. All of the big fellows seem to be very tired. I wish they were all fresher as weariness leads to friction.

Dined with Mrs. Harriman, Mrs. McCombs and Major Jim Mitchell, a doctor from Washington, and went to vaudeville given by the solders of 76th Regiment. The President and Mrs. Wilson and all Americans there. Seemed like Washington. Excellent show and well received.

JANUARY 17 (FRIDAY)—

Followed daily routine, which consists of being called at 8:00 A.M. Coffee, rolls and newspapers in my sitting room. Then to headquarters at Crillon in time for 10:00 o'clock conference with War Trade Board representatives. Lunched with Bill Delano. Conferences with Rublee, formerly of the Inter-Allied Shipping Commission; Taylor and Conger, formerly with the War Trade Board at Washington as foreign adviser, but now back at his old job of foreign representative of the Associated Press. Monet called with proposed organization for economic program as suggested by Clementel. Wanted me to present it to the President formally.

Dined with Dulles, Owen and Conger at French restaurant.

January 18 (Saturday)—
[Official opening of peace conference]
Conference at 10:00 A.M. Sheldon and I went to see Lord Reading by appointment at 11:00 to try to get blockade matters better organized from Inter-Allied standpoint. Found Reading still apparently uncertain as to his status with his own government. He frankly stated he did not know whether he would remain in Paris. He seemed rather peeved. We then called on Cecil. He said, as we knew, he was not in the Government, he having resigned, but was especially looking after League of Nations interests and was sorry he could not help us. There is much maneuvering going on in all the large delegations for place, and thus working organizations are held up. This will delay matters if not remedied soon. France is having her troubles and we have not yet co-ordinated our forces.

Lunched with Charge Bliss at his house. Present General Bliss, Deputy Marquis Chambrun, a brother of the nice Charles Chambrun, Charge of French Embassy at Washington, and Cabot Ward, head of the Paris U.S. Intelligence.

After lunch I went with Baruch to the Quai d'Orsay to attend the formal opening of the Peace Conference, assembled just forty-eight years to the day after the Versailles Council had established the German Empire with great military splendor.[20] The assembly hall was magnificent, yet dignified, and the conference was a great contrast to the former one in that it was free from any military display, all the delegates being in black coats, and the whole proceeding gave one the impression of great solemnity, more like the sitting of the highest court of a great nation, and the etiquette was the same, as there was no applause either upon the arrival of the celebrities or upon their remarks, which at any other time or place would have called forth some demonstration.

---

20. On January 18, 1871, William I was crowned emperor of Germany in the Hall of Mirrors at the Versailles Palace.

The delegates sat at the Peace Table in the shape of a U, with Clemenceau at the head as presiding officer, after President Poincare had made the opening speech and retired.[21] On his right hand sat President Wilson and the United States delegation. On his left Lloyd George and the British delegates. Twenty-seven nations were represented with seventy delegates about the table. A picturesque figure at the table was Prince Feisal, representing his father, King Hussein of the Hedjaz. His native costume of the Bedouin tribesmen added the only bit of color to the solemn assembly. President Wilson's advisers, like myself, sat behind him slightly to one side. After happy speeches of nomination by the President, Lloyd George and Sonnino, Clemenceau was made permanent chairman, who then stated the plan of procedure, and the Conference was ready for business, but soon adjourned after agreeing upon program for Monday. Wilson, Clemenceau and Lloyd George were all apparently on most friendly social terms, and the Conference was certainly started under most favorable circumstances. May it only continue.

We all stopped in the lobby adjoining the Conference Chamber for tea and I had an opportunity to talk with Clemenceau and only greet Foch and Pichon, French Foreign Minister, who do not speak English.

Went to Stetson's apartment to dine on invitation of Owen to meet Sir Esme Howard, British Minister to Sweden; a most agreeable man, great friend of America, and talked of as possible successor to Reading as Ambassador, as I think Reading will resign.

JANUARY 19 (SUNDAY)—

Motored down to Fontainebleau with Mrs. Harriman, Mrs. McCombs and Fred Sterling, Secretary U.S. Embassy, for lunch and had beautiful walk through the forest. I had no idea of the beauty of the forest and attractiveness of the Inn from my former visit with Anne[22] and Flemings on motor trip, as we had rushed through in typical tourist style.

Had tea at Barbizon, famous as home of artists who paint in forests.

Returned home in time for dinner and dined quietly alone in room, and had my first good read since the steamer.

---

21. At this session, Clemenceau was unanimously selected permanent chairman of the peace conference.
22. Probably referring to his sister, Anne McCormick (1879–1964)

JANUARY 20 (MONDAY)—

Conference at War Trade Board office. Called on Lord Reading and Cecil with Sheldon to try to work out Allied Blockade Committee that would have some authority. Not much success. Both these men still uncertain of their own standing with their governments and fearful of assuming authority.

Went to luncheon at Luxembourg Palace given by French Senate to President Wilson, held in Salon. Most gorgeous affair. Three hundred present. President made one of his best speeches and was most enthusiastically received. Hoover, Baruch, Hurley and I, being classed as President's advisers, get in on all these official occasions. The President's speeches are continually interrupted by the interpreter, and as the latter is the only one understood by the Frenchmen, he gets all the applause and the President's words are received in silence, which creates a most peculiar effect.

Worked in the office all afternoon. Dined with Lew Sheldon at Café Henri.

JANUARY 21 (TUESDAY)—

This morning we transferred our morning conferences from the Crillon to the War Trade Board office at the Embassy, as we have available there all cables, files, clerks, etc., and I think it will facilitate operations.

Lunched at the Majestic with Sir Hubert Smith, of the British Board of Trade; Fontaine, Secretary, and Captain Tufton, blockade man from the Foreign Office. Made some progress; think we are pretty well in accord. Had talk with Lord Robert Cecil and met his niece, Lady ———, a Salisbury. Worked in office until 5:30, when I had an appointment with the President at the Hotel Murat. Suggested the importance of his having weekly conferences with his advisers similar to War Cabinet meetings in Washington. He agreed to start them this week. It will help us all, I feel sure. Discussed organization plans for closer Allied co-operation. He has heard from reliable sources the Allies want to pool the total expense of the war and have us pay our proportionate share of the whole.[23] This, of course, is not to be considered, and the President was considerably exer-

---

23. This indeed was the plan of Lloyd George and Clemenceau, and it is well documented.

cised over this proposal and wanted me to tell the other advisers not to get mixed up in any of their committees by discussing this subject at this time; but we were to confine ourselves only to our own Allied financial or other problems in which the enemy countries are involved, thereby keeping clear of embarrassing discussions which have nothing to do with Germany. Colonel House has been getting about for the first time in ten days, but very weak.

Dined with Professor Rappard, of Switzerland, here as a delegate to the League of Nations and Red Cross. He introduced me to the President of Switzerland, who was staying at the Meurice, where we were dining.[24]

JANUARY 22 (WEDNESDAY)—

Conference at the War Trade Board. Cleaned up correspondence. Lunched with Lord Eustace Percy and his wife and Waterlow, blockade expert, and ———— at Viel Café. Conferences in the afternoon. Dined at Marquis de Polignac's. Present: Grand Duke Alexander of Russia, Princess de Polignac, Lady Johnston, Gifford Pinchot's sister, Baruch, Auchincloss and a few others. Went later to reception given by Lansing at the Crillon for President and Mrs. Wilson. Ambassador John W. Davis and wife of England are here for a few days visiting the Lansings.

JANUARY 23 (THURSDAY)—

War Trade Board conferences going more smoothly. Have Stuart overlooking details and handling cables from others countries; Owen serving on the Inter-Allied Committee; Sheldon, in addition to handling all London affairs, is assistant to Lansing; Paris office under Stetson; Taylor acting with me on general questions of policy while in Paris and now just back from trip to Austria-Hungary and soon off for Germany, reporting upon living conditions, particularly food.

Had for lunch today in my room at Ritz Secretary Lansing, Admiral Benson, Mr. Henry White, peace delegate with Dr. Taylor, Sheldon and Dulles to enlighten them on economic control, blockade, etc. A most fruitful meeting as we found them unfamiliar with questions of export and import control and blockade. Are holding other educational conferences and many memorandums are being referred to us. Conference with Davis, Auchincloss, House and President for a few minutes.

---

24. These men were particularly interested in the question of representation of neutral countries in the League of Nations.

Dined at the Hotel with Dr. Taylor and Mrs. Harriman. Just before dinner Henry White showed me the first draft of the League of Nations covenant and asked me to prepare a memorandum upon part pertaining to economic control as [a] weapon to enforce peace.

JANUARY 24 (FRIDAY)—

Morning conference at War Trade Board. Called at Embassy upon Robert Bliss, Acting Ambassador. Lunched with Gillet to meet Tardieu, Locheur, Minister of Munitions, Baruch and Summers at Voisin. Had interesting discussion on reparations and indemnities. Tried to get from the French the reason of delay in beginning reconstruction work. Both France and Belgium doing absolutely nothing in production line. In my opinion, the people are being spoiled and riding for a fall if governmental restrictions of all kinds are not removed and business permitted to become normal.

Went for tea with Marquise de Polignac at her sister-in-law's, Princess de Polignac. Most attractive apartment and seven children. Her husband lost in the war. Several good looking Countesses, relatives, and others present. A great treat to see the real French thoroughbreds in their own home surrounded by their children. I don't believe there is a more beautiful home life in any country.

Sheldon, Owen and I dined together and I spent quiet evening at home reading Harrisburg papers.

JANUARY 25 (SATURDAY)—
[*Peace delegates voted for League of Nations*]
Breakfast with Sheldon and then saw Sir George Riddell, one of the big publishers of England. Great personal friend of Lloyd George and handling his publicity at conference. Gave much valuable information. He will prove useful.

Lunched with Mr. and Mrs. Charpentier in their home. Met Mr. and Mrs. Girot, old acquaintances of former visit to Paris during the war, he a leading newspaperman and she an attractive woman, and a Madame ———, head of large hospital; three hundred babies under her charge. Walter Berry and Gillet also present.

Went to second meeting of the Plenary Peace Conference. The general plan of League of Nations proposed by the President. First speech in favor by President Wilson, seconded by Lloyd George also by Bourgeois for France. Adopted unanimously in principle but committee to be appointed.

Over this question interesting debate as small nations led by Belgium, aided by Sir Robert Borden, Canada, demanded greater representation on the committee. Old Clemenceau, a great parliamentarian, handled the situation well and put through the original proposal. The meeting was open and this informal and heated discussion will have a good effect, I believe, as it shows the public that all matters are not cut and dried and the small fellows have a voice at least. Baruch and I sit right near the President and are greatly interested. We were today appointed on the sub-committee on Reparations.

Dined with Dulles and Field, who wanted to discuss future of the Inter-Allied Maritime Council.

JANUARY 26 (SUNDAY)—

Late breakfast with Lew Sheldon. Church with Lansing and Dulles at American Church and heard the head of McCormick Seminary, Dr. ———, preach good sermon. With Dulles attended luncheon in honor of Ambassador Davis, served in my room at the Ritz. Pete Gross arrived in the afternoon and we had a good time gossiping about home. Pete is to be my aide. We walked in the afternoon to call upon Elizabeth Hudson and Miss Stillman. Dined with Bernie, Lew Sheldon and Pete.

JANUARY 27 (MONDAY)—

Started Pete in on his new duties. Conference War Trade Board. Lunched with Pete. Beginning to hold conferences with other advisers in connection with our new work on Committee for Reparations. Davis, a committeeman, sick, so Baruch and I have not been able to organize. Gordon Auchincloss says Baruch anxious to be chairman. I told him I was for him but wanted to talk to Davis. Called by appointment on Clementel and Vilgrain, food minister, to discuss Inter-Allied Blockage Committee and holding conference in relation to blockade, etc.

Dined with Mrs. Rublee, Mr. Rublee unfortunately ill. Other guests, Vilgrain and Monet, a nice little dinner party. The latter two men very attractive and able young Frenchmen, full of ideas and visions. I was interested in their belief in a world free trade; strong for a League of Nations, both very close to Clementel and Clemenceau. After dinner I went to grand opera upon invitation of Mr. Henry White, as the President's box had been presented to him. Not crazy about the opera but Russian Ballet beautiful. This was first night since the war regular box holders were out. Not very brilliant house; people still mourning.

January 28 (Tuesday)—

Conference at 11.00 o'clock. Stetson still sick. Stuart going to Italy to close out office and Taylor going to Germany Wednesday to report on food and economic conditions. Lunched with Pete Gross and Major Pete Schell. Worked in office in afternoon. Went to room early not feeling well. Had early dinner alone, went to bed.

January 29 (Wednesday)—

Slept late, still feeling below par. Attended conference of all advisers and experts of the Mission. Studied reparation matters and discussed informally plans for further research. Decided to hold weekly conferences in order to keep in touch with expert investigators. Had an interesting talk in afternoon with Gordon Auchincloss. Most amusing to note anxiety of Colonel [House]'s outfit over daily meeting of Council of five great powers at which Lansing sits with President. Colonel and Gordon both think things cannot possibly go right without the Colonel's presence and guiding hand. These little human weaknesses make interesting studies during these momentous days. Gordon insisted upon my seeing the Colonel to discuss meeting of our Economic Council of Advisers with the President which had not yet been started owing to the President's many other conferences. We decided to begin them at once and arranged one for the next day at the Colonel's office even if the President could not attend.

Dined with Pete in my room, still seedy. Pete had a great time talking home and showed me picture of his wife and baby.

January 30 (Thursday)—

Office all morning. Lunched with Billy Delano and Mrs. Havemeyer. Went to Hotel Murat to see the President by appointment to discuss with him, at Lansing's request, the Siberia railroad situation.[25] President agreed with me the whole story should be told to Congress of Japan's attempt to grab Siberia, the violation of ———— troops. Allied plans to reconstruct rail roads under Stevens. Need of money which if not granted might close open door to Siberia and Russia. Discussed reparation plans and also at my request President dictated cable to Tumulty about the postal zone. Attended at 5:00 P.M. the first meeting of the U.S. Economic Council at Colonel House's office. Present, Colonel House, General Bliss, Admiral Benson, Baruch, Hoover, Mr. Robinson, substituting for Mr. Hurley. Principal discussion relation of blockade. Agreed to prepare memorandum for the President which he was to try to get through Supreme War Council[26] Monday.

Dined at Lloyd George's house; met Mrs. Lloyd George and son. Present, Sir George Riddell, head of England's newspaper men in Paris, Baruch, Swope, of the *New York World,* Sheldon and self, and Lloyd George's secretary, Philip Kerr. After dinner Lloyd George, Baruch and I remained behind in the dining room and had an hour's solid talk with Lloyd George in the frankest manner. Openly discussed personalities of both countries. Seemed to admire President Wilson tremendously; sore at Northcliffe on account of recent attacks in *Mail;* gave us his opinion of our British conferees on Reparations committee. Hughes, Prime Minister of Australia, impossible but clever; Lord Cunliffe regular John Bull, no power of expression but straight and able; Lord Sumner judicial mind and great ability, no politician. Suggested he would make an excellent chairman.

Baruch and I both feel that we do not want to push America too much to front in seeking Chairmanship as Reparations Commission bound to disappoint everyone as to amount obtained from Germans.[27] After taking all Germany can give amount will fall below expectations so leadership in committee will not be a popular job. Interesting talk on Russia. Lloyd George defends Allied meeting at Principe Island and said he wanted Bol-

---

25. McCormick's notation of this problem indicates that he was privy to classified discussions of the most sensitive nature. Because the Japanese were attempting to control the operation of the Siberian railroads, Wilson sent John H. Stevens to investigate in 1917. Eventually, Stevens formally represented Russian railroad interests, but his position led to objections by the Japanese because the United States would then have indirect influence and control of the Trans-Siberian Railway and the Chinese Eastern Railway. As a compromise, Stevens named a Japanese railway expert to assist in the oversight of the Chinese Eastern. The Chinese had objections of their own to having Allied oversight of a railroad in their territory. An agreement on the Inter-Allied supervision of the Siberian Railway System was signed on January 9, 1919, by all the powers participating in the Siberian intervention. This agreement created a special Inter-Allied Committee to supervise the railways in the zones held by Allied forces. Stevens was appointed president of the newly created Inter-Allied Technical Board on March 9, 1919. This group served, in part, to protect the Chinese Eastern Railway from interference by the Japanese, who had large numbers of troops deployed in Siberia.

26. McCormick may be referring here to the Supreme Council or Council of Ten, the leadership group that devolved from the unmanageable number of delegates from the twenty-seven Allied and Associated powers who were in attendance at the Peace Conference. The Supreme Council was composed of the two ranking members from each of the five big powers: Britain, France, Italy, Japan, and the United States. Much work was done by specific committees of advisors who reported to the Supreme Council, who in turn reported to plenary sessions.

shevist leaders to come to Paris.[28] His theory if present plans fail is to let movement burn itself out in Russia so military invasion impossible. I suggested my relief plan of sending food to Petrograd with sufficient troops to protect distribution but he convinced me it would not work. His ideas of reparation possible for Germany to pay one hundred and twenty billion dollars same as his speeches during election. I doubt it but will wait until I see the figures. In questioning him as to how he got at these figures he states that before making them public he had gotten his information from Lord Cunliffe and other able advisers.

Felt after my visit that I could better see the power and success of the man as I was much impressed as he generally seemed to know what he was talking about and had great magnetism.

JANUARY 31 (FRIDAY)—

Still feeling under the weather. Meeting with Baruch in Davis' room where he is just recovering from pneumonia. Discussed plans for organization of Reparations Committee. Lunched with Mrs. Harriman, Mrs. Auchincloss, Sir George Lawrence, friend of Feisel and benefactor of Arabs, Oxford man and most interesting history, who has been pleading cause of Arabs and wants no French control of Syria. Also Sir William Tirrell present. Office all afternoon, conference with Hoover. Musgrove of Alabama called at my office with Methodist bishop. Dined with Bernie, Sumners and Sheldon.

---

27. McCormick was a key member of this key committee in the peace terms negotiations among the allied countries. When the armistice occurred on November 11, 1918, the Germans understood that they would not be assessed for the costs of war, only for damages. Since November 11, however, Lloyd George had been reelected prime minister in Britain by promising he would insist on huge payments from Germany as part of the war settlement. France's Clemenceau had made similar promises in his country for the harshest possible peace terms for Germany, which would include payment of all war costs. It was clear that Germany would be unable to pay the amounts demanded by Britain and France, thereby causing political repercussions for Lloyd George and Clemenceau, who joined forces against Wilson on this issue.

28. McCormick refers to a planned summit between Allied leaders and the warring Russian leaders to discuss terms of a cease-fire in Russia. The planned meeting failed to take place because Kolchak and Denikin refused to meet with the Bolsheviks. The proposed location for this was Prinkipo Island, which lies in the Sea of Marmara not far from Istanbul. Charles Seymour, *The Intimate Papers of Colonel House* (Boston: Houghton Mifflin Company, 1926), 4:347.

FEBRUARY 1 (SATURDAY)—

Office all morning. Conference with Hoover on relaxation of blockade. Lunched with Pete and Dulles. Conference in the office of Seydoux. Agreed on Inter-Allied Blockade Committee as a distinct organization; also approved of relaxation of blockade for Southeastern Europe, but not so sure of re-exports to Germany through bordering neutrals.[29]

Spent evening alone, having lost Pete.

FEBRUARY 2 (SUNDAY)—

Breakfast with Baruch; very late, due to oversleeping on account of bad cold. Talked with Jerome Greene to urge him to accept secretaryship of Reparations Commission for U.S. delegation. Went to lunch with General Churchill, living in Goelet apartment; Major Marsden, Helms, Colonel Grant, Tardier, Colonel Revall, on French Staff; Mr. Krech, a big French banker; ——— ———; Commander Howard, British Admiralty; Captain McNamee, Sheldon, Dulles and Fosdick.

Called on Stetson and Owen, who has been sick. Crillon to see Auchincloss. Tea with de Polignacs. Went to the President's house at 6 o'clock. Got him to present at Supreme War Council tomorrow program for a consideration relaxation of embargo. Discussed Congress' attack upon the Russian Bureau. He approved our proceeding with plans irrespective of attack, as he finds work more necessary now than ever, as the war is not over so far as Russia is concerned and they need our relief. He certainly has courage where criticism of himself is concerned. Discussed work of Reparations Commission and League of Nations as it concerned Economic Control. He seemed in great shape.

Dined with Mr. and Mrs. Alvin Krech and Sheldon. Mr. Krech wanted to tell us of his plan for helping to finance French reconstruction through a group of French bankers.

Bernie and Sheldon kept me up talking until a late hour.

FEBRUARY 3 (MONDAY)—

Maneuvering all morning with Davis and Baruch about organization of Reparations Committee; also conference with Cecil Harmsworth, Minis-

---

29. McCormick and other Americans were eager for Britain to drop the trade embargoes so that supplies could be moved to and from Europe—including Germany—allowing reconstruction and vital manufacturing to begin.

ter of Blockade for Great Britain; Sir William Mitchell Thompson and other blockade experts for England.

Lunched with Berenson, Laurent Café, with a Russian, Belgian and Frenchman. Most interesting conversation. Went to first meeting of Reparations Committee held at the Ministry of Finance in a magnificent salon. Table arranged similar to the Plenary Peace Conference, with delegates at U-shaped table and secretaries in the rear. Twenty-five delegates present. Finance Minister Klotz of France called the meeting to order and started to organize. He and Prime Minister Hughes, of Australia, evidently had organization divided between them. We blocked them on the secretariat as well as sub-committee. Meeting adjourned until tomorrow. Expect more trouble over organization.

Dined with Mr. and Mrs. Arthur James at their apartment, Carrie Slade's friends; with Krechs, Sterling and Mrs. James and Mrs. Thayer, of Boston.

FEBRUARY 4 (TUESDAY)—

Conference [at] Crilion with Baruch. Later I attended for the U.S. small meeting Minister Klotz' office with representatives of the Great Powers, including Belgium, to work out further plans of organization for Reparations Committee. Soon saw Belgium and France had formed combination to control situation, and I was not quite sure of Hughes, but he stood by and we put over two English-speaking secretaries and one French and one Italian, so minutes could not be misinterpreted; also broke up executive bureaus they planned of President and two Vice-Presidents, with one Secretary.[30] They are all playing for big stakes—billions—and want to control machinery of committee. Agreed on three sub-committees: 1st, Amount Germany will pay; 2d, Category of Damages; 3d, Guarantees. We tried for a fourth on "Principles," but only got them to agree to submit latter to the conference as a whole.[31] We will get the committee later, I am sure.

Gave lunch in my room at the Ritz to English delegates, Premier Hughes, Lord Sumners and Lord Cunliff. Hughes bright and active, but,

---

30. Here are vivid examples of the behind-the-scenes maneuvering and diplomatic detailing that constitute the work of advisors and diplomats. The more savvy and seasoned the diplomat, the more often the side so represented gains control, or at least equal footing.

31. The French and British representatives were more interested in hard practicalities than in Wilson's ideals; nevertheless, "Principles" refers to the understanding about reparations in the armistice agreement, which Wilson and the Americans felt should not be altered.

I am afraid, too sharp. The other two typical Englishmen, but I believe are pretty straight.

3:00 P.M. attended the full meeting of Committee at the Ministry of Finance to finish organization. Appointed secretariat. Agreed upon three sub-committees and determined to discuss Principles tomorrow in full Committee.

Captain Conway Howard, Mrs. Olmsted's brother, called at my Crillon office on his way from Czecho-Slovakia on relief work and looked very well.

Attended first meeting of Supreme Allied Blockade Committee at Ministry of Commerce, Clementel's office. Present, Clementel, Cecil Harmsworth, British Representative, with Sir William Mitchell Thompson and his assistant; Crespi, representing Italy, and self the United States. I was elected chairman of Council and we at least, after days of struggle, have an Inter-Allied Blockade Committee in Paris with full authority to act. Think the relaxations of the blockade will come fast and furious from now on.

Dined with Stuart, Ogden Mills and Sheldon at the Ritz. Worked after dinner with Baruch and Sheldon.

FEBRUARY 5 (WEDNESDAY)—

Meeting of full Reparations Committee at 11:00 o'clock to discuss principles of reparation. So many nations unprepared with briefs that conference adjourned until Monday, so that this most important question be decided before sub-committees can begin work.

Lunched with Sheldon and Lowenburg, a most influential Swede, who negotiated Swedish agreement with the Allies and United States Blockade Committees. Met the President with Hoover at 2:15 at the President's house to urge the President to strongly present at the War Council the need of relaxing embargo to relieve food situation in the enemies and neutral countries. Worked in office in the afternoon, having interview with Ray Stannard Baker, head of U.S. publicity for Peace Conference; also Mark Sullivan and Gilbert, of *The Tribune*.

Dined with Secretary and Mrs. Lansing, Allen Dulles and Hugh Gibson, latter just returned form Austria and Southeastern Europe. Represents frightful conditions as to food and industry. Our blockade certainly did the trick.[32]

---

32. McCormick was particularly interested here because the War Trade Board had been part of the execution of the American aspects of the blockade.

FEBRUARY 6 (THURSDAY)—

Office all morning. Lunched at Crillon as guest of Peter Schell to meet Sam Fleming, an officer friend, and Pete Gross. Enjoyed home gossip and war experiences of the boys.

Attended at 4:00 P.M. conference Allied Blockade Council, Clementel's office, Hot discussion on relations of exports to Northern neutrals. Could not gain point.

Dined at Mrs. Wood's, where Miss Helen Cameron is staying.

FEBRUARY 7 (FRIDAY)—

Conference in Colonel House's office with Davis, Strauss, Lamont and Sheldon to prepare resolution for the President to present at the Supreme War Council.

Lunched with Hill, correspondent of the *New York Sun*. Went with President to Supreme War Council to be on hand to advise if blockade matters come up. Meeting held in the French Prime Minister's office, Clemenceau presiding. Lloyd George, Foch and all other Allied representatives present. Sat directly behind President ready for action which never came, as Armistice terms took up entire afternoon and we adjourned until tomorrow afternoon.[33]

Conferred with counselor Miller and Dulles on the Reparations Principles; also later with Hoover, Davis and Sheldon on matters relating to blockade.

Dined with Miss Hudson and Miss Stillman in their apartment. George McFadden just arrived and was a midnight visitor. Henry Loomes, my new valet, recommended by Miss Hudson, is doing nicely.

FEBRUARY 8 (SATURDAY)—

Meeting in Dulles' room with counselor Miller, Davis, Strauss, Lamont and Captain Smith to discuss brief to be presented on Principles of Reparations for the full committee. Were all in accord. We meet in Hoover's office to discuss organization of new Supreme Economic Council. Sir John Beale, of England; Dr. Giovanni, of Italy, and Monet, of France, agreed upon draft of memorandum to be submitted in the afternoon at the Supreme War Council.

---

33. Because agreement on the terms for peace had not been achieved by the Allied nations, the November 1918 Armistice had to be regularly renewed.

Lunched at Crillon with McFadden and Owen. Went with President to Supreme War Council at the Quai d'Orsay. They discussed Armistice terms without agreement until after 5:00 o'clock. In the last few minutes the President put through creation of the new Supreme Economic Council for control of all economic questions affecting the Allies and enemy countries during Armistice. Clemenceau and Marshal Foch at meeting of Council had quite a tiff, and the Marshal angrily got up and slammed his papers down on the desk and left the room in great anger, followed by his aide. This difference between Foch and Clemenceau may become political issue in House of Deputies. Foch was very angry. He was followed out of the room immediately by Tardieu and Loucheur, who I think went out to try to pacify him, realizing the seriousness of the situation. Clemenceau had sided apparently with the United States on the question of some militaristic plan of Foch. I could not get the point exactly, as the heated discussion was not interpreted.

Dined with Dresel to meet Lady Hood, et al. Went to meet President by appointment at 10:00 o'clock P.M., only available hour during his day, to get his approval on Reparations Principles. Had good talk on matters generally. Went to dance at Jeffrey Dodge's apartment.

FEBRUARY 9 (SUNDAY)—

Pete Gross and Bill Clark breakfasted with me. Latter in route to London for two weeks' vacation. George McFadden also had his breakfast sent to my room.

Worked in my room nearly all day. Price Jackson and his brother called. Henry Gross and I called on Frank McCoy, who is convalescing from pneumonia in the hospital. Met his sister there, who goes to Coblenz Y.M.C.A. tomorrow. Pete and I and Mr. and Mrs. Auchincloss dined with Mrs. Harriman.

FEBRUARY 10 (MONDAY)—

Attended conferences Reparations Committee to discuss Principles. All the briefs were submitted. Only Prime Minister Hughes spoke. Then appointed committee to receive brief.

Lunched with Bernie, Strauss and Dulles. Went to conference of the Supreme War Council with the President. Worked afterwards until 8:00 o'clock. Dined with McFaddens.

Foch and Clemenceau seem to have made up, as at the meeting of the Supreme War Council this afternoon Foch was back in the meeting and in good spirits. French seem to be trying to kill time. President becoming very restless.

FEBRUARY 11 (TUESDAY)—

Meeting of the Reparations delegation of the U.S. in Secretary Lansing's office with U.S. Peace Commissioners to discuss Principles of Reparations. Later meeting in Baruch's office to discuss methods of aiding economic conditions at home, due to falling prices and lack of markets.

Lunched with Hoover. Hoover discouraged; Allies not playing the game. Thinks he will have to play lone hand in relief. Urges tying up with Belgium in Reparations clauses and giving them priority. Attended meeting of supreme Blockade Council. Cecil, Davis and others attended as special committee of the Supreme War Council to see if we could suggest other methods of pressure against Germany to make her live up to the Armistice terms. Long, windy meeting afterwards on blockade relaxation. French seem to block every effort in this direction.

Dined with Robert Bliss and went afterwards to the Opera in his box. Performance in honor of President and Mrs. Wilson. A great house. Opera "Damnation of Faust."

FEBRUARY 12 (WEDNESDAY)—

Mills, my new stenographer, came to room at Ritz to make up back work, also McFadden. Foreign Minister of Czecho-Slovakia called to present his nation's claim for financial assistance. Lunched with Monet. Told him of all our difficulties with the French, particularly unfair press propaganda against President and United States delegation.[34] The talk will prove helpful as he is near the throne.

Before lunch I was called by the President to the Supreme War Council at the Quai d'Orsay. Still discussing Armistice terms as the Armistice expires the 16th. The French seem panicky about Germany but I think new terms will please them. Met again at Quai d'Orsay in the afternoon. Agreed to not extend Armistice to definite date but indefinitely and with right to cancel on three days notice and to force Germany to make preliminary peace treaty concerning reduction of armament.

---

34. The press had been barred from the official meetings, and as a result of the closed doors, rumor and misinformation were fed to the press, particularly by the French anti-Wilson faction, which was designed to poison public opinion.

Dined at the Jockey Club with the Marquis and Marquise d'Polignac in honor of Lord and Lady Derby. Many Countesses and Baronesses present including Rothschilds, etc., and some good Americans—Admiral Grayson, Captain Tobin, Mrs. Harriman and Miss Sharpe, Ambassador Sharpe's daughter.

FEBRUARY 13 (THURSDAY)—

Lew Sheldon is back so Pete and I have company for breakfast before our wood fire. Attended meeting of the General Reparations Committee. Jumped on Klotz for leaks in the Press concerning our proceedings and the criticism of the United States in the French papers which were under government censorship, and this after his special request that no publicity concerning the Reparations Committee proceedings be given out by any member of the committee.[35] I was strongly supported by all the other delegates. Major Dulles presented our principles in an able speech and was answered by Lord Sumner in a weak speech because his case is a bad one. Dulles adhering strictly to International Law and the President's fourteen points as qualified by the Allies and made in agreement with Germany in Armistice terms.

Lunched with Clementel and Monet and continued discussion of the French methods of propaganda in the French Press and lack of frankness in peace negotiations. I think we made progress as Clementel is sympathetic. Worked in office in the afternoon. Mrs. Wilson sent for me at 5:30 to come for a cup of tea as she departs tomorrow for America. Had a good talk for an hour alone.

Dined in my room with Hoover and Lord Robert Cecil as guests. They wanted to discuss the new Economic Council of Conference.

FEBRUARY 14 (FRIDAY)—

[*Wilson presented the League Covenant*]

Attended meeting of Reparations Commission at Finance Ministry. Dulles answered Lord Sumner's argument of day previous, then Hughes made strong argument for total cost of the war without sticking to agreement of Armistice. Am afraid delegates are all against us although pri-

---

35. Censorship of the press was a touchy issue throughout the conference period. Censorship of press reports from France to the United States was removed on November 21, 1918, after Wilson's official request. Seymour, *Intimate Papers,* 4:236.

vately they claim they believe in our principles but are playing politics for home consumption and claiming the earth.

Lunched with Sanderson, whom Homer Cummings had me get over here, and Spellacy, to discuss politics. Went to the full meeting of the Plenary Peace Conference. President Wilson presented, under the most impressive conditions, the League of Nations covenant.[36] He made a wonderful speech, followed by Bourgeois and Lord Robert Cecil, et al. I had to leave early to attend a Blockade Meeting at the Ministry of Commerce. Making some progress.

Dined with Jack Boyd and Pete Gross. Jack blew in today for several days visit with me, well and hearty. Meeting my office with experts on claims for reparations, General McKinistry, Professor Young, Davis, Baruch, etc.

FEBRUARY 15 (SATURDAY)—

Attended meeting Reparations Committee at 10:30. Belgium, Serbia and several other states advocated full costs of the war; also Klotz, Finance Minister of France, in a vicious speech ignoring correspondence of President leading up to Armistice and stating Armistice agreement only agreement in evidence and that that permitted full war costs. At 3:00 P.M. attended organization of sub-committee of Reparations on claims. Lord Sumner made chairman. He and I alone wanted immediate action, all claims filed and approximation for basis of classification and estimates. The entire Latin group led by France against us, stating impossible to get figures for months. In informal conference after meeting I discovered from Minister Lebrun of France that they did not propose to ask a fixed amount from Germany but wanted Germany to sign a blank check and make annual demands upon the estimated cost of the war for each nation; this to be approved by Inter-Allied Commission. Am afraid it won't work. Will have to agree to maximum and minimum under such a scheme, otherwise, enemy countries will not know how to arrange financial and industrial life to pay indemnity.

Gave dinner to Polignacs, McFaddens and Baruch and we all went to a small dance at Ritz given by a number of us stopping at the hotel. Pete Gross enjoyed it immensely sailing around with Duchess of Sutherland, French Countesses, etc.

---

36. Wilson had been appointed the chairman of the commission to draft the covenant, and the group had prepared the draft in ten days.

FEBRUARY 16 (SUNDAY)—

Pete Gross returned to his Division and I shall miss him. Lunched with Jack and Jim Boyd at Ritz. Worked at Crillon until 5:00 P.M. Walked with Dulles. Dined with Hoover, Baruch, Davis, Strauss and other advisers to meet Belgium delegation, including Prime Minister de la Croix, Peace Delegate Hymans, etc. Think we succeeded in getting through their good graces, Van der ——— and Duprey, representatives on the Reparations Committee, to support U.S. on principles as against Great Britain and France.

FEBRUARY 17 (MONDAY)—

Meeting at the Finance Ministry of Reparations Commission. Klotz, Italians and Serbians strong for entire cost of war. Belgiums [sic] making weak attempt to support us. Loucheur called upon us to continue argument and answer argument of Hughes. Difficult to do without making embarrassing references concerning some of our Allies. Will be discussed Wednesday after debate on postponement. A leading Belgium [sic] present was disgusted with the weak position of their delegates. Asked us to lunch with the Belgium [sic] delegates Tuesday to try to get better support from them.

Lunched with Jim and Jack Boyd. Attended first meeting Supreme Economic Council at Ministry of Commerce. Clementel presided. Klotz, Loucheur for France, Lord Robert Cecil, Sir John Beale for Great Britain, Crespi and Ciesa for Italy, Hoover, Norman Davis and self for the United States. Organized and agreed to let Inter-Allied organization remain intact. Discussed relaxation of blockade; did not get anywhere. Crespi said would not agree to any relaxation unless Great Britain or United States helped finance food for his distressed country. Meeting getting hot over Crespi's statement so Lord Robert adjourned meeting. Lord Robert very angry at Crespi's hold up game.

Dined with McFaddens, Sheldon and Italian.

FEBRUARY 18 (TUESDAY)—

Conference at Lansing's room with Peace Commissioners White and Bliss. Conference with Davis, Strauss, Baruch and Lamont on policy of United States delegation on account of Allies holding us up on every hand for money whenever we asked for relaxation of blockade or anything else. I suggested we withdraw all our demands and play a waiting game. Think we can beat them to it. Agreed to.

We lunched as guests of Belgium [*sic*] delegation. Completed arrangement to support each other in full on reparations principles and reference back to heads of five governments who made them. Dulles and I got later in afternoon support of Italian delegates for reference. Hope thus save vote as the entire Reparations Commission against us except Belgium.

Dined with Major Kuntz.

FEBRUARY 19 (WEDNESDAY)—
[Wilson and Lloyd George both returned to home countries]

Conference with Lansing concerning the cable we proposed sending to the President, en route home on the *George Washington,* to get his interpretation of Reparation principles for use of Colonel House at Supreme War Council. Attended the Reparations Committee 10:30. The United States gave way to Japan and then Dulles followed making an able defence of our position but did not turn any votes. We then succeeded after considerable debate to have question referred to the heads of the five great powers.

We had a buffet luncheon at the Ministry of Finance, then worked in office with Sheldon, McFadden and Hoover. Talked to Colonel House about cable to the President. He was not enthusiastic and I thought rather resented cable being shown first to Lansing, but approved.

Dined with Sheldon, McFadden, Stetson and Owen. Goodby dinner to Owen, who leaves this week.

Dr. Taylor, just back from Germany, dropped in and we had a most interesting evening. He says the present government of Germany same old crowd with Kaiser gone. People unreconstructed yet he is not hopeless about proper leaders getting control as he thinks present government on very thin ice. Many leading men think Germany now in Kerensky period of Russia and Bolshevism bound to come. I doubt it. Too many people own their own property. Very different from Russia.

FEBRUARY 20 (THURSDAY)—

Worked in room until 10:00 o'clock. At 11:00 attended Blockade meeting. Sprang new policy of indifference on Relaxation of Blockade we have been working for. It worked like a charm. French and Italians are now the beggars as they want trade and we can sit back and let them worry. Think in a couple of weeks we will have accomplished our object. Worked in office all afternoon.

Dined at Ritz with Frank Hitchcock, Mrs. McCombs and Mrs. Harriman. Went to Casino afterwards.

FEBRUARY 21 (FRIDAY)—

My secretary, who by the way speaks French, Portuguese and Spanish, formerly of Lisburn legation, now comes to my room for dictation before going to the office. Easy day, because no committee meeting and have time for conference with advisers and House, particularly on Reparations solution.[37] Think I have convinced the crowd that to acquiesce in the plan not to name lump sum will be only thing Allies can stand for on account of having fooled their people by exaggerating promises of high indemnity and no taxes, otherwise governments will fall.

Dined in room for quiet evening with Harrisburg newspapers.

FEBRUARY 22 (SATURDAY)—

Office all morning. Invited to lunch with the Franco-American Club to make speech at farewell celebration for Ambassador Sharpe. Ducked speech and lunched with Rappard and Groutet, of Swiss delegation, with Taylor and Sheldon. Walked with Taylor to the War Trade Board at Embassy and at 4:00 went to tea with Mrs. Rublee to meet Russian Minister Titoff, formerly of Kerensky's cabinet, and Mme. De Maziaritz to discuss Russian matters. Present, Mr. and Mrs. Lamont, a Colonel of the French Army, Norman Angell and Mrs. Dillon, wife of writer.

Dined with Jesse Jones, of Texas, in Paris on Red Cross Work. As usual, McFadden and Sheldon dropped in for a little gossip before retiring. Arranged for tea at my room tomorrow for Colonel House and Tardieu for conference. Colonel trying to make preliminary peace reparation and asked me to arrange confidential meetings with French leaders. Hope something develops, as French have been behaving distressingly.

FEBRUARY 23 (SUNDAY)—

Church with Dulles at American Church. Heard minister from Texas. Met Julianna Wood and walked home with her. Lunched with A. W. Dulles in honor of Hugh Wilson, Charge at Berne; present, Lansing, Grew, Professor Charles Seymour. Conference with Hoover for two hours. Colonel House and Tardieu came to my room at the Ritz for a confidential conference and a cup of tea. Had very satisfactory talk and made progress in agreement as to pushing proceedings. Tardieu explained the great difficulties politically his government had in letting the people know the truth about the indemnity that can be collected from Germany. He fears the fall

---

37. House mentions this conference in his account. Seymour, *Intimate Papers*, 4:243.

of their government. England in same plight, and they are now hunting around for compromise to accept position of the United States. Tardieu stayed nearly an hour. If Clemenceau dies, he is the most talked of man for Premier.

I had to dinner in my room Lamont, Strauss, Davis, Baruch and Dulles to discuss plan of reparations which might be acceptable to Allies and yet adhere to the United States principles. Meeting broke up late.

FEBRUARY 24 (MONDAY)—

Reparations Committee at 10:30. Did not accomplish much. Decided to await discussion of the Supreme War Council on Principles, but also proceed with the sub-committee work.

Lunched with Oscar Strauss and Hoover and discussed League of Nations. Strauss thought the President's speech at the conference inspired. Best one he has ever made. Says Republicans must support the League.[38] Attended sub-committee on Claims. No progress to speak of.

At 5:00 o'clock meeting of Superior Blockade Council. Dined with Mrs. Harriman to meet Colonel and Mrs. House, Philip Kerr, Lloyd George's secretary,—a very nice fellow and most helpful to us—and Marquis and Marquise de Polignac. All went to Lady Hood's "at home," held on Mondays in February and March. Supposed to be for the purpose of gathering all the "lions" attending the conference—Balfour, Venizelos, Bakhmeteff, of Russia, present, including many charming ladies—Countess Brisaux (whom I dined with at the Country Club, Harrisburg, with Mrs. Olmsted and the Halls); Mrs. Whitridge, Mrs. Hyde, etc.; delightful evening. Lady Hardington, Lord Robert Cecil's niece, most charming.

FEBRUARY 25 (TUESDAY)—

Office all morning. 12:30 met Lord Robert Cecil on relaxation censorship. Lunched with Tardieu's assistant, Capt. Masson. Attractive fellow. Agrees in general way with our reparation views. Great change coming over French. Things get more hopeful every day. Supreme Economic Council at 3:00 P.M., Lord Robert presiding. Perfected organization and discussed relief matters. Hearing Hoover's troubles principally, which are

---

38. Republicans in Washington were opposed to the League of Nations as proposed by Wilson on the fourteenth. It was partially in answer to their opposition that Wilson had departed for the United States, and on February 26, 1919, Wilson met with Congress and was cross-examined concerning the league.

apparently endless. Our policy, however, of indifference on relaxation of blockade is having the desired effect and the Allies are now coming to us.

Dined with George McFadden and Monet. Later in the evening Lamont brought his report to show me, drawn by Loucheur and himself, on amount Germany can pay. Glad they are close together—around thirty billions. Another indication as to change in French attitude. Gordon and George McFadden kept me up until after midnight. Writing in room at 12:40.

FEBRUARY 26 (WEDNESDAY)—

Meeting of U.S. Reparations Committee at the Crillon with technical experts. Heard reports [of] sub-committees and after great discussion agreed to thirty billions in reparations—five billion in two years—seven hundred and fifty million per year for thirty-five years. Economists say it can't be done. French want forty billions. British not yet in accord. Can't agree among themselves.

At 12:00 M. met in Colonel House's office with Bliss, Benson and advisers Hoover, Baruch, Strauss, Lamont, Robinson, Davis and self. Discussed Italian holdup of relief to Austria and Czecho-Slovakia at Trieste, due to difficulties with Jugo-Slavia. Benson's reports show Italians on East bank Adriatic want war. We decided French, British and U.S. should read the riot act. Cable was sent to President. Colonel gave us political moves concerning Austria, Poland, Russia and Rhenish territory so our economic work would be guided right direction.

Lunched in Tardieu's apartment. Typical French home with side-whiskered waiter, etc. Finance Minister Klotz, Clementel, Davis, Baruch and Gann, et al. Satisfactory talk. Conditions improving daily with the French. Hope it continues. Certainly room for improvement. They certainly have been raw in the Press.

Office all afternoon. Carl Voorman called, also Major Bill Hickok. Townsend and Leith leaving for home. Disgruntled, I am afraid, but really no work especially in their line yet developed.

Dined with McFaddens, Mrs. Dr. Blake of divorce fame, formerly Mrs. Mackey; Sir Mitchell Thompson, Auchinclosses and Miss ———. Went to Follies [sic] Bergere and struck a championship wrestling match. One match thrilling. Swiss wrestler looked like Hun; lost his temper and struck opponent and all hissed and then threw seat cushions and anything they could lay their hands on at the wrestler. It looked like a riot for a few moments. Mrs. Blake nearly fainted and was taken home.

FEBRUARY 27 (THURSDAY)—

Meeting War Trade Board at Crillon. C. A. Richards just arrived from Washington, also Jones en route to Madrid as Commercial attache.

Gave lunch at Ritz to Minister of Commerce Clementel. Peace delegates Henry White, Alonzo Taylor, Monet, Sheldon and McFarland. Saw Ruby McCormick for a few moments.

Meeting of sub-committee Reparations. Discussed category of damages. Killing time discussing details. Must make peace and discuss details afterwards.

Dined at Gann's home with Tardieu, Baruch, Auchinclosses, Mr. and Mrs. Aubert, and a charming Miss Barclay and Madam ———, good looking, and Gillet. Good time singing and dancing. Madam Gann daughter of former manager of the Metropolitan Opera Company.

FEBRUARY 28 (FRIDAY)—

Usual dictating of letters in my room at the Ritz. Kept appointment Russian Ambassador Bakhmeteff and Mr. ——— upon Russian trade matters.

Lunched with General McKinstry and several officers at Officers Club, former home of Rothschild[39] to discuss Reparations categories prior to the meeting of sub-committee at 2:30. Committee met for four hours discussing categories, Lord Sumner giving delegates of smaller nations a chance to speak and air themselves. Hope to get minimum claims of each nation next week. Really killing time until sub-committee No. 2 makes report.

Dined with Sanderson to meet Mr. and Mrs. Vanderlip and General Atterbury.

MARCH 1 (SATURDAY)—

Both George and Lew breakfasted with me this morning. Attended meeting of American delegation Reparations Commission with U.S. experts. 11:00 o'clock meeting of the Blockade Council until 1:30. 3:00 o'clock met at Lord Robert's office with Lord Robert and Hoover. Lord Robert big as usual. How easy it would be if they were only all like him. Hoover's manners very brusque. I don't see how he holds his popularity.

---

39. Possibly the Hotel Talleyrand at Rue Saint Florentin, owned by several generations of Rothschilds, which is the present-day American Embassy and also served as the first NATO headquarters.

Meeting of Supreme Economic Council at Minister of Commerce office. Trying to put through financial plan for permitting Germany to buy food. French blocked every plan. England and America dread consequences, as we seem living on a volcano. Two hundred million people not producing in the world and many hungry. Interesting debate until 8:00 P.M. Got through modified relief.

Dined in room alone and read accumulation of Harrisburg newspapers.

MARCH 2 (SUNDAY)—

Overslept—did not get up until after 10:20. Wrote home. Lunched with Monet and Sheldon, trying to get real interpretation of differences at Supreme Economic Council meeting yesterday. Looks to me as though French will try to block food in Germany until Peace Treaty signed or we give in on Inter-Allied financial scheme to purchase food.

After lunch had appointment with Loucheur. Frank conversation about our differences. He spoke of the unknown propaganda against U.S. here, which accuses us of trying to unload pork, etc., in Germany and to get priority on German assets which reduces amount of indemnity French will get. Says he knows that it is not true but that is what they are up against politically. Finally agreed to work out satisfactory scheme in morning.

At 5:00, Colonel House and Tardieu came for tea, also Aubert with Tardieu. They agreed on plan for Rhenish Republic and discussed method of getting Lord George's approval, also on Saar Coal Basin.[40] Agreed Poland should have Danzig and Belgium Luxembourg, all of these, of course, with proper reservations. Agreed to push to conclusion work of committees so that reports would be ready for President upon his arrival the 4th, and Tardieu said Foch very anxious to get the Germans at conference, Versailles, 26th. Colonel agreed and they both hope it can be wound up May 1. This program is an ambitious one but I believe it can be done and should be, although I still see rocks ahead, particularly on questions of priority as to reparations payments.

---

40. The French wanted to create a neutral buffer state of the German lands west of the Rhine River; Lloyd George and Wilson opposed this. The French then proposed the territory be occupied for thirty years, but as a compromise, they agreed to a fifteen-year occupation. The French also demanded the annexation of the Saar Valley, which was predominantly German in population. Wilson opposed this, and eventually the French compromised and accepted the Saar coal mines as compensation for the destruction of French mines during the conflict. The Saar area was placed under the jurisdiction of the League of Nations for fifteen years, after which the inhabitants would have an election to choose their state.

Dined with McFaddens and Sheldon. Saw Jim McCrea and Irwin Laughlin and wife. Conference in my room with Davis, Baruch, Strauss and Lamont on Reparations and financing of the German food, in advance of meeting tomorrow when we expect trouble.

MARCH 3 (MONDAY)—

Now have another caller at room in the morning as C. A. Richards of the War Trade Board is here, so we have small W.T.B. cabinet meeting before leaving Hotel.

Attended meeting of the Supreme Economic Council to prepare for Marshal Foch instructions on terms for feeding Germans. Agreed upon the terms of draft to be submitted at afternoon meeting. U.S. advisers lunched together to discuss details of same. Went to session again at 2:30. As usual, French again balked. Same old trouble, apparently political and financial. Regret French so shifty—hot meeting. Lord Robert got after Clementel on a statement which looked like a threat. Finally agreed and delegates expected to leave tonight for Spa to meet German representatives. Hope they succeed as I believe we are facing another revolution in Germany and Bolshevism if they don't get food.

Dined with Sheldon at dinner at 8:00—Mr. and Mrs. Querre, Mr. and Mrs. Loufman and Countess Caracsa, Crosby's daughter. Went to dance afterwards at Ritz which number of us gave. Many dinner party guests present, mostly Italians and French—awful looking. Ladies were apparently trying to look like demimonde in dress and manners, and the odds were on the latter.

MARCH 4 (TUESDAY)—

Worked nearly all morning in my room at the Ritz on callers of War Trade Board, after dictating correspondence.

Lunched with Reggy Taylor, who is here on furlough. Splendid boy.

Went to sub-committee Reparations at 2:30. Wasted our time discussing category claims. Have not yet been able to get any figures after three weeks effort so I went after them this afternoon and think will have them by end of the week.

Dined with Oscar Strauss, Russian Ambassador Bakhemeff, Sasinoff, former Finance Minister to the Czar, Hoover and an American Colonel. Interesting discussion.

At Strauss dinner, proposed my scheme for economic relief of Russia by joint Allied and neutral action, distributed under proper military protection. Strauss had arranged the dinner to discuss this as I had broached it when Hoover and I lunched with him several days prior.

Walked home, beautiful moonlight night. First fine days. Beastly weather Paris in the winter.

Henry tells me Queen of Roumania is occupying suite next door. Things are certainly doing tonight.

MARCH 5 (WEDNESDAY)—

Started busy day at Ritz in room with Sheldon, Richards, McFadden still at Spa with commission arranging German food. Meeting of experts on Reparations with U.S. delegates at Crillon. Agreed to present as promised figures of our claim. Attended Blockade meeting at Commerce Ministry.

Lunched with Dulles and Davis—discussed Reparations. 2:30 went to Reparations meeting for half hour. Left Dulles and General McKinstry at 3:00 to go to Quai d'Orsay, to meeting of Council of Ten to be present at discussion of relief for Austria. Hoover presented his plan of improving bad transportation of food due to quarrel between Jugo-Slavia and Italy. Hoover wants to have under his charge enough railroad cars with full power to operate. Strongly supported by the British, less though by the French and strongly opposed by Italians whom I think are trying to make trouble on the Adriatic so they have an excuse for fighting Jugo-Slavia. The Council postponed action until next Friday. Italians were put in a hole by arguments and will have to show their hand.

First time I saw Clemenceau since he was shot.[41] He was presiding but did not seem as vigorous as usual and I noticed dozed off several times. Foch was on hand, keen as ever.

Dined at Minister Clementel's home in Versailles with Rublees and Monet. Delightful wife and home, small but full of beautiful things. He is a peculiar man; believes in spiritualism and mysticism and quite pleased with himself but extremely kind and hospitable. Am afraid not forceful as he has maintained his Ministry through too many changes of Government, but a capable, useful and attractive official.

Last night and today beautiful spring weather but it will not last.

The Queen of Roumania has asked for my sitting room for several days so I am writing in my bedroom and will be cramped for a short time

---

41. Clemenceau was driving to a meeting with Balfour and House on February 19, when he was shot and wounded by a Communist. One of the seven bullets fired at point-blank range lodged behind his shoulder blade, just missing the spine.

but we have to give way to Royalty, notwithstanding we hear so much of "Bolshevism."

French still blocking food deliveries to Germany. Situation there alarming. Cables all show state of revolution. Americans in Germany being attacked. My opinion we are living on top of a volcano; if relief not immediate, bound to have trouble and will affect France. English fully aware of situation and fighting hard with us to better conditions. French agree but don't help and really hinder whenever possible.

MARCH 6 (THURSDAY)—

War Trade Board at office, 10:00 o'clock. At 10:30 Plenary Committee on Reparations. Discussed questions submitted by the sub-committees. The U.S. delegates resent Klotz' unfair ruling. Went after him and made him crawl. Can see will not have report ready for President when he returns.

I had Lord Sumner to lunch to discuss matters concerning claims. Think we made progress.

Meeting of Supreme Economic Council 2:30, and announced trip of our delegates to Spa a failure, as Germany refuses to trade, because we had broken our former agreement under Armistice terms.

Dined with all officers of the Peace Conference and wives, about 50, as guest of Charge, Persian Legation in U.S., wife an American, in honor of Lansing. Persian commissioners were also guests. Speeches by host, Lansing and Persian Foreign Minister. I had a talk with General Pershing at the dinner, sat next to him. Looks very well. Later saw George McFadden, just back from Spa. Said it was most awkward. He found Allies had not lived up to agreement with Huns and Germans withdrew. Will learn more particulars tomorrow.

MARCH 7 (FRIDAY)—

Meeting in Lansing's office with U.S. Reparations delegates, Bliss and White being present with advisers to hear report of Spa delegates on Germans' turndown of Allies' offer. We discussed form of new proposal to be submitted to the Supreme Economic Council at 12:00 at Ministry of Commerce, meeting of Supreme Economic Council. Came to no agreement but considered certain drafts proposed by Cecil and House.

Lunched at Crillon with advisers.

At 5:00 P.M. met the sub-committee on Reparations. Finished up discussion on categories which we handed over to Lord Sumner to put in proper shape and finally got six nations to agree to file claims with figures by next week. French alone refused. Adjourned 7:30.

Dulles and I dined at Ritz. Appointment 9:00 o'clock with Dr. Giovanni, Italian Representative, to discuss the needs of Italy. Very short of ships, food and coal. Situation serious. Took opportunity to tell of U.S. disapproval of their action against Jugo-Slavia in the Adriatic.

MARCH 8 (SATURDAY)—

Morning in room at Ritz and office at Crillon until 12:00 noon, when attended meeting, Ministry of Commerce, of Supreme Economic Council to go over final draft of agreement with Germany for food in exchange for ships. British and ourselves in accord; Italians finally agreed; French still holding out on financial terms; still refusing to permit use of German gold for food, trying to force U.S. to supply money direct. We agreed to submit two proposals to the Supreme War Council in afternoon.

At 3:00 P.M. went to Supreme War Council. Lloyd George made great fight. Severely criticised Minister of Finance Klotz for blocking scheme to feed Germany for two months. Appealed for settlement now to save Germany and Europe from Bolshevism. Sonnino and Crespi for Italy agreed with Great Britain and U.S. and finally a compromise was worked out in which the French made big concessions and agreement approved.[42] I am still afraid, however, when final terms are decided we will find French throwing obstacles in way. The proposal which now goes back to Germany is the one she demanded at Spa. Looks like an acknowledgment that our first proposition was not a fair one.

Dined with Minister Koo of China, six Chinese officials, luxurious house. Present, Lansing, White, Grew, Patterson and myself. Delightful dinner. Chinese were most intelligent. Went to dance at Jeffrey Dodge's apartment.

MARCH 9 (SUNDAY)—

Slept late, Sunday. Went to Episcopal Church with Mrs. McFadden. Went to Versailles with Mrs. Harriman for lunch. Met many friends at

---

42. Another diarist of the period, Stephen Bonsal (probably the Major Bonsal who was part of the U.S. delegation to the Congress of Submerged Nationalities in Paris, November 1918) credits the day's reversal of policy to an "outburst" by Herbert Hoover directed at Lloyd George. It is also theorized that Europeans, in general, were wary of American humanitarianism, particularly as represented by Hoover. They felt it was a maneuver on the part of the United States to gain a position of power.

Hotel Reservoir. Afterwards went sight-seeing through Chateau with thousands of people doing the same thing. Many Americans and French soldiers and the usual Sunday parties of French people with all the family.

Dined with McFaddens and wrote home. Hoped to get to bed early but now 12:15. Am keeping very late hours—only time I have to read and write diary.

MARCH 10 (MONDAY)—

Usual morning of work in room and office. At 12 went to meeting of advisers in Colonel House's room. Discussed number of delegates to go to Brussels to meet Germans to negotiate food and ships. Decided on three—Food, Finance and Shipping. Informal talk over other matters. Nothing definite determined. I was interested in conversation on the side with General Bliss in discussing attitude of French on their reparations claims which they refuse to file. He said in course of conversation it would be a dangerous precedent to establish an international law in a Peace Treaty that victorious nations could impose all war costs of whatever nature, as it would lead to war in future. He further stated that before the signing of the Armistice the French generals and leaders were afraid the Germans would not accept the Allies' terms because they knew the German army was not yet beaten and could retire and hold out another winter if they had not broken at home and could only have been beaten by the United States troops the next year, as both the English and French armies were done, and that the French people could not hold out another winter of short food and fuel. This I consider a most important statement, coming as it did from a most conservative and level-headed man. As a matter of fact, I have read a copy of the proposal for surrender which General Bliss as U.S. representative proposed for the Americans and which was not accepted, and a weaker one was accepted because the French and British were afraid the Germans would not accept the American proposal.

Luncheon with Mrs. Havemeyer at Ritz.

Meeting Supreme Economic Council at 2:30. Discussed serious food and fuel shortage in Italy. Referred it to shipping section, as whole trouble now scarcity of ships. Seems as though we are in war again. I thought certainly all shipping troubles would be over. Discussed details of Brussels trip to meet Germans. Decided on three delegates each—Admiral Weymes, of British Navy, to head delegation. Discussed help and material for Railroads of Southeastern Europe and division of territory and responsibility. French and English fought over Roumania. Lord Robert and Clementel getting quite hot. Postponed entire action, as too many political questions involved.

Dined with Bernie Baruch and family; forty guests. I took out Countess de Rougement, delightful person, distant cousin of Brinck Thorne.

At 10:00 P.M. went to conference in Sir Joseph Maclay's room, Hotel Majestic, to discuss shipping shortage and get him to agree to go to Brussels to help with Germans.

MARCH 11 (TUESDAY)—

A morning's work in office and lunch with Russian Ambassador and Dulles to discuss Russian claim for Reparations. Lamont, Strauss, Baruch, Dulles and I held an interview in the morning to determine whether or not we should stand for joint or several liability of Central Powers. Decided in the affirmative. Meeting of Plenary Commission on Reparations at 3:30 to discuss question. Klotz absent. Hughes presided. Nearly all nations for it. France wanted to postpone action. Can't understand their game, as Loucheur, the French delegate, had subject put on agenda. Apparently trying to kill time. At 5:30 went into meeting of sub-committee No. 1. Started discussing figures of claims; United States first described theirs, which were discussed. Lebrun, for France, again refused to discuss figures, wanting to finish categories—same old game of delay,—possibly internal politics, as a warm financial debate now on in Chamber of Deputies.

Dined with Colonel Logan and Warburtons, who have the house across the river that Colonel House lived in at the time of the signing of the Armistice and in which many famous conferences were held with Prime Ministers, etc. Perfect spring weather and moonlight, which shows off the Seine at its best. Never weary of the beauties of this place. They grow on you.

MARCH 12 (WEDNESDAY)—

Meeting at 9:45 of U.S. delegates of Reparations Commission at Crillon to report work of sub-committee and determine policy. 10:30 Blockade at Commerce Ministry. Tried to put through relaxation of blockade on Austria and Hungary complete, and eliminate machinery for bordering neutrals, blockading only Germany. Blocked by the Allies. Will keep at it and hope for success when we get at the men at the top. Little fellows still fighting the war.

2:30 Reparations Committee. Four hours of discussion on valuation of damages, figures coming in slowly. Won't be ready to report for week yet. I can see every committee's work coming to a head for presentation to Supreme War Council at the same time, and great confusion unless some careful planning done immediately. Many important principles still to be decided.

I walked home today from Reparations with Lord Sumner at 7:00 o'clock through the Tuileries Garden. Perfect evening, beautiful summer weather.

Dined with McFaddens and went to Casino after dinner.

MARCH 13 (THURSDAY)—

Meeting War Trade Board at office—Strauss, Richards, McFadden and Sheldon. Sheldon and I went to lunch with Atalico at Hotel Eduard VII, Italian headquarters. Italians worried over serious food situation and apologetic for action of Crespi in trying to force us into helping them by holding back their approval of blockade relaxation. Atalico cleverest of the group—sees the mistake and is trying to correct error.

2:30 sub-committee on Reparations. Dull afternoon discussion on valuation of damages. Lord Sumner was convinced we will not get the French figures and is for going on without them.

Dined with Grempel and Richards at Ritz. Feel pretty tired and stale. Think will have to go away for few days.

MARCH 14 (FRIDAY)—

[*Wilson returns to Paris*]

The usual morning routine writing letters and office conferences. Went to Station Invalides to meet President and Mrs. Wilson, returning from U.S. Reception beautifully done as usual, with carpet from the street to railroad car and the railroad platform itself entire length decorated with potted plants. French soldiers lined up entire length of platform. French President and Committee of Reception with U.S. peace delegates and other dignitaries. President looked tired. Mrs. Wilson stopped on the platform to tell me she had a message for me from mother. Returned to Crillon and then lunched at Ritz with Beaver White, who just arrived from London, where he has taken his family to close up his personal affairs and move to America permanently.

Talked with Auchincloss in House's office. Arranged for conference of advisers. Called on Madame Gann, who was out, and then went home for rest before dinner, as I was very tired. Gave dinner to Ambassador Davis and wife—Guests, Mrs. Whitelaw Reid, Mrs. Harriman, Admiral and Mrs. Benson, Lord Robert Cecil, Marquis and Marquise d'Polignac. Good dinner and good company.

MARCH 15 (SATURDAY)—

Meeting of U.S. Reparations Commission, Crillon. Conference War Trade Board, including White and Baruch, to discuss control of export and imports to Germany during Armistice and afterwards. Conference with Lord Robert Cecil, Hotel Majestic, to discuss general policy of relaxation of blockade against enemy countries. We were in accord, but find his policy not in accord with certain sections of British Government, which developed later in the day in the Superior Blockade meeting.

Lunched with Mrs. McCombs at a most attractive little apartment.

Attended meeting of Blockade at Commerce Department. After considerable discussion, put through the lifting of blockade against Austria and Hungary, with guarantee against re-export to Germany. Italy will probably fight recommendation at Supreme Economic Council on Monday. Italy still misbehaving—trying to block everything until she gets her own needs cared for—also insisting upon carrying out of London Treaty by which she was brought to enter the war.[43] Lloyd George and other Allied leaders have expressed themselves confidentially as being disgusted with their attitude, and I look for a showdown soon. While pleading for coal and food, Italy apparently trying to break up creation of Jugo-Slavia. This is one of the difficult problems still to be solved. U.S. tried to free Poland, Esthonia, Lettland and Lithuania from further blockade restrictions owing to importance of resuming normal life to discourage Bolshevism. Great Britain withheld approval. Hope to straighten it out tomorrow. Afraid some trade advantage hoped for by Great Britain. Can see no other reason. These checks most discouraging.

Worked at office until 7:15.

Dined with Mrs. Whitelaw Reid to meet Bishop Brent. These reactionaries delightful socially, but have no vision and everything done by the administration during the war was wrong, and Mrs. Reid is so taxed that she can only give Jean Ward an income of $150,000 per year. Poor child!

MARCH 16 (SUNDAY)—

Very tired—slept late and worked in room.

Went to lunch at St. Cloud Country Club with McFaddens, Olbornes and Dev. Milburn. Cold and windy on course. Colonel Finney and son

---

43. The London Treaty was a secret separate treaty made by the Allies in 1915, which promised Italy enemy territory in return for Italy's joining the Allied effort.

and Hale Stineman called at Ritz this morning. Were here attending conference to organize the A[merican] E[xpeditionary] F[orces] Association, similar to the G[rand] A[rmy] of the R[epublic]. Am afraid from all accounts an attempt is being made to use it politically.

Went to have tea with Mrs. Wilson. President was there and we had a good talk over their American trip and things here in general. President seemed in good shape and ready for coming struggle. Henry White was calling also.

Dined with McFaddens, Sheldon and Colonel Moore, of the British Army.

Lew, George and I went afterwards to have conference in Baruch's room to discuss list of raw materials to be controlled in the exporting of commodities from Germany in payment for food.

MARCH 17 (MONDAY)—

Attended at 10:00 o'clock meeting of Supreme Economic Council. Heard report of delegates to Brussels to arrange food and shipping with the Germans. Discussed plan for assisting Central and Southern Europe to build up broken down transportation systems. We blocked the plan of Great Britain to divide up the territory between the Allies, which was to be looked after by each of them. Were afraid of political consequences, as Great Britain and France both wanted Roumania. Were also afraid of new countries becoming too dependent upon outside help. We won out and postponed definite action.

The U.S. advisers met with President at Colonel House's room at Crillon. I read the agenda showing subjects we desired instructions upon. Have arranged for weekly meetings.

Lunched with Mademoiselle Samovitch, who was in Harrisburg with Madame Groutich, at Bishop Darlington's, and is on her way back to Serbia to start a children's home.

Attended Reparations Commission sub-committee No. 1. Discussed categories; made little progress; still marking time.

Quiet evening at home reading home papers and getting to bed earlier than usual.

MARCH 18 (TUESDAY)—

Worked in office all morning. Had conference with Dr. Nansen, who called to discuss Russia. The Russians in Paris trying to get him to head international movement to help Russia get arms and munitions and one hundred million to down Bolshevism. He talks sensibly; wants more concrete information.

Lunched at Crillon with Dulles. Conference in afternoon with advisers. Dined Laperouse Restaurant across the river with the Osbornes, McFaddens, Miss Osbourne, Miss Sturgis, Ogden Mills and Dev. Milburn. Went afterwards to dance at Madame Brantes—beautiful French home— a good party. Dowager Duchess of Sutherland there, with whom Henry, my valet, served for some years.

MARCH 19 (WEDNESDAY)—

Meeting of Blockade Council. Still struggling to get relaxation for Poland and Baltic provinces of old Russia. British still blocking—trade reasons—pretending military; also discussed export control from Germany for food purposes. Adjourned until next day.

Lunched in Admiral and Mrs. Benson's apartment with Colonel House, General Bliss and Benson.

Dined with Terry Boal, now Major, staying in Paris with brother in law, ———— ————, and son. Met Mrs. Elsie Cobb Wilson at Ritz.

MARCH 20 (THURSDAY)—

All morning at Blockade; still on Poland. Put it over today after fight; also relaxed blacklist for German food purchasers.

Lunched with Countess Rougemont with most attractive and delightful guests; never can catch French names. Some particularly charming elderly ladies, keen minds, and reminded me of mother and Mrs. "Mertie."

Worked at office on blockade matters. Did not go to sub-committee No. 1 Reparations, as only marking time pending working out of plan with British which will let Lloyd George down from his outrageous claims in pre-election speeches about amount Great Britain was to get from Germany and now discovers it is impossible to collect one-third of amount. Afraid of political consequences when truth is known. France in same boat. Lloyd George claimed one hundred and twenty billions. Don't look like over thirty billions possible.

Dined with Grempel and met some interesting French people. Dulles and his wife, who has just arrived, were present.[44] Dulles has done excellent work as counsel for our committee on Reparations.

44. During the peace conference, wives of diplomats and delegates were "authorized" to accompany husbands, but the presence of wives of military personnel and other non–State Department individuals was not sanctioned.

MARCH 21 (FRIDAY)—

At 10 o'clock attended meeting Supreme Economic Council to discuss Brussels conference, terms and details of carrying them out. Got in a great wrangle over them and broke up without accomplishing much. Meet tomorrow afternoon.

Lunched with Beaver White and Dr. Nansen at Ritz.

Worked in office all day in conference with advisers to try to work out compromise for tomorrow's meeting on arrangements for German food negotiations. Auchincloss told me President wanted me to go to Syria for him on errand. Don't believe I can get away just now. Looks to me as though House and Auchincloss fear I am interfering with some of their inside political manipulations. Hoover also probably involved. Don't believe I can get away just now.[45]

Reparations sub-committees are simply marking time now. Still waiting for Lloyd George and Clemenceau to get out from under. No solution yet.

Dined with Louis Auberts, Auchinclosses and George McFadden.

MARCH 22 (SATURDAY)—

After meeting of Reparations committee experts at Crillon hearing reports on slow progress being made, spent morning in Baruch's office with Legge, Davis et al. trying to work out satisfactory solution of financial difficulties in connection with German experts to pay for food.

Lunched in Baruch's room with Hoover, Robinson, Legge, Sumners and Dr. Taussig.

Went to Supreme Economic Council 2:30. Lord Robert had to retire to another meeting. Clementel presided—after hours of discussion, still about our method of financing German exports to France and Italy in payment of foods; these countries trying to force us to obligate ourselves to finance dollars for francs and lires received for coal, etc. Will try again tomorrow for agreement.

Hoover and I returned to Crillon together and decided to get this question referred to Supreme War Council as a means of quick decision. Meeting of advisers to meet President at 6:00 P.M. He was tied up in long

---

45. This is a subtle reference to maneuvering on the part of Wilson's inner circle, who may have felt McCormick was gaining ascendancy. Along with Lebanon, Syria had been allotted to France as part of the 1916 secret agreement dividing the Turkish Empire among Russia, France, and Britain. The fire of Arab nationalism was in place and growing in strength, with Faisal fanning the flames.

session of League of Nations Committee. Hoover and I waited in outer room until he came out. Got his approval of reference to Supreme War Council and Hoover got his approval of strong cable to Shipping Board and Treasury Department concerning great need of ships for immediate supply of food, for Europe. Predicted no food [by] here June unless gets 500,000 tons of shipping immediately.

President asked me if I could go to Syria to report to him upon the preference of the people there as to mandatory. Told him I would think it over as Blockade work not yet quite finished here. President told me he had promised the Allies to try to get our country to agree to act on mandatory for Armenia and Constantinople. Could not guarantee they would do it, however. Suggested Charles R. Crane might go with me to Syria. Might be interesting trip but think I will decline until economic control policy entirely cleared up.

Dined with Beaver White, McFadden and Sheldon.

In talk with President he told me of program for next day, including appointment with Lloyd George, Clemenceau and himself to call upon Foch, who was very peeved and angry about not having his plan concerning Polish borders accepted.[46] The President was furious that such a thing was necessary yet amused at the whole proceeding. Foch is just like a child and must be humored or his feelings are hurt so the meeting of the five great powers was held up until the Prime Minister and the President placate the old Marshal.

MARCH 23 (SUNDAY)—

Church, at American Church. Dr. Goodrich, pastor, preached; Yale '86. Surprised to see the Grand Duke Alexander of Russia there sitting alone in a back pew.

Took ride in auto in Bois after church with Secretary Lansing. He is a bit disturbed at the way things are going with Colonel House, who is trying to "hog" it. Worried at the slow progress being made, and talked of resigning.

---

46. The question was how to define Polish borders; the argument was primarily between Lloyd George and Clemenceau. France wanted a strong—i.e., large—Poland, to include Danzig on the Baltic Sea, which would contain Germany from the east. The British position called for Danzig to be placed under the League of Nations and the surrounding areas be handed over to Poland and be subject to plebiscite. In the final outcome, these areas, which Wilson had been told were primarily Polish, voted for Germany rather than for Poland, but the point of self-determination was upheld.

Lunched at Majestic with Sir William Wiseman and friend. Read home papers after walk back to Ritz and dined with Monet and McFaddens. Monet showed cable finally sent to Huns today making offer of * * * black list exports in payment for foodstuffs. Should be accepted by the Germans and relieves what looked like a nasty tangle with the Allies. I am afraid we are too suspicious sometimes of our Allies.

MARCH 24 (MONDAY)—

Meeting Supreme Economic Council, Lord Robert presiding. Put through recommendation of Blockade Councils concerning relaxation Poland and Esthonia. Sir William Mitchell Thompson, M.P., got a good settling from Lord Robert for temporizing over trifles. Really trying to protect British trade. Nothing worse than a little Englishman.

Lunched with Dulles. Talked with Lansing concerning Russian situation and he asked me to prepare a cable for President. Went to sub-committee Reparations. More hot air on categories, getting nowhere. Marking time until the big fellows can agree on figures.

Dined with Belgium [sic] delegation, two cabinet ministers and leading powers, Hoover, Davis, Strauss and self for United States. They want Brussels as seat of League of Nations and priority of Reparations claim and they should have the latter.

Everyone greatly excited over the change of government in Hungary and Bolshevist control. I think it will hasten peace matters; U.S. doing everything to push it along. Some fear now of Germany not being able to trade with us upon Peace matters due to unsettled conditions and possible revolution. If we demand too much she may refuse to come across and tell us to come in and occupy her country and run it ourselves. I sometimes think that France would not object to this opportunity.

MARCH 25 (TUESDAY)—
[*Council of Four replaces Council of Ten*]
Instead of going to sub-committee on Reparations, worked in office. Interview with Morgenthau and meeting with War Trade Board and Commander Baker to discuss censorship.

Lunched with Mrs. George Meyer, Count and Countess Branbrilla, Countess ———, an Italian. Found they wanted to secure my support for the Italian position against Jugo-Slavia. I was a good listener.

Saw Secretary and Mrs. Daniels, who arrived this morning from Brest.

Morgenthau full of his trip West with Taft on League of Nations. Says the people are unquestionably back of it.

This afternoon took first exercise with Baruch. Tennis in enclosed court in the Bois. Good game but stiff tonight.

Dined at hotel.

MARCH 26 (WEDNESDAY)—

U.S. Reparations Committee at Crillon at 9:45. Then meeting Blockade Council 10:30. Started fight to get censorship relaxed also black list and much to my surprise Great Britain agreed to consider suspension of latter.

Lunched with Polignac and a few Frenchmen at Larnes Café.

In afternoon was called, by telephone, by the President to attend a conference at Lloyd George's house on Reparations. Sitting around the table in the dining room were the President, Lloyd George, Orlando, Loucheur, Davis, Lamont, myself, Lord Sumner and an interpreter. Discussed the claims of France and Lloyd George tried to break down the claims presented by Loucheur which amounted to sixteen billion dollars. Did not get very far; they did not have enough facts. Then the chiefs met in another room to discuss the capacity of Germany to pay and told us to continue to work out the proportion that Great Britain and France should get of total amount received.

We heard interesting trade between Lord Sumner and Loucheur, United States being the go-between and think they got pretty close. Loucheur wanted 2.2 to 1 while Lord Sumner 2 to 1. Adjourned about 7:00 P.M.

Dined with Henry Morgenthau and Baruch.

Oscar [sic] Garrison Villard came to my room after dinner. He is just out of Germany and gave most interesting discourse. Saw the murderer of Eisner in Munich leaving hall after the murder. Saw some of the shooting in the Assembly.[47] Says we may be too late with food to save Germany; may have no government to make peace with. He may be right but I have not much confidence in Villard's judgment. Talked until 1:00 A.M. I don't get enough sleep. Everyone drops in my room for final chat before retiring.

---

47. Kurt Eisner led the Independent Socialists in Bavaria. He was assassinated by a monarchist in February 1919, after which the Bavarian Communists and Socialists struggled, and the Communists took over with the Soviet Republic of Bavaria. Munich was put under siege by government forces from Berlin, and the Soviets were overthrown in May.

MARCH 27 (THURSDAY)—

Interview in my office with Lamont and Robinson before going to Reparations Committee Number One. Still discussing categories. Hope to get figures Monday.

Lunched with Henrietta Ely and Colonel Rice at Ritz, as Henrietta's guest. She is just back from south of France. Looks very well and is en route [to] Metz for few days, then comes back to Paris to take apartment.

Meeting at Davis' office with Lord Sumner and Lord Cunliff to discuss claims and principles reparations, principally to hear Lord Sumners's argument on putting principles in our interpretation of principles. I suggested this two months ago and was amused to see Davis and Lamont swing into line. Now have to get President's approval. Went with Lamont to see Loucheur to get permission to have General McKinstry review French figures. Took tea at Marquis de Polignac's to arrange about having German guns, helmets, etc., sent to America for French charity sale.

Dined with Reggy Taylor, Hale Stineman and Mrs. McFadden.

MARCH 28 (FRIDAY)—

Expected to attend meeting of sub-committee Reparations but was called to Supreme War Council which now consists of Pichon, Lansing, Balfour and Sonnino. The President, Lloyd George, Clemenceau and Orlando are now meeting alone trying to settle finally among themselves many disputed questions such as Fiume for Italy, Coal Basin of Saar for France, both of which in my opinion will be turned down by Chief and Reparations which we are insisting on.

We put through at meeting at Foreign Ministry, of the Supreme War Council, Austrian blockade relaxation also Poland and Esthonia and the Rhine as a route to Holland and Scandinavia from Switzerland.

Lunched with Henry White to meet chairman of the French Deputy Budget Committee and some other French politicians. Davis and Lamont also present. Discussed Reparations and French financial difficulties.

Was called by the President to his house, with Davis and Lamont, to discuss a new proposal of Clemenceau and Klotz on Reparations. Same old plan of leaving open in the treaty amount Germany is to pay, in other words, Germany is to give her signed check with the amount blank. We advised "Chief" it would not do, to which he assented.

Met Lord Sumner and Cunliff in Davis' office for further conference at 4:00 P.M. At 6:00 P.M. played two sets of tennis with Baruch, Sumner and Reggy Taylor.

Frank McCoy dropped in this evening and is spending night with me. We are having good talk over old times and Frank most interesting about war.

During the meeting at the President's house this afternoon the President told us of a spat he had at the morning meeting with Clemenceau. They were discussing the Saar Coal Basin and the President protested against it going to France and Clemenceau told the President he was pro-German; whereupon the Chief called him down and asked Clemenceau whether he wanted him to leave; whereupon Clemenceau cooled down and came off his high horse and everything was lovely again. I can see these final demands and decisions of peace negotiations getting on all the Chiefs' nerves and the President seems very tired.[48]

MARCH 29 (SATURDAY)—

Meeting at 9:45, U.S. representatives of the Reparations Committee at Crillon. 10:30 Blockade Council. Fixed dates of announcement for relaxation of blockade Poland, Esthonia and Austria. Hard fight on suspending black list. All against me but will bring it up at Supreme Economic Council. I will not take the responsibility of economic chaos in world due to artificial restrictions.

Lunched with Rappard, Dr. Taussig, Dr. Nansen and ————, representing Paraguay. Dr. Nansen and I discussed Russia. Hope he will agree to go in for survey. I believe he is the man to start a satisfactory neutral relief to aid Russia without recognizing Bolshevist Government.

President sent for Davis, Lamont and me to meet him at Clemenceau's office for reparation discussion. After sitting for some time in ante-room at Clemenceau's office, I sent in note and the President came out and advised us that we could not take up matter now as they had already discussed it and he would come to Crillon to tell us of Lloyd George's new plan. This he did, meeting Davis and Lamont, but I happened to be out when he called. I am convinced plan will not work. Lloyd George and Clemenceau trying to duck responsibility of telling people they cannot get what they had promised them before the election and this plan is simply putting off the evil day.

Called upon Mrs. Harriman, who is off tomorrow for America.

---

48. Admiral Grayson and other observers were noticing the same symptoms, as exhaustion began to affect Wilson's body, causing headaches, indigestion, extreme fatigue, and a short temper.

I took 8:00 P.M. train for Chalons to spend night, to make trip next day to Alexander Rogers' grave at Brizieux. Reggie Taylor was with me. Mills, my secretary, and Captain Howell, the guide, went by automobile to meet me at Chalons where I found them at 1:00 A.M., having secured a good room at the hotel and a hot cup of chocolate for Reggie and myself.

MARCH 30 (SUNDAY)—

Started at 8:30 in auto for Bar-le-duc where we were to meet Dr. Nolan who was with Alexander when he died. After picking him up we proceeded to Brizieux where we found the United States cemetery adjoining an old French one on the outskirts of the small village about a mile from the edge of the Argonne Forest and a most attractive location in an old apple orchard. After a search we found Alexander's grave well marked, and we also visited the hospital buildings, temporary frame ones, now abandoned, about one-half mile distant from the cemetery. It was a snowy, cold day, but even so the surroundings about the cemetery were attractive and everything looked as though it was well kept and someone had recently put laurel upon Alexander's grave as it was quite green. I met an old postman who lived in the vicinity and had helped to bury some of the soldiers and who spoke of the Americans as their saviors and wanted to do something for them so I arranged for him to care for Alexander's grave and fix up nicely with planting, etc.

We returned via Rheims and Chateau Thierry. I never saw anything like the miles and miles of desolation, old trenches, barbed wire, shell holes, ammunition lying about, tanks, aeroplanes, every conceivable war implement lying in the field; most desolate and depressing and nothing apparently done yet to clean up.

We lunched in Rheims in a partly destroyed hotel, with temporary roof and a temporary wall. About four thousand people had returned to their homes and the Boche prisoners had cleaned up the streets but no buildings repaired as yet. Apparently French waiting for reparations money and I can't see where it is to come from as Germany is broke until she can begin to produce and thus pay her debts.

Arrived at Paris 8:00 P.M. and dined with McFaddens, dinner party including General McCoy, Robert Blisses, Auchinclosses, Irwin Laughlins and self.

After dinner Dulles called to discuss with me Lloyd George's reparation plan to be ready to report to President tomorrow morning.

MARCH 31 (MONDAY)—

Met with Lamont and Davis on Reparations before going to President's house. Found the President, Lloyd George, Clemenceau, and Orlando closeted. President came out for a few minutes and gave us an opportunity to explain to him that under Lloyd George's plan we would still have to face the question of principle. We showed him the difficulties to be encountered. He told us to try to overcome them, that we should try to meet Lloyd George's and Clemenceau's suggestions, as otherwise, he was told by them, their ministries might fall and we would have no governments to make peace with for some time to come. Their plan is to postpone the fixing of the Germany cost to pay and leaving determination of claims to commission to report upon later. The Prime Ministers sent for their experts to meet with Davis, Lamont, Baruch and me, so Montague and Keynes for Great Britain, Klotz and Loucheur for France, and Crespi and Chesa for Italy, appeared at the President's house and we went at it. Nothing accomplished but hot air and we adjourned until tomorrow at 2:30. We were surprised at the appearance of Montague and Keynes, being back again in the conferences as they had been supplanted by Cunliffe and Sumner.

In the meantime, we made appointment with British for 3:00 P.M., namely, Montague and Keynes. Satisfactory arrangement with them but doubt if France agrees. Will know tomorrow.

Dined with Auchinclosses in their apartment in the Ritz; Sir William Wiseman and Mrs. Bullitt guests.

APRIL 1 (TUESDAY)—

Meeting of the War Trade Board in my office [at] Crillon where we had photograph taken of Staff of Peace Conference workers, McFadden, Dulles, Sheldon, Stetson and self and clerks, including Reggie Taylor, acting as orderly.

Was called into conference in Lamont's room to meet with Davis, Baruch and Dulles to consider Lloyd George ultimatum that Great Britain would insist upon putting in pensions as category of claims and would not leave question open for a future determination and arbitration. This made it necessary to get from President, after explaining to him the line upon which we had been arguing, principles of claims under 14 points and armistice terms, a definite statement as to whether or not he could accept pensions.[49] We called upon him at his house at 2:00 P.M. There were present Davis, Lamont, Baruch, Dulles and myself. We explained to him the limitations of the 14 points and armistice terms as the basis of peace in regard to its interpretations covering categories like pensions. He was very clear in his mind that there was no intention of including pensions when the peace and armistice terms were discussed and that particular categories of that character were not considered by themselves and that he felt that as pensions were such a just and equitable basis of claim, he would support them upon the French basis of valuations and it was particularly important to do this, otherwise England would not get what she was entitled to in proportions to the other countries. We all agreed to the Lloyd George proposal which established a commission to determine the amount Germany can pay and the amount of the claims before 1921 which will relieve Great Britain and France from their troubles of making public the small amount they are to get from reparations because both Prime Ministers believe their government will be overthrown if the facts are known. I am afraid this camouflage will not work but it may, as the people forget so easily. As far as the United States is concerned, it does not affect us, our claims are small and we do not violate any principles, as the claims are just.

We went to our office after our talk with the President to meet Montague and Keynes of the British Delegation. We told them of our agreeing to pensions and we prepared a report for the Prime Ministers to be submitted at 4:00 o'clock.

We went to the President's house again to meet the Big Four and Klotz, Loucheur, Montague, Keynes, Crespi and Chesa and the United States advisers, Davis, Lamont, Baruch, Dulles and self, and discussed Lloyd George's plan after telling French and Italian delegates President had agreed to pensions. Klotz, of course, had many modifications and new schemes. Loucheur had a few minutes to talk with Clemenceau in the hall and when he came back took Baruch aside and told him Clemenceau was with the British and ourselves on the Lloyd George plan but to let Finance Minister Klotz have his talk and get through with it and they would make it all right later. We adjourned to meet tomorrow morning for final action; United States to submit categories of claims they can agree upon to be presented to Germany.

---

49. The argument that pensions be included as reparations was based on the notion that the pensions would support the soldiers, who were really just conscripted civilians—temporary soldiers—and their wives would therefore be compensated for the damage they incurred as civilians. The American position with reparations was that the legitimate claim should be in the form of a bill for damages suffered by civilians as the result of German warfare on land and sea.

Worked at office with McFadden until 7.40 P.M. Dined at Robert Bliss's with Harry Lehrs, McFaddens, Laughlins and Rolands; the usual thing and I was very sleepy and tired.

APRIL 2 (WEDNESDAY)—

British, French, Italian and U.S. delegation on reparations negotiations went to Finance Ministry to discuss supposed first draft of reparations clauses for treaty with categories. Groups all met about 11:00 and discussed draft until lunch time. Looked as though we were getting closer together especially British and United States. After lunch Dulles and I went to meet Montague, Sumner and Keynes on categories to get them to expand their draft to suit ours. They stated Big Four had agreed to categories only on claims for destruction of property and destruction of life. I was worried considerably at this statement because I could see if true, that the British, after they got pensions in categories, were now trying to reduce the categories which would give France and others their just claims which we held had been admitted in 14 points and armistice terms. Dulles and I so stated but without effect.

We then started for the full committee meeting, at Finance Ministry. On the way down in the car with Montague he acknowledged to me if he could make his deal with France on the side as to distribution, he did not care what was in the categories. I saw the game Lloyd George was trying to put over on the President and I made up my mind to get busy. Met all afternoon discussing draft; made small progress; adjourned until 9:30 P.M.

I dined alone and was very tired.

At 9:30 we went at it again and argued until after midnight agreeing with British in draft of reparations except on categories. I cut loose with the British representatives about their discussing categories as a means of trading with the other Allies rather than upon the points of justice and equity of claims. I could see they sympathized and were embarrassed by the Chief's orders. Made up my mind to inform the President who had not been properly posted by Davis of the Finance Section.

Returned 1:00 A.M. after one of the most strenuous days of conference. I knew there would be difficulties over the division of the spoils but I could not foresee the political reasons of these countries keeping from their people the truth about Germany's ability to pay and now they have to work out a treaty clause which postpones the evil day and conceals temporarily the true situation. I wish we could blow up the whole plan, but the governments would fall and only Germany would benefit.

APRIL 3 (THURSDAY)—

[Big Four, except France, agree to draft of treaty]

Got started early this A.M. as Davis, Lamont, Baruch and I were to call on President, to explain situation in regard to categories as stated to us by the British. He acknowledged Lloyd George had nearly put it over on him and Davis, who with him had been present at all of the meetings and did not know enough about the categories to keep the President straight. President this morning, however, saw the point and approved the categories Dulles and I had worked out during the night and early morning, much to my relief, as we had what I believe was a just claim against Germany in accordance with the President's 14 points and for a proper distribution among the Allies. I went with Dulles to see Montague and Keynes to show our plan approved by the President. They agreed to submit to Lloyd George before afternoon meeting.

Lunched with Conger at Crillon. Conger, now Associated Press representative, just back from Berlin. He says unless peace made soon there will be a new government in Germany, and that a Soviet government.

Went to Ministry of Finance for meeting of Allied representatives on reparations to discuss draft for treaty and categories. Couple hours' discussion resulting in the French, Italian and U.S. for our categories and Great Britain delegates with no power to change from their former position. Great Britain, United States and Italy approved draft for treaty and France opposed.

Davis and I went to President to report. Found him in bed with a bad cold at 6:00 P.M., very tired and I know discouraged.[50] Allies acting like the devil. We are proposing most liberal terms and French particularly unreasonable. President told us he was willing French should take over Saar coal mines as reparations for destroyed coal mines of France, with freedom of operation, but could not take over territory as he only agreed to Alsace Lorraine; also agreed to most liberal military curtailment on Rhine; no fortifications within forty kilometers of Rhine, no troops or maneuvers east of Rhine and no rail road sidings or facilities for mobilization, active and military occupation by Allies for reasonable period. All

---

50. This was a serious illness for Wilson, causing high fever, vomiting, diarrhea, and coughing. After Wilson's threat to leave on the *George Washington* (as announced by Grayson), the other conference leaders became more moderate and willing to compromise. Various biographies of Wilson claim that his mental and emotional outlook was impaired by this illness and affected his behavior.

refused—he is at a loss to know what to do if impasse continues. Disgusted, threatening to go home as he must call Congress in May. I really pitied him as they are trying to make him the goat and he is powerless to fight publicly in the open because it would only help Germany by showing serious discord among the Allies.

Dined with Sheldon and two Dutch bankers, here to discuss German finances in regard to food purchases. Also present, Davis, Keynes and Sir Leverton-Harris. Sir Leverton complimented our consular service. Thought we were putting it over Great Britain. I was amused, knowing the opinion of our consular service in the United States.

APRIL 4 (FRIDAY)—

Worked in my room at the Ritz with Mills until after 10:00 o'clock. Worked at office all day. At 3:30 Lord Robert Cecil called to discuss with me the cable censorship. I told him we would have to cut out a lot of it and gave him our proposal which he agreed to consider and which he understood was our minimum. We discussed difficulties of freedom of trade in countries in Europe from which the blockade has been lifted due to blacklist and censorship restrictions and I gave notice of big fight on the subject at the next meeting of the Supreme Economic Council. He is sympathetic but has a difficult job to handle as their trade interests are powerful and unwilling to give up trade advantages afforded by British censorship and neutral blockade agreements, but they must go.

Met with Lamont, Davis and Dulles to discuss reparations and later went to Colonel House's office to discuss program for meeting with Prime Ministers in the morning, to try to force final settlement between British and French. They are playing a sordid game and playing for advantage in the division of the spoils and trying to lay the blame of the delay in making of the Peace Treaty on the President. The Chief is getting mad and I think we will have an explosion soon, which will be justified. President still indisposed today.

Dined with Mr. and Mrs. Harry Robinson.

Baruch and McFadden came in before bed. Baruch very sore at our Allies on account of unfair tactics at Economic meeting, also sore at Colonel's crowd, which he thought too free in criticising President to outsiders.

These are strange days and everyone tired and irritable and we will have to keep our heads and keep cool for we are just passing over the peak and still have some rough going before we land.

APRIL 5 (SATURDAY)—

Ritz until 10, then at meeting of experts, Reparations Committee, Crillon, discussing figures of claims. At 11:00 A.M. Davis, Lamont, Baruch and I went to President's house to meet Lloyd George, Clemenceau, Orlando, with their advisers—France, Loucheur, Klotz, and Great Britain, Lord Sumner. House took President's place as he is still indisposed in room although much better. We discussed draft of reparations text showing difference between us as to categories and United States holding out for the term of thirty years for payment. Lloyd George acknowledged to me he did not propose to present claims for loss of use of property, thefts and fines, which does not seem to me just to France and Belgium and I don't believe he can sustain his point.

Davis and I lunched with Henry White and two leaders of the Chamber of Deputies, one chairman of the Budget Committee.

Advisers met after lunch to prepare for 4:00 o'clock meeting at President's house with Prime Ministers for continuation of morning's meeting. We discussed categories and draft of text. Lloyd George and I had argument over claims for Belgium which he wanted to exclude. British and French insisted upon leaving undetermined the time for Germany to pay claims demanded. We succeeded in getting them to agree to specify categories under strict interpretation of our principles including pensions. This, in my opinion, is fair to put up to Germany. I don't see how she can accept it and there will be a hot discussion when her delegates arrive.

I am thoroughly disgusted with Allies' selfishness and constant effort to use the United States for their own selfish purposes and throw the blame for delay on us when we have been ready for some time and they are temporizing and playing politics; afraid to tell their people they cannot get them what they promised them at election time. I feel more discouraged today than at any time since I came over.

Dined with Sanderson, ———, Admiral Long and Frank McCoy, who dropped in this evening.

Am getting stale, glad tomorrow is Sunday although it looks like a busy one.

APRIL 6 (SUNDAY)—

Robinson of Shipping Board called before I was out of bed to discuss demand of Allies that ships taken by the United States by Act of Congress should be put into pool to be divided between all the Allies, raising difficult question and while I believe our title to ships good, yet we must consider our pledge to not get anything out of the war in a mercenary manner. We will have to discuss this with President as to policy. Robinson thought it might be possible to settle in reparations trade.

House sent for me at 11:00 A.M. so no church. He wanted to discuss categories of claims in respect to Belgium and we agreed tomorrow, if the present plan of reparations is agreed to, to accept same only with the reservation that Belgium be protected with satisfactory categories.

Lunched with Mrs. McFadden and the Bullitts. Bullitt very interesting about his recent trip to Russia. He is quite pro-Bolshevist. Talked to Lenine, [sic] whom he considers big man and able. Not so strong for Trotsky, who he claims is dominated by Lenine and not as popular with the people. He says Russians are behind Bolshevism and thinks we should lift blockade and recognize them and remove the military. He admits their government is not a Democracy, that their constitution permits only those who work with their hands and brains to have any part in it or have any rights. He admits the weak spots but compares failure with weakness of other countries. The general impression obtained is that Bolshevists are on their last legs and are ready to trade.[51]

Mrs. Bullitt and I drove out to Versailles and had a nice walk in the park and tea and then called on the Grempels.

Dined with Kirk, Lansing's secretary, who lives with his mother in a beautiful house across the river. Old part of Paris, dingy exterior but when you enter, delightful surprise with perfect interior of Louis XV period.

APRIL 7 (MONDAY)—

Another busy day, starting in the morning in Lord Sumner's rooms in Majestic Hotel on categories of reparations, then at Supreme Economic Council at Ministry of Commerce.

Lunched at Mrs. Linda Thomas' lovely apartment, who by the way is very good looking, Mrs. Ganott, Miss Willard, et al.

3:20, meeting at Lloyd George's house with Clemenceau, Orlando, Colonel House (President still resting) and advisers to try to approve reparations draft for categories. Had a long, windy meeting which sounded at

---

51. William Bullitt had been sent on a secret trip to Russia by Wilson. Upon his return, he recommended recognition of the Soviet government. His recommendation was rejected, and he resigned his delegate status. In later testimony before the Senate, he spoke against the Versailles Treaty.

times like a Bolshevist gathering, everyone standing up in the middle of the room and all talking at once in both languages. Progress very slow because Ministers are trying to decide matters without thoroughly familiarizing themselves with the details of the subject at hand and then attempting to make changes in the draft without mature consideration. Much time wasted. Some days I think they delay on purpose. Lloyd George, at his house, always serves delightful tea and cakes at 5:30 which is very nice break in our discussions which sometimes get quite warm. Were in sessions until about 7:15.

Dined with ———, Davis and McFadden. Read Harrisburg and New York newspapers all evening.

APRIL 8 (TUESDAY)—

Conference in the morning with Sheldon, McFadden and Peterson, of War Trade Board. 11:30, meeting with liquidation committee at Davis' office, also Hoover and food men to discuss sale of salvaged clothing of army to Poland and repatriated countries.

Lunched alone at Crillon. At 3:00 went to see Lord Robert Cecil and discussed relaxation censorship and blockade. Found him sympathetic but he frankly told me he had no governmental position and his influence was only as member of the Supreme Economic Council and he possibly might be fired for going against the policy of his government.

Went later to Reparations Plenary Commission; Prime Minister Hughes of Australia presiding as Klotz had left. Meeting called to adopt report of Committee No. 2 of which Lord Cunliff was chairman, on capacity of Germany to pay. No amount set in accord with wish of Big Four under plan of reparations decided upon. Report called forth sarcastic remarks from Hughes and he finally refused to vote for it, making a split in the British delegation.

Dined at Hotel Majestic with Lieut. McCormick-Goodhart, whose father was a son of Leander McCormick living in London. He had four of the lady secretaries of British delegates and Admiral Hoke and Captain Harding as guests. Funny dinner, and a poor one as the Majestic has English cooking instead of French.

APRIL 9 (WEDNESDAY)—

Supreme Economic Council 10:00 o'clock, Lord Robert presiding. Clementel, Loucheur, and the whole gang present. Had a good scrap over relaxation of blockade and difficulties of communication all over Europe choking trade and commerce, causing idleness and making Bolshevists. Think we made some progress.

Heard today Lord Robert returning to London to notify government unless he has more authority will resign.

Lunched with Charpentiers, the delightful Auberts, Sheldon and Foreign Minister of Greece.

2:30 meeting at Klotz's office on sub-committee on restitution, appointed at Lloyd George's house Monday.

3:30 Blockade Council and at 5:30 went to Mrs. Wilson's to tea, large crowd of distinguished guests including Lloyd George, Orlando, Prince Feisel of Hedjas, et al.

6:30 advisers met at Crillon; discussed whether United States should be on Inter-Allied committee to adjust reparations in years to come.

Dined at Ritz with Secretary Daniels and General Hayes of the 28th Division and Terry Boals.

After dinner, at 10:00 o'clock, went to meeting at the Ministry of Finance on restitution committee and worked until 12:00 o'clock, when Loucheur gave us little supper and I am now closing a busy day at 1:00 A.M., my usual bed hour these days.

APRIL 10 (THURSDAY)—

Worked in room until 10:30. Meeting in Davis' office with Lamont. Meeting in my office of War Trade Board staff discussing blockade and censorship relaxation.

Lunched with Mr. Henry White in his room with Davis, Lamont and Baruch to meet Chairman of Budget Committee, Chamber of Deputies, French Government, and Deputy ——— to discuss again French financial situation in reference to reparations.

After lunch we went to President's house to discuss with him question we had been discussing all morning, namely, should the United States be represented on the Commission of Reparations of the Allies to collect the debt and estimate claims against Germany. Baruch and I took the negative; Davis trimming but the President had previously made up his mind that we were committed to looking after interests of weak nations and in keeping a hand on the financial situation in Europe as well as protecting our own interests in the question of international exchange, etc., and our own only real reason for pulling out would be a selfish one in looking out for own interests alone. I am not yet sure he is right and Baruch was not convinced.

At 4:00 P.M. we went to session in the larger room with Lloyd George, Clemenceau, Orlando, Bonar Law and other advisers. The above gentlemen were delighted when the President announced we would join the Commission if desired. The Chiefs were all in good humor and spirits, much better than at last meeting, which was rather strained. They discussed whether the vote of the proposed Reparations Commission should be unanimous in the event of the cancellation of the amount Germany was to pay and on the amount to the first installment of bonds to be issued by Germany as a guarantee. President agreed to both, the latter, however, to be fixed in the instructions to Commission before Peace Treaty signed and sub-committee instructed to fix amount at once.

Dined with Baruch, Sam Fleming, Sergeant Taylor and Sergeant Post, young friend of Baruch's.

APRIL 11 (FRIDAY)—

After writing my morning's mail, I went to President's house to discuss with him some cables we proposed sending to State Department in regard to asking Congress to appropriate Twenty Million Dollars to Siberian Railroad with Russian co-operatives for Army salvage.

Lunched with Legge and some of Baruch's men.

Spent afternoon discussing reparations in kind with Loucheur in Baruch's office. Came to satisfactory understanding. Don't know whether President will approve but it certainly seems to me a fair principle to make Germany pay in kind for the restoration of devastated area.

6:30 played tennis in the Bois.

Dined with Admiral Long.

APRIL 12 (SATURDAY)—

Met at Crillon with advisers on reparation text and went to President's house at his call at 11:00 A.M. Found meeting had been postponed so we went back to Crillon to continue our work.

Lunched with Minister to Portugal and Mrs. Birch, Hotel Meurice, with Lansing, Berry Walls, the Andrews and Admiral Grayson.

At 2:30 met Captain Robinson of the Cruiser *Huntington* with whom I crossed during the war. Just in from Hamburg with most interesting tale. Says it is a two to one shot for a Bolshevist Germany. Food and raw materials, which mean work, may save it but he is afraid it is too late. Confirms the U.S. policy which we advocated.

Dr. Taylor just back from Russia and SE. Europe says while we have pulled down blockade, means of communication so bad as to cables and railroads that no trade moving. Also bitter against attempted exploitation by French with luxuries when staples are needed.

Attended meeting with Loucheur and Crespi in Baruch's office. Agreed upon restoration in kind for devastated areas.

At 6:00 the economic advisers with Bliss and Benson met in Colonel House's office. Had photograph taken.

Dined at Gremples with Bullitts, Madame deBilly, Davises and a couple of Frenchmen.

April 13 (Sunday)—

Arose early as I had a conference with the U.S. Economic Advisers to discuss with them economic treaty covenants to co-ordinate their work with our reparation covenants. Worked at Baruch's office until lunch time.

Lunched with Dr. Taylor and Henrietta Ely.

After lunch went out to an economic conference of a dozen men at Baruch's villa, which he has rented near St. Cloud, and not very attractive. Spent the entire afternoon working on covenants of treaty. Made good progress but showed considerable difference of opinion over plan of Bradley Palmer in disposition of the Alien Property Custodian Fund. Appointed a sub-committee of lawyers to discuss the matter further next day.

Stopped on my way home to call on Elizabeth Hudson. As there was no place to sit in her hotel, which was a small one just back of the Ritz, we took a short walk.

Dined with Belgium [sic] Prime Minister and Minister of Foreign Affaires Hymans, with several other members of the Belgium [sic] delegation. Baruch, Auchincloss and I the guests. Belgium anxious for priority of claims for reparations, also anxious to discuss terms of Reparations text as they have not yet been consulted by Big Four. They, like all other small nations, restive and express themselves frankly that they are looking to the United States to protect their interests.

April 14 (Monday)—

Usual morning in my room with Secretary and calls from Reggie Taylor and Richards.

At 10:00 attended meeting of Supreme Economic Council. As Lord Robert was absent, I presided. We rushed through the agenda in a couple of hours—nothing startling or of importance but better teamplay evidenced. The French are now much more amenable as they have their claims on the Rhine frontier, Saar Basin and reparations about agreed upon by the Big Four. I noticed great change in the atmosphere in negotiations. Things come easier and strain is less.

Lunched with Monet and Hoover at quaint little restaurant; supposed to be wonderful food. I could have done better at Ritz. Discussed relaxation blockade restrictions left bank of Rhine, proposing to treat it like Austria. Also planned to throw the responsibility upon Germany of seeing that all her exports should be used to secure food to feed her own people. We all feel we are assuming too much responsibility under our present plan of control and the failure to supply sufficient food, which is bound to occur, will be placed upon Allies.

Also discussed Russian plan of relief under Nansen, which we are now working upon but held up by the French. Monet interested, and I think will help, which he can do as he has great influence with Clementel and other ministers.

Worked at office until 6:00 and then attended reception in Colonel House's office to visiting U.S. Congressional delegates, who wanted to look over peace Commission and its work, which we explained in great detail.

Dined at Colonel House's to meet Paderewski and wife. Great function, one of a series, many notables present including Marshal Foch and wife, who by the way, stuck a napkin in her neck to save her dress. Orlando, Lansings, Persian Minister and wife, Venizelos, Garretts of Holland, Mrs. Williard and daughter of Spain, Blisses, Bensons, and other minor lights like myself. Mrs. Garrett, formerly Alice Warder, an old friend, called me up and asked me to take her to the party. Husband, who arrived today from Holland, came afterwards to the reception. Why he was not at the dinner I do not know.

APRIL 15 (TUESDAY)—

McFadden and Richards in room for usual blockade conference, then office to discuss with advisers the A.P.C. plan for disposition of German property in the U.S. and U.S. property in Germany. Decided not to write same in reparations clause but keep separate as matter was under control of the U.S. Congress.

Lunched with Commander Carter and Reggie Taylor.

Worked in office; quiet afternoon until 4:30 when attended meeting of Lord Sumner, Loucheur, Baruch, Dulles, Legge, Crespi and self to discuss further plan for restoration of devastated area by making Germans pay in kind if desired by government. United States, France and Italy agreed. Great Britain made reservation to be referred to Lloyd George. Don't know what President will do but think he should accept as proposal is fair one.

At 6:30 Baruch, Sumner, Reggie and I played tennis for an hour.

Had Dr. Nansen, Elizabeth Hudson and Miss Stillman to dinner at Ritz. A pleasant evening.

Had one of my frequent midnight conferences with Lew Sheldon, just back from London, and George McFadden. Lew says Great Britain War Cabinet will accept our blacklist suspensions and British Government, he thinks, will favor our plea for de-rationing bordering neutrals. When this accomplished, most of blockade machinery disappears.

APRIL 16 (WEDNESDAY)—

Stetson, of War Trade Board, in to say goodby, enroute to U.S., took breakfast with me in my room. Richards dropped in as usual to discuss War Trade Board matters.

Attended for short time at Crillon meeting of U.S. Reparations experts to discuss figures.

At 10:30 presided at Supreme Blockade Council at Ministry of Commerce. Made great progress on relaxation of restitution of blockade on bordering neutrals, particularly in de-rationing. If Great Britain agrees to removal of blacklist, the blockade is down everywhere except against Germany, Bolshevist Russia and Hungary, and these won't last long at the rate we are now going.

Lunched at President's house with President and Mrs. Wilson, Garretts, and Charles Crane. Had a nice informal time. President chatted with us for a long time after lunch. Talked freely about Clemenceau's characteristics. Says he seems to depend more upon his ministers for advice since his shooting. He really thinks he is not as vigorous mentally as formerly and has not quite the same confidence in himself. He suggests another reason for having ministers constantly with him at meetings is that he wants them to share his responsibility in the event of a fight in the Chamber of Deputies. President seemed in good spirits and told many stories. Charles Crane was making farewell visit before leaving for Constantinople and Syria to make report on conditions there for the President.[52]

---

52. This is probably the trip that McCormick had decided against taking.

Worked in office until 4:30 when I called upon Secretary of War Baker. He seemed rested and in good shape after his trip over—only here for a week and will spend most of the time at the front.

At 6:00 met with advisers at the Crillon, also Bliss and Benson.

Dined with Gertrude and Henrietta Ely, Dr. Taylor, Miss Sargent, of the *New Republic*, Mrs. Shaw and Swectzer. The Elys have taken Dick Strong's apartment. Gertrude returns to work soon.

APRIL 17 (THURSDAY)—

This has been an easy day and since the strenuous work of sub-committee is about over and the Reparations terms about ready for the Huns, I hope to have many more such days.

I dictated letters in my room at the Ritz until 11:00 A.M., then worked Crillon most of day. Interviewed Cyrus McCormick, just arrived and Minister of Switzerland, who wants some help to get coal contract with Germany in exchange for food; and Bradley Palmer on the A.P.C. clause in Treaty.

At 6:00 played tennis outdoors in the Bois for the first time with Bernie, Sumners and Reggie Taylor.

Dined with Robinson and wife, Hoover and Commander Baker, at Ritz as guest of the former.

Great change in sentiment in the French papers toward President and United States. Colonel thinks due to his calling them down but really due to the fact that their people are satisfied with the final terms of treaty. Lloyd George's Parliament speech topic of conversation. It was clever but think he made a mistake attacking openly Northcliffe papers, simply advertising press and shows criticism has hurt.[53]

APRIL 18 (FRIDAY)—

At 9:30 went to meeting in Legge's room at Ritz to attend meeting of experts of Economic Commission to go over draft of Economic clause of Treaty and clauses covering A.P.C. Fund.

Lunched with Minister Clementel at Larue restaurant.

---

53. Lord Northcliffe used the power of his press—the *Daily Mail* and the *Times*—to influence the actions of individual politicians and to shape the course of Britain during the war. The papers had been instrumental in supporting Lloyd George over Asquith, but they had now turned against Lloyd George.

Worked afterward at office in Crillon.

Played tennis at Tirer aux Pigeon in Bois with Mrs. Garrett, Miss Hudson and Richards.

Dined with McFaddens at Ritz.

APRIL 19 (SATURDAY)—

Meeting Blockade Council at 10:00. Adopted relaxation [of] our blockade machinery in the bordering neutrals and de-rationing of rationed commodities. In doing away with blacklist to which Sir Mitchell Thompson, Great Britain, had finally agreed to, practically puts the War Trade Board out of business as far as machinery is concerned so we will be able to reduce staff considerably in U.S.

Lunched with Robert Bliss, farewell lunch to Hugh Gibson, our new Minister to Poland. I wrote a letter for him to President and glad he got it as he deserves it, having worked up from the ranks in diplomatic corps.

At 3:00 went to meeting of five foreign secretaries at Quai d'Orsay at the request of Lansing to be present when they discussed blockade in Latvia and Lithuania. New complications. Germans who are in Lettland were asked to keep back Bolshevism are just reported to have turned out Lettland government and taken control of country. Query—shall we continue to feed country under German control and stop sending Germans supplies for military operations in which event they cannot hold back the Bolshevists. We decided to let no political difficulties hold back relief.

Attended meeting of the advisers in Benson's office—Bliss, House and Robinson present.

Dined at Mrs. Havemeyers and went to Williards for dance afterwards.

APRIL 20 (SUNDAY)—

Went to American Episcopal Church, Easter Sunday—stood all through service; crowded, largely soldiers. I am more impressed than ever with our troops; fine, manly looking lot of fellows and well behaved.

Drove out to lunch with Mrs. McFadden to Bernie Baruch's house near St. Cloud. Baruch had a house party, two French women, Swope, Irwin and self. McFaddens just for lunch. Went to St. Cloud golf club in afternoon. Ladies went home after dinner. We four men stayed until next morning. An ugly, modern, French house, attractive grounds but small. Paris for me.

APRIL 21 (MONDAY)—

When I got to office this morning I found my desk full of letters from home and many unfinished ends of reparations, blockade and Supreme Economic Council. I had sort of settled for easy time from now on but there are still many important decisions not unanimously agreed to which we are now negotiating and the Huns here Friday so we will have to hustle.

Went to Quai d'Orsay, meeting of Foreign Ministers to discuss the taking out of the hand of military power the economic questions arising in occupied territory. Much to our surprise, French agreed to proposal submitted.

Interview after meeting with Lord Robert who told me his government had finally given him full authority on Supreme Council matters except over censorship. He favored drastic relaxation of blockade as prepared by us so things will be easier sailing from now on.

Worked in office until 7:30. Russian Problem most interesting as we have agreed to relieve Bolshevist Russia and insist that the Bolshevists stop fighting, when the State Dept. comes along with another proposal to recognize the Omsk government, they getting stronger every day.[54] If we recognize Omsk, will it be breaking faith in regard to proposal of relief through Nansen. Lenine will not agree to stop fighting for food unless we get anti-Bolshevists to agree to stop also. This is hard on Kolchak as he is winning now. I am going to put this new situation to the President. Unfortunately, almost impossible to have satisfactory talk with President on this matter on account of other pressing peace terms now concluding.

Dined with Mr. Vanderlip, Mrs. Auchincloss and Admiral Long.

At 10:30 had meeting in my room with Lamont, Davis, Baruch and Dulles to discuss co-ordinating all work of respective committees. We have been sitting in on the final drafting this week.

APRIL 22 (TUESDAY)—

Meeting of Supreme Economic Council at 10:00 at Ministry of Commerce, Cecil presiding. Had warm discussion on relaxation of blockade against Germany. Cecil wanted to gradually relax as he has finally come

---

54. Aleksandr Kolchak was minister of war in the Siberian anti-Bolshevik government. He organized his own counterrevolutionary "White Army" and staged a coup d'etat in Omsk in November 1918, declaring himself supreme ruler of Russia.

to American position. French still holding out but considerable progress has been made, nevertheless. Great Britain and France announced their governments approved abolition of black list.[55]

Lunched with Richards.

At 3:20 Dulles and I met Lord Sumner and Loucheur to go over reparation draft of reparations in kind. Agreed upon most clauses with few reservations.

Meeting later with Baruch and Sir Hubert Llwellyn Smith to discuss control of dye exports from Germany after peace.

Swope came in office about 7:00 after talk with Italian delegates, who say they will go home tomorrow if they don't get what they want. I would let them go; I believe it is a bluff.

Dined with Garretts and Colonel Grant.

Went to Lansing's reception to our new Ambassador and Mrs. Wallace at Crillon. Hugh Wallace tells me he can't dine with me at Ritz as he thinks it undignified for an Ambassador to frequent hotels and restaurants in Paris. I am afraid he will not be able to live up to his principle.

APRIL 23 (WEDNESDAY)—

Meeting of Blockade at 10:00 o'clock to discuss plans relaxation, de-rationing neutrals. Reported to the Supreme Economical Council upon plan for simplifying machinery by cutting out German rations of foodstuffs.

Lunched with advisers Davis, Lamont, Baruch and Dulles at Crillon to get together on final reparations draft to be submitted to the President at 3:00 at his house.

Coached the President on points under dispute.

At 4:00 went to session with Lloyd George, Clemenceau and respective advisers in a large room upstairs in the President's house, Orlando being absent, still on a huff and threatening to go home over Fiume discussion.

During the conference Lloyd George left the room to telephone and when he came back he sat down on sofa with President Wilson and was heard to say that he thought Orlando was calming down and would not go. He walked across the room and whispered to Clemenceau, giving apparently the same information. Clemenceau seems to me to be aging rapidly.

---

55. Under the auspices of the War Trade Board, the Allies created "blacklists" in regard to international commercial trade. One list was public, one was classified, and one consisted of "cloak" businesses where a business was a "front" operation for German trade. By agreement, neither Ally nor neutral did business with these designated enterprises.

The Chiefs are all in a good humor and much progress made, practically settling all questions of difference. We called their attention to the fact that small nations must see the Reparations clauses, which they had evidently overlooked in the excitement of settling the differences among themselves, so we were divided up into sub-committees to break the news to the lesser powers and I can already hear the kicking. Was much impressed by good nature and cordiality of the Chiefs after the trying times they are passing through. Left President's house after 7:00 o'clock.

Dined at Hoovers with Paderewski; an interesting dinner as he told us all his troubles in Poland, the importance of Danzig. Says revolution if Poland does not get satisfactory settlement. Worried over Czecho-Slovak-Poland dispute over Teschen. He seems reasonable and has more force than I imagined.

April 24 (Thursday)—

Reggie Taylor and Sam Fleming had breakfast with me. Was late getting to Crillon.

Whole town excited over President Wilson's statement published this morning on Italian situation.[56] French Press inclined to blame President Wilson. Never mentioned that statement had full approval of Lloyd George and Clemenceau. Always trying to make the U.S. the goat. Many think, however, statement made most favorable impression and will call the bluff of Italians who have overplayed their game.

At 11:00 A.M. Lord Sumner, Jusserand, Dulles and I met Greece Reparation delegates, and Japan at 12:00 o'clock and Roumania at 1:00, for lunch, and explained the Reparations Clauses of Peace Conference treaty, preparatory to meeting Big Four. Another small committee of advisers was meeting simultaneously with Belgium, Serbia, Portugal, et al.

Worked in office all afternoon cleaning up much back work. Had interesting talk with Dr. Nansen, who called on Russian scheme. Said he had not yet been able to get his message through to Lenine. I rather hope it will be delayed as things are moving pretty fast with Kolchak government and I think some further thought should be given to recog-

---

56. Having been partner to the secret Treaty of London before the war, Italy was now asserting claims to additional territory, specifically Fiume, a strategic sea outlet in the newly created Jugoslavia. Inhabitants of the city were mainly Italian, but Jugoslavs were more numerous on the outskirts. Because of the right to self-determination, Wilson was against Italy's claim and took the question before the Italian people themselves, which angered the Italian leaders at the conference, and they left.

nizing Omsk government. Every plan in Russia, however, a gamble so present plan may be best, at least, this attempt will give more information as to actual conditions.

Dined with Morgenthaus. Dinner for Secretary and Mrs. Lansing, former absent. Davidson, Mrs. Cushman, Williards, Baruch, Flinn, and others.

At 10:00 went to meet Hoover at Davis' room to discuss new proposal of British for international bond issue to relieve financial distress in Europe and to use U.S. credit to guarantee bonds of bankrupt nations. Looks good but needs watching as there are many pitfalls, but of one thing I am certain, that if our great rich nation, practically untouched by the war, does not do something to help our bankrupt Allies, then we will come out of the war the most hated nation in the world.

APRIL 25 (FRIDAY)—

Papers still full of the Italian fracas. The President has called their bluff in good style. They can gain nothing by holding out. Looks to me as though their game is to save their Ministry by grandstand play and throw the responsibility on the Allies if they fail, which they will do.

Had busy morning in office on War Trade Board, Reparation and Russia.

I lunched at Countess Rougemont's with the Garry Lehrs, James Hazen, Hyde, Baruch and several friends. A queer bunch.

At office until 6:00 when I went to Bois to play tennis with Mrs. Garrett.

Dined with McFaddens, quiet dinner.

We are at a great disadvantage here in regard to publicity. French papers under strictest censorship and Government control and are antagonistic to the President whenever their Government wants to pass the buck. *Paris–New York Herald,* a rotten anti-Wilson sheet, evidently carrying on a distinct propaganda to embarrass the President. Chief is holding his own in great shape, has himself well in hand. Knows what he wants and is going to get it, in my opinion.

All advisers busy today discussing new financial scheme of British to consolidate debt and have all Allies guarantee interest and principal. That means the United States would guarantee all the bankrupt nations. The more the plan is studied the less enthusiastic our people become. It is the same old game they have been working on all through the conference, to get the United States to underwrite their debts. We will have to help but I don't believe in quite that way.

APRIL 26 (SATURDAY)—

The days are quieting down considerably and I have more time to get in War Trade Board cables and dip again into the Russian affairs. Had a talk with Bakhmeteff [*sic*]. Suggested cable to Kolchak to make food offer for relief to Bolshevist Russia and Siberia. Suggested it would have good political effect in Russia and outside just at the time of Nansen's relief offer. He jumped at the plan.

Heck, formerly of Rockville, our representative at Constantinople, a very intelligent person, called and reported on blockade conditions there. Same old game of British and French using situation to advance their own commercial interest at the expense of others.

Lunched with Dr. Nansen at the Norwegian Minister to France Wedel's house. A delightful American wife; living in Lafayette's old house; charming garden and court yard. Some very interesting Danish and Norwegian relations named Wedel. Guest of honor was Allah Kahn [Aga Khan], the God of Mohammedanism, head of that religion and ruler of India. In English clothes, speaks English perfectly and looks like a Russian. The Indians kiss his feet if they get a chance. He is friendly to the English and they use him to keep balance of power in India. The great rivals in India being the Mohammedans and Hindoos, the English keep their control by playing one against the other as they hate each other worse than the English. Allah told Dr. Nansen today he thought home rule would come for India in about ten or fifteen years.[57] They are not ready yet.

Was at office all afternoon. Mrs. Vera Cushman and Miss Spencer called to get me to assist them to get Y.W.C.A. workers into Siberia. I saw Secretary Baker later in their behalf and he (Baker) said President approved and would attend to it at home as he leaves tonight for United States.

At 6:00 o'clock met with U.S. advisers. Interesting discussion on the new British proposal to consolidate bonded debt. During discussion Benson displayed great animosity to English. Told us confidentially he had most difficult time with the British Admiralty in all negotiations about distribution of enemy ships. He told me that in the presence of the Minister of Navy, Long, and Secretary Daniels he told the Minister that his policy seemed to mean that Great Britain proposed to hold the supremacy of the sea both in Navy and Commerce at all hazards and the Minister

---

57. The Aga Khan was optimistic in his prediction, as independence for the states of India and newly created Pakistan came in 1947, nearly thirty years in the future.

acknowledged such to be the case. The Admiral said he replied that if that was to be the British policy they were building up a conflagration in America which could not be stopped and he was going back to America to tell the people all about it. The Minister replied he would have to report the matter to his Government.

Dined with Madame deBilly, and am just leaving to take 11:00 o'clock train to British front on French Government special train.[58]

APRIL 27 (SUNDAY)—

After a comfortable night on special train, rooming with General Bliss, I found in the morning that our special consisted of three carloads of distinguished guests, including all American Plenary Peace delegates and wives; House, Lansings, White and Bliss, Auchinclosses, French Ambassador Jusserand and wife, Ambassador Wallace and wife, Mezies and Morgenthaus; also some British, French and Canadian guests. Most comfortable train. Arrived at Lens soon after breakfast at 7:30. The second train over the railroad since it had been opened. Lens absolutely demolished. Nothing above ground and mines ruined and flooded underground. Such premeditated and systematic destruction of the mines and industries vital to France's very existence deserves the Reparations payment of the Saar coal basin, which the Peace Treaty will give France.

From Lens to Arras, then to Peronne and by auto to St. Quentin, then by train to Charleroi, Noyon and home.

Each destroyed town and surrounding country exactly alike, a desolate waste, churches, houses, everything gone. The destruction seemed greater than at Verdun and Rheims and I suppose it was as mines were used systematically by the Germans in destroying the cities, and the ground was all fought over every year of the war. I was glad to note the people were straggling back and beginning to clean up and re-build temporary quarters, particularly in the cellars, and I saw considerable land tilled and crops growing. I saw many German prisoners in their pens, looking well kept and fed. They were in the charge of the British.

I had some good talks with my roommate, General Bliss. Was interested in his estimate of the effect that the blockade had on ending the war. I told him of Marshal Foch's report to the War Cabinet in regard to

---

58. This trip was a semiofficial inspection of the damages in battlefront areas. It served to illustrate the destruction and underscored the French position in demanding full reparations and claiming the Saar coal area.

the victory due 50 per cent to the military and 50 per cent to the blockade and General Bliss remarked he would give the blockade the greater percentage. He said that the British and French were most anxious to make Armistice terms as they had gone about as far as they dared as they could not keep up to the Germans' retreat on account of the difficulties in getting up supplies and the German retreat was in such good order that if the pressure had not been so great at home, due to the blockade, they could have formed a new line of defense and held out for another winter, and it was this that the British and French feared because they were afraid of their own people not being able to hold out over another winter with lack of food and fuel, on account of nerves of the people being about gone, even with the knowledge that America was coming strong and they could win the next year.

We returned to Paris at 10:00 P.M. after a most instructive and interesting day, and full of sympathy for poor, devastated Northern France.

APRIL 28 (MONDAY)—
[Final covenant of the League of Nations presented]

I answered my mail in my room at Ritz before going to the Supreme Economic Council at 10:00 o'clock, Lord Robert presiding. Interesting discussion over an effort by the United States delegates to get the Danube opened up for trade and relief, now under British and French military control and commerce absolutely blocked. Did not make much progress. Also failed again in putting over complete relaxation of blockade against Germany but made some progress covering relaxation concerning occupied territory in Germany.

Lunched with Clementel and his son at the Ritz. He wanted to talk to me about Brazilian ships taken from Germans. He don't [*sic*] want them to be taken as were the ships in the United States harbors. It will be difficult to treat them otherwise. We may have to sell France some of our new ships now building.

At 3:00 o'clock went to Quai d'Orsay to attend a meeting of the Plenary Peace Conference to see the final passage of the League of Nations Covenant which was an historic event.[59] The President presented the amendments to the original draft which had been approved by the Commission and then the Japanese delegates stated their objection with a good argument about

---

59. The final document was worked out by a committee consisting of Wilson, House, Cecil, Smuts, Bourgeois, and Venizelos.

the equal treatment of all races, etc., but stated they would not press the issue at this time. Bougeois spoke for France; Hymans for Belgium, as did several others, and then Clemenceau declared the thing passed unanimously. Sir Robert Bordon [Borden], Canada, proposed amendment to labor clause of treaty which was adopted. Meeting adjourned.

The conference room was packed as more and more spectators are slipping in under the guise of advisers and newspaper men. I saw Mrs. Wilson and Miss Benham and Admiral Grayson present.

Some of the speeches were pretty long and as we sat close behind Clemenceau, Lloyd George and the President we could hear Lloyd George chaffing Clemenceau about permitting such long speeches and he asked him why he had not read over the speeches first, etc., much to the old gentleman's delight. They all seemed in good humor today and did not seem to miss the Italians, who, I think, will be back soon after they have blown off a little steam

Dined with Jannetta Whittridge and husband who live in Mrs. Alexander's apartment. Present, Duke of Dunston and Lady Hardingh, daughter of Lord Salisbury and niece of Lord Robert and a charming person. Reminded me a lot of Rachel Hale. Also Count and Countess Branbilla. We did not discuss Italy with the latter, being somewhat of an embarrassing subject at this particular time.

APRIL 29 (TUESDAY)—
[*German delegation arrived in Paris*]

Morning at office, interviewed Noyes and Day, just departing for Luxembourg to represent us on the Rhenish Inter-Allied Commission to look after all economic matters in occupied territory to get it out of military hands.

Lunched with Mrs. Whitehouse, mother of Henry and Sheldon Whitehouse; also Lansings, Andrews, ———, Rougemont, Mrs. Hyde, et al.

While working at office was sent for by the President to attend conference at his house with the Big Three and Belgians to discuss the latter's claim for reparations. Hymans, Foreign Minister Van der Heuval and Van der ——— representing Belgium. After some discussion and counter offers of minor changes in the categories, Hymans stated that as Belgium's proposals were not acceptable for war costs, etc., the Belgium [sic] delegates would have to return to Brussels and get instructions. This struck the Big Three like a bomb shell as the Germans have arrived and with the Italian mess it would be serious. I have felt all along Belgium would play a strong hand. She has a good case and a popular one and at a prior meeting of the Big Four at Lloyd George's house, where categories were dis-cussed, I made, during the President's absence in America, a reservation for United States until Belgium was satisfied. After some discussion, we having warned President Wilson to let Lloyd George and Clemenceau bear the burden of discussion, as this trouble is of their own making, the French and British suggested a proposal to have Belgium get from Ger-many payments sufficient to pay her war debt to the Allies. This was not made to Belgium but discussed among ourselves and was amusing to me because I can see Great Britain and France coming to what I said all along they would be compelled to do.

During the discussion one of Lloyd George's secretaries brought in the speech of Orlando in Italian, made in Rome today. It was a dramatic sight, seeing the President, Lloyd George and Clemenceau and others grouped about the interpreter in the middle of the room listening to the reading of Orlando's speech which might mean so much to the entire settlement of peace. It did not bring out anything new and there was not much comment.

While the Big Three seemed in good spirits, yet I could see underneath it all a great strain.

During the discussion the President mentioned to Davis on the side that both Lloyd George and Clemenceau had promised him to make a public statement on the Italian question but so far they had failed him. It has been unfair the way they have pushed him out into the light to bear the brunt of all the unpopular moves. Loucheur, French Minister of Reclamation, told me today that the propaganda of the Italians in French papers cost the Italians eight million francs. The French press is certainly rotten.

We did not get away from president's house until 7:30.

Dined with McFadden and Baruch and went to a show.

APRIL 30 (WEDNESDAY)—

Hoped to attend Blockade meeting this morning but was detained at office by Loucheur, who wanted to get British to agree to reparations clause making immediate return of horses and cattle stolen from Belgium and Northern France by the Germans.

We lunched with Davis, Baruch, Lamont, Keynes and Dulles and agreed in principle to proposals. In afternoon discussed details with Belgium rep-resentatives, Loucheur and Dr. Taylor, and had Dulles make draft, which was approved by Keynes, to submit to Lloyd George.

Minister Cartier of Belgium called to try to have me arrange an appointment with the President for the Belgium [sic] delegation tomorrow. Hymans, Foreign Minister, telephoned he had heard from Brussels and the Belgium [sic] government could not accept British and French proposal and two members of the cabinet were leaving for Paris tonight. I talked to President over telephone about appointment. He feels he should not meet them alone as it might make matters worse for them as Lloyd George and Clemenceau are quite excited over situation and very firm in their position. I am not sure the President has sized the situation up. I think it most important to give the fullest opportunity for Belgium to present its case.

Some of the advisers went to the President's house with Dulles to discuss joint and several liability of enemy states. I stayed behind to talk to Baruch.

Dined with Madame de Billy at Union Club. Met the Grempels, a Miss Skinner, Colonel Grant and several French, male and females.

MAY 1 (THURSDAY)—

The famous "May 1st" has come and gone. It is the day of Labor and Socialists and Paris always looks for trouble and this year more than ever as great plans for a general strike were made with "red" parades, etc. The strike was a quiet one but most effective; not a car, bus or taxi running in Paris; not a restaurant open, not even in the Ritz. We ate in our rooms and only cold food as all cooks are out today. Front doors of hotels barred and we used side door, care was used. The Government made no effort to stop strike but had thousands of soldiers and police stationed all over the city. Place de la Concorde and Rue Royale principal gathering place of the people. Red parade started but did not get very far as police separated it. Some few fights and broken heads. I walked around in the crowd for a couple of hours much interested. Crowd generally doing what I was. Police and soldiers calm and in good humor. I think tonight, however, everyone glad it is over and no serious disturbances.

I had a busy day at Crillon with Loucheur on his animal restitution clauses of reparations and later in afternoon in Davis' office with Belgians, who are still raising a rumpus for their share of the spoils.

Worked until 8:00 P.M. and dined alone in my room on cold meats.

Peace officials met Germans today to go over their credentials. Tomorrow some informal conferences begin on some of the financial matters. Nothing new from Italy today although Loucheur told me that President

Poincar's statement in the papers expressing sympathy with Italy had made Clemenceau very angry and he and Tardieu had advised Clemenceau to make public the statement that he and British had given Orlando stating they did not approve of Italy getting Fiume. I still cannot help but think Italians will be heard from in a few days as they have too much at stake to pull out.

MAY 2 (FRIDAY)—

I was engaged all morning with War Trade Board and Russian cables trying to work out with Dulles and Williams, the head of the Eastern affairs, our plan for financing U.S. share in Siberian Railroad out of assets of old Russian Government in Washington. Finally decided it could not be done and we would have to use the War Trade Board Russian Bureau's funds temporarily until Congress will appropriate, and we prepared a cable to that effect. I don't know whether Lansing and Chief will approve. I am beginning to believe Nansen's relief expedition a mistake as Kolchak is making such progress and it might become necessary to recognize Omsk government in which event embarrassments might arise.

Lunched with Heck, from Hecton near Harrisburg, U.S. Commissioner to Constantinople and War Trade Board representative. He is enroute home after five years' absence.

After lunch Loucheur called up to have me go with him to Quai d'Orsay to meet Big Three to have approved the clauses in the treaty for immediate restitution of breeding animals stolen from Northern France and Belgium. We put the thing over in about five minutes after a little arguing with Lloyd George; the other two being agreed. Loucheur and I also discussed briefly Belgium's claims, which are up in the air, and Belgians still threatening to pull out. Lloyd George was very vehement in his declaration that Belgium would have no more than other nations, that they had lost few lives and would come out of the war with their debts paid as they had borrowed the entire cost of the war from the Allies and that Scotland, their great commercial competitor, hindered with a great debt and also having lost thousands of lives in fighting to save Belgium, could not defend it at home and he would not stand for it. I never saw him so exited. I think he will have to come down a bit.

I had a meeting later with Lamont, Davis, Hoover and Loucheur to discuss Belgium. We worked out a plan to submit to Chief which I hope will prove satisfactory.

Bernie and I drove out to his house in the country for a quiet dinner together. Still raining. I never saw such a late spring and very cold. Have no warm weather yet.

MAY 3 (SATURDAY)—

A quiet morning at the office.

Lunched with Lady Ward, formerly Jean Reid, and her husband, and sister-in-law.

After lunch was called to meeting in Davis' room on Belgium claims— Cunliff, Keynes, Loucheur, Lamont, Dulles and self holding a preliminary conference. Then met Belgium [sic] delegates, headed by Hymans, foreign minister. Situation somewhat strained but made progress during the after-noon, Great Britain being loathe [sic] to give up, French and United States liberal. I believe made a satisfactory proposal but Hymans compelled to go to Brussels to calm the rising populace and is to report tomorrow.

Dined with Mrs. Williard, wife of U.S. Ambassador to Spain. Present, Grews, a French count and Countess ———, Mrs. Carlton, of Boston, Miss Saltonstall, Kirk, Dawson, et al. Went to Majestic Hotel, British head-quarters, afterwards to dance. Saw Lloyd George, Balfour, Lord Robert and a funny looking crowd of men and women. Typical English dancing with all sorts of steps and clothes—a most democratic affair.

MAY 4 (SUNDAY)—

Bill Clark dropped in for breakfast. Here on three days' leave from LeMons enroute home. This week they received orders delaying their trip home, maybe waiting outcome peace negotiations at Versailles.

Went to church with Bill and then returned to Crillon where I lunched, and worked until 3:00 o'clock.

Took a walk with Miss Hare to the Notre Dame along the Seine.

Dined with the McFaddens, Bill Clark and Miss Hare. Grand Duke Alexander joined our party after dinner. His family has just gotten out of Russia and enroute to England. British Government will not give him passport to England. Bill and I had a good talk in my room after party broke up.

MAY 5 (MONDAY)—

Called on Admiral Benson at 9:30 at his request to discuss with him proposal for the Government to control radio cable system around the world to protect commercial interests and the Navy. Daniels wanted any suggestions we might have from a world trade point of view.

At 10:30 met with Supreme Economic Council. Had the pleasure of showing to Council how France, who has been insisting upon maintaining the blockade against Germany, has been shipping carloads of cotton and wool materials into Germany through Alsace Lorraine. I had the goods on them from our representatives in the border and it created quite a stir in the Council.

Had a quiet afternoon in the office and a walk alone through the Tuileries Garden. Watched the children play and the United States soldiers playing ball. I was crazy to get into it. The first real spring day we have had.

Reggie Taylor and I dined together and went to a vaudeville show.

MAY 6 (TUESDAY)—

Henry Morgenthau called while I was at breakfast and we had a long talk about mandatories and politics. He wanted me to go with him to Salonica and Macedonia[60] on Venizelos' invitation to investigate the true state of affairs there as situation has been misrepresented according to Venizelos and he wants impartial report for the Allies. It would be interesting and is tempting as work here about concluded unless the Huns buck on us.

Worked on mail and cables at office.

Lunched with Dresel, just back from Berlin to report on conditions there. He says too drastic treatment will make German delegates refuse to sign and then the present government will be kicked out and Independent Socialists control which will mean extreme radicalism, communism, disorder, etc., and no hope of reparation. Then the consequent reaction with a military government finally. I don't take a pessimistic view. Hope for better luck.

Loucheur called in afternoon at the request of Big Four stating that he, Lord Cunliff and I had been appointed a committee to pass upon the new clauses in the treaty for Poland. We went to Quai d'Orsay to see about its insertion by drafting committee. While there we saw Tardieu just coming out of big room where Plenary Peace Conference was in session dis-

---

60. A reference to an area that was inhabited by Greeks and had been held by the Ottoman Empire until the Balkan Wars of 1912–13, when it was annexed by Serbia. With the collapse of Serbia in 1915, the Bulgarians took over Macedonia.

cussing complete treaty clauses. Tardieu was quite excited and told Loucheur that Marshal Foch had just made a strong speech criticizing the military clauses because they did not contain the permanent military occupation of the left bank of the Rhine. Loucheur thought that this would make trouble but said Clemenceau would stick to the present treaty clauses. He said the whole Cabinet had met Sunday and after hearing Marshal Foch were unanimous for the present arrangement of fifteen years' occupation. I am waiting anxiously results tomorrow.

Loucheur also told me Orlando and Sonnino were enroute to Paris to be present at the presentation of the treaty to the Germans. Said their sudden return was due to the fact that they had told Signor Crespi, who was in Paris, that Lloyd George and Clemenceau had decided that in view of the attitude of the Italians in regard to Fiume and London Pact and had withdrawn voluntarily from the conference, that the British and French were released from their obligations not to sign the treaty without Italians. Crespi at once telephoned this to Rome and the gentlemen were soon on their way back to Paris without having any concessions from the Big Three.

This morning Henry Morgenthau gave me interesting account of Frank Cobb's return from Paris after his accompanying Colonel House at the time of the signing of the Armistice. Cobb evidently discovered new traits in House which have apparently been developing rapidly this trip, of most interesting nature. This entire history of the inside conference will make interesting reading some day.

MAY 7 (WEDNESDAY)—
[*Treaty presented to Germans*]

After mail in room at Ritz, went to Crillon to see if there was any chance of anyone but five U.S. delegates admitted to room at Versailles when the Germans are handed the Peace Treaty.[61] Found the rule was cast iron so made no further attempt.

Presided at a meeting at 10:30 of the Supreme Blockade Council. Routine work. Decided to postpone further relaxation of blockade until we see how Huns take the Treaty.

---

61. The Germans, led by Count Ulrich von Brockdorff-Rantzau, chief of the delegation, protested vigorously that the terms were not consistent with the conditions under which Germany had laid down arms, and that many of the clauses would be impossible to satisfy.

Lunched with Dr. Nansen and had an interesting discussion upon Russian situation. I suggested that as his message had not gotten through and in view of apparent success of Kolchak, he might withdraw offer and make new one, offering relief to Petrograd without conditions as to stopping fighting, which otherwise might become embarrassing if we want to recognize the Omsk government. We went to talk to Hoover and heard report from Commander Baker, just back from Esthonia and Baltic States. Says they are making great fight against Bolshevists and with little help and if we don't send assistance immediately they will fall into the hands of the Bolshevists. Hoover has sent letter to President and he and I will go to see him about this matter, probably tomorrow.

Dined with Madame deBilly and Bernie Baruch and went to a show.

Nothing came out this morning in the papers about Foch's attack on Treaty. *The Herald* was censored, as evidenced by a blank quarter of a column.

Everything passed off all right at Versailles today. The Huns received the Peace Treaty at the Hotel Trianon in the presence of the Plenary representatives of the Associated Governments. Only Clemenceau and Brockdorff-Rantzau spoke. Both apparently affected, the latter particularly nervous and did not stand up in making his statement. Some say intended as an insult, others say a very ill man. Whole proceeding took only an hour.

MAY 8 (THURSDAY)—

The reaction after the rush of closing days of drafting treaty has set in and it is difficult to settle down to routine of War Trade Board and work on further liquidation. We studied this morning plan of blockade in the event Germany refuses to sign Treaty.

In the afternoon discussed in Davis' office with Dulles the omissions and changes in treaty which we felt should be corrected and which slipped in at the last minute.

Dined at d'Avray at a most attractive café, on small lake on road to Versailles, with Mr. and Mrs. Dulles and Mrs. Lansing. Tables out of doors; beautiful moonlight night.

Treaty seems to have made good impression in France. Hoover's experts, first out of Germany, think German delegates will not sign. If they don't, I shall support military occupation instead of blockade. The latter will only make revolution and distress and make it all the more difficult to get anything out of Germany, while if we occupy the territory we can get something out of the wreck by permitting her to have freedom of trade and restore her economic life and then whatever she produces we can take for reparations.

MAY 9 (FRIDAY)—

As usual, this morning before I was through breakfast McFadden, Richards and Baruch dropped in, the latter to say there will be a meeting of representatives of the Supreme Economic Council at the President's house with Council of Four to discuss certain economic questions. At meeting, there big as life, was Orlando, apparently as though nothing had happened and he had not been away. Lord Robert Cecil opened the meeting by speaking of distress in Europe due to shortage of food and raw materials saying that only relief by the former made matters worse as idleness sure breeder of trouble. High prices part of the trouble, transportation also part of the difficulty but finances principal need. It was then suggested by the President that each nation appoint two representatives on committee to discuss problem and report immediately to Council of Four. Lord Robert also asked for permission to announce publicly the complete removal of blockade on Germany if treaty was signed. Agreed to.

Went to special committee of the Supreme Blockade Council at the Commerce Department to discuss for blockade in the event of Germany refusing to sign Treaty. We came to agreement. I notified Council, while approving the plan, that I hoped the Allies would not use it as it would make more chaos. In my opinion, the only solution of the question would be military occupation.

Lunched with the Bullitts, Grempels and McFaddens, guests of the Bullitts.

Worked in office in afternoon until 4:00. Attended meeting of Council of Foreign Ministers to discuss relief of Baltic States, over which Lansing and Balfour had a warm tiff, also Hungary blockade which it was decided not to relax for the present.

Played tennis with Baruch at 6:00.

Dined with Mr. and Mrs. Beekman, Rector of the American Episcopal Church; dinner given for Ambassador and Mrs. Wallace; Mrs. House, Mrs. ———, Mr. and Mrs. Monroe and Bishop McCormick.

After returning from dinner, Swope called to discuss the issuing of licenses to newspaper correspondents to enter Germany.

MAY 10 (SATURDAY)—

Jim Neale arrived from America before I was out of bed. I secured him a room adjoining so he can use my sitting room and it seems like old times being together again.

I met with Special Blockade Committee this morning and approved final draft of report for the Council of Big Four in the event of Germany's not signing Treaty.

Jim and I lunched with Dr. Taylor at Larue's.

Worked in office and then took walk with Jim and we dined with Elizabeth Hudson and Miss Stillman, Café Paris, and then took in Follies, etc. Had altogether gay evening.

MAY 11 (SUNDAY)—

Had a quiet morning in my room writing to Mother.

Went to lunch with Miss Hare, Miss Kane and Colonel Moore and then the races. Great crowd and remarkable dressing.

Dined with McFaddens, farewell dinner, as they leave in the morning.

Meeting in Bernie's room after dinner to discuss new financial plan to assist stricken Europe.

Nothing new from Huns today. Everyone getting restless to get home. If something does not develop soon, I think most of the experts will be pulling out for home.

MAY 12 (MONDAY)—

Jim, Lew and I breakfasted together, and at 10:00 o'clock I went to meeting of Supreme Economic Council. Lord Robert quite put out because Loucheur left meeting early and left his veto against certain matters coming up regarding feeding the Germans and exemption lists. Lord Robert insisted upon having special meeting tomorrow with Loucheur present.

Lunched with the Richards and Madame Waddington, a famous Paris character of eighty years of age, wife of former Ambassador to England, also French General Tauffileb and American wife. General commanded French Army corps, now retired and going to his birthplace in Alsace to run for Senator.

Worked in my office all afternoon. Interview with Bakhmeteff discussing recognition of Omsk Government, trying to get Bakhmeteff to urge Kolchak to hold a Constituent Assembly so U.S. could recognize their government.

Jim and I dined with Grempels, Auberts, deBillys, Auchinclosses, and several French friends.

MAY 14 (WEDNESDAY)—

We are having congenial breakfasts with Lew and Jim and Richards usually drops in for a blockade conference before going to office.

Was called to the President's house at 11:00 to submit to Big Four our plan for blockade in the event of Germany refusing to sign. While waiting for our turn I had a good talk with Lord Robert on many subjects, among them Russia. I was interested to see he agreed with me that the Omsk Government should be recognized as a de facto government and said he thought so long ago. When we started meeting I handed the President a letter I had just written him strongly recommending the use of military occupation instead of blockade in the event of Germany not signing and told him of Lord Robert's opinion that for financial and other reasons he thought military occupation impossible. I told the President this could not be and that the alternative was starvation and revolution in Germany. Everything would be lost to the Allies while occupation would save something out of the wreck. President made this statement to the Big Four and urged occupation. Lloyd George at once said that it would only be a blockade of several weeks and did not say that military occupation was impossible. President also stated that in our blockade plan he thought we should adopt the formal (legal) blockade because to return to the old one might recognize England's blockade operations which we had always held as illegal. He joked with Lord Robert about it, who said nothing about legality but agreed with the President a formal blockade was now possible and should be adopted.

Lord Robert read the notice to Germany we had agreed upon yesterday at Supreme Economic Council in regard to removal of blockade if Germany signed and giving also our relaxations up to date. This was approved.

Am always impressed with the cordiality and harmonious workings of the Four even with Orlando present. They are apparently frank with each other, differing frequently and earnestly but always in a most friendly spirit. Three big men trying to do the big thing in the proper spirit. They could not have gotten as far as they have if this spirit had not been present.

Worked at office most of afternoon and took a little walk. Jim at races with Elizabeth Hudson. Dined with Lamonts, Auchinclosses, Jack Carters and Mrs. Corbin. Had a hot discussion on Russia. Can see by Gorden

Auchincloss talk he has been somewhat influenced by Bullitt's talk. Says he is down on Bolshevism but don't [*sic*] want to have anything to do with Kolchak.

MAY 15 (THURSDAY)—

After usual breakfast with Jim and Lew went to office until 11:00, then attended Supreme Blockade Council at Seydoux' office. Agreed upon method of shipping to neutrals with license, also upon identical note to neutrals in regard to re-opening blockade if necessary.

Lunched with Jim and Dulles at Crillon.

At 2:00 went to President's house with Hoover, Davis and Baruch to discuss with the President the blockade policy as to food if Germany refused to sign. Hoover urging food should go to Germany in any event, he being worried because millions had been contracted for and if stopped suddenly Relief Committee would be broke. President told him of our conversation with Big Four yesterday and that he advocated military occupation rather than starvation methods. President discussed freely his difficulties with his colleagues in Council—called them mad men, particularly Clemenceau, whom he now understands better since he has read some of his earlier writing in which he advocated the "survival of the fittest." He says he has a great pity for them. They have such fear of the Germans and such great self pity. He spoke feelingly of his struggles with Clemenceau and Lloyd George to hold them down to justice and reason and could not vouch for his being able to convince them that military occupation was better than the starvation method because the military occupation would cost more in money. He discussed certain proposals for the Fiume dispute, one is that plebiscite be held as to whether the people of Fiume would be willing to remove to a nearby port if built by the Italians. This was suggested by Jugo-Slavia. He says he will propose it but doubts if Italians will accept. When it was suggested that Sonnino had been the trouble, the President stated that he thought he had played fair as he had signed the London Pact which really gave Fiume to Croatians and he had never heard him claim Fiume. I gathered he rather blamed Orlando. As a matter of fact, I blame Lloyd George and Clemenceau for not supporting more strongly the President as I believe they could have called the bluff of Orlando and changed the tide before it had gone so far.

The President seemed rested and discussed some of the points of his message to Congress. We had an hour and a quarter's talk with him.

At 5:00, I went to the office of Minister of Finance to meet with Reparations Commission to discuss one of the many German notes on the Peace Treaty clause, this one concerning reparations, which had to be answered.

I have been appointed as the United States representative on this subcommittee and this was our first meeting today.

Jim and I dined with Elizabeth Hudson and Miss Stillman at Larue's. Just to give an idea of prices in Paris today, our simple little dinner cost 230 francs or about $40.00.[62]

MAY 16 (FRIDAY)—

Worked in office all morning and cleaned up a good deal of War Trade Board work.

Lunched with Bill Hickok and Jim Neale.

Talked with Noyes, our commissioner on Rhine Allied Commission. Told me of lack of co-operation in administration by French playing their own game and he is very much afraid of their exploiting territory for own interests.

Met with Dulles at 4:00 to attend meeting of experts on Austrian reparations clauses. Italians fighting for art treasures and Adriatic ships. British objecting, particularly to the latter; we sitting by watching them scrap it out.

Dined with Legge to meet British Rhine Commissioner, Sir Harold Stewart; and Mr. Tirrand, the French representative. I think the dinner bore fruit and we will get better co-operation. We think the attitude of the Allies, particularly the French, towards occupied territory means much to the future peace of the would. Any policy of revenge or exploitation is bound to make trouble in the future.

MAY 17 (SATURDAY)—

I had hoped to get off by motor in morning on tour to see Frank McCoy but decided to wait until afternoon on account of meeting with experts to discuss Austrian Treaty clauses.

At 1:00 I lunched with advisers at the Crillon, it being first regular Saturday lunch to discuss Supreme Economic Council agenda for Monday's meeting. I found Jim Neale could not go to Tours as he is going with Noyes to Rhine for several days so I picked up Elizabeth Hudson,

---

62. Translated in today's dollar values, the cost would be $453.63.

Miss Stillman and Reggie Taylor and after late start, about 3:30, and a beautiful run, arrived at Frank's house about 8:45. Found Frank out at farewell dinner to Atterbury and dinner at his house over. General Conner, Cheney, Bill Hickok and another Colonel acted as our hosts and got together a warmed over dinner. We then went to Hotel Univers, where we had a comfortable night.

MAY 18 (SUNDAY)—

At about 10:00, we went out to Reggie's German prison camp, where he had spent the night and picked him up and started on a sight-seeing tour of the chateaux. Beautiful weather and country at its best. Lilacs, wistaria, fruit trees, all in blossom and country wonderfully green. We visited both Chateaus at Azay le Rideau; particularly delighted with the small one which I did not remember before.

Lunched at an attractive little inn there in charming garden. In afternoon stopped at Chenonceau, Cheverny; saw "blest" pack of hounds being fed at Chambord, and then to Fontainebleau for dinner and home to Paris late in the evening. There were soldiers everywhere, principally French and Americans; billeted in nearly every small town. It will certainly be a good thing when demobilization is complete and the men can get home and begin to produce, for it is production the world needs today worse than anything else. I was impressed with the numbers of old people working, practically no young men.

MAY 19 (MONDAY)—

Attended the regular Monday meeting of the Supreme Economic Council. Principally routine work except report of German Commission, which called attention to Marshal Foch's refusal to accept action of Rhenish Commission without his approval, raising question of military vs. civil authority over occupied territory. French made plea to save the Marshal's feelings after cleaning the room of everyone except the members of the Council. We finally worked out a compromise. It looked as though there might be an interesting scrap as we had filed protest against French shipping goods into Germany through the French army zone, violating blockade, while the English and Americans are living up to it. I think this great tenderness for Foch is due to suggestions from certain Cabinet Ministers, who want to play a lone game, in German commerce.

Lunched with Legge, Baruch and Davis. Afterwards discussed financial plans for relief of Europe. Lamont also present. Senator Gerry called to discuss United States politics and at 4:00 o'clock Davis, Baruch, Lamont and I went to discuss with the President the financial plan. President willing to recommend to Treasury and Congress postponing of interest for three years provided Allies agree to a financial plan that is satisfactory.

President in good shape today. Told us of his message to Congress and plans for returning home. Expects to get away about the 1st of June. He will be disappointed, I am afraid. Hopes to be here until Austrian treaty is ready for presentation and expects to carry back with him the signed German treaty.

Dined with Lord Robert Cecil at Majestic with about a dozen guests; his attractive niece, Lady Cranburne, et al. One of the guests Madame Neufflies invited me to her Opera box Monday.

MAY 20 (TUESDAY)—

After an hour's reading of papers in my room I went to Crillon to clean up my routine work reading cables, etc.

Had an interesting talk with Colonel Riggs just out of Russia. Has been with General Denekin's army.[63] Says situation is better. British gave them considerable equipment. Thinks he will be able to hold Bolshevists. Says people in Russia as they turn from Bolshevism are tending toward monarchy. He thinks Bolshevism failing.

Lunched with Dick Crane, new minister to Czecho-Slovakia, Colonel Duncan and Treadwell, also just back from Russia and Turkestan.

Worked for several hours at office.

Dined at large dinner of the Baruchs, followed by dance at the Ritz. About 100 guests, principally French, run by his friend Count Rougemont. Good party.

MAY 21 (WEDNESDAY)—

Meeting of the Supreme Blockade Council at 10:30. Nothing important.

Lunched with Jack Ridgely Carters. Guests, Henry White, Colonel Hart, Mrs. Cooper Hewitt, Lady Hood and Mrs. Stuyvesant and Sir Eyre Crow. These lovely May days make lunching at Ritz quite attractive with garden now in use.

---

63. This was the Volunteer Army, or White Army in southern Russia, which was committed to the overthrow of Soviet power. Denekin's forces were to move north to Moscow while Kolchak's moved west from Siberia. In early May, Denekin's army was advancing with success.

Everyone is now speculating on what the Germans are going to do with the Treaty. Today they have asked for a week's extension which looks hopeful. I suppose it will be granted. Some of us are suggesting that the advisers find excuses for informal discussions on reparations clauses which appear pretty drastic but which upon explanation will seem possible of fulfillment.

Late this afternoon Bernie and I played tennis with Balfour and Sir Malcolm. Balfour is really good and remarkably active for a man his age. We expect to have some more. Bernie and I dined together alone, pretty well tired out after our exercise.

MAY 22 (THURSDAY)—

Reggie Taylor and I breakfasted together to talk over Reggie's future plans as to his homegoing. Worked at office all morning, and conference in Baruch's room with advisers on reparation payments of new formed countries and we agreed we would recommend should not be assessed for ceded territory as [these?] new countries would have to pay pre-war debt as well as war debt for the [peace?] of Austria and Hungary acceded.

Lunched with Hoover and Davis in Hoover's room. Hoover very much exercised because he had had a talk with General Smuts of British delegation who said he would not sign the Peace Treaty as his conscience would not permit him to do so and reported that Barnes, another British delegate, would not sign and that there is a revolution on, and among our delegates also, and that he had talked with House, Lansing and Bliss and that they did not approve of the Treaty and were considering not signing. I suggested the latter was incredible as all the above discussed the Treaty with the President and approved it before it was submitted to all the Allies at the Quai d'Orsay and voted for it in the Plenary session and I thought this was a pretty late date to criticize and balk. Hoover had nothing to say, except he said everyone was displeased and the Treaty was unworkable and would never be signed and he thought Lloyd George would attempt to take the world leadership away from President Wilson and come out in about a week and denounce the Treaty and stand for a new deal. I told Hoover I did not think he had the courage to do this and besides he was largely responsible for the clauses most criticized. It is amusing to hear criticism from Davis, Keynes and others who, when they have been talking to the Big Four, agree with everything they say and make no strong protest. I told them the time to fight is before they are committed.

At 4:00 o'clock went to the President's house to discuss Austria reparations clauses. The Big Four did not agree with us about relieving new countries from reparations for ceded territories and I guess they are right; otherwise treaty clauses accepted.

The Big Four were all present and seemed still to be working harmoniously. I thought Lloyd George looked old and tired. The old "tiger" [Clemenceau] as spry as could be and as usual wore gray gloves which he does at all the meetings.

I had a chance to say a word to the President about my conversation with Hoover. He said he had heard about some of the British delegates not signing but did not take much stock in the report about the American delegates. He said they certainly would have told him as, in fact, he showed them all the clauses and they said they approved. He asked me to talk to Mr. Lansing and sound out the situation.

Dined with Bernie, who gave dinner of forty to Economic Commission at the Ritz; Crespi, Sir George Foster of Canada and Clementelle spoke.

After dinner I went to Lady Hood's dance and am writing in the small hours of the morning after a busy day.

Impression seems to be growing in certain quarters that the Treaty too drastic and Germans will not sign. I have given up guessing. I know all the military and blockade plans are ready.

MAY 23 (FRIDAY)—

Had a farewell talk with Richards, who leaves War Trade Board today for several days' private business and then home.

Called on Lansing about General Graves' withdrawal from Russia and took occasion to question him about Hoover's statement that he and other American delegates were going to refuse to sign and as I had supposed Hoover let his imagination run wild which I find is frequently the case. Lansing said he told Hoover he did not approve of all the treaty but he had no thought of raising any objection to signing; in fact, he said they were appointed by the President and as Plenary Commissioners would, therefore, have to sign unless they resign. I could see Lansing was a bit sore at not being consulted more. He also told me that Lloyd George was largely responsible for the giving up of the Council of Ten and substituting the Big Four because he, Lansing, argued to a finish too many of the questions in dispute and thereby blocked Lloyd George's game. He said this information came from an English source. As a matter of fact, my own guess is that Colonel House was largely instrumental in breaking up

Council of Ten because it left him out and the Colonel could not bear it as he and Gordon have certainly been obsessed to be the whole show.

Lunched with Baruch, Robinson, Hoover and Sumner to discuss coal shipments to Europe. Worked at office all afternoon until 5:00. Tea with Miss Kane and Princess Guicka of Rumania at Laurents. Dined alone and went to opera with Grempels, who had Baron Rothschild's box.

I am feeling more hopeful today. I believe the Huns will sign after few more bluffs. Allied armies are mobilizing and we have blockade machinery ready to spring which I hope will not be necessary.

MAY 25 (SUNDAY)—

At 8:30 A.M. Miss Dorothy Kane, Miss Polly Hare, Reggie Taylor and I, with Captain Parker, of the 42nd Division from Roanoke, as guide, in an Army car, started for the battle fronts. We first visited Belleau Woods and Chateau-Thierry, studying that phase of the American advance, following their movements North to the Ourck and then to the Vesle. I also saw Dormans, South of which the 28th was stationed and where several companies held the Germans until there were very few Americans left.[64]

After lunching at Chateau-Thierry we went to Rheims and Fort Pompel just East on the road to Chalons; this a most interesting and demolished fortification. The tourists have already begun—every place crowded. Big auto busses full of excursionists and very different from my first visit, also many more signs of reconstruction; masons at work, shell holes being filled, fields cultivated and stores starting up in nearly all devastated towns and more and more people returning.

We had a good run to Chalons where we had dinner and as our next day was to be a big one we decided to press on to St. Minnehauld on the edge of the Argonne Forest although we were told that satisfactory hotel accommodations doubtful. An hour more, at 9:30, brought us to our destination and sure enough the only hotel packed to overflowing. We started out to scour the town and met some old French women on the streets who took pity on us and found us rooms. Miss Hare, Miss Kane and Reggie had rooms over a notion store, very clean and comfortable. I was over a blacksmith shop and our Army friends found quarters some-

---

64. McCormick refers to the U.S. 28th Division, which was composed in part of four companies of the Pennsylvania National Guard, men who would have been known to him. Robert Grant Crist, ed. *The First Century: A History of the 28th Infantry Division* (Harrisburg, PA: Stackpole Books, 1979).

where else. We all breakfasted together at hotel after an eventful night, particularly for the ladies who proved themselves good sports.

MAY 26 (MONDAY)—

Up at 6:30, breakfast at 7:00, and off at about 7:30 for Verdun. We did the citadel, saw the destroyed city and ran out by Fort Souilly which I had visited December 1st of 1917, when a bombardment was on—to Fort Douament which was tremendously interesting. French soldiers now occupy it and are patching up the damage apparently getting ready for the next time. I think this particular territory probably the most devastated spot in France; more dead to the square yard than anywhere else and more acres of churned up ground. The French soldiers pointed out in the distance where the Germans in their hasty flight left many of their soldiers unburied and now the smell is so great that he says they cannot send the Hun prisoners to bury their own dead. Hun prisoners working everywhere, smiling and apparently contented. From Fort Douament we returned through Verdun en route for the Argonne-Meuse Sector. Started in where the American troops relieved the French and moved North through Mount [blank] and Ems along the road over which the U.S. Army supplies moved on the way to Montfaucon where the Crown Prince had his concrete tower in a house on the top of a hill overlooking the entire country. He was well protected with his concrete and deep cellars.

We picnicked here and then we crossed the Argonne Forest through Varennes where King Louis and Marie Antoinette were captured on their flight from Paris, and most of this ground was fought over by our troops, including the 28th. We visited in the forest the wonderfully constructed concrete shelters built underground, quite palatial, window glass, paneled walls, heating apparatus, running water, certainly occupied by royalty. Regular villages with board walks, flower beds, all hid in the woods. The German cemeteries were remarkable in their permanent appearance, carved stones, large monuments, etc. The Germans were in these wonderfully protected woods for nearly four years and must have had a difficult time in keeping their men occupied. The hillsides in the valleys of the forest were regular nests of dugouts and trenches.

We got back to St. Menehould about 2:30 P.M. and started on an uneventful but comfortable trip back to Paris after two days of good weather and a most interesting experience. I was impressed with the rapidly changing appearance of the devastated areas; foliage, grass and human hands are changing the looks of the country and while it will always be badly scarred,

I am afraid by the time the millions of tourists arrive much will have been covered up and repaired, although some will never be restored.

Jim Neale, who I found back from Coblenz when I returned, Reggie and I had dinner, then I went to the opera with the Baroness deNeufflies.

MAY 27 (TUESDAY)—

It is good to have Jim back for breakfast. A busy morning in the office trying to catch up with yesterday's cables. A conference of advisers in Lamont's office on question of charges against liberated countries for ceded territories which is a burning question of Austria-Hungary settlement.

Lunched with Baroness deNeufflies' sister and ———.

Office until 4:00 then to the Ministry of Finance to sit with the Allied Committee on liberated countries and their reparations claims. We were trying to work out satisfactory arrangement for them so that while they would not pay reparations for part of enemy territory they take, they could make some kind of contribution for war costs. Did not come to definite agreement. Decided to try to make separate agreement with each nation.

Dined with the Richards and Jim Neale, farewell to Richards who leaves in the morning for London, en route home.

Went to Baron Rothschild's house to dance. Wonderful place, but guests a poor lot. The kind that make Bolshevists. If I went to many such I am afraid I might become a socialist or worse.[65]

MAY 28 (WEDNESDAY)—

Meeting of Blockade in the morning; not much of importance. Lunched with Jim Neale and Noyes, prior to their departure to British front, Brussels and Coblenz.

Attended a meeting in the afternoon at the Ministry of Finance on Austrian Reparations; not making much progress, still struggling with new liberated countries and have not yet worked out satisfactory manner in which they can make contributions for their acceded territory.

---

65. McCormick spent most of his social evenings with a group of extremely intelligent and accomplished men and women; here he may be commenting on another social set in Paris at the time, a group that was the basis of "the Lost Generation." Many were wealthy and chose a life of sybaritic leisure. Cole Porter, resident of Paris, was part of this set, and a description of his parties may also describe what McCormick encountered: "The parties during these years were elaborate and fabulous, involving people of wealthy and political classes. His parties were marked by much gay and bisexual activity, Italian nobility, cross-dressing, international musicians, and a surplus of recreational drugs." www.coleporter.org/bio.html.

Dined with deBillys at Union Club for Colonel and Mrs. House, Tardieu, Venezelos [*sic*], Auberts, several French and Colonel Grant.

MAY 29 (THURSDAY)—

I had an interesting conference with Bakhmeteff, Russian Ambassador, who came in to see what could be done to relieve situation in Siberia, with General Graves, whom Omsk Government claim is not co-operating and encouraging the Bolshevists.[66] I told Bakhmeteff the reports are exaggerated and due to activities of Japanese, British and French representatives trying to get us out of Siberia and it had to stop. Russia would be the greatest loser and Siberia would be turned over to Japan. He agreed and said he would try to convince Omsk Government.

Meeting at 10:30 of Reparations and Responsibility Committee to discuss answer to German note. The answer that the America delegates presented was accepted almost in toto.

Gave lunch at Ritz to Secretary and Mrs. Lansing, Mr. and Mrs. Charpentier, ——— Cooper Hewitt, Miss Hare and Tom Lamont.

Afternoon at office until 6:00, when we had another meeting of Reparations Committee on the Austrian treaty. Did not get very far, as Italians balking. Keynes, of Great Britain, stirred thing up by saying Austria dead broke and we ought not to ask reparations like Germany, but send Commission to Vienna and arrange financial assistance, otherwise Austria bankrupt and cannot buy food. Adjourned until tomorrow afternoon, as meeting lasted until after 8:00 o'clock.

Dined with Admiral Long, Miss Reid, Miss Parmentier, Mrs. Norris, Baruch and Grayson.

MAY 30 (FRIDAY)—

Bakhmeteff at office at 10:00 to see cable about conditions in Siberia in re Graves and railroads. The conditions much improved.

Conference in Davis' room on Austrian Reparations clauses. Loucheur came in, said he had been reading nearly all last night Germans' answer and did not like it. Said he thought we should not enter into extended discussion. Said Clemenceau had confidence in Wilson to stick, but was afraid of Lloyd George; afraid he may swing to extreme liberals if it looks

---

66. General Graves, without updated orders, was attempting to maintain absolutely neutral status in relation to both Soviet and Omsk governments.

popular at home. When I intimated such a contingency to the President some days ago, he said he would not dare.

Bernie and I lunched with Miss Hare. Sorry we could not attend Memorial Day exercises at the United States Cemetery, as the President spoke, but had a Reparation meeting at 3:00 o'clock. Keynes and Lord Sumner, of the British delegation, continued fight over Austrian reparations clauses, Keynes trying to modify them considerably, saying Austria broken and ought to be helped financially. Lord Sumner saying that the present clauses fair and flexible. Committee agreed with Lord Sumner, and Keynes stated he would fight it out before Big Four. Loucheur and Crespi seemed to be getting thick; there is some deal on and I have not discovered it yet.

Dined alone, and called on Miss Clara Alricks at Hotel d'Iena. Am trying to help her get home. Wrote letter to Mother.

MAY 31 (SATURDAY)—

Office, then to meeting of Blockade at Seydoux's office to discuss Sweden's guarantee against re-export. Later arranged organization at Paris War Trade Board office with Hale, Garlin and Thayer.

Lunched in my room with advisers, General Bliss, Hoover, Lamont, Davis, Dulles and Shepherdson. Discussed agenda for Supreme Economic Council Monday. Discussed informally Germans' answer, the one topic of conversation now. Some of our crowd, principally Davis and Hoover, think we should make concession. We all agree that lump sum for reparation, which we always advocated, is the right thing, and I think would agree on Twenty-five Billions if we could get the French to agree also. Looks as though the British are weakening. We discussed Germans' answer most of the afternoon and Baruch, Dulles, Sumners, Newton and I went out to Baruch's house for a night in the country to have a quiet time studying the note further and trying to come to some agreement on recommendations to the Chief.

JUNE 1 (SUNDAY)—

Drove in from Baruch's house to American Church, Communion Sunday. Saw Ambassador and Mrs. Davis with Lansings.

Lunched at Auberts with Tardieu and Mademoiselle Chovet. After lunch Tardieu drove us out to Louvecienes, where Loucheur lives, he having bought the pavilion of Madame Dubarry, Mistress of Louis XV. Lovely location overlooking the Seine; beautiful grounds, not well kept; house done in poor taste. Loucheur self-made, very rich.

Dined at Ritz; saw Pershing, Minister Morris and wife, Mr. and Mrs. Gary, of Washington, U.S. Diplomatic Agent at Cairo.

JUNE 2 (MONDAY)—

Started the day at office and then to Supreme Economic Council at 10:00. Interesting discussion on French evasion on carrying out Brussels agreement which is getting to be a scandal, concerning the coal sales by Germany to France, for purchase of food, the French having not yet paid one cent. We also made it hot for France when she made a break in her answer to my charge upon the shipping of cotton goods to Berlin by Alsace-Lorraine, contrary to blockade regulations. We get pretty well discouraged sometimes with the business morals of our Allies.

Lunched with Davis, Baruch and Dulles to discuss the German counterproposal and our answer thereto. Spent the entire afternoon continuing discussion and Dulles and I dined together for further consideration. Lamont and I favor fixing sum at Twenty-five Billions. Baruch, I think, agrees; Davis fearful it is too much. I don't think French will accept any fixed amount. We hear today British have agreed to fixed amount and told President so. Lloyd George wants President to make fight with Clemenceau—again passing the buck. It looks like interesting times ahead next few days. Germans really made better offer on reparations than we expected. Looks as though some small concessions will be agreed to. Will know more tomorrow when we meet with President and Commission.

JUNE 3 (TUESDAY)—

Started busy day at 9:30 with meeting Tardieu in Lamont's office with Baruch. We suggested advisability of taking this opportunity of fixing lump sum for reparations in German treaty, it being the thing we had always stood for and better for the Allies, and the British now for it. Tardieu very firm we should make no change. Said the changes proposed by Lloyd George all against France. He said you notice Great Britain does not suggest giving up any ships of German colonies. Said Clemenceau would stand pat; that President Wilson had said nothing while Lloyd George was making his statement at the meeting of the Big Three except took exception to what Lloyd George said about Saar Basin. Tardieu said U.S. and French should stand together and Lloyd George would change his mind again. Before he left he intimated French might discuss reparations changes if only questions of machinery and not of principle but not until Lloyd George withdrew his proposal for concessions, which were— Upper Silesia, period of occupation, League of Nations and Reparations.

At 11:15 went to meeting with the President and the four other U.S. Peace Commissioners and all the U.S. technical advisers in Lansing's office. President presided and spoke of proposals of Lloyd George for concessions in treaty and asked for our opinion on same. Dr. Lord, expert on Poland, saw no reason for changing treaty clauses about Upper Silesia. Our reparations group advocated lump sum, and it was determined we should endeavor to get French to come to our point of view. General Bliss discussed occupation and strongly opposed to 15 years. Said he did not see how occupation could continue after Germany admitted to League of Nations, which was a good point. Dr. Haskins and the President did not think Saar settlement needed modifying. Hoover spoke of necessity of making concessions for expediency sake to get Germany to sign. President said he did not want to be arbitrary, but thought it was not a question of expediency but one of being satisfied in our own consciences that we were doing the just thing and then stick to our demands whatever the result. He said he knew the Treaty was a hard one, but a hard one was needed on this occasion, and what he wanted us to do was to point out any injustice that in our opinion existed. He was quite severe on the British, without mentioning any names, for getting in a state of funk after insisting upon terms which we opposed and now coming around after the Treaty has been handed Germany and proposing concessions. Lloyd George is playing a weak game in my opinion and can only help the Boches [Germans]. The papers are beginning to say he is weakening, and also say they are burning bonfires in Berlin tonight.

Lunched with Countess Limur, nee Crocker, of California.

At 5:00 o'clock met Loucheur and Tardieu. Tried to get them to agree to lump sum. Both of them said they had just seen Clemenceau and he would consider no change until Lloyd George withdrew his proposed concessions. They were positive and very sore at British and begged us to stand with them and said they might discuss reparations with us in a couple of days, after Lloyd George withdrew proposal. We argued a long time for a lump sum. They answered amount of reparations will probably have to be smaller than the claims of the Allies, and when known by the French people they would turn out Ministry. We could not convince them to change their position.

Dined with Mr. and Mrs. Norman Davis at the Meurice, Italian Ambassador and wife, Stettinius, Simons, etc. Party of a dozen.

JUNE 4 (WEDNESDAY)—

Jim Neale and I had a comfortable breakfast. I then went to office before going to President's for meeting of advisers with Big Four to discuss Austrian treaty reparation clause. The Chiefs approved our draft, and just about the time we thought everything O.K., Lloyd George, as usual, changed his mind and made a new proposal for settlement with Jugo-Slavia and Roumania, which threw the whole thing up in the air again and started a general discussion among the separate groups all over the room. We got Lloyd George aside and tried to persuade him to stand by arrangement made, but he thought it was too liberal for Jugo-Slavia and Roumania on account of territory ceded them. What he was really trying to do was to work out a scheme so those countries would get nothing or very little from German reparations and thereby it would be possible to name a smaller lump sum in reparation settlement with Germany. The meeting broke up at 1:00 o'clock and advisers were told to get together again in the afternoon and try to work out a plan. The President seemed tired and told us he had a headache. I don't wonder.

The situation today—Clemenceau standing pat, President firm unless someone can show him mistake in Treaty which causes great injustice, and Lloyd George wobbling all around the lot. His trouble is two schools among his advisers: one for the present Treaty, another group wanting concessions. It is the last crowd always gets him, but he is, in my opinion, coming around to Clemenceau and the President, although they may agree on some concessions as to occupation and reparations, but not very great.

Lunched with advisers at Meurice Hotel. Discussed negotiations entire afternoon. Met Loucheur at 5:30. His plan is to make separate settlement with Italy and small states and, therefore, have less to come out of Germany. I don't see it, but it may work. We have dropped the negotiations with small countries which we have been carrying on and told him to go to it.

Dined with Jim and went to a dance afterwards at the Van Henkelons.

JUNE 5 (THURSDAY)—

A good morning's work in office cleaning up Blockade matters and discussing German proposals with Lamont, Davis and Baruch. Tom Lamont went to see Lloyd George and Loucheur about Lloyd George's new proposals.

Davis, Jim Neale and I lunched at Laurent.

Bakhmeteff called about rifles for the Omsk Government. We have not yet been able to get them released as State Department wants answer from Kolchak.[67]

Lamont, Davis and I went to see the President to tell him about Lloyd George and Loucheur's proposals. They want to postpone for ninety days fixing definite sum suggesting in the interim Germans estimate the cost of their restoring devastated areas and then agree on sum for pensions and other damages—in this way postponing the evil day of telling their people the truth about the small amount they will ultimately receive. Lloyd George and Loucheur agreed to leaving Germany working capital and ships for trade, also to define the constructive duties of the Reparations Commission. Agreed to work on statement to be presented to Germans. Lloyd George anxious for experts to have informal talk. Loucheur says Clemenceau opposed. The President is just as cool and collected as can be, has his nerve right with him. I think we will agree to Lloyd George's proposal if it means a peace, otherwise, we would stand for a fixed sum and the present treaty in toto. He agrees with Lloyd George that a real explanation of the treaty to Huns would probably clear the atmosphere.

Dined with Mrs. Thomas, Mrs. Garrett, Miss Warder, Mrs. Matthews, Colonel Logan, young Warburton, et al., at Madrid Café in the Bois.

JUNE 6 (FRIDAY)—

Jim Neale left for Coblenz for a few days.

Usual morning at office and then at 11:00 met in Seydoux' office with Sir William Thompson to discuss note to Big Four on future blockade plans in regard to Hungary and Bolshevist Russia. After a tiff with Sir William, whose manner at times most overbearing, we agreed on form of note.

Lunched with Dulles. Interviews during the day with advisers and Loucheur on answer to Germans, reparations proposals. Loucheur seems reasonable as to changes but doubts Clemenceau's agreeing. At 5:00 went to office of Klotz to meeting of special committee on answer to German reply, with Lamont and Dulles; also Klotz, Hughes and Morey of Japan

---

67. A dispatch sent from Paris to Omsk by the Big Five in late May had offered assistance to Kolchak provided he agreed to certain conditions. Apparently, his answer had not yet been received. Peter Fleming, *The Fate of Admiral Kolchak* (London: Rupert Hart-Davis, 1963), 135.

present. Hughes and Klotz submitted proposed draft of answer; we submitted comments. It was determined to consider same tomorrow. These meetings wasting time because Big Four now settling things on the side through their advisers.

Dined at Precatelain Café in the Bois with Lamont; dinner to Countess Branbilla. Several titles present, Princess Guicka, Countess ————, Grews' ————, Herters, Miss Beecher, Mrs Shaw, et al. Good party.

Stopped at Mrs. Owen Johnson's party on the way home. Very gay week.

JUNE 7 (SATURDAY)—

Office in morning with meeting of advisers in Lamont's office, on reparations. Davis and I went to Ministry of Finance to attend meeting of special Reparations Commission for answering German note, Klotz presiding. Appointed committee to prepare draft of reply to be submitted at afternoon meeting. Loucheur very amusing about time wasted at these meetings as work being done on the side. He returned to Crillon with us to meet with the United States advisers in my room at lunch as we postponed the regular Saturday lunch on Supreme Economic matters until Monday. We discussed answer and tried to get Loucheur to agree to modification which might be accepted by Huns. Hoover made a strong speech saying present treaty crushes Germany and is unworkable. I think he over-stated as he usually does. Loucheur says he personally agrees with much Hoover said but Clemenceau is adamant and will not give in to important changes. Loucheur agreed to most of our memorandum.

Tom and Bernie went to see Lloyd George to submit our views. Met Bonar Law. The British still very unsettled. Tom thinks they won't consider fixed sum. Bernie thinks they may come [around]. Lamont, Davis, Dulles and I went to Reparation Commission at 5:30. Got nowhere; could not agree on form of draft, differences too fundamental. Adjourned until Monday.

Found Lew Sheldon in my room when I returned. Elizabeth Hudson and I dined at Laurent.

JUNE 8 (SUNDAY)—

An easy morning and a letter home to Mother with an hour at the office after going over Dulles' draft of our proposals as to changes in reparations clauses.

Lunched with Morgenthau and wife at Ritz and afternoon at St. Cloud at golf.

I don't believe really after thinking it over the Big Four will make any modifications. My own opinion is the answer should go back at once and firm with an ultimatum. Lloyd George's wobbling has already weakened the situation in my mind. I don't believe the people of France or England will stand for any modification—any other course will mean a change of Ministry. What the Huns will do nobody knows.

Dined with Count and Countess Branbilla at Hotel Eduard VII, Italian Headquarters. Several Countesses present and the good looking and attractive Princess Guicka of Roumania.

JUNE 9 (MONDAY)—

At 9:30 we went to meeting at Ministry of Finance to hear report of subcommittee on draft of conclusions of Reparations Commission for Big Four which was in the form of a statement showing our differences. We agreed to disagree. Americans for lump sum, British, French and Italians for certain modifications but against a lump sum on account of political reasons in their respective countries because they are afraid to tell their people the truth about the amount they can get out of Germany and still want to put off the evil day. We sent our differences up to Big Four and we went at once to tell President Wilson about the situation so he would be advised. He said he had tried his best to get Clemenceau and Lloyd George to agree to fixed sum but absolutely failed. Lloyd George always said when alone that he thought it was right but when they were together he never supported the President's arguments. It don't [sic] look to me like any serious changes and I think Lloyd George making an awful mistake temporizing and not sending an ultimatum to Huns at once.

Lunched at Mrs. Hyde's with French and Italian titles. There are so many of them about that they seem cheap and common but some people choose them. If I saw much more of this kind I believe I would become a real out and out Socialist.

Hoover, Baruch and I discussed future of Supreme Economic Council and all are unanimous we should not continue its control after peace. Our Allies want us tied up to them; Italy through fear of her other Allies; France for somewhat same reason and hope to use us and Great Britain to hold us down to her level in trade until she gets on her feet as she fears our competition. I am afraid I am getting stale for I am pessimistic these days about the attitude of our Allies. Their leaders are not all grasping but the underlying pressure of self preservation is very strong and their attitude today reminds me of the organization which wants to hold the skilled laborer down to the level of the inefficient and unskilled man. This has left them crippled and they must be helped but not by killing initiative and holding back the production of the enemy countries or any other country.

Attended dinner of Lord Robert Cecil and British members of Supreme Economic Council to their fellow members. Lord Robert, Clementel, Hoover, Crespi and Cartier made speeches. All very gloomy about future outlook and revolutionary tendency in world. Lord Robert's speech was opening gun for continuing Allied organization. He made quite a radical speech for a Salisbury and conservative leader in England and urged fair treatment of labor classes. He is emotional, fair and just but at times goes off half cocked and the more I see of him I am not quite sure always of his judgment but believe him to be sincere.

JUNE 10 (TUESDAY)—

An informal talk in my office when Lamont, Baruch and Davis dropped in to discuss attacks in the United States Senate on the leak of the Peace Treaty in the hands of New York bankers and the subpoenaing of Lamont, trying to involve Morgan & Company.

Lunched with Eugene Meter of War Finance Corporation, just from Washington to study financial situation here for couple of weeks, also Hoover, Baruch, McDowell and Sumner.

At 3:30 went to meeting of Supreme Economic Council, very full meeting. Indications of something important being up. Lord Robert brought up question of continuing Supreme Economic Council after peace, and removal to London. United States opposed action and after heated debate we referred entire matter to special committee which will report in two weeks. Lord Robert very much disappointed as he leaves for London tomorrow and wanted to carry Council back with him. I am more convinced than ever that we want to move slowly as what Europe needs is freedom of action and to learn to stand on its own bottom, cut out paternalism and let the economic laws assert themselves. I believe they will all come to this but mentally they are still in the old war days and can't adjust themselves to normal peace times.

Another interesting and intense moment was when Lloyd George cleared the room of all the delegates, except the members of the Supreme Economic Council, when the Italian coal question came up for discussion, and told the Italians of the many reports concerning Italy sending in arms to Bolshevist Hungary for use against the Czecho-Slavs. Of course

Crespi denied it and agreed to investigate. Rumor has it Italy already playing with Germany, Austria and Hungary to build up a barrier between Czecho-Slovakia and Jugo-Slavia. From all signs it looks like troublesome times ahead for that part of Europe for many days to come.

Dined at Whitridges with Lady Edward Cecil. Whitridges now living in Lizzie Camerson's old apartment. Also a Miss Towne, just returned from visiting Lizzie C., adopted niece of Henry Adams, and other guests.

When I got to my room found final proposal of Big Four in answer to the Germans on reparations clauses which we are to read over night and comment on in the morning to the President. I saw the fixed sum eliminated, which I regret, but which I knew Clemenceau would never agree to. Lloyd George had not enough courage in the matter, so I suppose this is the best that can be done. The important thing now is to get it in the hands of the Huns at the earliest possible date.

June 11 (Wednesday)—

Bernie, Tom Lamont, Davis and I had another talk over final proposed answer to Germans on reparations which was sent us by the President. Lamont also discussed his troubles about the leak of Peace Treaty. He is considerably worried, but was greatly pleased by a letter from the President showing his confidence in him. I told Tom that was always the way— the Chief stood by his friends, and I could see Tom was deeply affected.

Bernie and I lunched with Princess Guicka II, a former American, to meet a Roumanian General.

Heard after lunch Big Four had agreed on Reparations answer to Huns and all other clauses would be ready by tomorrow night, so Germans will have answer and ultimatum Friday morning.

Dined with Morgenthaus to meet Lausannes; father, mother and daughter, he the leading man on *The Matin,* and like more French newspapermen anti-American. Met Bishop Darlington in America and quite enthusiastic about him; the Bishop had evidently told him a great deal about his own greatness. Madame Lausanne told me that the Bishop had said his ambition was to preach in the Notre Dame, because he liked the Catholics so much better than his own Church. Nicholson, English expert on Balkans, also at dinner. He had heated and interesting argument on Peace Treaty, European politics, etc. I had an opportunity to tell Lausanne some plain truths about the reaction taking place in America due to French criticism of President and our country. Henry Morgenthau rambled on in his usual easy manner, not always accurate and most indiscreet.

JUNE 12 (THURSDAY)—

An easy day before me. Jim and I loafed at breakfast. Our blockade work all over and resting on our oars as to blockade until we know what the Huns are going to do. Interviewed Edwards, our Holland War Trade Board representative from The Hague, about blockade matters.

Lunched with Davis. Played golf with Jim, Lamont and Davis.

Jim, Sumner and I dined and went to show. I will stay around for couple of days cleaning up details and then will probably go to Coblenz awaiting German answer. French think now Germans will sign. Everybody guessing; nobody knows.

Colonel House leaves today to get League of Nations started at London.

President expects to make short trip to Belgium after answer in hands of Germans, probably Saturday or Sunday.

JUNE 13 (FRIDAY)—

While Jim and I were eating breakfast in our cozy apartment I was called upon the phone and told the President wanted to see economic advisers at 10:00 A.M., before the 11:00 o'clock meeting of the Big Four, now the Big Five, as the Japanese joined Council this morning. When we, that is, Baruch, Hoover, Davis, Lamont and I, arrived the President told us Lloyd George was again arguing importance of Allied control of all purchases of foodstuffs, otherwise prices would get too high and European countries ruined. President, of course, opposed to principle, but wanted our opinion and practical arguments against same. We strongly advocated no price control and no Inter-Allied combination. The President said he thought Allies would do collective buying in any event and wondered how we could break it. Baruch and I did not think it would last as it would defeat itself. Hoover said that Lloyd George should be told that if they attempt to control and lower food prices the production would fall off seriously, and he feared the result. The President said Lloyd George never argued from real hard facts, but depended on his eloquence. He said he made him mad by intimating we were not willing to join because we wanted higher prices for our food. He said he and Lloyd George had a hot argument and Lloyd George later apologized for his insinuation.

The President seemed just as calm and clearheaded as though he were not passing through the most anxious days of the Conference. He discussed calmly the report of the Germans' refusal to sign and I think we all feel that the present delegates will not sign. He said Pershing told him some of the British generals proposed dropping bombs on the German cities. He was very indignant about it and said our soldiers would not stand for that kind of tactics and he would order them home if they did. We left the Chief so we could go into the Big Five meeting. He said the answer would not be ready before Monday or Tuesday, and then five days for the Huns and the story is told.

Lunched with Robert Bliss; guests, Hoover, Lamont, Davis, General Squires, Wood, Minister to Tiflis; Coolidge, just from Vienna; General Allen, and others.

Golf at St. Cloud-Davis, Dulles, Jim and I.

Dined at Ritz with Jim, afterward went to Mrs. Rutherford Stuyvesant's dance with Miss Elsie DeWolf and Mrs. Ogden Mills. Weird people and gowns, many of the most undesirable type of French society frequently seen at such functions. Met Nicholson there, of British delegation, Balkan expert. Very bitter against Lord Sumner; said he influenced Lloyd George and made treaty clauses too drastic; said all British delegation against Sumner. Keynes gone home. I asked him why Lloyd George listened to Sumner rather than others. Said Lloyd George listens to Parliament, and I was interested to have him say what President Wilson said today, that Lloyd George and Clemenceau seem to be making a treaty for their Parliaments and not one which represented their people because the present British Government was an accident and does not represent Great Britain's thought. The President is convinced that the Parliaments don't represent the opinion of the countries. He can't make a fight in the open for the things he wants because it will show a divided Council and can only help the Germans who are waiting for a split.

JUNE 14 (SATURDAY)—

After cleaning up routine in office, I attended the final meeting of the Blockade Council on preparations for re-imposing blockade in event the governments decided it wise to do so. The machinery is all set and we are ready to shoot. I hope it may not be necessary. I am convinced that military occupation is the real thing and blockade unnecessary.

Lunched with advisers in my room—General Bliss, Admiral Knapp, Hoover, Baruch, Davis, B. Palmer present. Hot discussion on treaty and blockade. Hoover and Bliss think it too hard; Baruch and I think it just and workable. Hoover says if blockade imposed he will resign. I find Hoover very exaggerated talker and premises not always accurate.

Bakhmeteff called about recognition of Kolchak. Feels the action of Big Four not recognition. Very anxious to have Morris go to Omsk.[68] I believe myself it was a pity to recall him.

Played tennis with Mrs. Garrett and niece, Miss Thoron, and Jim, at St. Cloud.

Dined at grandee dinner of Mr. and Mrs. J. Ridgley Carter, private room at the Ritz; Italian Ambassador Imperiali and wife, Rachel Hale's old friend; Grecian Minister and wife, formerly Miss Cockrell, American, daughter of former Missouri Senator, very pretty; Sir Ian Malcolm and wife, Duchess ———, Gratz, Duchess ———, and Kahn [sic], the Mohammedan God; Mrs. Garrett, Mrs. House and Mrs. Harjes, formerly Miss Berwind, and most attractive. A very refreshing gathering after last night's dance with the Rothschilds et al. of the dancing set.

Jim and I after dinner put on our best and started for the soiree of their Royal Highnesses, Duke and Duchess Vendome, she being the sister of the King of Belgium. We were so late in arriving we found everyone had gone home except the family, and as we did not want to be received alone, although we had entered the hall, we turned tail and ignominiously ran for home, much to the surprise of the dignified servants, who must have thought we were housebreakers, as they followed us to our taxi, but we never stopped to explain.

JUNE 15 (SUNDAY)—

A late breakfast with Jim, then church at the American Church, and we found ourselves in the same pew with Miss Clara Alricks, whom we took for a little drive in the Bois after church. She is just as uncertain as ever about oging home and talks now of spending the summer here. I urged her to go home at once, but I am afraid without avail.

Lunched with Mrs. Hyde, Jack Ridgely Carters, Princess Guicka, Walter Berry and Commodore Nelson and wife. Went to Elsie DeWolf's beautiful house she shares with Miss Anne Morgan at Versailles for afternoon party. Topped at Tirer-au-Pigeon to play tennis with Mr. Balfour. We sat around on the grass for almost an hour waiting for a court without getting one, so we had to postpone our game until tomorrow afternoon. He is a delightful gentleman, kind and affable always, even under disappoint-

---

68. Roland S. Morris was the ambassador to Japan but spent some time at Vladivostok and was involved with the Russians because of U.S. involvement with the Trans-Siberian Railroad.

ment. Sir Ian Malcolm, his secretary, is very anxious to come to America on diplomatic missions. He is a nice fellow with a beautiful wife, and I hope he lands.

Jim, Sheldon and I dined together at Ritz.

Answer will probably go to Huns tomorrow afternoon.

Met Louis Slade at church; hope to have Carrie and him lunch with me tomorrow.

JUNE 16 (MONDAY)—

Jim had Henry pack for him, thinking he was going to London with Lew Sheldon to sail from England. He found later he could get sailing at Brest about the middle of week, so changed plans.

I cleaned up work in office, as Hale was sick. Met Leeds Anwyll just outside of Crillon. Looked very well and said he was getting ready to close up at Nevers.

Lunched with Louis and Carrie Slade.

Went to meeting of Supreme Economic Council at 3:00; Clementel presiding, as Lord Robert Cecil has gone to England. Nothing very important on agenda. While there called by messenger to President's house on Austrian reparations. Waited some time while the Military, Foch, Bliss and General Wilson with Big Four were discussing military plans of occupation if Germans don't sign. When we all went into room we found it getting late and the Chiefs were anxious to get out, so after brief discussion of question in dispute, namely, settlement with small nations, Poland, etc., and questions of disposition of private property in ceded territory, both referred to small committee for drafting, principles having been agreed to in latter case.

Big Five want everything ready by tomorrow for Austrian treaty. Grayson told us President wanted us to go to Belgium with him tomorrow night. Orlando not present today, Sonnino substituting. Japan present now.

The big fellows are ending strong, their spirits and courage unshaken, and they have come through a most trying six months in most friendly and cooperative manner which only big men could do. Have their scraps and differences, making their apologies to each other and going at it again and, I believe, with really a liking for each other.

Everyone here disgusted with the partisanship of Knox and Lodge et al.[69] It must certainly soon begin to react at home.

Played tennis at 6:30 with Balfour, Sir Ian Malcolm and Baruch. Very close today.

Dined at Madrid with Colonel Logan, Mrs. Thomas, Duchess of Sutherland, Mrs. Ogden Mills, Mrs. Mathews, et al.

JUNE 17 (TUESDAY)—

An uneventful morning in office. A call from the Norwegian Minister to France about mail censorship from the United States to Norway. Was glad to tell him all mail censorship removed after June 21.

Talked with Secretary Lansing about future plans of War Trade Board which we turn over to State Department June 30, and also about again taking up with President the sending of Morris to Omsk notwithstanding agreement with Kolchalk [sic] because he can pick up most valuable information and could give good advice to Omsk Government as to United States aims and purposes. Lansing asked me to talk to President at first opportunity about this matter.

Jim Neale and I lunched with Auberts and Miss Chovet, of Buenos Aires. Office in the afternoon and tea with Grempels.

Dined at Ritz at dinner given by Reily and McDowell to Callaway, cotton manufacturer, Lagrange, Ga.

At 10:30 P.M. went to station with Baruch to join President's party to Belgium.[70] In the party were President and Mrs. Wilson, Miss Margaret Wilson, Miss Benham, Admiral Grayson, General Harts, Baron de Cartier, Minister of Belgium to United States, and Secretary Hoover, Baruch, Davis, Commander Baker, Lieutenant Irving and several aides and newspaper men and self. Complete train, consisting of President's car, compartment cars and diner. Every man his own compartment and most comfortable.

JUNE 18 (WEDNESDAY)—

I got up early, at 7:30, as I wanted to see Dunkirk which so barely escaped capture and was frequently bombarded. It was a short ride from Dunkirk to Adinkerque where we were met with much ceremony by the King and Queen and their retinue. The station platform was covered with carpets and lined with flowers and with many flags flying. The Queen's guard were lined up the entire length of the platform and a military band played "The Star Spangled Banner" as we drew into the station. The King

---

69. In his diary, Colonel House states that he had wanted to recommend the appointment of Republicans Knox (Pennsylvania) and Knute Nelson (Minnesota) to the Peace Commission as a method of guaranteeing congressional support for the treaty.

70. The French and Belgians had wanted Wilson to make this trip before negotiations began so that he could witness firsthand the devastating results of the war. He was criticized for delaying the trip. Seymour, *Intimate Papers*, 4:243.

and Queen walked along the platform to the President's car, followed by the Burgomaster and town council, who have the formal welcome. After introductions all around we were then put in automobiles and started for the front line trenches. I was glad to be in a car alone with Brand Whitlock as I had an opportunity for a good talk with him. I find he had formed the same opinion about the French as had I, which after six months negotiating was not very complimentary, we agreeing that their besetting sin was avarice; courageous and brave to a degree, give their lives for their property but will not stand taxation. We could not quite explain the propaganda against Wilson and the United States which they have been carrying on in the press of France and Belgium.

We were driving through the little bit of Flanders that the Belgians kept out of the hands of the Germans and skirted their line of trenches and by the flooded lands which held back the enemy. Our first stop was at Nieuport after passing through Fairnes at which place the King explained to us the plan of flooding of the land by the control of the tide with flood gates. It was the King who determined that the Belgium [sic] army should make the final stand at Nieuport. He said he would rather lose his army than be driven from Belgium soil so they held out until relieved by the French and British with only a remnant of their original army left.[71] The country we passed through was the typical battle front, a frightful scene of desolation and destruction, not a house standing, villages completely effaced, no trees left and ground literally covered with shell holes.

From Nieuport we passed through Dixmude and stopped at Ouken which was on a hill with a commanding view and held by the Germans against repeated assault until driven out in 1918. Then to the Forest of Houthult where we stopped for lunch. This Forest was the scene of some of the fiercest fighting of the war. The British and French made several unsuccessful attempts to dislodge the Germans and it was only in the drive of 1918 that the Belgians drove them out of the woods.

Here in the middle of the woods we had our picnic lunch; an awning was spread over the table and the King and Queen were as informal as could be and entered into the spirit of the occasion and we had a good opportunity of becoming acquainted. They are most gracious, simple in their manners and most democratic, and you can see why they are so

---

71. With sixty thousand men, the Belgian Army held its position along the Yser, until Belgian king Albert decided to flood the area after they had lost another twenty thousand men. After the sluices were opened to let in the sea, the area was impassable between Nieuport and Dixmude.

beloved by their people. We had a very simple lunch of cold chicken, sandwiches, salad, cake and strawberries, usual white and red wine, mineral water and coffee.

After an hour's rest we started for Ypres. I found at this time the Belgians had forgotten to feed the U.S. newspaper boys and they were very sore.

Ypres was the usual devastated town, more so if possible. Halles, which the guide book says is the most considerable edifice of its kind in Belgium, a complete ruin, the Cloth Hall, Town Hall and Cathedral all gone. Still many British soldiers about as they are still in control of zone and we saw them directing hundreds of German prisoners in cleaning up the battle fields and picking up unexploded shells.

From Ypres to Menin, then North through Roulers and Thourout and Bruges towards Ostend. Our car broke down and we missed main party so gave up Ostend and made direct line for Zeebrugge where we arrived ahead of party which gave us time for cup of tea at café on roadside.

President and King had the usual reception at each place, the school children always playing a prominent part.

We drove out on the Mole and were received by British Naval Officers and Captain Carpenter of the *Vindictive,* who explained their bold attempt to close the channel, which was thrilling. We saw some of the sunken ships still in place although others have been removed and they were at work while we were there. They also showed us the marks on the Mole where the grappling irons caught.[72]

I was glad again to meet Captain Evans of the Destroyer *Broke* who did such gallant work when with the *Broke* and another destroyer he captured six German destroyers.[73] He carried the House Commission over the channel in 1917 at which time I met him.

---

72. On April 23, 1918, the British Navy had staged a two-part raid on Zeebrugge. Marines landed on the Mole to created a diversionary action, while three ships filled with concrete were maneuvered in place and sunk at the entrance to the Brugges Canal to block the waterway against use by German U-boats. The *Vindictive* was used to rescue personnel after the mission was completed. Under extremely heavy German artillery fire, many lives were lost, but the mission was considered successful by the Allies. After the war, several U-boats were found trapped in the canal, and it took salvage crews twelve months to clear it.

73. On April 20–21, 1917, two six-ship groups of German destroyers sailed into the Straits of Dover to bombard Dover and Calais. Two British ships, *Broke* and *Swift* were on patrol and engaged the German ships in battle. The *Broke* rammed German ship G-42, and the British sailors were forced to fight hand-to-hand to repel the German sailors who attempted to board her. German ships G-42 and G-85 were sunk at the Goodwin Sands, and *Broke* was towed back to port. Both *Broke* and *Swift* were awarded battle honors for the engagement.

Here we took our special train again en route to Brussels. We had a most interesting day and were charmed with our host and hostess. The President and King always rode together in one car and Mrs. Wilson, the Queen and Miss Wilson in another, the rest of us following without any particular order except Hoover, who is much beloved for his great relief work, and always had the place of honor. Baruch, Davis and I had much merriment over our ranking which while Ministerial was sometimes obscure in the minds of some of the aides and I don't blame them.

We all had dinner in the train and arrived in Brussels at 9:00 o'clock. The usual elaborate reception at the station, carpets, plants, flowers, band, soldiers lined from the cars to the street and then along both sides of the street from the station to the Palace, the streets crowded with people behind the troops, who gave most enthusiastic welcome. Hoover, Baruch, Davis and I went to the Astoria leaving the President and Mrs. Wilson at the Palace.

We soon dropped our "royal manners" and went out on the town to the Savoy Café for late supper before turning in.

At 9:00 the next morning we went over to the Palace to join the President and King, the ladies remaining at home, who led us a wild ride at over fifty miles an hour down to Charleroi passing by the battlefield of Waterloo. At Providence, a suburb of Charleroi, we saw some of the destroyed iron and steel plants. Every piece of machinery removed by the Germans and that which could not be removed blown up. A deliberate attempt to ruin a competitor. This destruction more appalling than that due to military action. Immense crowds at works and most enthusiastic. Typical laboring people, well behaved and no signs of starvation, in fact, I was surprised to see the healthy condition of the Belgians and particularly the bright, cheerful faces of the children.

The King and the President without special precautions walked about among the works, surrounded by the people in a most informal and democratic manner. The President was very much impressed. He was shown about by the local committee wearing high hats and frock coats and to see this committee with the King and President climbing over debris and destroyed blast furnaces was a unique sight and one long to be remembered.

Back from Charleroi at break neck speed, we arrived dusty and dirty.

After lunch we joined the party at the Palace and were driven to the House of Deputies where they were to receive the President. We entered the Chamber by one of the side doors with the Queen and Mrs. Wilson, while the President entered with the King from the other side of the hall, preceded by the troops carrying the colors which took their places on a raised platform behind the speaker's desk and stood during the ceremony, making a picturesque sight.

The President of the Deputies made a speech of welcome as did also Foreign Minister Hymans which the President answered in an excellent speech, showing how the Belgians' desecration aroused the world and gave birth to the League of Nations. Also received applause when he said he would ask Congress to raise our Minister to an Ambassador. After speech the entire Chamber remained standing while we all proceeded out to the cars and started off to Malines on another wild auto ride of about an hour. Every small town gave us a warm welcome as we flew by—flags flying and children yelling, Vive la Wilson, Vive la Roi, Vive la Reine.

The entire country bursting with crops and beautiful. Farmers making hay. Only thing not prosperous [was] manufacturing towns and in them there was very little smoke coming out of the chimneys.

We soon saw the steeple of the Cathedral of Malines, the seat of the Primate, and soon we were driving through thousands of people lining the streets, the greatest demonstration yet. A delightful old city of narrow streets. We drove right to the home of Cardinal Mercier and there had a most enjoyable tea with him; a charming personality, with a kindly and gentle face and most hospitable. While we were having tea the old Malines chimes were played for our benefit, most famous in Belgium and very beautiful and this was the first concert since the war and was called "Carillon," a concert by Jef Denyon.

After tea we said goodbye to the Cardinal and started out through the cheering crowds en route to Louvain, here to pass through the same crowds up to the town hall where we were formally welcomed by the Burgomaster in a set speech of welcome which the President answered for his third. We were then presented to the Alderman and shown to the Hotel de Ville. We next proceeded on foot to the destroyed Library of Louvain, part of the University and there took place the most impressive ceremony of the day.[74] While standing in ruins with only the sky above

---

74. On August 25, 1914, German troops set fire to the streets and buildings of Louvain, and after three days of fire and looting, the university's library, which had housed a treasure trove of old paintings, manuscripts, and books, had been burned out, along with more than a thousand other buildings. The world united in condemning the German Army for this unprecedented assault, and committees were formed to collect money and books to restore the library, including a committee officially created by the Paris Peace Conference.

the President of the University in gown, surrounded by the University officials, conferred upon the President the degree of Doctor of Civil Law. The President answered with a gem of a speech, inspired by the surroundings and occasion. He was much impressed by the deliberate and wanton destruction of the former old library which his University training made him feel keenly.

Everywhere Mrs. Wilson was presented with flowers.

The King and Queen were delightful in their anxiety to always keep the President and Mrs. Wilson to the fore and you could see their desire was that the welcome should be for the President. It was evident everywhere the deep affection the people have for their Sovereigns and I don't blame them as they certainly grow on you.

From Louvain we dashed for Brussels as we were fifteen minutes behind our schedule. We were due at 6:00 o'clock at the Hotel de Ville, Brussels, and were welcomed by the Burgomaster [sic] and Aldermen and a great sight it was, a fitting climax of many official welcomes. We drove into the old market place or Grand Place of the Hotel de Ville with its delightful old Flemish houses, one of the finest medieval squares in existence, and found there a hollow square formed by the troops behind which were thousands of enthusiastic people and every window crowded, making it easy to picture the old festivals and tournaments for which the Square was famous in the olden days.

In the hall the ceremony was impressive, all the diplomatic corps being present. The usual address of welcome by the Burgomaster and reply by the President. Then to another room where the President and Mrs. Wilson, King and Queen and Hoover signed the golden book. Refreshments were quickly served so we could pass out on the Royal Balcony, overlooking the Square, which was decorated with red and gold plush drapings.

When the President and King appeared a great shout went up and from across the Square on a balcony of the Maison du Roi, directly opposite, a number of trombones started to play and were answered by a similar band from our building. Then the large military band played "The Star Spangled Banner" and "Marseillaise." This was followed with music by two large men's choral societies, several hundred voices and I never heard anything more inspiring. The whole sight was thrilling and made me fill up and I found I was not the only one because I saw as President Wilson walked off the Balcony into the room his eyes were filled with tears.

Brussels had done itself proud and this reception was a fitting climax to an eventful day of public receptions.

We returned to the Palace and then hurried off to dress for the Court banquet at 8:00 o'clock. When we arrived at the Palace and were depositing our hats and coats, they told us to take our high hats with us upstairs as it was Court etiquette to carry them with you. We found ourselves in a large reception room where a number of dignitaries were waiting. We, that is, Hoover, Baruch, Davis and I, were at once taken into another room where we found about twenty distinguished guests such as Cardinal Mercier, and others. Here we waited the arrival of the President and Mrs. Wilson, and the King and Queen. They soon arrived and we all stood behind them while the other hundred guests were then admitted into the large reception room to pass before them in single file, having each name read off as they were presented, and then passed on into the next room. After this greeting the King and Mrs. Wilson and the President and the Queen led the procession into the large dining hall and what a beautiful sight it was—tables, set for 150 guests, covered with nothing but beautiful silver service which had been presented by Queen Victoria to Leopold, and pink roses. I never have seen more beautiful decorations or in better taste. The President and King sat side by side, Queen on President's right and Mrs. Wilson on the left. The little Queen was looking pretty tired by this time and I don't blame her after two strenuous days. I was well placed between a Baron ———— and Madame Frank, the latter most attractive, wife of Colonial Minister, and spoke English perfectly. A waiter for nearly every diner and you had to eat fast to keep up to the waiter. All palace attendants in gorgeous crimson coats and short breeches.

Dinner quickly served and we repaired to reception room where guests were taken up to speak to King and Queen and President and Mrs. Wilson, one by one. This did not last long as we had to leave at 10:30 for train. The King and Queen were most cordial as usual and as we started to bid farewell they announced that they were going to the station to see us off, which they did, and they could not have given us a better send off and made us believe they were really sorry to see us go, and the last we saw of them was standing on the platform as the train pulled out waving a good old fashioned democratic farewell. The party was certainly to my way of thinking, a most congenial one and we flattered ourselves by believing that they would like to have seen more of us.

We were ready for bed and did not waste much time in getting into our berths.

June 20 (Friday)—
We arrived in Paris at 9:00 A.M. and when I arrived in my room at the Ritz I found it filled with flowers, a wrist watch from Jim Neale and a cake from Henry in honor of my birthday which I had forgotten was the day before. I also found a cable from home at my office.

I had a very busy time at the office catching up.

Lunched with Jim at Laurent. Late in the afternoon at my room in Ritz I was called upon by Colonel Recant, one of Marshal Foch's aides during the war, now with Tardieu, who presented me with my certificate of appointment as a Commander of the Legion of Honor and also the Order.

Jim and I dined at Madrid with Mrs. Harriman and had quite a quiet evening in the Bois.

June 21 (Saturday)—
All the news we have been getting from Germany is good. The Scheidemann Government has fallen and our advices are that the new government will appoint new delegates who will sign.

This morning the reparations advisers had a new note from the Germans to answer in regard to whether the note in answer to their proposals would be embodied in treaty as a protocol or would be binding in present form. We were all called before the Big Four on these questions and it was decided to put same in protocol and other would stand as bringing instructions to Commission. The big room in the President's house was full of experts trying to settle eleventh-hour problems on Austria, etc. There seemed to be great confusion, and I am always fearful on these occasions of our French and British colleagues putting over some of their pet schemes in the midst of the confusion. Orlando was missing as his Ministry fell a few days ago, but Sonnino was on the job.

I had an interesting talk with Bakhmeteff about Russian matters. He asked some very pertinent questions about real meaning of Kolchak's recognition, and I promised to get definite reply from President.

Lunched with the Economic advisers. Talked with Dr. Taylor, just back from Vienna, Warsaw and Prague; still disgusted with lack of trade; says military have situation tied up as badly as though strict blockade still on.

Played tennis at St. Cloud with Mrs. Garrett and niece and Jack Carter.

Dined with Garretts. I think most of the U.S. foreign diplomats have been here or are coming, trying for Italian Ambassadorship, soon to be vacant.

Went to Majestic Hotel with Davis, Baruch and Lamont for Saturday night dance.

JUNE 22 (SUNDAY)—

Slept late, and then to church at the American Church. Harry McCormick's classmate, Chauncey Goodrich, preached.

After lunch went to opening of new Pershing Stadium with Mrs. Harriman; most impressive sight, forty thousand people. President Poincare, Pershing, Cabinet Officers, Peace Delegates and many other celebrities, but the soldiers and similar decorations; thousands of children lining the streets and singing of different nations aroused the enthusiasm of the crowd as they passed by, and our troops were magnificent. The athletes of the Allied nations all paraded by and made an attractive show.[75]

I dined at Meurice with Davis, Hoover and Baruch to determine policy concerning U.S. attitude on continuing Supreme Economic Council. We were all a unit in agreeing it should be abolished, although we thought we had better not make definite announcement as to our position until after peace treaty signed. We are all convinced it is only a question of a few days now. The change of Ministry and vote of the Assembly have made it certain.

The sinking of the German ships the chief topic of conversation everywhere; the French are furious and rather blame the British. The British are sheepish about it, but really it is a good thing, in my opinion, because it clears up a serious question, although you can't say so openly. It also shows the crookedness of the Germans—most characteristic.[76]

JUNE 23 (MONDAY)—

Attended meeting of Supreme Economic Council at Ministry of Commerce. May be my last. Clementel presiding. Discussed blockade matters pertaining to Hungary and Bolshevist Russia, also Hoover relief plans. Italians tried to explain shipment of arms to Hungary to fight Jugo-Slavia,

---

75. Gen. John Pershing believed that linguistic and cultural barriers could be broken on the sports field and organized this friendly competition, which in the end involved fifteen hundred military athletes from eighteen nations and five continents, who competed in twenty-four sports. Similar games were held in 1948 following World War II.

76. At Scapa Flow on June 21, German crews under the command of Adm. Ludwig von Reuter scuttled the German fleet, consisting of about five hundred thousand tons. This act of naval defiance kept the German ships from Allied possession and negated many hours of diplomatic wrangling, solidifying a punitive attitude on the part of Allied leaders.

also shipments of gold to Vienna to pay for Italian food. Explanations not satisfactory, but plausible. Attitude of meeting was one of liquidating organization. We all believe Treaty will be signed by Wednesday.

Lunched with Mrs. Linda Thomas, Duchess of Sutherland, Marquis and Marquise Polignac and an English officer, friend of the Duchess.

At 2:45 went to keep appointment at "White House." Discussed with President his understanding as to meaning of the Kolchak correspondence. He said the papers had interpreted it as being a recognition of the Kolchak Government, which it was not, but only making certain conditions under which they would continue to send supplies and munitions to the anti-Bolshevist forces. I argued the difficulty of furnishing money unless you could recognize some governmental obligation, particularly in Siberia for railroad development. He agreed with me the importance of telling Congress the whole story and said he would appeal for funds upon his return, as he also recognized the opportunity of a great constructive program in aiding Russia through Siberian road and keeping open door by preventing Japan from creating sphere of influence and monopolizing Siberia, which will also jeopardize Chinese interests.

He asked me to prepare a cable for him stating reasons why Roland Morris should go to Omsk, which I had advocated; also plan for financing Siberian road.

Just as I was going out Herbert Hoover was coming in and he asked me to remain. We discussed the question of maintaining Supreme Economic Council after signing of peace treaty. President agreed with us it should be abolished and agreed he would have to go to the U.S. to talk with Department heads before discussing any new Inter-Allied organization. We all discussed Russia; President said in answer to Hoover's statement that Russia could not rehabilitate itself without economic aid, which should be given without political interference; that it was impossible for an Inter-Allied body to give such aid without getting mixed up in politics to some extent, which is true, considering who Allies are. The President further said the Russian people must solve their own problems without outside interference and that Europe had made a great mistake when they attempted to interfere in the French Revolution. He said it seems hard on the present Russian generation, but in the long run it means less distress for Russia, and I believe he is right.

He told us of his having turned down the request of the Germans for forty-eight hours more time to consider Treaty and said in three hours we will know the answer, it then being nearly 4:00 o'clock.

He said the French and British were wildly excited about the sinking of the German ships and he had spent the entire morning trying to hold down Lloyd George and Clemenceau to reason, as they were figuring what else they could get out of the Germans in payment for their loss, and he said most confidentially that the British and himself were relieved by the sinking of the ships of a most embarrassing question, as the French wanted some of the German ships for their own navy.

Returned to office. In a short time was told by Conger that Germany had agreed to sign.

Went out on the boulevards, as the celebrating had begun. Soon the cannons were firing salutes and the streets began to fill up with happy people, as to them it now looked as though the war was really over and the soldiers would not have to advance into Germany tonight, but could return home.

Dined at Madrid Café in the Bois. Had as guests the Auberts, Mademoiselle Chovet, of Argentine, and Grempels.

All the people very happy; band played national airs and everyone sang and danced. Miss Wilson joined us later to dance. Coming home the boulevards crowded with cheering crowds, singing and pulling around the streets the captured cannon. Soldiers and girls having good time. It looked like an all-night celebration.

JUNE 24 (TUESDAY)—

We began to plan for home and the closing up of our work here, and we are wondering now whether the Commission and President will let us go or make us stay for the completion of the Austria-Hungary treaty.

I attended a meeting of the Blockade Council to plan for dissolving it and to make arrangements to cancel all neutral agreements at the signing of peace. We did not complete our work, so arranged for last meeting for next day. I was instructed to try to get a definite answer from Heads of States as to the date of signing and date of pulling down the blockade.

I caught the President at the Crillon after meeting with the Commissioners and asked him to bring up the question at the next meeting of the "Chiefs." He said he thought it bad policy to do so, as Clemenceau was in such a rage at the action of the Germans in sinking the fleet and lowering the flags that he was having great difficulty in preventing him from making war again on the Germans, and that this was the wrong time to submit the question of removing the blockade.

I lunched with Bainbridge Colby, who gave me the inside of many matters concerning Shipping Board. I cannot understand how Hurley has held on as long as he has and why the President does not see through him. We are riding for a fall soon if he stays in office much longer.

Just before lunch I had a talk with Lansing, who told me he might go home and let Polk come to take his place, as he said Frank [Polk] had broken down and must be relieved, and he thought the trip might be helpful. He said the State Department was being badly broken up, as Phillips wanted to go and other changes were contemplated and he ought to be home to make his plans for the future. He asked me what I thought of getting Roland Morris to take Frank Polk's place. I told him he could not get a better men, but doubted if he would accept. He wondered if Frank would take Belgium, as Whitlock was going to Italy. I told him when we got home that I would be on call at Harrisburg if anything turned up in which I could help upon any of the hangovers of the war, and would be glad to run down if he needed me. He seemed very grateful and I am afraid he will need help after Polk goes.

I notice now all the Mission conferences are held in Lansing's office and not in House's as early in conference, and the Colonel is not permitted to monopolize the "Chief" as much as he and Gordon would like.

I had a busy afternoon working on Russian cable with Dulles for the Chief, and other War Trade Board matters and did not leave the office until nearly 7:30.

Dined at Ritz with Baron de Cartier, Belgium Minister. Dinner for Miss Margaret Wilson. Mrs. Carey, Mrs. Brooks, Mrs. Harriman, Miss Benham et al. Bernie and I got some music afterwards and we had a little dance.

JUNE 25 (WEDNESDAY)—

At 9:30 met Sir William Mitchell Thompson to go over with him resolution for pulling down the entire blockade. Meeting with Davis, Lamont, Dulles and Baruch on Bulgarian reparation clauses. We agreed to oppose effort of Allies to have commission of British, French and Italians take over the customs and taxes to collect reparations and insisted that these be turned over to the reparation commission also against right of any country having monopoly of commerce.

Made a settlement this morning with Benes of Czecho-Slovakia in regard to their share of the cost of the war in consideration of their liberation under Austrian Treaty if Poland, Roumania and Jugo-Slavia agree to our proposal that the reparation clauses are complete. It is another case of where the Allies have gone back to the original proposition we made for a settlement after wobbling all over the lot in the usual L. G. [Lloyd George] style.

Bernie, Davis and I lunched together. At 2:00 o'clock went to Lansing's office to have photograph taken with the President, Commission, advisers and experts.

President told me again today Clemenceau still too hot to bring up date of pulling down blockade. He said also he thought the Treaty would not be signed until Saturday as the German delegates would not get here until Friday morning and their credentials would have to be most carefully scrutinized. He said he wanted to talk over with us tomorrow our future plans as to staying or going home with him. I think I can convince him my work is over in Paris and I can accomplish more at home.

Perfected my plans for liquidating War Trade Board affairs here; Gaulin takes charge at embassy. Dr. Taylor and Hale will be here until about July 15 so can determine any questions of policy that might arise.

At 5:00 P.M. went to last meeting of Allied Blockade Council. Agreed upon resolution for cancellation of Neutral Agreements and had farewell speeches from the heads of different delegations, expressing our appreciation of cordial and harmonious co-operation that existed and regrets at the severance of associations that have been so agreeable under difficult and trying circumstances. I was particularly sorry to say "Good Bye" to Mr. Seydoux, the French representative, who is paralyzed and walks with great difficulty but a man of courage and great ability and in my opinion perfectly honest and fair. He is one of the ablest men in the French Foreign Office and has been a big factor in helping to win the war in a modest and unobtrusive manner.

Had tea with the Auberts in their attractive home, Rue Vanlau, their garden overlooking the old Austrian Embassy. Dined at Pre Catelan.

JUNE 26 (THURSDAY)—

Busy morning in my office getting everything in shape for my departure if President says we can go Saturday with him, after signing of the Peace Treaty.

I was invited by the heads of the Armenian Delegation, Norve and Mr. Malcolm, to lunch with them at Larue. They are most anxious to have United States accept the mandatory of Armenia, and much worried over the fact that the Turkish question may not be settled for six months as they say six hundred thousand refugees will starve and very serious consequences will follow. They would rather be the lone mandate of the United States, England or the French but not Italy or Greece which they say impossible. They do not want to be under the same mandatory as Turkey. Say the Turkish influence bad and ultimately contaminates anyone living in or under Constantinople. They think Armenia with Cilicia will in time be self supporting. Mediterranean port more important than Black Sea. Say it will not take more than thirty thousand U.S. soldiers to control the country with local troops organized.

At 3:00 went to President's house to talk with him, along with Baruch, Davis and Lamont to see whether it would be wise for us to go home with him Saturday. He said he recognized that the principal questions of policy had been decided but wanted someone here with good judgement who, if anything new developed, would know enough to act intelligently or refer to higher powers at home. He asked us each what we had done to close up our work and who we proposed to have represent us. We all agreed that on reparations and financial clauses Foster Dulles was the best man with his complete knowledge of the subject, he was perfectly reliable and safe in every respect and we asked the President to write him a letter requesting him to stay, which he said he would do. He was in a good humor and told us one of Lincoln's stories which he is so fond of doing. He quoted him several times and you can see continually signs of his being a close student of Lincoln's war time experiences.

At 5:00 o'clock Lloyd George and others came in so we got out, delighted with his final consent to our all sailing with him on the *George Washington* Saturday. He was convinced the Germans would send their delegates Friday and we could have the ceremonies on Saturday afternoon.

I dined with Grempels and said "Good Bye" to a number of our good French friends, who really seemed sorry to have us go and I felt also many regrets at leaving them as they have been most cordial and hospitable during our stay and I had a real affection for many of them. It was the first time I had worn my button as Commander of the Legion of Honor and much to my surprise when I went into the room Major Grempel kissed me in his delight.

JUNE 27 (FRIDAY)—

After my usual office routine was attended to I went to the President's house to attend, with the other advisers, a meeting of the Big Four or rather Big Five, as Makino, the Japanese, was a regular attendant these days. This was to be our last meeting with them and was to settle the terms upon which we should settle with the smaller states in the reparations settlement with Austria. We were given certain latitude in this settlement after there was considerable discussion, it being determined that all of the States should make some contribution on account of having secured their freedom and also for the territory acquired in addition to assuming part of the war debt. Serbia would, however, have a considerable claim for reparations which gave them a good balance; Roumania probably a smaller balance in the settlement while the others, with the possible exception of Greece, would have to pay something, such as Poland and Czecho-Slovakia, which they can afford to do as they will be rich countries.

I worked out with Clemenceau and President Wilson the form of statement Clemenceau was to hand the German delegates on Saturday after the signing of the Treaty, telling them the blockade would be removed upon the ratification of the Treaty by the German Assembly.

I lunched at Ambassador Wallace's and sat next to Admiral Frueier, Minister of Marine Leygues was the honor guest—Lansing, Senator Saulsbury, Baruch, Minister Garrett and other French and Americans present.

After lunch I saw Whitehouse on Russia; Taylor and Hale on blockade, and generally cleaned up my desk.

Dined at Ritz and Bernie and I gave a little dance after dinner, a sort of farewell to our friends. Margaret Wilson came in for the last part.

JUNE 28 (SATURDAY)—

I was busy in the morning with Henry about paying bills and packing and with my secretary, Mills, about closing up my office.

After an early lunch with Frank McCoy and Mrs. Harriman, Frank McCoy took us out to Versailles to see the signing of the Peace Treaty. Frank left me at the gate of the Chateau as the others did not have tickets of admission to the Hall of Mirrors where the ceremony was to take place; Frank having none and Mrs. Harriman only a ticket to the terrace. I felt it very unjust that a brave soldier like Frank was unable to see the ceremony when he had played such an important part in making a peace possible and some of the rest of us, not so deserving, could be present.

An impressive sight awaited us upon our arrival at Versailles. At the front of the Chateau in the court extending out the main avenues as for as you could see were lines of soldiers, French chasseurs with their

Little Vance McCormick, in the 1870s, seated at the far left in a skull cap. To the right are brother Henry, his sister Mary Cameron, and cousin Eliza. HISTORICAL SOCIETY OF DAUPHIN COUNTY

Annie Criswell McCormick, Vance McCormick's mother, in a photograph taken about the time he was born, 1872. HISTORICAL SOCIETY OF DAUPHIN COUNTY

Col. Henry McCormick in his military uniform. He raised Company F, Twenty-fifth Regiment, Pennsylvania Volunteers, at the outbreak of the Civil War, led troops in the Antietam campaign, and was a staff officer at the Gettysburg battle. HISTORICAL SOCIETY OF DAUPHIN COUNTY

The McCormick mansion at 101 North Front Street in Harrisburg, Pennsylvania. PHOTO BY MICHAEL BARTON

Vance and his dog Frank, when knickers and high-top shoes were the fashion. HISTORICAL SOCIETY OF DAUPHIN COUNTY

The fictional Dink Stover strides into the stadium for the big game. Vance McCormick and his Eli teammates were inspiration for such gridiron myths. ILLUSTRATION FROM *STOVER AT YALE*

Vance posing on the fence, an honor accorded only to the captain of Yale's football team. The photo was autographed in 1894, although he played in 1891 and 1892. HISTORICAL SOCIETY OF DAUPHIN COUNTY

The Yale Campus in Vance's senior year, 1893. HISTORICAL SOCIETY OF DAUPHIN COUNTY

Yale's 1892 undefeated team, which outscored its opponents 435–0. In the center of the picture, holding the ball, is Captain McCormick, All-American quarterback.
HISTORICAL SOCIETY OF DAUPHIN COUNTY

*The young McCormicks, in 1894, gathered outside the family mansion at 101
North Front Street in Harrisburg. Front row: Robert, Anne, and Eliza. Middle
row: Henry Jr., Vance, and James Jr. Back row: Donald, Harold, Henry Buehler,
and Stanley.* HISTORICAL SOCIETY OF DAUPHIN COUNTY

*The McCormick family at Rosegarden on July 4, 1897. Front row: Vance McCormick,
Anne McCormick, Henry McCormick Gross, Edward Gross. Middle row: Lilie
(Cameron) Bradley, James McCormick, Henry McCormick, Annie (Criswell)
McCormick, Mary (Boyd) McCormick, J. D. Cameron Bradley, Rachel (Cameron)
Hale, Hannah (Gross) Campbell, Donald McCormick, James McCormick Jr. Back
row: Henry B. McCormick, Henry McCormick Jr., James McCormick Cameron,
Robert McCormick, J. Gardiner Bradley.* HISTORICAL SOCIETY OF DAUPHIN COUNTY

The entrance to Rosegarden, the McCormick country estate and working farm in Cumberland County. HISTORICAL SOCIETY OF DAUPHIN COUNTY

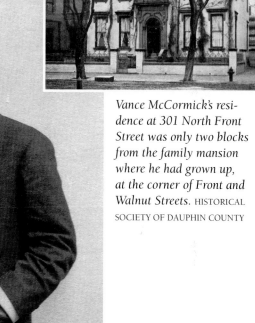

Vance McCormick's residence at 301 North Front Street was only two blocks from the family mansion where he had grown up, at the corner of Front and Walnut Streets. HISTORICAL SOCIETY OF DAUPHIN COUNTY

Vance in 1906, in his typical attire of double-breasted suit and starched high collar shirt. He had just completed his term as Harrisburg's youngest mayor. HISTORICAL SOCIETY OF DAUPHIN COUNTY

McCormick campaigning for governor of Pennsylvania in 1914. HISTORICAL SOCIETY OF DAUPHIN COUNTY

Vance McCormick, country gentleman, dressed to judge livestock at the Hogestown Cattle Show, which he established. HISTORICAL SOCIETY OF DAUPHIN COUNTY

President Woodrow Wilson's war cabinet in 1917. Front row: *Benedict Crowell, Assistant Secretary of War; William G. McAdoo, Secretary of the Treasury; Wilson; Josephus Daniels, Secretary of the Navy; Bernard M. Baruch, Chairman of the War Industries Board.* Back row: *Herbert Hoover, Food Administrator; Edward N. Hurley, Chairman of the Shipping Board; Vance McCormick, Chairman of the War Trade Board; Harry A. Garfield, Fuel Administrator.* SPENCER G. NAUMAN JR. COLLECTION, HISTORICAL SOCIETY OF DAUPHIN COUNTY

This photograph of President Woodrow Wilson hung on McCormick's office wall in Harrisburg, along with other photographs of European heads of state and diplomats he had worked with at the Paris Peace Conference in 1919. SPENCER G. NAUMAN JR. COLLECTION, HISTORICAL SOCIETY OF DAUPHIN COUNTY

David Lloyd George, Prime Minister
of the United Kingdom, 1916–1922,
and one of the "Big Four" at the Paris
Peace Conference. There, he said, he
"was seated between Jesus Christ and
Napoleon," meaning Wilson and
Clemenceau. SPENCER G. NAUMAN JR.
COLLECTION, HISTORICAL SOCIETY OF
DAUPHIN COUNTY

Georges Clemenceau, Premier of
France, 1917–1920. Nicknamed Le
Tigre (The Tiger), he was opposed to
leniency toward Germany in the peace
negotiations. Trained as a physician,
he was also a newspaper publisher, and
had once lived in the United States.
SPENCER G. NAUMAN JR. COLLECTION,
HISTORICAL SOCIETY OF DAUPHIN COUNTY

Vittorio Orlando, Italian Prime Minister, 1917–1920. He clashed with Wilson
at the peace conference over Italy's territorial demands. McCormick remarks
that he did not speak English and
required a translator, which slowed
the proceedings. SPENCER G. NAUMAN JR.
COLLECTION, HISTORICAL SOCIETY OF
DAUPHIN COUNTY

Economic advisors to the American Commission to Negotiate Peace, at the Hotel Crillon, in Paris, April 11, 1919. Sitting: Herbert Hoover, Gen. T. H. Bliss, Adm. H. S. Benson, Bernard Baruch, H. M. Robinson. Standing: T. W. Lamont, W. H. Shepardson, Norman Davis, Col. E. M. House, Gordon Auchincloss, Vance McCormick.

Bernard Baruch—financier, philanthropist, advisor to presidents, and friend of Vance McCormick. "Bernie" and he shared a cabin on the voyage to Paris, and played tennis when the conference was not in session.

Andre Tardieu, assistant to Clemenceau during the peace conference and ardent defender of the Versailles Treaty. In their correspondence, he and McCormick appear to be genuine friends. He presented McCormick the medal of the Legion of Honor. SPENCER G. NAUMAN JR. COLLECTION, HISTORICAL SOCIETY OF DAUPHIN COUNTY

Etienne Clementel, economic advisor to the French delegation at Paris. Mentioned often in McCormick's 1919 diary, his picture hung on the wall in McCormick's office. SPENCER G. NAUMAN JR. COLLECTION, HISTORICAL SOCIETY OF DAUPHIN COUNTY

Louis Loucheur, a French member of the Reparations Committee on which McCormick served. Like Clementel, he is mentioned often in the diary, and his picture also hung on McCormick's office wall. SPENCER G. NAUMAN JR. COLLECTION, HISTORICAL SOCIETY OF DAUPHIN COUNTY

Robert Cecil, British representative to the peace conference. He first worked with McCormick in setting up the blockade of Germany. After the war he championed the League of Nations, receiving the Nobel Peace Prize in 1937. SPENCER G. NAUMAN JR. COLLECTION, HISTORICAL SOCIETY OF DAUPHIN COUNTY

Silvio Crespi, economic advisor to the Italian delegation in Paris, member of the Reparations Committee, and among the photographs hanging on McCormick's office wall. SPENCER G. NAUMAN JR. COLLECTION, HISTORICAL SOCIETY OF DAUPHIN COUNTY

Gen. John J. Pershing, Commander of the American Expeditionary Force in France and member of Vance McCormick's photographic collection. SPENCER G. NAUMAN JR. COLLECTION, HISTORICAL SOCIETY OF DAUPHIN COUNTY

Mrs. Gertrude McCormick in a portrait by Sir John Lavery, 1925. ART ASSOCIATION OF HARRISBURG

Pine Street Presbyterian Church in Harrisburg, Pennsylvania, where the McCormicks worshiped and were leaders. HISTORICAL SOCIETY OF DAUPHIN COUNTY

Westward Way, the McCormick's estate at Northeast Harbor, Maine, where Vance and Gertrude spent summers, entertaining and sailing. SPENCER G. NAUMAN JR. COLLECTION, HISTORICAL SOCIETY OF DAUPHIN COUNTY

Vance with stepdaughter Gertrude Olmsted Nauman, on board the great ocean liner Mauretania *in 1927.* SPENCER G. NAUMAN JR. COLLECTION, HISTORICAL SOCIETY OF DAUPHIN COUNTY

Gertrude McCormick in her Girl Scout uniform. She was vice president of the national organization from 1923 to 1941. HISTORICAL SOCIETY OF DAUPHIN COUNTY

McCormick in later life, distinguished in his three-piece suit with gold watch and chain. This photo was used for his newspaper obituary. HISTORICAL SOCIETY OF DAUPHIN COUNTY

lances, and with the setting of the Chateau in the background it made a most magnificent sight.

After entering the building from the court I checked my hat and coat and then proceeded up the large stairway, flanked on both sides with the brilliantly uniformed chasseurs, with brass helmets with long black tassels and drawn swords, then through a series of rooms which led to the front of the building to the Hall of Mirrors and there in the end of the room were the tables for the delegates making three sides of a rectangle with a smaller table in the center upon which rested the peace document which was to be signed, a wonderful looking work of art. Inside the rectangle there were seats for many secretaries as well as behind the delegates' tables. At the other end of the room from where we were sitting there were four hundred or more press correspondents.

It was very interesting seeing the big men come in to take their seats and we had a chance to shake hands with Clemenceau, Lloyd George and the other notables. Our seats were with the Cabinet Ministers of the other countries, and it seemed like a gathering for a church wedding with the usual subdued chatter and curiosity and desire to get aisle seats. There was no applause, however, when any of the big figures appeared and the whole impression was more that of a religious ceremony than anything else.

The entire U.S. delegates [*sic*] had only sixty seats, so there were many disappointments, and I must say I was sorry to see some of the mothers and wives of certain minor secretaries present when many a brave general and soldier, who offered their lives for their country could not get in. Mrs. Wilson, Miss Wilson, Miss Benham, Mrs. House and Mrs. Lansing were present.

The crowds in the grounds and on the terraces were enormous and made a striking picture, massed around the fountains, and standing crowded behind the blue coated poilu.

It was a solemn moment when the two lone German delegates walked in. You could have heard a pin drop. Both were pale and ghastly looking; dressed in black frock coats of old style. With straight backs and heads held high in the air, but looking like death, they walked up to their vacant seats at the table where sat the delegates of the other nations and quietly sat down. Then Clemenceau made a short announcement about the manner of signing the Treaty. It was interpreted by Montou and the Germans were escorted, by a French officer, around to the table upon which lay the treaty and there signed and immediately returned to their seats. The

President then led the United States delegates to the table to sign, and upon their return to their seats they were followed by Great Britain, France, Italy, Japan and Belgium and all the representatives of other nations who were parties to the Treaty.

It was quickly over, lasting about a half hour. We all left the Hall of Mirrors and strolled out on the terraces and watched the crowds cheer the big fellows when they came out.

After a cup of tea at the Reservoir, we returned home.

It was impressive and yet did not have the thrill you might have expected and you could not help but feel that the two German delegates, Mueller and Bell, in their insignificance typified in a way the new German government, which is certainly an unknown quantity these days, and no one knows what a day may bring forth.

A hurried dinner at the hotel and then off to the station for the President's train. At the station the usual royal sendoff, red carpets through the station from the street to the train, wonderful plants lining the side of the awnings and canopy, right to the cars. Troops galore with the army band; President of France Poincare, Clemenceau, all the French delegates, Italian Ambassador and American friends. A great sendoff and I can see the President had made real and sincere personal friends, and especially Clemenceau, with whom he had formed a strong attachment.

On the special train going to see us off at Brest were Foreign Minister Pichon, Tardieu, Naval Minister Leygues, et al. American Ambassador Wallace, etc.

Our party consisted of President and Mrs. Wilson, Miss Wilson, Miss Benham, Admiral Grayson, Baruch, Davis, Lamont and wife, McDowell and wife, Clive Day, Seymour and wife, several other experts and Ambassador and Mrs. Jusserand. We turned in early.

JUNE 29 (SUNDAY)—

In the morning as we passed through small towns we were greeted by cheering crowds. Peasants lined the railroads along the entire route waving American and French flags. There is no question but President Wilson has the affection and confidence of the plain people of France, notwithstanding the efforts of so many of the leading newspapers of the country to belittle him.

At 11:40 we pulled in to Brest, our train running right up to the wharf, where we were met by the French and United States Commanders of the Port. The band played "The Star Spangled Banner" and "Marseillaise" and at once we were taken on board the tender to be taken out into the harbor where the *George Washington* was anchored. All the ships in the harbor had their pennants and flags flying and made a beautiful sight, and the guns from the fort boomed a salute as we went by.

When we arrived on board the French officers and United States Ambassador said farewell and after the loading of the baggage, we weighed anchor, at 2:00 P.M., and started out of the harbor with more booming of cannon from the men of war in the harbor. Our temporary escort consisted of a light U.S. cruiser with Admiral Knapp on board and four destroyers and a French man of war and four French destroyers. We had for a permanent escort the *Oklahoma* battleship and four destroyers. Our temporary escort accompanied us for a couple of hours and then turned back after giving the proper salutes. A very different departure from Brest when in 1917 our War Mission slipped secretly out of the harbor at dusk and made a rush through the submarine zones.

The weather was beautiful and it was a happy crowd turning their faces towards home although leaving France at its very best, the coast presenting a beautiful picture.

We have a couple of thousand soldiers on board and a number of casual officers. I have Reggie Taylor along detailed as courier.

We are all comfortably placed in large staterooms with baths and eat in a small dining room. The President and family eat in their own suite.

We all went to the movies in the main saloon tonight.

JUNE 30 (MONDAY)—

A very comfortable and quiet night. Sea calm with just enough breeze stirring for pleasant sailing.

At 8:00 in the morning we met *Northern Pacific* from America which stopped to send out President's mail by one of the destroyers serving as our escort. In this way we got the United States newspapers of June 24.

Uneventful day, everyone still feeling the effects of the strenuous conference life and the reaction has set in with much resting, napping, etc. We have practically the same crew as coming over—Captain Ed. McCauley and Executive Officer Perkins in command. The one lasting impression I have received from my war and peace conference experiences abroad was the wonderful impression made upon me by the men of our Army and Navy—fine manly men, simple and strong. It does your heart good to see them, wherever they are, under whatever conditions, cheerful and good natured and standing out in every way head and shoulders above the men of the other nations. It drives away all doubts as to the future of our country when you think of this material as a foundation to build upon.

We all attended the movies again and saw a sentimental war film "Hearts Humanity" and rather tiresome.

JULY 1–2–3 (TUESDAY, WEDNESDAY AND THURSDAY)—

Every day very much alike—pleasant sailing weather, smooth and sunny, rather warm.

We have interesting talks with Dr. Taussig, Professor Day, Seymour, et al. Whenever we find ourselves together the conversation drifts back to the Peace Treaty and it is interesting to hear these territorial experts talking over their problems as we had very little time to go into these matters in Paris.

Bernie and I lunched with the President Tuesday and nearly every day we meet him on the deck and have interesting chats. One day we discussed with him Dr. Taussig's theory that all the railroads, public utilities and hard coal mines should be nationalized in the near future as Taussig thought we could not escape it. The President said he also felt that the necessities of life, like water, electricity and railroads, which are as much a part of our national life as air for our lungs, would ultimately bring about governmental ownership or control and he thought the time was soon ripe for a well worked out scheme. I suggested it might come and was really upon us because the Government now attempts to fix the price at which the railroads sell their commodity and also attempts to fix the price of labor which certainly [would] be the wrong time to advocate it.

I have enjoyed reading Brand Whitlock's German occupation of Belgium and was delighted with his description of some of the places visited by us with the President, particularly Louvain, Grand Place in Brussels and ceremony in the Hotel Ville receiving King and Queen of Denmark. The reception being practically the same.

We were all very sorry when we heard today the Chief had decided to land in New York Tuesday instead of Monday, because we are very anxious to get home. It, however, gives him time to work on his message and at the same time have the much-needed benefit of an extra day's rest at sea.

JULY 4 (FRIDAY)—

This was a great day for sailors and passengers. The day was given up to deck sports and speeches. The racing, boom fight, boxing matches, etc., by the sailors and soldiers were a great success and the President's speech was most inspiring; standing on the deck in the midst of the sailors and soldiers, who covered every available space within sight, even up on the rigging and astride the booms. He made an excellent speech and later with Ambassador Jusserand spoke to the sailors in their hall on E deck.

The usual movies in the evening in the main dining hall. I can't see how the regular movie fan stands it every night. The President and Mrs. Wilson go every night as does the Captain. One interesting feature every evening at the movies is the singing by everyone of the popular airs, the words of which are thrown on the screen. The President and Mrs. Wilson enjoy this immensely.

JULY 5 (SATURDAY)—

A perfect day but warm, drifting along at about 315 miles per day. We have settled down for the long voyage and everybody knows everybody else by this time.

The President sent for Lamont, Davis, Baruch and me with Dr. Taussig to come to his room after lunch to read us his message to Congress to get our suggestions and criticisms. Mrs. Wilson, Miss Wilson and Grayson were also present in his stateroom.

We had few changes to suggest as it was an excellent general statement of the situation at Paris and the problems that confronted him. We raised the question as to the praise given his colleagues and developed from him a real feeling of friendship for his colleagues whom he said privately were in accord with the principles we were fighting for but were hampered and restricted by their own political conditions at home, due to the temper of their people. He said he was surprised to find they had accepted the Fourteen Points not for expediency only but because they believed in them. He told us frankly of the Shantung settlement because it was in his opinion the most criticized and most difficult party of the Treaty to defend. He referred to the agreement made by France and England with Japan, binding them absolutely to the Shantung agreement.[77] This he said Lloyd George criticized himself and said it had been made by Asquith when Gray was sick, that the War Cabinet was astounded when it was pre-

---

77. Japan sought to acquire Germany's economic rights in Shantung. In a secret pact in 1917, Japan had agreed to support British claims to Germany's islands south of the equator in return for Britain's support of Japan's claims in Shantung to the German islands north of the equator.

sented but had to accept it. He said it only gave Japan an economic con-trol, not political in any sense, and by this settlement they kept Japan in the conference and made her a party to the Allied policy toward China in all other respects and by getting her in the League of Nations will main-tain the open door policy in China and make it possible to compel Japan to give up an exclusive sphere of influence in that country, and you could see he was far from satisfied but felt it was the best that could be done under all the circumstances. He further stated Japan had agreed with him verbally to pull out of Shantung but would not put it in writing as it reflected on their good faith.

We all discussed the advisability of reading message to Congress as a whole or to Senate alone. He said he had cabled to Tumulty to get advice from friends in Senate on this point. He also told us he was ready to make a tour of the country if necessary to speak for the League of Nations and read us topics of his speeches.[78]

Baruch, Davis, Grayson and I dined in Captain McCauley's cabin on the bridge and had an excellent dinner. Captain McCauley is a fine young officer and is one of the reasons for the great success of the Navy. It makes you proud of our country when you get close to the men who really run our Army and Navy. They have attained their leadership because they delivered the goods.

The usual movie show and a very warm night as it is extremely close and sultry.

JULY 6 (SUNDAY)—

Went to church in morning at which Chaplain preached, named Bloomhardt from Altoona, also communion service.

Quiet day; smooth sea; usual talks on deck; President always appearing in the afternoon; we having good chats and he telling many good stories.

JULY 7 (MONDAY)—

The last full day was passed in usual way, very hot. Cooler towards evening. Miss Wilson and I had a little shuffle board. We have not missed an evening at the movies and I must say am getting quite bored with them and glad we are landing tomorrow.

---

78. Wilson presented the treat to the Senate on July 10, 1919, for its approval. The opposition was led by Wilson's political enemy, the Republican majority leader from Massachusetts, Henry Cabot Lodge. In order to gain public support for approval, Wil-son arranged a tour of the United States, which departed on September 3, 1919. It was cut short on September 25, when Wilson suffered the first of his strokes.

JULY 8 (TUESDAY)—

We were all up bright and early to complete our packing and anxious to get the first glimpse of land. It was not long before we saw what seemed like a swarm of flying machines sailing out over us to be the first welcome for President Wilson upon his return to America. The air seemed full of them, some of them lighting on the water and then rising again.

During the entire three hours nearing port the seaplanes maneuvered over the *George Washington* and exchanged greetings. Before reaching Ambrose Channel we slowed up to take advantage of the tidal conditions and were saluted from Fort Hancock, Wadsworth and Governor's Island.

At about 10:30 a Naval escort, headed by the U.S. Battleship *Pennsylvania*, met the *George Washington* at sea. We with our convoy which consisted of U.S. Battleship *Oklahoma* and destroyers *Yarnell, Woolsey, Conner* and *Tarbell* were greeted by an escort of five battleships, forty destroyers, dozens of submarine chasers, a number of airplanes and a dirigible.

The *Pennsylvania* led this escort with Vice-President Marshall, Secretary Daniels and other Cabinet officers, Congressmen and personal guests aboard. The escort moved up the harbor in a single column three miles long, the destroyers following the *George Washington*. The *Pennsylvania* gave the twenty-one gun salute when the *George Washington* passed. She passed quarantine about 1:45 and turned into the Government Pier at Hoboken docking about 3:00 o'clock.

Bernie Baruch, Admiral Grayson and I were on the bridge with President Wilson during the interchange of good will messages. A number of Municipal steamers had Mayor Hylan and members of Citizens' Welcoming Committee aboard. American and British liners at the piers were all "dressed" for the ceremony.

The welcome was a hearty and noisy one and the President was particularly pleased with it.

As we neared the dock, I recognized Harry and Anne at one of the windows, also Mrs. McAdoo and Mrs. Sayre and a number of other friends.

We stepped ashore about 3:30 and I decided to go directly home to see Mother instead of joining the parade of the President to Carnegie Hall where he was to have a formal welcome at a big meeting presided over by the Mayor of the city.

Our baggage was passed through without examination and Harry, Anne and I were soon on the train for Harrisburg, arriving home the same evening.

A Glossary of Names and Places

Adinkerque (June 18)
Small town on English Channel near the Belgian border with France.
Aga Khan III (April 26; June 14)
Born in Karachi, India, Aga Sultan Sir Mohammed Shah (1877–1957), as the direct descendant of Mohammed, was primarily a religious leader who became a statesman representing Muslim interests internationally. He was the first president of the All-India Muslim League (1906–12) and later represented India at the Assembly of the League of Nations, serving as president in 1937. Aside from his sterner roles, the Aga Khan was active in European society and bred and raced Thoroughbred horses.
Albert, King (June 18)
King Albert (1875–1934) of Belgium had maintained the nation's neutrality until Belgium was invaded by German forces on August 4, 1914, after which he became the active commander in chief of the Belgian forces.
Alexander, Grand Duke of Russia (January 22)
Grand Duke Alexander Mickhailovitch (1866–1934) was a member of the Russian royal family. Until the revolution, he was an admiral in the Imperial Navy, and he had overseen the development of the Russian Navy and created the Russian Air Force. He escaped death at the hands of the Bolsheviks and sailed for France in December 1918. During the Paris conference, he lobbied for Allied food and monetary support for Russia against the Soviets.
Alricks, Clara (August 30; June 15)
Clara Bull Alricks (1848–1933) was Vance McCormick's aunt's sister.
American Episcopalian Church (January 26; February 23; March 9, 23; April 20; May 4, 9; June 1, 15, 22; July 6)
The American Episcopalian church at 23 Avenue George V in Paris, called Cathedral Church of the Holy Trinity, was founded in the 1830s by a group of wealthy expatriate Americans. The congregation built a cathedral that was dedicated on November 25, 1886, while a simultaneous dedication of the Statue of Liberty was taking place in New York.
Andrew (April 12, 29)
Abram Piatt Andrew (1873–1936) was a Harvard graduate, associate of J. P. Morgan Bank, and director of the American Ambulance Field Service. Before the war, he was one of the advisors in drafting the Aldrich Plan, which led to the creation of the Federal Reserve System. He was

appointed first director of the Mint (1909–10) under Taft, and then assistant secretary of the treasury (1910–12).

Anwyll, Leeds (June 16)

The son of McCormick's secretary, William E. Anwyll (1863–1944).

Argonne Forest (May 25)

A wooded ridge about ten miles wide that extends about forty-five miles, forming a geographic barrier that was the site of a major American offensive during the fall of 1918.

Arras (April 27)

This town in northern France was the focus for some of the most severe trench fighting involving British forces. The cellars of destroyed houses were used as bunkers by Allied troops.

Asquith (July 5)

British statesman Henry Herbert Asquith (1852–1928) was a progressive of the Liberal party. He served as prime minister of England from 1908 until his resignation in 1916. Although he was an outstanding parliamentarian, he was not a good wartime leader, causing weaknesses in Britain's military and diplomatic endeavors, and leading to a loss of confidence in his governing and the rise of Lloyd George. He continued to lead the Liberal Party until he resigned from political activity in 1926.

Atterbury (February 28; May 17)

Brig. William Wallace Atterbury (1886–1935) was sent to Europe by Wilson when Pershing telegraphed for "best railroad man in the U.S." Atterbury supervised the reorganization of European railroads to better transport and supply Allied forces. He had joined the Pennsylvania Railroad just after college, and in 1925 he became president of the railroad, serving until 1935.

Aubert, Mr. and Mrs. Louis (February 27; March 2, 21; April 9; May 13, 28; June 1, 17, 23, 25)

McCormick is possibly referring to the author of *The Reconstruction of Europe*, published in 1925.

Auchincloss, Gordon (January 11, 13, 22, 23, 27, 29; February 2, 9, 25, 26, 27; March 14, 21, 29, 30; April 13, 27; May 13, 14)

Secretary to and son-in-law of Colonel House, Auchincloss (1886–1943) was ranked as special assistant in the U.S. Department of State and secretary in the American delegation to the peace conference. He also was law partner of David H. Miller, with whom Auchincloss prepared "an elaborate memorandum . . . on the President's draft of the League of Nations Covenant," containing comments and suggestions, the essence of which was that the league would destroy the Monroe Doctrine. The memo especially called into question the legitimacy of the International Court of Justice. Auchincloss "incurred the dislike of [Wilson] when he accompanied Wilson to London at the end of 1918."

Auchincloss, Mrs. (January 13, 22, 31; March 21, 29, 30; April 21, 27; May 13, 14)

Wife of Gordon Auchincloss and daughter of Colonel House, she accompanied her husband to the Paris Peace Conference.

Azay le Rideau (May 17)

Small chateau in the Loire Valley.

Baker, Commander (March 25; April 17; May 7; June 17)

Probably Lt. Cdr. George Barr Baker, USNRF, who, representing Admiral Sims and Lord Eustace Percy of the British government, had met Hurley on his arrival in England. He was part of the British Shipping Committee.

Baker, Newton (April 16, 26)

Newton Diehl Baker (1871–1937) was mayor of Cleveland, secretary of war from 1916 to 1921, and served on the World Court at the Hague in 1928. He appointed General Pershing head of the U.S. Army.

Baker, Ray Stannard (February 5)

A journalist by occupation, Ray Stannard Baker (1870–1946) worked on *McClure's Magazine* long enough to gain a reputation as a crusading journalist. He served as a special commissioner of the State Department in Europe and was Wilson's press secretary during the peace conference. He served as Wilson's emissary to China, with apologies for not doing more for China to protect its interests from Japanese "rapacity."

Bakhmetev (written as Bakhmetiff, Bakhmeteff), Ambassador Boris A. (January 15; February 24, 28, 30; April 26; May 13, 29, 30; June 5, 14, 21)

The last Imperial ambassador to the United States, 1911–17. After the first Russian Revolution, he stayed in America to represent the interim government of Aleksandr Fyodorovich Kerensky. Later he became involved in Soviet efforts to gain possession of gold deposits once owned by the tsarist government.

Balfour (February 24; March 28; May 3, 9, 21; June 15, 16)

British secretary of state for foreign affairs from 1916 to 1922, Arthur James Balfour 1st Earl Balfour of Whittinghame (1848–1930), had served as prime minister (1902–05) in an early government. He was an active leader of England's Conservative Party, whether in office or out.

Barbizon (January 19)

A small town about one hour's drive southeast from Paris, Barbizon is known as "the painters' village" because of the famous French painters who worked there, including Jean-François Millet and Rosseau. These painters featured scenes of the nearby forest.

Baruch, Bernard (January 2, 11,12, 13, 14, 18, 20, 22, 24, 25, 26, 27, 30, 31; February 2, 3, 4, 10, 11, 14, 15, 16, 18, 23, 26, 27; March 2, 10, 11, 15, 16, 22, 25, 26, 28, 29; April 1, 3, 4, 5, 10, 11, 12, 13, 15, 20, 21, 22, 23, 24, 25, 29, 30; May 7, 9, 15, 19, 20, 22, 24, 29, 31; June 16, 19, 21, 22, 25, 26, 27, 28; July 5, 8)

One of America's best-known financiers and philanthropists, Bernard Mannes Baruch (1870–1965), served as commissioner for raw materials and then chairman of the War Industries Board in 1918. Baruch was a member of the Committee of Economic Advisers and Chairman of the Supreme Economic Council in Paris. As chairman, he unsuccessfully lobbied for greater war reparations for Germany. Personal advisor to Wilson and friend of McCormick.

Beale, Sir John (February 8, 17)

Beale was a representative of the British Food Ministry and counterpart to America's H. J. Heinz on the Shipping and Food Relief Committee. He was opposed to relaxing the food blockade "until the Germans learn a few things."

Bell (June 28)

German Catholic Reichstag member since 1912, Johannes Bell (d. 1949) remained active in the German government, even after the Nazis assumed political dominance.

Belleau Woods (May 25)

An area along the western front five miles northwest of Château-Thierry, successfully defended by two brigades of Americans from the 2nd Division. One was a marine brigade that suffered losses of 55 percent, but they halted the German drive toward Paris and gave the French troops new energy, as this was the first deployment of American forces in battle.

Benes (June 25)

Eduard Benes (1884–1948) was the head of the delegation for the newly created Czechoslovakia. He later served as president of the Assembly of the League of Nations and as president of his country. During World War II, he served in London as head of the Czech government in exile.

Benham, Miss (April 28; June, 17, 24, 28)

Private secretary to Mrs. Woodrow Wilson, Edith Benham Helm had a nervous breakdown and left her position during Wilson's confining illness after his stroke, with all the concurrent criticism of Mrs. Wilson. (She was possibly Edith Wallace Benham, the daughter of Rear Admiral Andrew Benham.)

Benson, Admiral (January 23, 30; February 26; March 14, 19; April 13, 14, 16, 19, 26; May 5)

Chosen in 1915 as the first U.S. chief of naval operations, Adm. William S. Benson (1855–1932) developed improved naval operations, which were in place at the time of the U.S. entry into the war. After the war, Benson was active in the leadership of the U.S. Shipping Board. He served in Paris as a member of the Committee of Economic Advisers.

Berenson (February 3)

Bernard Berenson (1865–1959) was an American art historian, critic, and connoisseur. He was a graduate of Harvard (1887) and an authority on Renaissance painting. Brother in law of Bertrand Russell.

Berry, Walter (January 25; June 15)

Probably referring to the wealthy expatriate lawyer who lived Paris and became the close companion of Edith Wharton. He was a cousin of minor poet Harry Crosby.

Bliss, Charge (January 12, 18, 24; February 11, 18, 26; March 7, 30; April 1, 12, 14, 16, 19, 27; May 22; June 13, 14, 16)

Counselor (secretary) of the U.S. Embassy in Paris, 1916 to 1920, Robert Woods Bliss (1875–1962) dealt with alien relief matters during and after the war. Charge d'affaires in France from December 23, 1919, he later served as the U.S. ambassador to Sweden (1923–27) and Argentina (1927–33). He donated his extraordinary estate, Dumbarton Oaks, in Georgetown, the site of the conference that led to the creation of the United Nations, to Harvard University. It is now a research center.

Bliss, General (West Point 1875) (January 18, 30; March 10, 19; April 27; May 31; June 3, 14, 15)

Charles Howard Bliss (1853–1930) was born in Lewisburg, Pennsylvania. As a military representative on the Supreme War Council in 1917, he urged disarmament of Germany. He was a member of the American delegation to the peace conference with little influence; he was not highly enthusiastic about the treaty. A member of the Committee of Economic Advisers who served in Europe during World War I, Bliss had the confidence of Wilson and firsthand European experience.

Boals, Terry (April 9)

Col. Theodore Davis *Boal* (1867–1938) was a gentleman farmer and sometime architect from Boalsburg, Pennsylvania, who organized a private unit that became part of the 28th Division. During the war, he served as aide-de-camp to Gen. Charles Muir, the division commander until October 1918, and may have been serving as escort officer or aide to General William Hay. He was married to a European woman, Mathilde de Lagarde. Near Boalsburg, he built an officers' club for the division. This building and land was later purchased by the commonwealth of Pennsylvania and now serves as the Pennsylvania Military Museum.

Bonar Law, Andrew (April 10; June 7)

A staunch conservative, he served as chancellor of the exchequer, the number-two position in the British government, during the Lloyd George government. Andrew Bonar Law (1858–1923) was born in Canada, but moved to Scotland, where he was involved with the family business. His firm was said to have sold iron to Germany for armament prior to the beginning of the hostilities. He served for a brief period as prime minister after Lloyd George.

Borden, Sir Robert (January 25; April 28)

Canadian prime minister from 1911 to 1920, Robert Laird Borden (1854–1937) effectively represented Canadian interests on the international scene. He led the active Canadian involvement in World War I, and his advocacy gained independent status for Canada in the League of Nations. He served as the Canadian representative during the 1917 Imperial War Conference in London and at the Paris Peace Conference.

Bourgeois, Leon (January 25; February 14)

Léon Victor Auguste Bourgeois (1851–1925) was a French statesman and philosopher who won the Nobel Prize for Peace in 1920. He served as a member of the French Parliament, as secretary of state, and later, as president of the Council of the League of Nations.

Boyd, Jack (February 14, 16, 17)

Andrew Jackson Herr Boyd (1892–?) was a Harrisburg friend of McCormick's. He and his brother Jim lived at 124 Pine Street. He returned to Harrisburg and the family business—coal interests, several large farms east of Harrisburg, and land in North Carolina—after the war, eventually residing in his childhood home.

Boyd, Jim (February 16, 17)

James Boyd (1888–1944) lived a more public life than his brother. A writer, he worked briefly as a reporter for McCormick's paper, the *Harrisburg Patriot,* but after college settled at Weymouth, the Boyd family estate in Southern Pines, North Carolina. He authored several books, and in 1941 purchased and developed a newspaper in Southern Pines, the *Pilot.* He married Katharine Lamont, daughter of Daniel S. Lamont, on December 1917.

Brent, Bishop (March 15)

Canadian born but an American citizen, Charles Henry Brent (1863–1929) was a visionary Episcopalian priest who founded the Episcopal Church in the Philippines, as well as introducing a Western system of education. During World War I, he served as chief of chaplains. His ecumenical interests led him to later become one of the founders of the World Council of Churches.

Brest (January 2, 10; March 25; June 6, 29, 29)

French seaport town on a landlocked bay with a naval harbor that was developed by Cardinal Richelieu in 1631. It served as the official port for debarkation of the U.S. troops during World War I.

Brockdorff-Rantzau

Count Ulrich Brockdorff-Rantzau (1869–1928) was prime minister of Germany, representing Germany at Versailles. Later, during the 1920s, he served as Germany's ambassador to Russia and was instrumental in solidifying German-Russian diplomatic relations.

Bullitt (March 31; April 6, 12; May 9, 14)

From Philadelphia, William Christian Bullitt (1891–1967) was a U.S. delegate and served as a diplomatic emissary for Wilson. He was later appointed the first ambassador to the USSR (1933–36), and served in other diplomatic positions as well.

Callaway (June 17)

Probably referring to Fuller Earle Callaway (1870–1928), a successful cotton manufacturer and businessman in La Grange, Georgia. He was the father of two sons, one of whom was Carson Jewell Callaway (1894–1961), who served in the navy during the war. He and his wife developed the extensive Callaway Gardens at Blue Springs, Georgia, from a family retreat where they frequently entertained neighbors such as FDR.

Cameron, Helen (February 6)

From Princeton, New Jersey, and related to Vance McCormick, whose aunt married Sen. J. Donald Cameron (1833–1918).

Camp, Walter Chauncey (January 2)

McCormick's football coach at Yale. Walter Chauncey Camp (1859–1925), a pioneer in physical training and in American football, helped revolutionize the game by instituting the conventions that are still in place. As an expert in exercise, Camp was put in charge of keeping cabinet members and congressmen in shape. He authored more than thirty books.

Cannon, Bishop James, Jr. (January 15)

A Southern Methodist preacher who was a member of the Virginia Anti-Saloon League, and founded the *Richmond Virginian*, a dry newspaper. Bishop James Cannon (1864–1944) was in Paris as a U.S. delegate to the International Congresses Against Alcoholism conference in 1919, concurrent with the peace conference. He was successful in procuring the League of Nations' support in limiting the trafficking of alcohol. As a very effective Washington lobbyist, he led a movement that ended in the Eighteenth Amendment.

Cardinal Mercier (June 19)

Desiré Joseph Mercier (1851–1926) was appointed cardinal in 1907. His was considered the leading voice in opposition to the German occupation of Belgium during World War I.

Carter, Commander (April 15)

Aide to Admiral Benson, Commodore A. F. Carter, USN, also served on the shipping committee under Hurley.

Cathedral of Malines (June 19)

St. Rumbold's Cathedral of Malines (now known as Mechelen) is the seat of the Roman Catholic Church in Belgium. The enormous tower, which dominates the skyline of the city, is well known for its set of bells. The chief architect of the cathedral was Sébastien Vauban.

Cecil, Lord Robert (January 12, 14, 18, 20, 21; February 11, 13, 17, 24, 25; March 7, 14, 15; April 4, 8, 22; May 9, 19; June 9, 16)

England's assistant secretary of state for foreign affairs in 1918–19, Lord Edgar Algernon Robert Gascoyne Cecil, first viscount Cecil of Chelwood (1864–1958), was a founder of the League of Nations. He was awarded the Woodrow Wilson Foundation Peace Prize in 1924 and the Nobel Peace Prize in 1937. Lord Cecil drafted the "Memorandum on Proposals for Diminishing the Occasion of Future Wars,"

which became the basis for the British draft of the covenant (constitution) of the League of Nations. He later helped in writing its final
draft in September 1919. In Paris, Cecil often argued for and supported Wilson, while going against wishes of his own government and
Lloyd George.

Chalons-Sur-Marne (March 24; May 25)

About twenty-five miles southeast of Reims (northeast of Paris), this
city is a vital road, railway, and canal hub for northern France. It was
held briefly by the Germans in 1914 but was regained in the battle of
the Marne.

Chambord (May 18)

A 440-room castle in the Loire Valley, Chambord was constructed
between 1519 and 1547 and used by royalty, particularly Louis XIV, as
a retreat. It features a stairwell designed by Leonardo DaVinci.

Chambrun, Charles (January 18)

Great-great-grandson of Lafayette, Chambrun was in charge of the
French Embassy in Washington.

Chambrun, Marquis (January 18)

Probably Aldebert Chambrun, brother of Charles, and another great-
great-grandson of Lafayette. The marquis, a colonel in the French
artillery, served as liaison officer to Gen. John Pershing. Later he served
as deputy at the French embassy in Washington, D.C. He was born in
Washington when his father, Adolphe, was on an earlier diplomatic
mission.

Charleroi (April 27; June 19)

Belgian town forty-two miles due south of Brussels near the Sambre
River to which it links by canal. In the coal region of Belgium, it is a
manufacturing center for iron and steel.

Charpentier, Mr. & Mrs. (January 25; April 9; May 29)

Probably referring to son of Georges Charpentier and his wife. Mrs.
Charpentier, senior, and her children were the subjects of the Renoir
painting, exhibited in 1879, that made Renoir's reputation as a society
painter. The Charpentiers were in the publishing business and collected Renoir paintings.

Chateau-Thierry (May 25)

A town along both banks of the Marne River east of Paris that was
successfully defended, in part by American troops, in the first week
of July 1918.

Chenonceau (May 18)

Castle in the Loire Valley, at Indre-et-Loire, eighteen miles east of Tours. Built in 1515, it was transformed into a temporary hospital at the end of the war where more than two thousand wounded were treated.

Cheverny (May 18)

Castle in the Loire valley. Today the feeding of the dogs can still be viewed at Cheverny, where they are fed sides of horsemeat.

Churchill, General (February 2)

Marlborough Churchill (1878–1942) was an American army general who was serving as assistant chief of staff in the Military Division. He was the chief of Army Intelligence Services (M18) and general military liaison and coordinating officer to the commission to negotiate peace. In June 1918, Churchill became head of the Military Intelligence Branch of the War College Division, which became the Military Intelligence Division of the War Department. He remained head of Military Intelligence until September 1920.

Ciesa (February 17)

Italian representative to Supreme Economic Council at Peace Conference.

Clemenceau, Georges (January 16, 18, 25, 27; February 7, 8, 10, 23; March 5, 21, 22, 18, 31; April 1, 15, 7, 10, 16, 23, 24, 28, 29, 30; May 1, 6, 7, 15, 30; June 2, 3, 4, 5, 6, 7, 9, 10, 13, 23, 24, 25, 27, 28)

Georges E. B. Clemenceau (1841–1924) lived briefly in the United States as a young man, becoming sympathetic to American democracy. He was prime minister of France (1917–20) and president of the French Council of Ministers and War during World War I. He took a hard line on Germany during the peace conference to ensure French autonomy in Europe and negotiated the evacuation of the Rhineland, not bowing to extremists from France who wanted more territory to protect from Future German invasions. He advocated the balance-of-power theory in Europe and Britain's Cecil plan. His aggressive debating style led to his nickname "The Tiger," and he wore gray gloves in public to cover eczema.

Clementel, Etienne (January 16, 17, 27; February 4, 6, 13, 17, 26, 27; March 5, 10; April 9, 14, 18, 28; May 22, June 9, 16, 23)

A statesman and career politician, Etienne Clementel (1864–1936) was French minister of commerce, industry, and posts and telegraphs, and a member of the Allied Maritime Transport Council. He was also the French representative on the Inter-Allied Relief Commission. During the conference, he served as the economic advisor to the French delegation.

Cobb, Frank (May 6)
American journalist (1869–1923).

Colby, Bainbridge (June 24)
Bainbridge Colby (1869–1950) was a member of the U.S. Shipping Board. He served as secretary of state for a short period, after which he returned to law practice.

Conger (January 17; April 3; June 23)
Arthur Latham Conger Jr. (1891–1971) was the foreign advisor to the War Trade Board in Washington. He had resigned in October 1918 to become a foreign representative of the Associated Press.

Crespi (February 4, 17; March 8, 13, 31; April 1, 12, 15; May 6, 22, 30; June 9, 10)
Silvio Crespi (1886–1944) was the Italian minister of provisions (food controller) and Italian chair of the Commission on Ports, Waterways, and Railways. In Paris, he was a member of the Reparations Committee and an economic advisor for the Italian delegation to the peace conference. He was a signatory of the treaty for Italy.

Crillon, Hotel (January 11, 13, 14, 17, 21, 22; February 1, 4, 6, 8, 16, 26, 27; March 5, 7, 8, 12, 14, 15, 17, 18, 22, 16, 29; April 1, 3, 5, 8, 9, 12, 16, 17, 18, 22, 23, 24; May 1, 4, 7, 15, 17, 20; June 7, 16, 24)
The Hotel de Crillon on the Place de la Concorde has lost little of its eighteenth-century splendor. It was the headquarters for the American Commission to Negotiate Peace during the Paris Peace Conference and was designed by Jacques-Ange Gabriel for Louis XV in 1758.

Cummings, Homer Stille (January 14; February 14).
Homer Stille Cummings (1870–1956) was mayor of Stamford, Connecticut, for several terms; served as vice chairman and then chairman of the National Democratic Committee from 1913 to 1920; and was the U.S. attorney general.

Cunliffe (January 30; February 4; March 27, 28, 31; April 8; May 3, 7)
Financier and governor of the Bank of England, Lord Watler Cunliffe (1855–1920) and Lord Sumner were labeled "the heavenly twins" because of the astronomically high reparations figures they advocated. Cunliffe, the first baron of Headley, was a member of the Reparations Committee and economic advisor to the British delegation.

Daniels, Secretary (July 8)

Josephus Daniels (1862–1948) was from North Carolina and the editor of the *Raleigh Observer.* He served as secretary of the navy for the United States from 1919 to 1921, and was the U.S. ambassador to Mexico from 1933 to 1941.

Darlington, Bishop (June 11)

Diocesan bishop at St. Stephens (Episcopal) Cathedral in Harrisburg, Pennsylvania, from 1905 to 1930, James Henry Darlington (1856–1930) lived at 321 North Front Street, not far from the McCormick residence. He served as the chaplain at Fort Totten, New York in 1916 and was active in numerous organizations. Because of his interest and involvement with nature, a central Pennsylvania mountain trail that was projected to be a part of the planned Appalachian Trail was named for him.

Davis, Ambassador (January 22, 26; March 14)

John William Davis (1873–1955) served as U.S. ambassador to Great Britain from 1918 to 1921. He was a strong supporter of the League of Nations and a close friend of Lansing. As the U.S. delegate to the Rhineland Commission, he is given credit for persuading France to allow civilian control of the Rhineland, and he drafted the section of Versailles Treaty dealing with Rhineland issues. He was a presidential candidate in 1924.

Davis (January 11, 23, 27, 31; February 3, 7, 8, 11, 14, 16, 17, 18, 23, 26; March 2, 5, 22, 24, 26, 27, 28, 29, 30; April 1, 3, 4, 5, 7, 8, 10, 12, 21, 23, 24, 29, 30; May 1, 2, 3, 8, 15, 19, 22, 30; June 1, 2, 3, 5, 7, 10, 11, 12, 13, 14, 17, 19, 21, 22, 15, 26, 28; July 5)

A staunch supporter of the League of Nations, Norman Hezekiah Davis (1878–1944) was the U.S. Treasury representative in London and Paris in 1918, finance commissioner of the United States to Europe from 1919 to 1920, and undersecretary of state from 1920 to 1921. In Paris, he served as assistant to Hoover, a member of the Reparations Committee, and a financial advisor to the American Commission. Davis defended Germany against gross demands of war reparations while holding the Allies to their own war debts, and negotiated postwar relief politics. He was president of the American Red Cross from 1938 to 1944.

Day, Clive (June 28)

Dr. Clive Day (1871–1951) was a regional specialist for the Balkans from Yale University. He was a member of the House Inquiry.

de Cartier (April 30; June 9, 24)

Baron de Cartier de Marchienne, commander of the Order of Leopold and the Order of the Crown, was Belgian Ambassador to Washington from 1928 to 1946.

de la Croix (February 16)

Elected in Belgium's first election by universal male suffrage, Léon Delacroix (1867–1929) was the first designated prime minister of Belgium, serving simultaneously as minister of finance.

de Polignac, Marquis (January 12, 22, 24; February 2, 12, 15, 24; March 14, 26, 27; June 23)

The marquis (1868–1937) was a wealthy resident of Paris who had a broad range of interests. He created a College of Athletes in Rheims in 1913, which focused on a natural method of training later adopted by the French Army. The school was destroyed in 1914, and there is now a park at the site. The marquis also was involved in fund-raising in America for various war-related causes and was a member of the International Olympic Committee.

de Polignac, Princess (January 22, 24)

Possibly the Marquis's sister. The descendants of Prince Auguste Jules Armand Marie (1780–1847) bear the titles prince and princess of Polignac.

Derby, Lord & Lady (February 12)

Edward George Villiers Stanley, seventeenth earl of Derby (1865–1948), succeeded his father as chancellor of the University of Liverpool (1909–48). He was a conservative member pf Parliment. He was the British ambassador in Paris from 1918 to 1920, served as the secretary of state for war from 1916 to 1918 and 1918 to 1920, and retired from political life in 1924.

DeWolfe, Elsie (June 13, 15)

A major New York designer of the time.

Dillon, Mrs. (February 8, 22)

The wife of English correspondent Dr. E. J. Dillon, who was a member of the British Commission, and later authored his own account, *The Inside Story of the Peace Conference.*

Dixmude (June 18)

Also spelled Diksmude. Belgian city near the "Trench of Death," where Belgian troops resisted the German advance toward France from 1914–18.

Dormans (May 26)

French village on the Marne River midway between Chateau-Thierry and Epernay.

Dresel (January 12; February 8, May 6)

Ellis Loring Dresel (1865–1925) was the director of the Special Commission of Study in Germany, commission to negotiate peace. He worked for State Department and was head of the U.S. intelligence mission in Berlin, sent early to Berlin to prepare for peace. Served as U.S. Charge d'Affairs in Germany from 1921 to 1922.

Dulles, Allen, (February 5, 23)

Allen W. Dulles (1893–1969) was grandson of John W. Foster, former secretary of state; nephew of Robert Lansing; and brother of John Foster Dulles. A federal administrator, he was the second secretary of legation in Switzerland and was attached to the commission to negotiate peace. Later in his career, he was head of the CIA (1953–61).

Dulles, John (January 12, 17, 23, 25, 26; February 1, 2, 7, 8, 10, 13, 14, 16, 18, 19, 23; March 5, 17, 11,18, 20, 14, 30; April 1, 2, 3, 4, 15, 21, 22, 23, 24, 30; May 2, 3, 8, 15, 16, 31; June 2, 6, 7, 8, 13, 24, 25, 26)

John Foster Dulles (1888–1959) was a commissioned army officer assigned to the War Trade Board in Washington, where he served as an assistant to McCormick. In Paris, he was appointed counsel to the reparations section of the American delegation. A nephew of Secretary of State Robert Lansing and an expert in the field of international law, Dulles was also sent by Wilson to Central America to secure the defense of the Panama Canal during World War I. Dulles remained in Europe after the peace conference to handle reparations from Austria, Hungary, and Turkey. Eventually, Dulles became secretary of state under Dwight D. Eisenhower, from 1953 to 1959.

Dunkirk (June 18)

French port on the Straits of Dover at the edge of the area of Belgium and France known as Flanders. It received even greater fame during World War II.

Eduard VII, Hotel (March 13; June 8)

Italian hotel "headquarters" for the conference.

Eisner (March 26)

German Editor of Social Demoractic Party (SPD) newspaper *Vorwaerts*, from 1900 to 1906, Kurt Eisner (1867–1919) at first supported the war, but moved to the pacifist opposition. After an imprisonment in

1918, he led the November 1918 revolution in Bavaria, where he was made prime minister. He was shot and killed in February 1919 by Count Anton Arco-Vally.

Elizabeth, Queen (June 18)
Wife of King Albert I of Belgium.

Ely, Henrietta (January 12; March 27; April 13, 16)
Possibly the wife of Richard Ely, who was the acting director of the Bureau of Enemy Trade of the War Trade Board. This person was likely Richard T. Ely (1854–1943), a prominent American economist who had studied and traveled extensively in Germany and Europe. He was an expert on European economics and had written about various aspects of it.

Evans, Capt. Edward (June 18)
British naval officer and commander of HMS *Broke*. He was known as "Evans of the *Broke*," and his destroyer engaged six German destroyers off the Dutch coast in April 1917, sinking three.

Feisel, Prince Emir al Husein (January 18, 31)
The third son of King Husein bin Ali of Morocco, *Faisal* (1885–1933) was commander of the army of Hedjaz. He hoped to rule occupied Syria and had worked with T. E. Lawrence to capture Jerusalem and Damascus. Britain brought him to Paris in a warship and helped him get a seat at the peace conference. He became the king of Iraq in 1921.

Field (January 25)

Fiume (March 28; April 23; May 1, 6, 15)
An ancient seaport city on the Adriatic Sea now known as Rijeka. Now part of Croatia, the city has been claimed by every nation in the area in its history. During World War I, it was held by Hungary until seized by Croat troops in 1918, followed shortly after by an occupation by Italian forces.

Fleming, Samuel (January 15, 19; February 6; April 10, 24)
Samuel Fleming was commissioned as a first lieutenant in the U.S. Infantry Reserve Corps in March 1917. He was promoted to captain in the 315th Infantry, 79th Division, in August 1917, followed by promotion to major in the same command in October 1918. He became a lieutenant colonel of the 104th Infantry/104th Cavalry in October 1921. Fleming served in France from June 1918 to June 1919. After the war, he became a licensed engineer partner in the Pennsylvania firm of Gannett, Seelye, and Fleming.

Foch (January 18; February 7, 8, 10; March 2, 3, 5, 22; April 14, 27; May 6, 7, 19; June 16, 20)

A career military officer, Marshal Ferdinand Foch (1851–1929) served as commandant of the Ecole du Guerre (the French West Point). He was Commander of the French Northern Army on the western front through the summer of 1916, then supreme Allied commander on the western front during latter part of the war. He was an influential military advisor during the peace treaty process in Paris.

Folies Bergere (February 26)

Famous Parisian music hall.

Fontainebleau (January 19; May 18)

A town thirty-five miles southeast of Paris, famous for the spectacular, ornate royal palace and for the forest of forty-two thousand acres that surrounds it. The palace served thirty-four sovereigns, and during the Third Republic (1871–1940), it served as the summer residence for the presidents of France.

Fort Douaumont (May 26)

Thought to be an impregnable fort in defense of Verdun, Douaumont was taken by the Germans in February 1916 after a long period of shelling. It was recaptured by the French in November.

Fort Souilly (May 25)

During the Verdun battles, French military headquarters were in Souilly, a town eleven miles southwest of Verdun.

Fosdick (February 2)

Raymond Blaine Fosdick (1883–1972) was a lawyer with an interest in social welfare. He was chairman of the committee on training camp activities from 1917 to 1918 and became undersecretary of the League of Nations in 1919. Climaxing a long association with the Rockefeller Foundation, he served as its president from 1936 to 1948.

Gann (January 14; February 5)

Gann served under Hoover in Europe with the American Relief Administration from November 1918 to April 1919.

Gary (June 1)

Hampson Gary (1873–1952) was a Texan who served as U.S. chief of mission in Cairo from 1918 to 1919, and was appointed envoy extraordinary to Switzerland in 1920.

Gerry, Senator (May 19)

Harvard graduate and a senator from Rhode Island, Peter Goelet Gerry

(1879–1957) served as Democratic whip in the Senate from 1919 to 1929. He was a supporter of the League of Nations.

Gibson (February 5; April 19)

Hugh Gibson (1883–1954) served under Herbert Hoover in Europe with the American Relief Administration from November 1918 to April 1919, when he became U.S. ambassador to Poland. He was later ambassador to Switzerland, Belgium, Brazil, and Luxembourg, as well as ambassador-at-large, and led the American delegations at several disarmament conferences throughout his career.

Gillet (January 2, 14, 24, 25; February 27)

Representative of the French high commissioner.

Giovanni (February 8; March 7)

Dr. G. Giolotti Giovanni (1842–1928), prime minister of Italy from 1911 to 1914 and 1920 to 1921, opposed Italy's entry into World War I.

Goodrich, Chauncey (June 22)

Chauncey Goodrich (1836–1925), Williams College class of 1861, was the college's second missionary to China, where he served for sixty years.

Grant (February 2; April 22, 30; May 28)

Col. Ulysses S. Grant III (1881–1968), grandson of the eighteenth president, was an American military representative in the Paris Peace Conference secretariat. He had a long, successful military career and served as vice president of George Washington University. He married the daughter of Elihu Root.

Graves, General (May 23, 29, 30)

Handpicked head of the American expeditionary forces in Siberia, William S. Graves (1865–1957) of West Point class of 1889 was given command of forces without clear military orders in a volatile, ambiguous situation. He performed as directed in secret orders from Wilson and kept U.S. forces in as neutral a position as possible between two Russian armies. He ended his military career as commander of the Panama Canal.

Grayson (February 12; April 12, 28; May 29; June 16, 17, 28; July 5,8)

A naval officer, Adm. Cary Travers Grayson (1878–1938) had served as President Wilson's personal physician from early in his presidency. Grayson prescribed a diet and exercise regimen that exacerbated Wilson's tendency to digestive troubles and respiratory problems.

Greene, Jerome (February 2)

Jerome Davis Greene (1874–1959) was American businessman and a trustee of the Brookings Institute.

Grew (January 12; February 23; March 8; May 3; June 6)
> State Department officer and secretary general of the American Commission to Negotiate Peace, Joseph C. Grew (1880–1965) was in Berlin when America entered World War I. He was the acting chief of the State Department's Division of Western Affairs and official secretary to the U.S. delegation. Dubbed "father of the career diplomatic service," Grew served the U.S. government for more than forty years, with a career that included two ambassadorships, two secretaryships, two ministerships, and every junior rank in the service.

Grey (July 5)
> After his appointment as England's secretary of foreign affairs (1905–16), Sir Edmund Grey (1862–1933) conducted secret diplomacy with other European countries against Germany. It was he who said, "The lamps are going out all over Europe." Although a liberal, Grey was removed from his position in 1916 by Lloyd George, partially because it was believed that Grey's secret agreements had turned other countries against England.

Gross, "Pete" (January 26, 27, 28, 29; February 1, 6, 9, 13, 14, 15, 16)
> Henry (Pete) Gross was Vance McCormick's first cousin. Their mothers were Criswell sisters Nancy and Annie. They grew up together on Front Street in Harrisburg, Pennsylvania, and as boys, Vance gave Henry the nickname "Pete" based on the influence of a Civil War song called "Pete McGonigle's Knapsack No. 62." A captain while in Paris, Gross eventually became a brigadier general and served as head of the Pennsylvania Selective Service from 1945 to 1970. He was one of the last American officers elected to the rank by the soldiers in the unit.

Hale (May 31; June 16, 25, 27)
> Associate of the Paris War Trade Board office.

Harmsworth, Cecil (February 3, 4)
> Nephew of Lord Northcliffe, Esmond Cecil Harmsworth, Viscount Rothermire of Hemsted (1898–1978), was aide-de-camp to Lloyd George during the conference. He was also the minister of blockade for Great Britain. After the war, at age twenty-one, he became one of England's youngest members of Palimient (MPs). He signed the Neuilly-sur-Seine Treaty as MP, undersecretary of state for foreign affairs. As owner of the *Daily Mail,* he was later involved with newspaper owner-publisher organizations.

Harriman (January 16, 19, 23, 31; February 9, 12, 20, 24; March 9, 14, 29; June 20, 22, 24, 28)

Born to a wealthy New York family, Florence "Daisy" Harriman (1870–1967) married J. Borden Harriman in 1889. She pursued a career in social work and was an advocate for suffragism. During World War I, she was sent to Paris by the Red Cross as the second in command of a large unit of women ambulance attendants. She supported the League of Nations and was the "social whip" for the American community in Paris. Active in the Women's National Democratic Club, Harriman was appointed by Wilson to the Federal Industrial Relations Committee and in 1937 was appointed V.S. Minister to Norway by FDR.

Harry (July 8)

Henry McCormick (1869–1941), Vance's brother.

Haskins, Dr. (June 3)

Charles Homer Haskins (1879–1937) was America's foremost medievalist, a professor at Harvard (1902–31), and the dean of graduate studies (1908–24). He was a member of House's Inquiry and then was appointed chief of the Western European Division of the American Peace Commission by Wilson.

Havemeyer, Mrs. (January 30; March 10; April 19)

Probably Mrs. Louisine Havemeyer (1855–1929), widow of American sugar baron Henry Havemeyer. She was a benefactor of the Metropolitan Museum of Art.

Hayes, General (April 9)

This person was Gen. William H. *Hay* (b. 1860), West Point class of 1886, who served briefly (October 1918–April 1919) as commander of the Pennsylvania 28th Division, after which he assumed command of the Intermediate Section of the Supply Service until July 1919.

"Hearts Humanity" (June 30)

A Canadian film made in 1918, directed by Allen Holubar, and classed as a war drama. The prerelease title was "Dawn of Reckoning."

Heck (April 26)

Lewis Heck, American vice counsel stationed at Constantinople and an expert on Turkish matters. After the war, he went into business there, possibly the oil business. He was originally from Heckton, a small village named for the family, just north of Harrisburg. His father, J. Lewis Heck, was in the lumber business, producing all the ties for the Reading Railroad.

Heinz (January 2)

Serving as chief of the Near East Division of the Inter-Allied Food Council, headquartered in Constantinople, H. J. Heinz (1844–1919) was a successful food manufacturer from Pittsburgh, famous for his ketchup and known for his interest in the welfare of his workers.

Hickok, Maj. Bill (February 26; May 16, 17)

An infantry officer assigned to the Peace Commission to assume responsibilities for military attachés and the investigating commissions for Central and Eastern Europe and Asia Minor.

Hill (February 7)

Correspondent for the *New York Sun*.

Hitchcock, Frank (February 20)

A Republican, Frank Harris Hitchcock (1867–1935) was the former postmaster general (1909–13) who had instituted air mail service.

Hollister (January 14)

J. James Hollister, of Gaviota, California, (d. 1940) was the secretary of the Democratic National Committee.

Hood, Lady (February 8, 24; May 21, 22)

From a letter by Gen. Tasker Bliss to his wife on February 26, 1919: "A great many of the old French families were represented. I met Lady Hood who has come over with her children from London."

Hoover (January 2, 11, 13, 14, 20, 30, 31; February 1, 5, 11, 13, 16, 17, 19, 23, 24, 25, 26; March 1, 4, 5, 21, 22, 24; April 8, 14, 17, 23, 25; May 2, 7, 8, 15, 22, 23, 31; June 3, 7, 9, 10, 13, 14, 17, 19, 22, 23)

Herbert Clark Hoover (1874–1964) organized and directed the American Relief Committee, based in London which led to his appointment as head of the Commission for Relief in Belgium. In 1917, Wilson appointed him U.S. food administrator, in which capacity he worked in the United States to increase food production, stabilize prices, eliminate waste, and improve food distribution. As director general of the American Relief Administration, Hoover was a member of the Committee of Economic Advisers and economic director of the Supreme Economic Council. As a personal advisor to Wilson at Versailles and chairman of the European Coal Council (he had the reputation of rescuing economically troubled mines), Hoover is given great credit in directing the economic reorganization of Europe. Although he was a big supporter of the League of Nations, Hoover later criticized Wilson and the Democrats for making the League a partisan issue. Hoover noted that "Vance [McCormick] probably had more personal influence with the President than any other American in Paris." After the war, Hoover served as secretary of commerce (1921–28) and became the thirty-first U.S. president (1929–33).

House, Col. (January 13, 14, 21, 23, 29, 30; February 17, 19, 21, 22, 23, 24, 26; March 2, 7, 10, 11, 14, 17, 19, 21, 23; April 4, 5, 6, 7, 12, 19, 27; May 6, 22, 24, 28; June 12, 24)

Born in Texas and advisor to several Texas governors, honorary colonel Edward Mandell House (1858–1938) became Wilson's friend and closest advisor. House was appointed as Woodrow Wilson's representative on the Supreme War Council and left for Paris on October 17, 1919. He was instrumental in winning consent of Allied leaders to establish fourteen points as basis for peace settlement, and he oversaw practically all political and economic work of peace delegation. Before going to Paris, House organized the Inquiry, headquartered in Washington, D.C., at the National Geographic Society, whose executive officer, Dr. Isaiah Bowman was a member of the committee. This Inquiry enlisted the service of geographers, historians, statisticians, ethnologists, international lawyers, and government experts. They studied issues for a year before going to Paris, then took a council of advisors in international law, including Baruch, Davis, Lamont, McCormick, Taussig, David Hunter Miller, and James Brown Scott.

House, Mrs. (January 13; February 24; May 9, 28; June 14, 22, 28)

Neé Loulie Hunter, she married Edward House in 1881.

Howard, Capt. Conway (February 4)

McCormick's future brother-in-law, Howard, was brother to Florence Howard Olmsted.

Howard, Sir Esme (January 18)

Sir Esme William Howard, first baron of Penrith (1863–1939), British minister to Sweden and expert on Poland. He also served as British ambassador to the United States.

Hudson, Miss Elizabeth (January 26; February 7; April 13, 15, 18; May 10 14, 15, 17; June 8)

Elizabeth Hudson (1885–1973) was an American from New York who assisted in relief work for destitute children in France during the war.

Hughes (January 30; February 3, 4, 10, 14, 17; March 11; April 8; June 6)

William Morris Hughes (1864–1952), prime minister of Australia (1915–23), represented Australia at the conference. He was appointed to the Reparations Committee by Lloyd George and pushed for full reparations from Germany. His anti-Asian views caused a stir among nonwhite delegates.

Hurley (January 11, 13, 20, 30; June 24)

Edward Nash Hurley (1864–1933) served on the U.S. Federal Trade Commission (1914–17) and was then appointed chairman of the U.S. Shipping Board, in charge of "procuring and operating" merchant ships for war and commerce and overseeing the construction of new vessels. He became a member of War Council of the American Red Cross. In Paris, Hurley served as chairman of the shipping section of the Supreme Economic Council.

Husein (January 18)

Husein Ibn-Ali, sharif of Mecca and king of Hejaz (1856–1931), was a direct descendent of Mohammed. With British help, he led an Arab uprising in Syria, which weakened the Turkish enemy. Husein came to Paris to seek British-promised help in forming an Arab state.

Hyde, Mrs. (February 24; April 29; June 9, 15)

Very possibly, McCormick is referring to Florence Louise Rowley Hyde, wife of the English painter Frank Hyde (1849–1937). This artist painted some World War I battle scenes, including *1st Battalion the Queens Own, Royal West Kent Regiment, Going into Action at Neuve Chapelle on October 28th, 1914.*

Hylan (July 8)

John F. Hylan (1868–1936) was the mayor of New York City from 1918 to 1925.

Hymans (February 16; April 13, 28, 19, 30; May 3; June 19)

Belgian minister of foreign affairs, Paul Hymans (1865–1941) was an active plenipotentiary at the peace conference. He was a spokesperson for small states.

James, Mr. & Mrs. Arthur (February 3)

Head of the American Near East Relief Committee.

Jim, see Neale, James.

Jockey Club (February 12)

An exclusive private club in Paris, founded in 1863 at the Hotel Scribe but relocated to another site in 1913, possibly the present location at 2 Rue Rabelais. The club developed a valuable private library. Clemenceau was a frequent visitor to the library.

John Bull (January 30)

A personification of England, or used to describe the prototypical Englishman.

Jones, Jesse (February 22, 27)

Jesse H. Jones (1874–1956) was a Houston real estate baron and politician appointed by Wilson as director general of military relief for the American Red Cross until 1919. He then served on the Reconstruction Finance Corporation (RFC) and was tapped by FDR to head the Federal Loan Agency. He also served as secretary of commerce under Roosevelt.

Jusserand (June 28; July 4)

French ambassador to the United States (1902–25), Jean Jules Jusserand (1855–1932) was a highly respected diplomat and author. His was the first work about American history to received the Pulitzer Prize (1917), and he served as the president of the American Historical Association in 1921.

Kerensky (February 19 & 22)

Aleksandr Fydorovich Kerensky (1881–1970) was a Russian revolutionary, trained as a lawyer, who was head of the provisional Russian government from July to November 1917. Upon the Bolshevik uprising, he fled to London, France, and finally New York. During the conference, he lobbied for Allied anti-Bolshevik support for Russia.

Kerr, Philip (January 30; February 24).

Philip Henry Kerr, eleventh marquess of Lothian (1882–1940), was a British statesman and journalist. Before the war, he was editor of the British liberal scholarly journal *Round Table* and gained a reputation as a theorist of international politics. He served as Lloyd George's secretary and advisor on foreign policy matters in Paris. In 1939, he became British ambassador to the United States.

Keynes (March 31; April 1, 2, 3, 30; May 3, 22, 29, 30; June 13)

John Maynard Keynes (1883–1946) remains one of the leading figures in the realm of economics. During World War I he served in the British treasury department and was sent as part of the British delegation to the Versailles Peace Conference in 1918. He believed the reparations demanded of Germany were punitive to the extreme and would cause serious repercussions. He resigned from the conference then published *Economic Consequences of the Peace* (1919), denouncing the Treaty of Versailles.

Klotz (February 3, 4, 13, 15, 17, 26; March 6, 8, 11, 28, 31; April 1, 5, 8, 9; June 6, 7)

French minister of finance Louis-Lucien Klotz (1868–1930) was the supposed source of leaks about committee work to the French press. He was a member of the Reparations Committee. He proposed a financial committee of the league, which was popular idea in France and constantly insisted on full repayment from Germany.

Knapp (June 29)

Harry Shepard Knapp (1856–1928) was then a rear admiral serving as the naval attaché in London. Prior to the armistice, he had directed naval activity against German U-boats in the Caribbean.

Knox (June 16)

Philander Chase Knox (1853–1921) was a former attorney general of the United States. He had been a possible Republican candidate for president and was serving as senator from Pennsylvania. He was a determined opponent of the Versailles Peace Treaty and the League of Nations, because he believed they violated the Constitution.

Kolchak, Aleksandr Vasiliyevich (April 24, 26; May 2, 7, 13, 14; June 5, 14, 21, 23)

A Russian admiral and counterrevolutionist, Aleksandr Kolchak (1874–1920) was an officer of the Imperial Navy who served with distinction in the Russo-Japanese War and in World War I. He created and led the White Army in an attempt to overthrow the Soviets but was eventually defeated and ultimately shot by the Bolsheviks.

Krech (February 2, 3)

Alvin W. Krech was a New York City financier, at one point a trustee for Equitable Trust.

Kuntz, Major (February 18)

Lamont (February 7, 8, 18, 22, 23, 25, 26; March 2, 11, 26, 28, 29, 31; April 1, 3, 4, 5, 10, 21, 23, 30; May 2, 3, 14, 19, 27, 29, 31; June 2, 3, 5, 6, 7, 10, 11, 12, 13, 21, 25, 26, 28; July 5)

Thomas William Lamont (1870–1948) was a partner with J. P. Morgan which was involved in war loans to the British and French. Lamont served on the Liberty Loan Committees and advised Colonel House in efforts to coordinate the U.S. war effort with the Allies. He represented the U.S. treasury with Norman Davis and served as financial advisor to the American delegation; he was a member of the Reparations Committee. Lamont owned the *New York Evening Post* during the war years.

Lamont, Mrs. (February 22)

Wife of Thomas Lamont.

Lansing (January 11, 13, 22, 23, 26, 29, 30; February 5, 11, 18, 19, 23; March 6, 7, 8, 23, 34, 28; April 6, 12, 14, 19, 22, 24, 27, 29; May 2, 8, 9, 22, 23, 24, 29; June 1, 3, 17, 24, 25, 27, 28)

Robert Lansing (1864–1928) was then the U.S. secretary of state

(1915–20) and a delegate to the peace conference. He grew distant from Wilson at the conference because of ideological differences over the right of the Germans to negotiate and over the League of Nations. He was asked to resign from cabinet in February 1920. In 1921, he authored *The Peace Negotiations: A Personal Narrative* and *The Big Four and the Peace Conference.* The proper diplomat, Lansing bowed to Wilson during important international matters and was overshadowed by Col. Edward House during informal negotiations.

Lansing, Mrs. Robert (February 5; April 24; May 8; June 28)

Laperouse Restaurant
Restaurant located in Paris at 51 Quai des Grands. Still in business as of 2002.

Lausannes (June 11)
Journalist for the French newspaper, the *Matin,* which was considered anti-American.

Lawrence, Sir George (January 31)
McCormick surely means "Lawrence of Arabia," *Thomas Edward Lawrence* (1888–1935), an Oxford-educated man who had served as British liaison officer during the Arab Revolt of 1916–18. He was a friend of Faisal, and while a member of the British delegation to the peace conference, became a spokesman for Arab interests. He was opposed to French control of Syria. He also left a noteworthy body of writing.

Lebrun, Minister (February 15; March 11)
Albert Lebrun (1871–1950) was a member of the French government who held a variety of positions from 1910 to 1920, including minister of war, minister of blockade, and minister of liberated districts (1917–19). He became the president in 1932 and served as the last President of the Third Republic.

Legge (March 22; April 11, 15, 18; May 16, 19)
Originally from Wisconsin, Alexander Legge (1866–1933) was the general manager of International Harvester Company. He had served on the Red Cross mission to Russia in 1917 and was the vice president of the War Industries Board in Washington, D.C. In Paris, he served as a U.S. representative on the Economic Committee.

Lens, France (April 27)
A town south of Ypres in an area of coalfields. It was held for much of the war by German forces who used the slag heaps as protection until the heaps were destroyed by Allied forces.

Lettland (March 15; April 19)

McCormick's term for Latvia, which became independent in 1918 and remained so until 1939. The country's history has been one of domination by other nation-states, most recently the USSR.

Lew, see Sheldon, Lewis P.

Leygues (June 27)

George Leygues (1857–1933) was France's minister of marine, head of the navy.

Lloyd George (January 18, 25, 30; February 7, 24; March 8, 15, 20, 21, 22, 26, 28, 29, 30, 31; April 1, 2, 3, 5, 7, 9, 10, 15, 17, 23, 24, 28, 29, 30; May 2, 3, 6, 14, 15, 22, 24, 30; June 2, 3, 4, 5, 7, 8, 9, 10, 13, 23, 25, 26, 28; July 5)

David Lloyd George, first earl of Dwyorf (1863–1945), was head of the British delegation. He was British prime minister (1916–22) and first lord of the treasury. He was a longtime member of Parliament (1890–1922) and had won the election to power just before the peace conference began. At Versailles, he sought to maintain the peace through a treaty that would contain Germany and involve the United States, a position that placed him in opposition to Clemenceau.

Lloyd George, Mrs. David (January 30)

Lloyd George married Margaret Owen in 1888.

Lodge (June 16)

Henry Cabot Lodge (1850–1924) was a Republican senator from Massachusetts who criticized Wilson's foreign policy.

Loomes, Henry (February 7)

Valet to Vance McCormick.

Lord, Dr. (June 3)

Robert H. Lord was an expert on Poland from Harvard University. He was a member of the House Inquiry and served as a member of the Peace Commission. His advice led to the facet of the treaty—a larger Poland—that was the most objectionable to the Germans.

Loucheur (January 14, 24; February 8, 17, 25; March 2, 11, 26, 27, 31; April 1, 5, 9, 11, 12, 15, 22, 29, 30; May 1, 2, 3, 6, 12, 30; June 1, 3, 4, 5, 6, 7)

Louis Loucheur (1872–1931), minister of industrial reconstruction, was an advisor on economic questions and French member of the Reparations Committee. He served as the French minister for social welfare and labor from 1926 to 1930.

Louvain (June 19)
A university town on the Dyle River east of Brussels, Louvain was
known as the "Oxford of Belgium."
Louvecienes (June 1)
An area about ten miles west of Paris Louis XV presented his mistress
Jeanne Bécu du Barry (1743–93) with a small chateau located there.
She "outgrew" the chateau and had a small pavilion built for entertain-
ing. It is probably this pavilion that Loucheur owned. The scenic area
was a favorite subject for French Impressionist painters.
Luxembourg Palace (January 20)
A palace on the Left Bank now housing the French Senate. It was orig-
inally built for Marie de Medicis, regent of France, and took the name
Luxembourg from the hotel that had stood on the same location.
Majestic Hotel (January 14, 21; March 10, 15, 23; April 7, 8; May 3, 19;
June 21)
The Majestic served as British diplomatic headquarters during the
peace conference.
Makino (June 26)
Baron Makino [Nobuaki (1861–1949?)] was Japan's representative in
Paris. His best-known proposal was that the preamble to the Covenant
of the League of Nations include an agreement on basic human equal-
ity and nondiscrimination among member nations. (The clause was
not approved for inclusion by all of the Council of Ten.)
Malcolm, Sir Ian (June 15, 16)
Secretary to David Balfour, British secretary of state for foreign affairs.
Marshall (July 8)
Then vice president Thomas Marshall (1854–1925) was the former
governor of Indiana.
McAdoo (January 14)
Named secretary of the treasury in 1913 by Wilson, who became his
father-in-law the next year, William Gibbs McAdoo (1863–1941) also
served at various times as chairman of the Federal Reserve Board, Federal Farm Loan Board, and War Finance Corporation. He was most
important in arranging financing of American war efforts. Trained in
law, McAdoo achieved recognition by his leadership of the Hudson
River tunnel ventures. He resigned from the cabinet in January 1919,
made two unsuccessful attempts at the Democratic nomination for
president, and later served as senator from California (1933–38).

McAdoo, Mrs. (June 14)
Woodrow Wilson's daughter, Eleanor Randolph Wilson (1889–1967), married William McAdoo in May 1914.
McCaulay, Captain (January 2)
McCaulay was navy captain of the USS *George Washington.*
McCombs, Mrs. (January 16, 19; February 20; March 15)
Wife of Wilson's former campaign manager, William F. McCombs.
McCormick, Cyrus (April 17)
This son of inventor Cyrus Hall McCormick continued to expand the harvest machine business and combined with other manufactures to create the International Harvester company in 1902. He served on the Root Commission, which traveled to Russia in 1917; International Harvester provided $200,000 to underwrite the commission.
McCormick, Harry (June 22)
Vance's older brother, Henry Buehler McCormick (d. 1939).
McCormick-Goodhart (April 8)
A son of Leander McCormick-Goodhart, who lived in London. Leander McCormick-Goodhart was a great-grandson of Cyrus McCormick and the grandson of Leander J. McCormick, manager of McCormick Harvester Works. Born of a British father and an American mother, McCormick-Goodhart spent his career in Britain's diplomatic service. From 1921 to 1942, he served at the British Embassy in Washington, first as a commercial secretary, and then as a special assistant to the ambassador, Lord Lothian. On retiring in 1942, he remained in the United States, although he maintained his British citizenship.
McCormick Seminary (January 26)
A still-functioning Presbyterian seminary located in Chicago, McCormick had been moved there from New Albany, Indiana, in 1859 by Cyrus McCormick Sr. Cyrus and his family were the main financial support for the seminary which took the McCormick name at his death in 1884.
McCoy, Frank (February 9; March 28, 30; April 5; May 17; June 28)
McFadden (February 7, 8, 9, 10, 12, 15, 17, 19, 22, 25, 26, 27; March 2, 5, 6 12, 13, 16, 18, 21, 22, 23, 30; April 1, 4, 7, 8, 15, 18, 20, 25, 29; May 4, 9, 11)
George McFadden (1873–1931) was the War Trade Board representative in Paris in 1918. He was in France with U.S. Food Administration. He worked with Treasury Department assistant secretary Oscar Crosby.

As an economic advisor, he was one of two civilian American members of the Armistice Committee in November 1918.

Mcfadden, Mrs. (March 9, 27; April 6, 20)
Wife of George Mcfadden.

McKinstry, Gen. C. H. (February 28; March 5, 27)
Head of the War Damages Board, McKinstry had been detailed to estimate the damages done in Belgium and northern France by the Germans.

Mercier, Cardinal (June 18)
Désiré Joseph Mercier (1851–1926) was the Roman Catholic cardinal of Malines and a leading Belgian voice against German occupation of Belgium, for which he was held under house arrest by the Germans.

Meurice, Hotel (January 11, 21; April 12; June 3, 4, 22)
The Meurice Hotel, situated at 228 Rue de Rivoli, is known for its elegance and traditional French flair. It could be regarded as a smaller version of the Ritz.

Mezies (April 27)
Referring here to Dr. and Mrs. *Mezes*. Dr. Sidney Edward Mezes (1863–1931) was the president of the College of the City of New York (1914–27) and former president of the University of Texas (1908–14). Colonel House's brother-in-law, he was a member of the House Inquiry and in Paris served as director of the U.S. section dealing with territorial, economic, and political intelligence.

Miller (February 7, 8)
David Hunter Miller (1875–1961) was serving as an advisor on legal questions to the American delegation in Paris. He was an international lawyer and worked on final draft of the Charter of the League of Nations.

Mills (February 12; March 18, 29; April 4; June 28)
Mills was McCormick's stenographer.

Mills, Ogden (February 4)
Ogden L. Mills (1884–1937) was a wealthy businessman and a Republican state representative from New York State. He served as a captain during the war and was one of the initial members of the American Legion, which was founded in March 1919 in Paris. He was appointed the fiftieth secretary of the treasury during the Hoover administration.

Mills, Mrs. Ogden (June 13, 16)
Ogden Mills married Dorothy Randolph Fell in 1924.

Mole (June 18)
A man-made harbor wall forty feet high and eighty yards wide that extended in a curve one and a half miles into the sea, protecting the

harbor and the entrance to the Bruges canal against storms on the North Sea. At the time, this harbor wall, or mole, created the world's largest man-made harbor. See www.navsource.org/archives/01/013020.jpg.

Monet (January 15, 17, 27; February 8, 12,13, 25, 27; March 2, 5, 23; April 14)

Jean Omer Marie Gabriel *Monnet* (1888–1979) served as secretary to Clementel and coordinator of Anglo-French supplies during World War I. He was a French member of the Allied Maritime Transport Executive, and at the conference, he was advisor to the French delegation on economic questions. He was deputy secretary general of the League of Nations (1919–23) and became an advocate for western European unity. Monnet had a noteworthy ability at persuading national governments to seek negotiated solutions to differences, and later in his life, he was highly sought after by foreign countries as an economic advisor.

Montfaucon (May 26)

Built in the eleventh century, this castle had a commanding view of the surrounding land. It was enlarged and modernized during the nineteenth century by Baron Louis de Montfaucon. In an area held for a long period by German forces, the castle housed the 5th Army commander, the German crown prince.

Morgenthau (March 25, 26; April 24, 27; May 6; June 8, 11)

Henry Morgenthau Jr. (1891–1967) was the owner of a large commercial farming enterprise in New York State. He worked with Hoover's Farm Administration in an effort to send tractors to France. He is better known as a friend of Franklin Roosevelt, who later appointed him secretary of the treasury, which post he held for eleven years.

Morris, Minister (June 1)

Possibly Ira Nelson Morris (1875–1942), who was appointed minister to Sweden in 1914.

Morris, Roland S. (June 14, 17, 23, 24)

From Pennsylvania, Roland S. Morris (1874–?) was U.S. ambassador to Japan from 1917 to 1920 and served as president of the American Philosophical Society from 1932 to 1942.

Mother (July 8)

This refers to Annie Criswell McCormick (1843–1922), daughter of J. Vance Criswell, a successful contractor in Harrisburg. She was an active participant in the social and charitable activities of Harrisburg, giving time and money to various projects.

Mueller (June 28)

Brockdorff's Social Democrat successor, Hermann Müller (d. 1930) was head of the German Social Democratic Party (SPD), and nine years later, on June 28, 1928, became head of Weimar Germany's "Great Coalition," which held office until 1930.

Murat, Hotel (January 13, 21, 30)

Residence of Napoleon's marshal, Joachim Murat, and President Wilson's official residence during the peace conference. Wilson worked behind a Napoleonic desk. McCormick refers to it as the "White House." The address on official presidential stationery was printed, 11 Place des Etats-Unis. It was in the Parc Monceau.

Nansen (March 18; April 14, 15, 24)

Norwegian-born Dr. Fridtjof Nansen (1861–1930) was a scientist and arctic explorer who traveled in Russia and wrote about Siberia. He became involved in international politics and served as head of the Norwegian delegation to the United States (1917–18). He was in Paris as the Norwegian representative to the peace conference and acted as lobbyist for adoption of the League Covenant and on behalf of all small nations. He was a renowned humanitarian and was later appointed high commissioner for refugees by the League of Nations. Nansen was awarded the Nobel Prize for Peace in 1922 for the implementation of model agricultural stations in the Volga area and in the Ukraine, which aided in the fight against starvation.

Neale, James (May 10, 12, 13, 14, 15, 16, 17, 26, 27, 28; June 4, 5, 6, 12, 13, 14, 15, 16, 17, 20)

Associate and good friend of McCormick. He graduated from Yale in 1897 and was tapped for the Skull and Bones secret society.

New York Sun (February 7)

The Sun (1933–50) was known for its high journalistic and literary standards. The editorial policy supported advocacy of reform in government and the exposure of corruption. On March 19, 2002, a new newspaper bearing this name was launched in New York City.

New York World (January 30)

Established in 1860, the paper was purchased by Joseph Pulitzer in 1883 and in 1919 was run by his son. The paper was known for its concentration on human-interest stories and sensationalism.

Nicholson (June 11)

Harold Nicholson (1886–1968) was a British junior foreign officer with a special knowledge of the Balkans. After World War I, he married Vita Sackville-West, authored several books, entered politics, and became a member of Parliament.

Nieuport (June 18)

Small town, on land subject to flooding, at the mouth of the Yser River in Belgium. It was at the northernmost end of the battlefront line in 1914.

Northcliffe, Lord (January 30; April 17)

Born Alfred Harmsworth, Lord Northcliffe (1865–1922) served as head of British propaganda during the war and was chairman of the British war mission. He was critical of Lloyd George's conciliatory approach with the Bolsheviks. Through his newspapers, Northcliffe maintained a strong political influence in Britain throughout the war.

Noyon (April 27)

A town fifty-five miles northeast of Paris held for most of the war by French troops and then lost in the German offensive in the spring of 1918.

Olmsted (February 4, 24)

Mrs. Gertrude Howard Olmsted was from Harrisburg, the widow of Congressman Marlin E. Olmsted. She and Vance were married in January 1925.

Omsk (April 14, 21; May 2, 7, 13, 14, 29; June 5, 14, 17, 23)

A city in Siberia where the railroad splits into two branches. It was the seat of a temporary anti-Bolshevik government.

Orlando (March 26, 28, 31; April 5, 7, 9, 10, 14, 23, 29; May 1, 6, 9, 14, 15; June 16, 21)

Head of the Italian government through the Paris Treaty process, Premier Vittorio Orlando (1860–1952) resigned in June 1920.

Ourcq (May 25)

A small tributary to the Marne River.

Owen (January 12, 17, 18, 23, 24; February 2, 8, 19)

Scandinavian representative to War Trade Board.

Paderewski (April 14)

Famous as a pianist and composer, Polish-born Ignace Jan Paderewski (1860–1941) was also a nationalist and diplomat who became involved in politics on behalf of an independent Poland. He served the interests of Poland during the Paris conference and was instrumental in raising large amounts of money for Polish war relief.

Percy, Lord Eustace (January 14; February 14)

Eustace Sutherland Campbell Percy, First Baron Percy of Newcastle (1887–1958), was private secretary to Balfour and later British ambassador to Washington. He also served as president of Britain's Board of Education (1924–29).

Péronne (April 27)

Town on the Somme River where British and French forces joined.

Pershing (January 14; March 6; June 1, 13, 22)

Gen. John Joseph Pershing (1860–1948) was the commander of the American Expeditionary Force in France in 1917. In September 1919, he was promoted to general of the armies of the United States. He insisted that American troops be deployed as American units, and not just used as reinforcements in existing Allied units. After the war, he became chief of staff of the army and is today regarded as one of America's greatest generals.

Pershing Stadium (June 22)

A stadium built under the direction of General Pershing to house the Inter-Allied games, which he proposed on January 9, 1919. When French workers went on strike during the construction, American soldiers were assigned to complete it. Working three shifts around the clock, they completed the stadium within two months.

Phillips (June 24)

William Phillips (1878–1968), a foreign service officer who was serving as assistant secretary of state at the time of the conference. He later served as undersecretary of state as well as in several ambassadorships.

Pichon (January 18; March 28; June 28)

Stephen Jean Marie Pichon (1857–1933) was the editor of the *Petit Journal* and, from 1917 to 1920, the French minister of foreign affairs, (the equivalent of the U.S. secretary of state). He was an ardent nationalist, a follower of Clemenceau, and a plenipotentiary at the Paris Peace Conference.

Poincare, President (January 18; June 22, 28)

Raymond Poincare (1860–1934) began his career as a lawyer, became involved in politics, and served as president of the Republic of France from 1913 to 1920. During the Paris negotiations, he served as the chairman of the Reparations Commission, McCormick's main concern.

Polk, Frank (Jun 24)

A close friend of Robert Lansing, Frank Lyon Polk (1871–1943) was from New York State. He was appointed undersecretary of state in June 1919, and then served as interim secretary of state in 1920, following Lansing's departure from the post.

Principe Island (January 30)

An island off the west coast of Africa in the Gulf of Guinea.

Quai d'Orsay (January 18; February 9, 12; March 5; April 19, 21, 28; May 2, 6, 22; June 18)

The street in Paris that runs along the Left Bank of the Seine River. The Ministry of Foreign Affairs, where many of the committee sessions and meetings were held, is at 37 Quai d'Orsay.

Rappard, Professor (January 21; February 22; March 29)

William Emmanuel Rappard (1883–1958) was a Swiss economist who later gained an international reputation for excellence in the field of international studies and founded the Graduate Institute of International Studies in Geneva. He was born in the United States to Swiss parents and served several diplomatic missions for Switzerland, including representation of Switzerland in Paris. Rappard impressed Wilson, who later advocated Geneva as the site for the League of Nations, based on Rappard's recommendation. Rappard published extensively.

Reading (January 11, 14, 16, 18, 20)

Lord Rufus Daniel Isaacs Reading (1860–1935) served as an advisor to the British war cabinet on financial matters and represented his government during financial negotiations in Washington. He was appointed British ambassador to Washington in 1918 and later served as viceroy of India (1921–26).

Recant, Colonel (June 20)

French officer who was once an aide to Marshal Foch but served on Tardieu's staff at the time of this writing.

Reims (May 25)

City northeast of Paris.

Richards (February 27; March 3, 5, 13; April 14, 15, 16, 18, 22; May 9, 12, 14, 23, 27)

C. Arthur Richards was a member of the War Trade Board as a representative of the food administrator. He was director of the Bureau of Exports under the Trade Board.

Riddell, Sir George (January 25, 30)

Sir George Allardice Riddell (1865–1934) was associated with the *News of the World,* a sensationalistic Sunday publication and founded and financed *Country Life.* He founded the Newspaper Publishers Association in Britain.

Ritz Hotel (January 11, 12, 15, 23, 26; February 4, 12, 15, 16, 20, 23, 27, 28; March 3, 4, 5, 7, 8, 10, 13, 14, 16, 19, 21, 23, 27, 31; April 4, 5, 9, 13, 14, 15, 17, 18, 22, 28; May 1, 7, 20, 21, 22, 29; June 1, 8, 13, 14, 15, 17, 20, 24, 27)

> Hotel where McCormick and other Americans stayed while in Paris. On the historic Place Vendôme, the elegant Ritz opened on June 1, 1898; it was constructed by Hardouin-Mansart, the architect of Versailles. The Ritz provided unofficial space for many of the small conferences, working meals, and social events hosted by members of the peace conference.

Robinson, Henry M. (January 30; February 26; March 22, 27; April 4, 6, 12, 17, 19; May 24)

> A member of the Committee of Economic Advisers and the Supreme Economic Council at the peace conference, Robinson was a member of the Shipping Board and later a member of the Dawes Commission.

Roosevelt (January 2)

> Franklin Delano Roosevelt (1882–1944), then the assistant secretary of the navy, was present in Paris chiefly as an observer and became an active advocate for the League of Nations. He later was elected the thirty-second president of the United States.

Rothschild (February 12, 28; May 24, 27; June 14)

> Lord Lionel Walter Rothschild, Second Baron Rothschild of Tring (1868–1937), was a British politician, a Zionist, and a zoologist with the largest collection of birds in the world. The Balfour Declaration, written to Rothschild in November 1917, expressed official support for the creation of a Jewish Palestine. The text of the Balfour was included word for word in the League of Nations mandate document ratified in 1922.

Rublee, George (January 17, 27; March 5)

> A wealthy politician and lawyer, George Rublee (1868–1951) was the U.S. Shipping Board representative in London. He was sent to Paris in 1918–19 as the American delegate to the Allied Maritime Transport. He was a member of the Commercial Economy Board of the Advisory Council of National Defense, the Priorities Committee of the War Industries Board, and special counsel to the Treasury Department. His contact with Jean Monnet and experience in Europe made this progressive Republican a supporter of the League of Nations. Rublee was the director of the Intergovernmental Committee on Refugees in 1938.

Rublee, Mrs. George (January 27; February 22)

Juliet Rublee (1876–1966), a free-thinking socialite with an exotic and exciting life of her own, was the best friend of Margaret Sanger, as well as a financial supporter of the crusade for birth control.

Sanderson (February 14, 28; April 5)

George Andrew Sanderson (1850–1925) was a graduate of the Naval Academy, class of 1871, who resigned from the service for a career in business in Chicago and in 1904 became a railroad builder in the Sonoran area of Mexico. He served as the appointed secretary of the U.S. Senate from 1919 to 1925.

Saulsbury, Senator (June 27)

Willard Saulsbury Jr. (1861–1927), a member of the Democratic National Committee, was a senator from Delaware. He was a member of the Advisory Committee of the Conference on Limitation of Armaments in Washington, D.C., in 1921–22.

Scheidemann (June 21)

Philipp Scheidemann (1865–1939) led the organization of the government of the Weimar Republic when the German monarchy collapsed in November 1918. He served as the first chancellor and resigned on June 20, 1919, in protest of the treaty. A few years later, he became a member of Germany's pre–World War II government, but he emigrated to Denmark as the Nazi Party took power in Germany.

Scheidemann Government (June 21)

The German government led by Philipp Scheidemann, which stood from February 13 to June 20, 1919.

Schwab (January 2)

Owner and savior of Bethlehem Steel Company, Charles Michael Schwab (1862–1939) helped make the company a major supplier for the Allied powers. His European Allied contacts secured him large war contracts. In 1918, Wilson named Schwab director of the Emergency Fleet Corporation, where he successfully resurrected America's shipbuilding program.

Seydoux (January 14; February 1; May 15, 31; June 6, 25)

Jacques Seydoux, who was France's emissary to Germany and Russia. After the war, he reoriented French diplomacy. As emissary, Seydoux arranged for Germany to pay three billion gold marks yearly for five years, but the French reneged and in 1924 sent Aristide Briand, who advised Germany they had to pay at least six billion gold marks every year for forty-two years.

Seymour, Dr. Charles (February 23; June 28; July 1)

> The Sterling professor of history at Yale University, Seymour (1885–1963) was a specialist on Austria-Hungary. A member of the House Inquiry and chief of the Austro-Hungarian Division of the American delegation in Paris, he noted that McCormick was "a very fine man and very intelligent." Seymour was the curator of the House Papers at Yale and authored several books with and about House. He served as Yale's president from 1937 to 1950.

Sharpe, Ambassador (February 12, 22)

> Born in Ohio, William Graves Sharpe (1859–1922) was a state representative in Congress (1909–14) and ambassador to France during World War I (1914–19). Sharpe managed German, Austrian, and Turkish affairs. He visited prison camps and did relief work.

Sharpe, Miss (February 12)

> Ambassador Sharpe's daughter.

Sheldon, Lewis P. (January 11, 12, 14, 18, 20, 23, 24, 25, 26, 30, 31; February 2, 4, 5, 7, 13, 17, 19, 22, 27; March 2, 3, 5, 13, 16, 22; April 1, 3, 8, 9, 15, 29; June 7, 15, 16)

> Assistant to Robert Lansing, Sheldon was a member of the War Trade Board and Food Administration representative for the London Peace Commission in France. Winner of the bronze medal in the triple jump in the 1900 Olympics, he was a frequent companion of McCormick.

Smith, Sir Hubert (January 14, 21; April 22)

> Sir Hubert Llewellyn Smith (1885–1935) served as director general of economics security in the British delegation. Smith was the permanent undersecretary for the British Board of Trade (1907–1919).

Smuts, General (May 22)

> Formerly an enemy of the British in the Boer War, during World War I Gen. Jan Christian Smuts (1870–1950) served as commander of the Allied forces in East Africa. He was appointed to the British Imperial war cabinet and served at the conference as part of the British delegation. In August 1919, he became premier of South Africa. He was active as a statesman throughout the remainder of his life and served as a field marshal during World War II.

Sonnino, Baron Giorgio Sydney (January 18; March 8, 28; May 6, 15; June 16, 21)

> Baron Giorgio Sydney Sonnino (1847–1922) was Italian minister of foreign affairs and plenipotentiary at the Paris Peace Conference.

Spa (March 3, 5, 6, 7, 8)

Fashionable resort in Belgium for medicinal, water-based cures and for casinos. It was from this city that the generic noun *spa* originated. It was visited by Russian and Swedish royalty, as well as other fashionable Europeans. The German general headquarters were located in Spa at the end of World War I.

Spellacy (January 2; February 14)

Thomas J. Spellacy was an attorney. He was an assistant attorney general in 1920 and served as mayor of Hartford, Connecticut, from 1935 to 1943.

Sterling, Fred (January 19; February 3)

Frederick Augustine Sterling (1876–1957) was a career diplomat. He served as U.S. minister to Ireland (1927–34), to Bulgaria (1933–36), and to Sweden (1938–41).

Stetson, Charles C. (January 11, 12, 18, 23; February 2, 19; April 1, 16)

Stetson was on the Superior Blockade Council. He was U.S. representative of War Trade Board in Paris, as well as acting secretary.

Stettinius (June 3)

Edward Reilly Stettinius Jr. (1900–49) served as U.S. secretary of state (1944–45) and the U.S. representative to the United Nations (1945–46).

Stevens, John. F (January 30)

John F. Stevens (1853–1943) distinguished himself in railroads, the building of the Panama Canal, and his years in Russia. In 1917, he went as head of an American railroad commission to investigate the Trans-Siberian Railway and to oversee the forwarding of American supplies through Vladivostok. He became president of the Interallied Technical Board of the Siberian Railways, serving from 1919 to 1923.

Stillman, Miss (January 26; February 7; April 15; May 10, 15, 17)

Companion of Elizabeth Hudson and occasional dinner partner of McCormick. He never notes her first name.

Stineman (March 16, 27)

James Hale *Steinman* was a newspaper publisher from Lancaster, Pennsylvania. He was active in Democratic politics and a Pennsylvania member of the Democratic National Convention in 1936. Conestoga House, his home in Lancaster, is a local tourist attraction known especially for the gardens.

St. Menehould (May 25, 26)

A town due west of Verdun.

St. Quentin (April 27)

Small city in the area where British forces lost ground to the German offensive during the spring of 1918.

Strauss, Albert (February 7, 8, 10, 16, 18, 23, 26; March 2, 11, 13, 24)

A prominent New York banker, Albert Strauss (1864–1929) was vice chair of the Federal Reserve. He was a member of the War Trade Board, representing the Treasury Department. Strauss was a member of the Financial Commission and advisor on financial questions for the American delegation.

Strauss, Oscar (February 24; March 4)

Oscar Strauss (1850–1926) was a representative in 1919 of a private organization called the League to Enforce Peace. He was a member of the Permanent Board of Arbitration from 1902 to 1908 and served as ambassador to Turkey in 1909.

Stuart (January 12, 23, 28; February 4)

War Trade Board representative.

Stuyvesant, Mrs. Rutherford (June 13)

The wife of the wealthy American builder who constructed the first apartment building in New York City, she had begun a "One-Dollar Fund" in the United States, which collected $20,000 by the end of 1917. Mrs. Stuyvesant was assisting the French organization known as the Charité Maternelle de Paris, which was probably involved with the hospital referred to in the January 25 diary entry.

Sullivan, Mark (February 5)

Mark Sullivan (1874–1952) was an American journalist and historian.

Summers, Leland L. (January 24)

Chairman of the U.S. War Industries Board Mission in Europe; member of the Inter-Allied Munitions Council.

Sumner (January 30, 31; February 4, 14, 15, 28; March 6, 7, 12, 13, 22, 26, 27, 28, 31; April 2, 5, 7, 15, 17, 22, 24; May 24, 30, 31; June 10, 12, 13)

John Andrew Hamilton Sumner, the right honorable lord of Ibstone was a lawyer and judge. He was a member of the Reparations Committee and supported the push for heavy reparations from Germany.

Sutherland, Duchess of (February 15; March 18; June 16, 23)

Lady Millicent Fanny St. Clair–Erskine, duchess of Sutherland (1867–1955), was an independent woman of independent means who established a hospital called Millicent Sutherland Ambulance during the earliest states of the invasion of Belgium. The hospital was subsumed by the Red Cross but remained under her supervision. She was a collector of sculpture and art, and is the subject of a famous portrait by John Singer Sargent.

Switzerland, President of (January 21)

Gustave Ador (1845–1928) was the president of Switzerland in 1919. He was president of the International Committee of the Red Cross from 1910 to 1928.

Swope (January 30; April 20, 22; May 9)

Herbert Bayard Swope (1882–1958) was a newspaperman and foreign correspondent with the *New York Globe*. He won the Pultizer Prize for reporting in 1917 and later became editor of the *New York Herald Tribune*. Swope was a New York delegate to the Democratic National Convention in 1936 and 1940 and was an advisor to Franklin Delano Roosevelt.

Tardieu (January 14, 24; February 1, 8, 23, 25, 26, 27; March 2; May 1, 6, 28; June 1, 3, 20, 28)

French high commissioner to the United States 1917–18, Andre Pierre Gabriel Amedee Tardieu (1876–1945) served as a plenipotentiary at the Paris Peace Conference. He acted as Clemenceau's principal advisor and chief lieutenant and commissioner of Franco-American affairs. Tardieu was one of the principal framers of political and territorial clauses in the treaty, and its leading French defender. Tardieu believed France's first goal, was to guarantee her security, and reparations were a secondary goal. He also worked to minimize leaks to the French press. He was a member of the Chamber of Deputies from 1914 to 1924 and premier of France in 1929–30 an 1932.

Taussig, Dr. (March 22, 29; July 1, 5)

Frank W. Taussig (1859–1940), an international economist and free trade advocate, was a professor of economics at Harvard University (1885–1935). He served as an economic advisor to Wilson from 1917 to 1919.

Taylor, Dr. Alonzo (January 16, 17, 23, 28; February 19, 22, 27; April 12, 13, 16, 30; May 10; June 21, 25)

A professor at the University of Pennsylvania and a representative of the secretary of agriculture on the War Trade Board, Taylor was a chemist and food specialist. He worked with the American Embassy in Berlin, and his focus was on protecting the food interests of British prisoners of war. After the war, he helped create the Hoover Institute for Food Research at Stanford University.

Taylor, Reggie (March 4, 27, 28, 29; April 1; May 5, 17, 22, 25; June 29)
Also spelled Reggy. A young soldier who acts as orderly and courier for McCormick and sometime companion.

Teschen (April 23)
Now known as Cieszyn, town in southern Poland on the border with Czechoslovakia.

Thomas, Mrs. Linda (June 23)
Linda Thomas (1883–1954) was a wealthy divorcée living in Paris. She was said to be the most beautiful woman in the world. In December 1919, she married Cole Porter, the American composer, who was also living in Paris at the time.

Thompson, Sir William Mitchell (February 3, 4, 26; March 24; April 19; June 6, 25)
Sir William Mitchell-Thompson was a British blockade expert, later Chief Civil Commissioner during the general strike of 1926.

Tiflis (June 13)
Old or alternate name for the ancient city of Tbilisi in the country of Georgia.

Titoff (February 22)
Ivan Titoff was Russian minister at the conference.

Tobin, Captain (February 12)
Possibly Robert Gibson Tobin, U.S. Navy, who was promoted to a rear admiral and received three navy crosses for surface engagements during World War II.

Tours (May 17)
A medieval town southwest of Paris in Indre-et-Loire where the Cher and Loire Rivers meet.

Townsend (February 26)
Possibly geologist Charles Kenneth Townsend (1867–1960). A professor at the University of Wisconsin, he was a proponent of seeking outside mineral resources for America before totally depleting national sources.

Townsend (February 26)
Maj. Gen. Sir Charles Vere Ferrers Townsend (1861–1924), expert on Mesopotamia.

Trianon Hotel (May 7)
Also called simply Trianon. A separate building on the ground of the Versailles Palace, the Grand Trianon was built by Mansart. The build-

ing was used during World War II, after the invasion of Normandy, as Eisenhower's headquarters.

Trotsky (April 6)

Leon Trotsky (1879–1940) was born Lev Davidovich Bronstein, assuming the name Trotsky in 1902. A disciple of Marx, he eventually joined the Bolsheviks. He was appointed the commissar for foreign affairs in 1917, and then in 1918, the commissar of war, in which capacity he created the Red Army which struggled against Kolchak's White Army of non-Soviets. He eventually left the Soviet Union and was assassinated on Joseph Stalin's orders.

Tuileries Garden (March 12; May 5)

This public garden in the center of Paris was once the site of a royal palace which was attacked several times, and ultimately destroyed, by the citizenry of Paris. The palace was named for the tile works that originally stood on the site.

Tumulty (January 14, 30; July 5)

Joseph Patrick Tumulty (1879–1960) was Wilson's advisor during the latter's New Jersey gubernatorial campaign. He became Wilson's secretary in 1911 and remained so until 1921. Tumulty served as president of the Shipping Board. His critics, who included his rival for influence with Wilson, Col. Edward House, felt he was politically timid, but Tumulty and Grayson formed a close association with Edith Wilson after Wilson's incapacitating strokes.

USS *Conner* (July 8)

A destroyer (1918–40) that was transferred to the United Kingdom as HMS *Leeds*.

USS *George Washington* (January 1, 2, 19; February 19; June 29; July 8)

A German ocean liner (1909–51) interned in New York in 1914, at the outbreak of the war. It transported the American Commission to Negotiate Peace to the Paris Peace Conference and back again. In April 1919, radio equipment was installed on board to enable President Wilson to engage in direct telephonic communication with his officials in Washington during his return voyage from the peace conference. After the war, it was part of the U.S. mail transport system.

USS *Leviathan* (January 1)

This ship was confiscated from the German Hamburg-American like in Hoboken, New Jersey, in 1914. She was the largest ship afloat at the time, at 54,282 tons. (For comparison, the *George Washington* was

23,788 tons.) She carried up to 10,000 troops at a time to Europe or 10 percent overall of those shipped. Launched on April 3, 1913, she was scrapped in 1938.

USS *Northern Pacific* (June 30)

A transport ship that ran aground at Fire Island during rough seas on January 1, 1919, while carrying wounded veterans back from France. The troops were rescued by other ships.

USS *Oklahoma*, BB 37 (July 8)

Built in 1912 in Camden, New Jersey, the *Oklahoma* escorted the presidential ship for both the 1918 and 1919 trips. She was heavily damaged while anchored at Pearl Harbor during the attack in 1941. She was sunk in the Pacific Ocean in 1947.

USS *Pennsylvania*, (July 8)

Built in 1913, she became the flagship of the U.S. Atlantic Fleet in 1916. She remained in service through World War II and was used as a target ship in the atomic bomb tests at Bikini during July 1946. Decommissioned in August 1946, she remained in Kwajalein Lagoon for radiological and structural studies until February 10, 1948, when she was sunk off Kwajalein.

USS *Tarbell* (July 8)

Destroyer built at Cramp and commissioned in 1918.

USS *Woolsey* (July 8)

In 1921, this ship sank off the Pacific coast of Panama.

USS *Yarnell* (July 8)

Destroyer-class ship that was commanded by Adm. William F. Halsey during the World War I period.

Vanderlip (February 28)

Washington Baker Vanderlip (1867–?) was a mining engineer. He represented a mainly Los Angeles–based investor group. In 1920, the United States and Vanderlip won concessions of nearly $3 billion in oil, coal, timber, and fishing resources on Kamchatka.

Varvennes (May 26)

Village in Lorraine associated with the history of Louis XIV and Marie Antoinette as mentioned by McCormick.

Venizelos (February 24, May 6, 28)

Greek statesman Eleutherios K. Venizelos (1849–1936), also spelled "Venezelos" by McCormick, supported the Allied cause during the war, in opposition to the pro-German position of King Constantine I, who was forced to abdicate in 1917. At this time, as premier, Venizelos brought Greece into the war on the Allied side.

Versailles (January 18; March 2, 5, 9; April 6; May 4, 7, 8; June 28)

A planned city located about twelve miles west-southwest of Paris, Versailles is the seat of a catholic bishopric and also the place of residence of the kings of France. During World War I, Versailles was the seat of the Allied War Council. The early château was enlarged and perfected between 1665 and 1683 by a series of famous architects and landscapers. The Hall of Mirrors, where the Peace Treaty was signed, was designed by Le Brun and connected the original state apartments of the king and queen. Versailles has been the site of many significant events, both French and international, before and since World War I.

Vesle (May 25)

A river in France. On this river, at the town of Fismette, the 28th Division of the Pennsylvania National Guard lost seven thousand men killed, wounded, and missing.

Vilgrain (January 27)

The French undersecretary of state for Ravitaillement worked with the Civilian Relief Board (Hoover's organization) to bring supplies into liberated areas. Between November 1918 and May 1919, 108,000 tons of supplies were imported.

Villard, Oscar Garrison (March 26)

The son and grandson of journalists, *Oswald* Garrison Villard (1872–1949) also became a newspaperman and crusader-reformer like his grandfather, William Lloyd Garrison. He owned and operated the *New York Evening Post* and the *Nation*. Because of his strong pacifist views, readership of the former paper declined. He sold it but retained the *Nation* as a means of promoting his radical views. He was one of the founding members of the NAACP and crusaded on behalf of universal suffrage and trade union reform.

Wallace, Ambassador (April 22; May 9; June 28)

Hugh Campbell Wallace (1863–1931) served as U.S. ambassador to France from 1919 to 1921.

War Trade Board (January 11–13, 15, 17, 20–24, 27; February 22, 27; March 3, 4, 6, 15, 25; April 1, 8, 10, 16, 19, 25, 26; May 2, 8, 16, 23, 31; June 12, 17, 24, 25)

The War Trade Board was created in the fall of 1917 to oversee control of U.S. international trade during the war. Vance McCormick was chairman of the board. The board was subsumed by the State Department on June 30, 1919.

Ward, Cabot (January 18)

Head of Paris U.S. Intelligence.

Waterlow (January 22)

Probably Sir Philip Hickson Waterlow, son of former Lord Mayor of London, Sir Sidney Waterlow.

Wedel (April 26)

Norwegian minister to France.

White, Beaver (March 14, 21, 22)

Born in Milroy, Pennsylvania, Beaver White was a resident of England before the war and became involved with the American Committee of Relief of Belgium, which led to his assoication with Herbert Hoover, the food administrator. Beaver was a Member of the War Trade Board as the representative of the food administrator.

White, Henry (January 23, 27; February 18, 27; March 7, 8, 15, 16, 28; April 5, 10, 27; May 21)

Henry White (1850–1927), U.S. ambassador to France from 1906 to 1909, was the only Republican appointed to the Peace Commission. A member of the Credentials Committee for the conference, he strongly advocated American entrance to the League of Nations.

Whitehouse (June 27)

Probably referring to Sheldon Whitehouse (1883–1965), a U.S. Foreign Service officer who was later envoy extraordinary and minister plenipotentiary to Guatemala in 1929 and to Colombia in 1933.

Whitlock, Brand (June 23; July 1)

A journalist by trade, Brand Whitlock (1869–1934) became active in politics and for several terms (1906–14) was elected mayor of Toledo, Ohio. During World War I, he was ambassador to Belgium. He authored eighteen books.

Wilson, Elsie Cobb (March 19)

A famous New York decorator for the homes, ranches, offices, yachts, hotels, and clubs of the rich and famous.

Wilson, Hugh (February 23)

Hugh Robert Wilson (1885–1946), a career U.S. diplomat who became envoy extraordinary and minister plenipotentiary to Switzerland in 1937, served as assistant secretary of state, and served as ambassador extraordinary and plenipotentiary to Germany.

Wilson, President Woodrow (January 1, 13, 14, 16, 17, 18, 20, 21, 22, 23, 25, 29, 30; February 2, 5, 7, 8, 10, 11, 12, 13, 14, 15, 19, 24, 26; March 2, 6, 14, 16, 17, 21, 22, 24, 26, 27, 28, 29, 30, 31; April 1, 2, 3, 4, 5, 6, 7, 10, 11, 12, 15, 16, 17, 19, 21, 23, 24, 25, 26, 28, 29, 30; May 7, 9, 14, 15, 19, 22, 24, 30; June 2, 3, 4, 5, 9, 10, 11, 12, 13, 16, 17, 19, 21, 23, 24, 25, 26, 27, 28, 29, 30; July 3, 4, 5, 6, 8)

Woodrow Wilson (1856–1924) considered Vance McCormick a personal friend as well as a vital advisor; they had become acquainted through the workings of the National Democratic Committee. Before he was elected president of the United States (1913–1921), Wilson had served as president of Princeton University (1902–10) and governor of New Jersey (1911–13). He was awarded the Nobel Peace Prize in 1915.

Wilson, Miss Margaret (June 19, 23, 24, 27, 28; July 5, 7)

Eldest daughter of Woodrow Wilson, Margaret Woodrow Wilson (1886–1944) never married.

Wilson, Mrs. (January 13, 15, 16, 22; February 11, 13; March 14, 16; April 9, 16, 28; June 17, 19, 28; July 4, 5)

Woodrow Wilson married Edith Bolling Galt (1872–1961) in 1915, within two years of the death of his first wife, Ellen Axson Wilson. The second Mrs. Wilson accompanied her husband to Paris. She gained political influence of her own after Wilson's debilitating strokes, when she assumed even more than the routine duties of the presidential office. She was a good friend to Vance McCormick and corresponded with him after the war.

Young, Professor (February 14)

Dr. Allyn Abbott Young (1876–1929) was chief of the Division of Economics and Statistics for the American Commission. He was an international lawyer, a specialist on economics and statistics, and a faculty member at Cornell University.

Other Documents

Edited by
Michael Barton and
Cherie Fieser

"Harrisburg Elects a Football Mayor"
Clippings from Vance McCormick's Political Scrapbook, 1902

V ance McCormick collected in a scrapbook political advertisements (possibly handbills) and newspaper stories from his 1902 campaign. On the spine is stamped "Democratic Candidate for Mayor 1902," and on the cover, "V. C. McC." The exact dates of the documents were not always provided, but one can safely presume that they are from 1901 and 1902 (the election was held on February 18, 1902). Likewise, the identities of the newspapers were not always provided, but the source was often the Patriot of Harrisburg, which McCormick purchased after the election. What stands out is the partisan, sensational style of the political journalism of a hundred years ago; also obvious is the reporters' portrayal of Vance McCormick as a winning athlete.

Worth special attention is item 14, an article that either paraphrases or quotes a good deal from a speech on success that mayor-elect McCormick gave to the Messiah Lutheran Boys' Club of Harrisburg. The address shows that McCormick could use his football experiences for effect as vividly as any reporter could. It also includes his impressions of a fellow progressive from the opposite party—President Theodore Roosevelt, with whom he had recently dined.

1. ADVERTISEMENT

DON'T GIVE THE CITY A BLACK EYE.

A Greater Harrisburg?

To-day will decide!

The campaign for the proposed municipal improvements has closed!

The voters hold the fate of the city in their hands!

Will they strike a blow at the good name and fame of their home?

It is no exaggeration to say that to-day Harrisburg is "the observed of all observers." Towns and cities not merely in our own state, but in many other states are looking to see if the voters of Harrisburg will adopt the scheme (in its general outlines) which has been planned by trained and experienced experts, and which has been named the "Harrisburg plan," and has done more to call attention to our city than anything else in a generation.

It is not a question of details; an honest capable and thoroughly practical board of public works will look after those, and consult the best interests of ALL PARTS OF THE CITY.

It is a truth, however disagreeable it may be to admit it, that in the last few years typhoid fever has increased very largely; it is also a truth, that as the noted authority on the subject, Dr. Osler, has stated, "effective [*sic*] drainage and contaminated water" are the two chief things which spread the disease. The opportunity is now offered to do away with these conditions in Harrisburg, and at a cost (NOTHING IN 1902) which is trifling when compared with a doctor's bill for one's self or his family.

Harrisburg is "beautiful for situation" and its position as a railroad center makes it an attractive point for people to come to love or to set up manufacturing plants; but when it is found that our water supply is impure, that our sewer system is defective, and that we have few places for children to play in, those who would otherwise come here, decide to go elsewhere.

It is not to be expected that all will equally approve all that is proposed, but each feature has its hearty supporters and each should be willing to sacrifice something, in order to get all that so many earnestly believe is vital to the prosperity of our town.

Our children are to be considered for the little ones are concerned. When the grown-ups were young, the town had more open lots, where the children could play. Now they have to play in the streets.

Of this day, it may be truly said, in the poet's words:
"This day's propitious to be wise in."
Be wise! Don't give your home a black eye! Vote for the loan!
Vote for a progressive city, a Greater Harrisburg.

———————————

2. ADVERTISEMENT

VOTE FOR THE PUBLIC IMPROVEMENTS
by George F. Ross
Tune: "Marching Through Georgia"

Harrisburg the capital of this grand old Keystone State,
Has been asleep for many years, but now she's struck her gait,
And she's going to keep it too, and be right up to date
By voting for the public improvements.

Hurrah, hurrah, we'll sing the jubilee.
Hurrah, hurrah, it's up to you and me,
To help along the good work for our town's prosperity,
By voting for the public improvements.

The water that we have to drink from city reservoir
Is mixed with sewage, culm and dirt and typhoid germs galore,
But we can have a filter plant and drink such stuff no more,
By voting for the public improvements.

Hurrah, hurrah, etc.

Paxton Creek's a nuisance and it often overflows,
When we have to cross that stream we always hold our nose,
But now's the chance to rid it of the filth that in it goes,
By voting for the public improvements.

Hurrah, hurrah, etc.

When you scratch a man who is against the river dam,
Who thinks it wrong in theory and a veritable sham,
You will find that he's the kind that's generally called a clam,
And won't vote for public improvements.

Hurrah, hurrah, etc.

When we stroll on river front upon a summer's day
The perfume that we must inhale is not like new-mown hay,
And this smell that stinks like ———— well, it can be driven away,
By voting for the public improvements.

Hurrah, hurrah, etc.

Let us then on Tuesday next this city fairly sweep
By such a vote as will denote that we are not asleep,
To all the people of this State who tabs on us they keep,
By voting for the public improvements.

Hurrah, hurrah, etc.

———————————

3. UNIDENTIFIED NEWSPAPER REPRINT OF A NEW YORK *EVENING JOURNAL*
ARTICLE, FEBRUARY 11, 1902

AS OTHERS SEE HIM
"New York Journal" Recognizes the
Importance of McCormick's Candidacy
for Mayor of Harrisburg.

Under a two-column, full-length half-tone foot ball picture and vignette
portrait the New York "Evening Journal" to-day prints the following special dispatch which emphasizes the popularity of Mr. Vance C. McCormick, the democratic candidate for mayor

Hold the fort, McCormick's coming,
Barbour signals still,
Hefflefinger's in the centre,
Win we must and will.
—Old Yale Foot Ball Chant.

Harrisburg, Pa., Feb. 11.—Vance C. McCormick, the old Yale quarter back,
varsity captain and goal kicker, the only man that "Billy" Bull ever succeeded in teaching the heart breaking spiral twist to a punt which meant
death and sudden destruction to Harvard hopes and an extra kink in the
Tiger's tail, is bucking the political center with the vim which made him
famous as a gridiron star.

McCormick is the democratic candidate for mayor of Harrisburg nom-
inally. Really he is the candidate of the good government party and the

backers of the immense public improvements which are to make Harrisburg hold up her head along with her sister state capitals.

The mayoralty election will take place Tuesday, February 18, and the odds are on the young Yale ex-athlete, who is popular alike with the machine politicians and the church people. McCormick has long ago solved the secret of retaining popularity without a sacrifice of principle. Harrisburg is normally republican, but it looks as if Vance McCormick would win out on his personality. A feature of the campaign is the energetic electioneering that is going on at afternoon teas and country club dinners and dances, where debutantes vie with one another in endeavoring to secure society republican votes for their favorite.

The voters of Harrisburg will ballot for an increase of $1,090,000 in the city debt for the purpose of better sewerage, paved streets, parks and an improved river front. Two years ago Mr. McCormick was elected to common council by a large majority in a republican ward, and since being in office he has become prominent because of his interest in a better Harrisburg.

Mr. McCormick was graduated at Yale, class of '93. He was captain of the freshman base ball and foot ball teams, and played full back and quarter back, on the university team in the seasons of 1891 and 1892. The latter year he was captain. While on the team he was never scored against. Since his retirement from college he has each season officiated as coach with other former Yale captains.

---

4. UNIDENTIFIED NEWSPAPER EDITORIAL, FEBRUARY 17, 1902

IT WILL BE A LANDSLIDE
FOR VANCE C. M'CORMICK.
He and His Democratic Col-
leagues Will Win Out.
Republican Leaders Are Panic-Stricken At the
Headway That Has Been Made Against
Them and Have Given Up Hope.

Mr. McCormick's first initial is also the initial of Victory. There is now no longer any doubt about the outcome of the campaign which will close tomorrow with the election of the entire democratic ticket. Even the republican leaders have wearied with the task of boasting vauntingly of victory when the last shred of confidence in their ticket has been torn from them in the closing days of the campaign. Men high in the councils of the republican city machine privately hope that the triumph of the democratic party shall not be a landslide while they publicly profess confidence in the outcome.

On Saturday night Mr. McCormick made a tour of the upper wards of the city and came into personal contact with hundreds of railroad men. Railroaders live a strenuous life and they have taken kindly to the candidacy of the democratic candidate for office. They want a man who can do things and will not be hampered in the discharge of the duties of his office by the behests of any machine.

All over the city the closing hours of the campaign are seeing new recruits come forward to the standard of the young candidate for mayor. The assertion is now made that every ward in the city will be carried by the democratic municipal ticket to-morrow and the candidates for minor offices in the various wards are confident that they will win out in the struggle to-morrow.

The democratic city committeemen will meet this evening in the grand jury room of the court house, when the watchers' certificates will be distributed. It is expected that the meeting will be largely attended, as the party interest in the coming election is greater than it has been for years.

TO-MORROW.

Action to-morrow will follow a long and not unprofitable season of argument. All good citizens must hope that action will be such as will commend itself to the subsequent good judgment of the right-thinking and right-doing people of this community.

No citizen anxious for the future progress of our municipality and for the betterment of all its affairs can conscientiously set aside his convictions as to the matter of needed public improvements at the behest of party bosses and for the purpose of strengthening and enlarging the power of a corrupt political machine. The plain truth is that the election of McCormick to the mayoralty would be a greater victory for good government than has ever been accomplished in this city at a single election. In thus asserting we do not exaggerate, we but state a ponderous truth in the mildest way.

Will not, then, every good citizen cast aside partisan feeling for a little time and use his best endeavors for the success of McCormick. His election would not mean and could not honorably be claimed as a party victory. It would be something much greater and higher—a triumph of sensible men of business, of men of honesty and unselfishness over petty politicians and scheming spoils-men.

Isn't such a triumph worth working for and contributing one's ballot to? Let to-morrow be made Harrisburg's day instead of the politicians' day.

---

5. NEWSPAPER ARTICLE, *BALTIMORE SUN*, FEBRUARY 17, 1902

END OF A HOT FIGHT
McCormick Expects To Be Next
Mayor of Harrisburg.
FAMOUS FOOTBALL PLAYER
The "Harrisburg Plan" of Extensive
Public Improvements-Democratic
Candidate's Personal Work.

[*Special Dispatch to the* Baltimore Sun]

HARRISBURG. PA., Feb. 17—At the close of the most exciting municipal campaign this city has ever known the Democratic candidate, Vance C. McCormick, one of the greatest goal kickers the Yale football team ever had, stands an excellent chance of being elected by from 300 to 500 majority. He expects to kick the winning goal over his opponent Dr. Samuel F. Hassler, the Republican candidate.

The former Yale quarterback and captain of the eleven of '92 has personally visited every industrial plant employing male labor in the city and made addresses at many ward and district meetings. He has had efficient help from Hickok, the noted ex-Yale hammer-thrower, and other fellow-collegians now in Harrisburg, and letters of encouragement from members of the Yale football team of 1892.

Mr. McCormick, who is in his thirtieth year, was graduated from Yale in 1893. He was captain of the baseball and football teams, and played fullback and quarterback on the elevens of 1891 and 1892. His team was never scored against while he was on the gridiron, and he never failed to assist in coaching the Yale teams for the big annual contests with Harvard. He is one of a board of three managers of the large McCormick estate, and is now serving his first term in the City Council, having been elected by a majority of over 200 in a strong Republican ward.

Mr. McCormick was one of 60 citizens who raised a fund of $5,000 with which to secure opinions of experts from New York, Boston and other cities on the various improvements whose fate rests with the voters tomorrow, and he introduced the ordinance submitting to the people the question of increasing the city debt to $1,090,000 for the following purposes: $310,000 for the extension, improvements of the sewerage system, including the deepening of the channel of Paxton creek, a small stream flowing through the city, which overflows its banks at every little flood; $65,000 for the construction of a dam in the river that will keep the stream about four feet above low-water mark, and thus cover the mouths of sewers at all stages of the river; $250,000 for acquiring lands for parks and for making park improvements, including the extension of Reservoir Park, and the purchase of Wetzel's Swamp, a wooded tract of about 465 acres in the upper part of the city; and $100,000 for the creation of a paving fund.

The improvement campaign has been pushed with much vigor and has the indorsement of all the daily newspapers. One or two features of the "Harrisburg plan," as it has been termed, have stirred up considerable opposition in certain quarters, and may bring about the defeat of the whole proposition. There seems to be little objection to the sewerage and filtration features of the plan.

Should the improvement plan go through the money is to be expended by a Board of Public Works, made up of three gentlemen who are to serve without pay. If the loan is authorized there will be expended in Harrisburg during the next five years about $6,000,000, of which $4,000,000 will go into the new State Capitol building, plans for which, modeled somewhat after the Capitol at Washington, were recently adopted

---

6. NEWSPAPER ARTICLE, HARRISBURG *PATRIOT*, FEBRUARY 18, 1902

SWEEPING VICTORY FOR
GOOD GOVERNMENT TICKET

McCormick and Royal Carry the City by Overwhelming Majorities
and a Bigger and Better Harrisburg is Assured by the Great
Vote Given by the People for Public Improvements—
Most Propitious Day in History of the City.

Returns from eighteen precincts at 11:40 o'clock to-night indicate that Vance C. McCormick has been elected mayor of the city over Dr. Hassler, Republican, by a majority of at least 1–500. John K. Royal, the Democratic candidate for city treasurer, will be elected by a majority of 1,500, and perhaps by much larger figures. Indications at this time, although the returns are imperfect, indicate the election of Gough for controller by about 100. Mr. Moore, the Democrat, made a gallant fight, but it looks at this time as though he cannot win.

Returns from every precinct are in favor of improvements. Even the strongest of the opposing districts record but a small majority against the loan. The indications are that the public has endorsed improvements by a majority of 3,000. At this time no estimate can be made on the remainder of the ticket on account of the slowness with which the returns are being counted, due mainly to the fact that tickets were cut in every ward.

Clean politics and good government yesterday won the greatest victory in the history of Harrisburg. Vance C. McCormick was chosen mayor, John K. Royal city treasurer and public improvements carried by an overwhelming majority.

Harrisburg has awakened from her long slumber and from this on it will be all and everything for a bigger and better city. The citizen who has taken no active interest in the fight that was yesterday brought to such a satisfactory conclusion can scarcely realize the true meaning of the great victory. Harrisburg is to have for its mayor one of the brightest and most able men in the state. The mayor-elect is a Democrat in every sense of the word and what is more, he is a thoroughly honest business man of high standing and a student of municipal government. Under his guiding hand Harrisburg will go forward along all lines.

Mr. Royal is to be city treasurer. His past record speaks for itself and his election was not once in doubt. Even the most ardent supporters of the machine candidates had not the courage to even hint at his defeat. The overwhelming majority he received yesterday is a tribute to the worth of the man and an encouragement to all honest and upright citizens. Harrisburg is to be congratulated upon electing such a man as he for the high and important office of custodian of the people's money.

The Municipal League for Public Improvements is deserving of the greatest praise. Worthy motives prompted a band of public spirited citizens to set aside their own private interest and to give time and money for the good of the city at large. Their fight was not so much for themselves as for the great body of people who did not at first understand the loan and for that reason opposed it. The "Harrisburg Plan" will become famous. It emanated from the Municipal League and was the direct cause for yesterday's great victory for a bigger and better city. Public spirited citizens contributed $5,000 in order that experts might be employed to formulate plans for the improvements proposed. When these were completed headquarters were opened by the league and a campaign of education begun. The newspapers of town were united in favor of the loan and devoted columns of space to setting forth the advantages of it. One by one the public local organizations, such as the Civic club and the board of trade, endorsed the plan and on Monday evening the last vestige, almost, of opposition vanished and the great victory of yesterday resulted.

The campaign was one free of personalities. The high character of the Democratic candidates prevented personal attacks. In the Democratic management pure politics and honest methods was the war cry and the results of tactics based on these watchwords have emply [sic] justified them. Honest candidates and honest work met hesitating candidates and machine methods on open ground and defeated them by an overwhelming majority. Harrisburg is through with the Gang. Harrisburg stands for progress and all that is progressive. Harrisburg is a good city and is going to be a great city. The people won their victory yesterday and it will redound to their credit and welfare in the years to come.

The liveliest municipal campaign in the history of Harrisburg was that of yesterday and heavier votes were polled at many of the precincts than ever before at a spring election. The vote was got out early in the day and the surprises in the various precincts were many and frequent. At noon a majority of the voters had cast their ballots and the afternoon hours were the quietest of the day.

Towards evening the voting became heavier again and at 7 o'clock when the polls closed the number of votes cast in many districts exceeded that at the last presidential election. The result of the election became apparent after the voting booths had been open for only a few hours and early in the day the Republican leaders in the various precincts began to acknowledge the defeat of the head of their ticket.

The 2d precinct of the 2d ward was one of the centers of the fight and the scenes around the polls were lively in the extreme. Early in the morning trouble was threatened among several of the watchers and four deputy sheriffs were sworn in. Although there was some little trouble after that time the officers were entirely unnecessary.

In the 8th ward there was also a threat of "rough house" on several occasions and the favorite weapons of "de ward," razors, were flourished. The principal disturbance was at the close of the polls in the 4th precinct of the ward. The voting place at Briggs and Seventh streets was crowded with watchers and workers and when the hour for closing arrived there were four voters within the space for the election board. The point was raised that it was too late to vote the men and the argument became so heated that barber implements were called upon to support the points at issue. The fracas did not result in any bloodshed, however.

In the 1st precinct of the 4th ward the vote polled was heavier at 3 o'clock in the afternoon than it was at the close of the polls at the last presidential election.

The heavy voting was also evident in the 5th ward and in the 2d precinct 135 votes had been cast at 1 o'clock while at the same time the year before the number cast at that hour was but 90. The voting continued in the same way throughout the afternoon and at the close of the polls the vote registered was a record breaker.

The Republican leaders saw how the election was going and many left the polls early in the afternoon. At 5 o'clock in the 6th ward prominent Republican workers said that the ward would go at least 250 for McCormick. In the 1st ward the voting seemed to indicate a similar result and some of those who had tried to stem the current and make a respectable showing for their ticket left their places and practically acknowledged defeat.

The reports for almost all the precincts in the city early in the afternoon indicated the complete victory of the Democratic ticket.

Shortly before the close of the polls at the 1st precinct of the 9th ward a heeler attempted to vote a man not on the registry list. A candidate on the Republican ticket who had been working with the heeler until that time challenged the vote. The two came to blows and the counting of the ballots could not be started until more than half an hour after the close of the polls.

The voting for the improvements was a surprise to many of those who had opposed the scheme. Many of the districts which had been apparently against the increase in debt early showed that the sentiment was strong for the improvements. The manner of voting for the increase permitted the watchers to know pretty well how the vote was going and early in the afternoon it was seen that the increase in debt would be carried by a safe majority. Even in the districts which had practically been conceded to be against the plan the vote was a surprise in many ways.

---

7. EDITORIAL, HARRISBURG *PATRIOT*, FEBRUARY 18, 1902

PICKING FROM THE POLLS

Three years ago when Dr. John A. Fritchey was elected mayor for the third time The Patriot said: "Well if Harrisburg isn't a Democratic town Mayor Fritchey will make it so." The Patriot is inclined to think it is something of a prophet.

Notwithstanding the snappy weather the saloons observed the law and kept closed doors yesterday. But the sideboards of the social clubs were not shut down.

Didn't Capt. McCormick make some beautiful touch-downs yesterday!

He is the McCormick mower, for sure, the way he cut down the enemy's grass and made of it hay for himself. And he's a thresher, too, as Dr. Hassler will admit.

If they were for McCormick they never minded the weather. But if they were the other way they feared pneumonia chills and the like. The McCormick men were exceedingly healthy fellows.

Three years ago Mayor Fritchey carried the city by 410 majority, six of the ten wards giving him majorities ranging from fourteen in the 10th ward to 270 in the 7th. The largest majority for Sheeslev, his opponent, was 183, which was given by the 4th ward.

Scenes around the polls reminded those who gathered there of a presidential election.

A great crowd of members assembled at the Harrisburg club to hear the returns. Returns favorable to McCormick and the loan chiefly received the applause.

And you will observe City Treasurer Royal is something of a sprinter, also.

It didn't wait to snow the next day. The prospects looked so fine that it turned in the day before.

McCormick runs like sixty. And he's only thirty.

When Dr. Hassler learned he had lost his own precinct he concluded it wasn't worth while to look for anything more.

It is in order now for somebody to be first to propose Vance McCormick for governor.

Charles B. McConkey, who was the head of the advisory committee in behalf of McCormick and his colleagues, did most excellent work. His ability and industry went far toward bringing about the handsome results.

The bulletin service of The Patriot attracted continuous crowds last night and the reports of the victory for good governments were enthusiastically received. It was a late hour when the cheering crowds went to their homes happy over the great good news The Patriot had carried to them.

Upon the closing of the polls it was pretty generally conceded by the enemy that McCormick had won. The trend was his way all day and no boasting of the Hassler followers could delude those who watched with care.

At 10 o'clock the first strains of a band of rejoicing musicians sounded in front of The Patriot office. And there was music then for several hours later.

It was a cold day. That much the defeated mayoralty candidate admitted at the outset.

Did bosses ever get such a beating. The people rule even in Harrisburg! There are some Republican "leaders" looking for a job this morning.

It's no use fooling with these modern athletes. They are bound to get there.

---

8. NEWSPAPER ARTICLE, *NORTH AMERICAN*, FEBRUARY 18, 1902

HARRISBURG ELECTS
A "FOOT-BALL MAYOR"
Vance McCormick, Famous Yale Quarterback,
Beats Machine Candidate by 2000 Votes

Special Dispatch to The North American.

HARRISBURG, February 18.

Vance C. McCormick, formerly captain and quarter-back of the Yale foot-ball team, is elected Mayor by an unprecedented majority of 2000 over Dr. Samuel F. Hassler, Quay Republican. McCormick was the Democratic nominee and was endorsed by the Union party and the Central Labor Union.

McCormick's large majority helped elect Democratic Councilmen in the Sixth and other strong machine wards.

In the Eighth ward Edward Moesline, Democrat, who was running for Select Council against Henry Walter, Republican, was severely beaten at the polls this evening in an attempt to prevent an alleged repeater from voting.

The proposition to increase the public debt $1,090,000 for sewers, parks and other public improvements, will have a majority of nearly 5000. McCormick was the author of this movement, and had charge of it in Common Council, of which he is a member. Hassler lost hundreds of votes by his refusal to commit himself for this proposition.

McCormick is a nephew of former Senator Donald Cameron, who came to Harrisburg yesterday to help along the improvement question. Mr. Cameron is alleged to have contributed $5,000 to the committee in charge of the campaign for this movement.

The normal Republican majority in Harrisburg is 1200, and Hassler's managers confidently expected him to win by 500. Both sides were well supplied with money, and it is estimated that $15,000 was spent for campaign purposes.

In the First precinct of the Second ward voters were paid as high as $15 for their votes.

At midnight Republican City Chairman Middleton conceded the election of the entire Democratic city ticket. William H. Moore defeats City Controller Gough.

William M. Gastrock, George W. Leissman, Jr., and James H. W. Howard, a negro, are elected City Assessors.

It is the most crushing defeat ever administered to the Quay ring in Harrisburg.

---

9. UNIDENTIFIED NEWSPAPER EDITORIAL, FEBRUARY 19, 1902

CONGRATULATIONS!

The good people of Harrisburg were well entitled to rejoice last night. They may well rejoice to-day and continue for a decade. They won a great victory for improvement and progress.

The chief closing meeting of the interesting and instructive campaign which ended yesterday made clearer than at any previous time the certainty of the coming victory. In that meeting men of both or all political factions united in urging the voters to give the loan their approval and by so doing send Harrisburg forward in all that stands for the highest and best in municipal advancement. The Republican governor of the commonwealth stood beside the Democratic mayor of the city in endorsement of the general improvement plans submitted to our people while from the same platform pulpit and laity asked that personal opinions and selfish views be subordinated to the public good and demanded that every voter who has pride in our city, anxiety for its growth, a desire for its immediate and future prosperity go to the polls and give practical expression to such pride, anxiety and desire.

Had yesterday's vote failed to endorse the loan the true friends of progress would have become discouraged, perhaps dismayed. A like opportunity would not have been given us again for a generation to come. Had our people been deluded by the snare that if the loan measure be defeated yesterday they would be given a chance a year hence to vote upon the several improvement plans separately the next year chance in all probability would never have come.

Happily the Harrisburg plan is not much longer to be a theory. The people have risen above narrowness, selfishness, niggardliness and partisanship and have manfully asserted their freedom from the vices which so often palsy or destroy the noblest purposes of good citizenship. Congratulations, indeed! Harrisburg is saved!

---

10. NEWSPAPER ARTICLE, *PHILADELPHIA PRESS*, FEBRUARY 1902

THE "HARRISBURG PLAN" APPROVED

Philadelphia Press

One of the most hopeful signs of the times in municipal affairs is the overwhelming vote cast in Harrisburg on Tuesday in favor of the new city loan of $1,090,000. It is not exaggerating the importance of this action of the majority of the citizens of the Capital City in the least to say that they have started a new chapter in civics in Pennsylvania and have set the voters in other centers an example that is worthy of the closest imitation. It is true, other cities have voted loans before, we do this rather frequently in Philadelphia, but the high value of the Harrisburg vote is that it represents the popular indorsement of one of the most practical and most admirable projects for the improvement of the city that has ever been presented to any community in the State.

The novelty in the Harrisburg loan proposition lies in the fact that the voters of the city were not asked to approve of a municipal pig in a poke. On the contrary, as will be remembered, a committee of sixty public-spirited citizens raised a fund of $5,000 with which the services of three experts were secured, who mapped out an admirable and consistent plan of public improvement. This plan embraced the modernization of the water supply and sewage system, the sanitary improvement of the Susquehanna River front and the protection of the city from floods in Paxton Creek at the relatively moderate cost of $660,956.40, and also included the study of streets and roadways and mapping out of a park system. With this plan in hand the authorities were able to determine the amount of a loan which would give a minimum increase in indebtedness with a maximum of results.

The effect of all this public-spirited effort was that every voter could see for himself just how the money he was asked to authorize the city to borrow was to be spent. Nothing was hidden, everything was above board, and it is a credit to the intelligence of the average voter in Harrisburg that the loan so presented received so amazing an endorsement. Of course this result was not secured without hard work. And after the foresight shown in the report of the "Executive Committee" on the "Proposed Municipal Improvements in Harrisburg," the thing done by the committee that calls for unstinted praise is the common sense way in which they carried their campaign of education to so successful a conclusion. The opposition, at first so decided as to make it probable that the loan would have been defeated had the election taken place on January 18th instead of February 18th, was met not by partisan rancor, not by calling hard names, but by a steady, persistent appeal to facts that in the end won the day.

Indeed, just as the November report on the improvements plan was a model which all municipalities might follow, so the way in which the issue was laid before the Harrisburg voters is a lesson in the management of a campaign that all those interested in the business administration of civic affairs may well take to heart. And not the least happy result of this significant election is the choice also by a large majority of the man for Mayor who stood more than any other man in Harrisburg for the projected improvements and the loan that will bring them into being. All that is left to be done now is for Mayor and Councils to begin to realize the "Harrisburg plan" and make the capital the model city which it may very well be if it lives up to the light and the lessons of the campaign just closed.

11. NEWSPAPER ARTICLE, *NORTH AMERICAN*, DECEMBER 27, 1902

MAYOR GIVES TURKEYS
TO CAPITAL POLICE

Vance McCormick, Surprised by
Group Photograph of His Department, Reciprocates.

Special Dispatch to The North American.

HARRISBURG, December 27.

Mayor Vance C. McCormick's popularity with the Harrisburg police department was attested Christmas Day, when he received as a gift from the force a splendid group photograph of the members handsomely framed in heavy gilt. The photograph was made by Frank E. Musser, the official city photographer, while the Mayor was absent from the city on business, and is an excellent likeness of the patrolmen and their superior officers.

The Mayor was very much surprised when the photograph was presented to him, and he reciprocated by giving a turkey to every member of his department.

The police are not allowed by the present city administration to take part in politics, and as a result the force is the most efficient this city has ever had.

———————

12. UNIDENTIFIED NEWSPAPER ARTICLE, DATE UNKNOWN

A QUARTETTE OF DRUNKS.

The First to Appear Before Mayor McCormick
Charged With Minor Offences.

A quartette of defendants charged with drunk and disorderly conduct were the first to appear before Mayor McCormick at a hearing this afternoon at 3 o'clock. Daniel Donohue was the first to fall into the hands of the police under the new administration and Patrolman Wolfield was the officer who is credited with the arrest. John Ford was later picked up by Patrolman Berry and David Fitzgerald fell into the hands of Sergeant O'Donnell. Patrolman Corcoran, at Third and Market streets, got Martin M. Bankler.

Chief Lutz, in observance of the new regulations governing the fire department, this morning arrested a trespasser at the Friendship fire engine house. Several ex-members of the company have been in the habit of making that house a headquarters to sleep off a drunk and while in the act of carrying out this practice one of this number was arrested this morning and locked up.

"Is the m'ah in," asked a colored girl in a green shawl at the door of Chief of Police Kautz's office this morning. "He is not in now, but can I do anything for you?" asked the chief. "No, I wants to see the m'ah privately. I wants to git a pass to go to Atlantic City," and she left determined to see the "m'ah."

---

13. UNIDENTIFIED NEWSPAPER ARTICLE, DATE UNKNOWN

RUNS CITY ON A BUSINESS BASIS
A GROUP ABOUT THE REFRESHMENT TABLE;
MAYOR MCCORMICK AT THE RIGHT. MAYOR VANCE
MCCORMICK, JAMES B. REYNOLDS OF HARRISBURG,
SEC'Y TO MAYOR LOW OF NEW YORK

Vance McCormick, Mayor of Harrisburg, the youngest man who has occupied the office of Mayor in that city or any other city of equal size in the country, was given a reception in the Penn Club last night by the Municipal League.

Mayor McCormick was to have shared the hospitality of the League with James H. Reynolds, secretary to Mayor Low, of New York, but the New York official was prevented from attending by illness. The youthful Mayor was an interesting and entertaining guest.

He is the political wonder of his home city. Two steps carried him from private life to the highest civic position in Harrisburg. Mr. McCormick has been Mayor a year, and for two years he was a Councilman. That is his whole political career. He began it with an office that usually requires long and arduous work in the ranks before it can be attained.

He Is an Athlete.

Mayor McCormick is short in stature, but sturdy of build. He has the physique of a hardened athlete and a fresh, ruddy complexion that adds to his youthful appearance. In 1893 he was captain of the Yale football team. When his college career was completed he took up a business life, in which the responsibilities were of weight sufficient to tax the capabilities of veteran business men. Mr. McCormick occupies in Harrisburg a position in the business world similar to that of young Cornelius Vanderbilt in New York.

When he took up political work and set about reforming conditions in his home city he spent much of the time fighting his best friends. He opposed franchise grabs and lessened the profits of relatives who were investors in railroad companies. And he did it with as little hesitation and as much determination as he fought dishonest political methods.

Mayor McCormick did not say much about his work last night, but he told a picturesque story of his entry into politics, giving the credit for his rapid advancement to the voters, claiming no glory as the result of his own efforts.

His Funny Start

"I have simply done what is the duty of every American citizen—taken an interest in my city's government," he modestly explained. "It was rather funny, how I got into politics. I had been doing a lot of kicking about political affairs in general.

"'What right have you to kick?' inquired a local politician, who had overheard some of my remarks. 'Did you ever do anything for the city?'

"I had to admit that I never had.

"'Will you do anything?' he suddenly asked, and in the enthusiasm of the minute I replied that I would.

"He promised to 'fix' me, and before I knew it I was Councilman from the Fourth Ward. I have been 'fixed' ever since. In Councils I went in [with] the idea that the municipal government was a business concern whose books showed property worth $30,000,000, and I worked on that idea from the start.

"I simply acted as a business man who had taken an interest, a proper interest, in local affairs. And I say to you all that this give-up policy, this sitting down with folded hands and saying 'We can't do anything' is bound to be the ruination of government wherever it is practiced."

Though Mr. McCormick disclaimed any credit for himself in the improvement of Harrisburg's politics, his hearers noting his firm, square chin and determined eye, were of a different opinion.

Before luncheon was served Mayor McCormick was introduced to the following gentlemen:—

George Burnham, Jr., Captain F. Wesenberg, Clarence L. Harper, William T. Innes, Jr., Odin R. Edwards, S. Water Foulkrod, Colonel George E.

284

OTHER DOCUMENTS

Mapes, F. D. Witherby, E. I. Stearns, William Kirkbride, Edward Wiener, Charles T. Byrnes, George H. Peace, James E. Dwyer, John Story Jenks, Magistrate David T. Hart, J. W. Crawford, T. S. McIlhenny, Reverend Oscar B. Hawes, Edwin F. King, H. C. Carlisle, Reverend Joseph May, E. P. Morris, Jr., Dr. L. J. Lauterback, R. G. Warner, Reverend H. F. Phillips, Dr. J. A. Bolin, John C. Trautwine, Jr., A. Rulon Foster, John E. Baird, John C. Lowry, Thomas Hare, Walter Wood, J. Aylward Denlin, J. P. Mumford, Reverend E. B. Palmer, John J. Wilkinson, Robert Pearsall, Colonel James M. Whitecar, Thomas S. Williams, R. S. McNutt, C. J. Trumbull, Dr. Ferris, Henry J. Gibbons, Andrew M. Shute, Albert Kelcey, Clinton Rogers Woodruff.

---

14. UNIDENTIFIED NEWSPAPER ARTICLE, DATE UNKNOWN

M'CORMICK TELLS BOYS OF HIS DINNER WITH TEDDY
TAKES ROOSEVELT AS AN EXAMPLE
OF DETERMINED MANHOOD.
MAYOR-ELECT MADE AN INTER-
ESTING AND PRACTICAL AD-
DRESS TO THE MESSIAH LU-
THERAN BOYS' CLUB.
HIS EARLY TRIALS AT FOOTBALL

"This pleasantest day I have ever spent was last Saturday a week ago when I took dinner with President Roosevelt at the White House," said Mayor-elect Vance C. McCormick in his talk to the Boys' club of Messiah Lutheran church, last evening, in citing instances of what determination will do for men, in the course of his remarks on the subject of "Success."

"At the table were seated General Funston, the man whose determination resulted in the capture of Aguinaldo, and Edward Everett Hale, and Senator Beveridge and Attorney General Knox, all of whose works in their several walks of life are examples of what perseverance and determination will accomplish. Their every movement showed the determination which they possess, and this is especially the case with President Roosevelt, who showed his teeth, just as he is described as doing in the thick of battle, with his every utterance."

Mr. McCormick was greeted with great enthusiasm when he was introduced by Dr. Fager to the boys of the club and their guests, to the number of a hundred all told. After the introduction the boys all rose to their feet and sang a song of welcome to the tune of "Blest Be the Tie That Binds," with appropriate words composed for the occasion, and this was followed by an oft rehearsed military salute.

The mayor-elect arose with the graceful response of "Gentlemen, I salute you," and proceeded to tell them that their military demeanor had solved for him in an instant the momentous question in regard to selecting the police force, as he saw before him abundant excellent material to fill every position.

Mr. McCormick said that he was not much older than many of the boys of the club and did not feel very well qualified to speak to them on the subject of "Success," which had been assigned to him. Speaking as a boy to boys, however, he would give his idea of how true success should be acquired.

There are two kinds of success. The first kind is the selfish, win-at-any-cost success. It is true that many persons succeed in gaining wealth and position in this world by always looking out for themselves alone, and overriding the rights and liberties of others in order to gain their ends. The speaker cited Jay Gould as an example of a man who had gained success by self-seeking methods, and said that the world is better without such men.

There is another kind of success that is gotten, by our making the world better for our having lived in it. That is the kind of success that he urged the boys to seek. Character is the underlying principal [sic] in its acquisition. A boy must have sand [sic], not alone the kind that helps to win foot ball games, but the kind that leads a boy to say "no" when he is lead [sic] into temptation. It is moral courage that is necessary. Many boys think that refusing to do wrong will make them unpopular, but in reality continued persistence against temptation will lead others to respect a boy. It comes hard at first, but the hardest part is in first taking the stand.

"I went to Andover to attend school when I was 15 years old," continued Mr. McCormick, "and although I knew nothing about base ball or foot ball at the time, I tell you boys, I made up my mind that I was going to make the teams before I got out of school. It came very hard at first to go out and try. I did not have the courage to put on a regular suit to practice in because I was afraid the boys would think that I thought that I was a good player. During the first season I wore nothing but ordinary long trousers and my knees and body were cut and bruised all the time. But I was determined to stick it out, and at the beginning of the next season the school rewarded my perseverance by giving me a suit."

Mr. McCormick said that the next step after the foundation of a character was the exercise of tact and common sense. The best definition of tact that ever occurred to him was to do the right thing in the right place—to seize opportunities. A young man may have a position in an office and may do his routine work satisfactorily, but if he does not take advantage of the opportunities which come to him and exercise his determination he will never acquire real success.

"We have a great county, a great state and a great city, and it depends upon you and boys like you to keep them great. You will soon be voters and although you cannot all hope to be office holders you can by the power of your ballots see that the country is governed as it ought to be. You must not stand aside and see professional politicians run things to suit themselves.

"But the greatest element of all toward gaining success is to keep the love of God in your hearts. It is only then that you will have grasped the right idea of success."

The speaker then thanked the boys for their attention and said he would come up and coach their foot ball team for them next fall if they wanted him to. After shaking hands with Mr. McCormick the club gave their yell for him as follows: Boom-alacka boom-alacka rah rah rah Messiah Lutheran Boys' club rah rah rah.

Records from the 1914 Gubernatorial Campaign of Vance McCormick

Vance McCormick ran for governor of Pennsylvania in 1914 against Republican Martin G. Brumbaugh. It was not a very close race: McCormick won 453,880 votes to Brumbaugh's 588,705. Brumbaugh even took Dauphin County, where McCormick hoped for a favorite-son advantage.

The following letters, newspaper items, and pamphlets from McCormick's papers show the moralistic political style that he and his allies brought to their battles. For them, the enemy was Bossism and the machines, or as one crusader simply put it, "evil." The materials also provide a brief narrative of the campaign itself.

---

1. ADDRESS OF VANCE C. MCCORMICK BEFORE THE DEMOCRATIC STATE COMMITTEE, JUNE 3, 1914

I stand before you today particularly to make an appeal for a United Democracy. There has never been presented to our party such an opportunity to serve our state as now, and the responsibility for its acceptance rests entirely upon us. My earnest prayer is that, realizing this responsibility, all good Democrats may bury their differences, eliminate all factional strife and bitterness and in a spirit of liberality and true patriotism, co-operate with each other in building up our party so that it may become, in very truth, an instrument with which decent citizens of our State may regain their government, at the same time repudiating the insult which Senator Penrose cast upon it several weeks ago when he publicly announced that one hundred thousand Democrats would vote for him in November. . . .

The great issue today in Pennsylvania is Penroseism and all the political and public ills for which it stands. There never has been presented to the voters of this State a clearer issue. Those responsible for the corruption and misrule in our State government are making their last stand.

Under this system of Republican misrule, which has been in existence for many years in our state government, these political bosses, to check a popular uprising of citizens protesting against graft and extravagance, have frequently attempted to shield themselves behind a nominee of eminent respectability and presumably an honest man, brought forward as a lure to the voters.

This game will work no longer. The people are at last aroused, for they recall too vividly how this system has cost them million of dollars as in the Capitol graft and Rittersville hospital scandals, occurring under the administration of some of these honest Governors. They see again the pitiful spectacle of some of these Governors, as they renounce at the behest of their political masters the ringing recommendations of their own inaugural messages. . . .

It is perfectly apparent that the handpicked governors of political bosses who do not repudiate their sponsors before the election have neither the courage nor strength to do so after. Consequently, the state government is manipulated by and under the absolute control of a political machine, whose sole desire is to serve its own special interest.

This old game is being attempted again but the people today will demand of the candidates that they publicly and openly declare themselves on Penroseism. They must either endorse or reject it. Silence will be unavailing. What will be the answer of my opponent on the Republican ticket, the candidate of Penrose and the contractor bosses of Philadelphia? Will he endorse or reject Penroseism? There can be no evasion; the people demand a direct anser.

We demand, will enact and put into execution, if given the opportunity, a constructive program of legislation for the better security of human rights, the uplift of mankind and the moral welfare of the citizenship of the state.

---

2. LETTER FROM WILLIAM DRAPER LEWIS TO VANCE MCCORMICK,
AUGUST 18, 1914

William Draper Lewis was former dean of the University of Pennsylvania Law School and ran for the Progressive/Washington party nomination for governor in 1914. In this letter, he proposes to McCormick that one of them might drop out of the party contest if they had identical views. McCormick answers courteously, humoring him, it would seem, and Lewis later withdrew.

3400 Chestnut Street
Philadelphia, Pa.

Hon. Vance McCormick
Harrisburg, Pa.

Dear Mr. McCormick:

I followed your campaign speeches with interest. We apparently agreed that the issue which overshadows all others in this campaign, is the destruction of the corrupt political machine now in control of the state government. The saloon, the corrupt politicians of all parties, the denizens of every tenderloin, and those individuals and corporations who want to make money by getting things out of the state that they should not have or to continue for their own profit bad industrial conditions, are with few exceptions enthusiastically behind Dr. Brumbaugh.

The forces of evil being thus united I believe that you and I should consider carefully whether it is not possible to prevent the forces making for the regeneration of the state, from being divided.

Any action which would involve the retirement of one of us is of course only possible if we are in accord, not only on the necessity of cleaning up the state government and defeating a candidate picked out by the gang now controlling that government, to perpetuate their power of evil, but also if we are in accord on constructive measures of legislation and state administrative reform.

I send you a copy of the statement which I am having printed defining with exactness my position on what I believe to be important state questions.

If you care to pursue this matter further I shall be very glad to hear from you.

Sincerely yours,
William Draper Lewis

P.S. My address for the next week will be Northeast Harbor, Maine. In the statement referred to, several definite measures were part of the State Legislative Program of the Progressive or Washington Party which passed the House and was defeated in the Senate in the 1913 Legislature. I send under separate cover a copy of these bills.

---

3. LETTER FROM VANCE MCCORMICK TO WILLIAM DRAPER LEWIS, AUGUST 25, 1914

Personal
Wm Draper Lewis, Esq.,
Northeast Harbor, Maine.

Dear Mr Lewis:—

In reply to your letter of eighteenth inst., I would state that I absolutely agree with you that the issue in this campaign which overshadows all others is the destruction of the corrupt political machine which now controls our state government and am convinced this could be more easily accomplished if our decent citizens were united.

I have read with interest the personal statement which you so kindly enclosed and can safely say that I am in substantial and entire accord with the position you have taken upon the economic problems facing our people.

I have not reached these conclusions hastily. As a member of the Democratic Legislative Committee, I studied carefully the bill framed by your committee and joined in urging the passage of the Workmen's Compensation Act prepared by the State Industrial Commission. It was a great disappointment to me that this legislation was defeated by a hostile Senate. I also labored earnestly for the passage of the Child Labor Law which your committee drafted and which the Democratic committee adopted without change. I am not as confident as you are that the Minimum Wage Bill for Women will in practice accomplish the results which we both seek. I have been interested for years in the problems which the advent of women in wider fields of industrial life has produced. Certain distress in conditions already existing must be remedied and I am sure that further discussion and the location of additional facts would enable us to find the solution. I should welcome the opportunity to work with you on these lines.

I fully recognize the weaknesses of the present Corrupt Practices Act. While the act of 1906 was a step in the right direction, it has been painfully inadequate. It permits of easy evasion and thus real injustice to the man whose conscience will not permit him to hide behind a Manufacturers Protective Association or a fictitious committee. During the recent primary I certainly would have welcomed any law that would have assisted me financially in securing publicity to refute the vicious attacks made upon me and the cause I represented. To reach the individual voters in the interest of the progressive movement in my party I decided to write directly to every enrolled Democrat. This plan cost me for postage and the mailing of letters alone over $17,000.; along with advertising in three hundred newspapers at a cost of nearly $7000, and almost a like amount for the free distribution over the state of The Patriot; and convinced me that the method of publicity for all candidates and at state expense, such as you suggest, must be adopted if our valuable primary system is to be preserved.

It seems hardly necessary to tell you how thoroughly I agree with your position on Woman Suffrage, Local option, the abolition of the voter's assistant and the amendments to the Public Service Commission measure.

Three departments of our state government are in peculiar [sic] need of a thorough reorganization and overhauling. For years I have fought the present system of charitable appropriations as being the chief source of our legislative corruption. I have opposed bitterly the present system of road building. The extravagance, graft and incompetency of the Bigelow administration has not only retarded the development of our state but has done infinite injury to the good roads movement, in which I have always been so deeply interested. I agree with you that the very powers conferred on the Department of Labor demand for their exercise and administration representatives of labor, as well as in sympathy with it and familiar with the needed reforms of working conditions.

I have not attempted to cover all the points of your statement. Some that I have not mentioned are covered by the Democratic Platform, which I have unqualifiedly endorsed, and others will be found in my personal platform, copy of which I enclose.

There is one subject I do not think you have touched upon, that of the conservation of our agricultural resources. I have always been particularly interested in the agricultural development of our state and, as a member of the Board of Trustees of State College, have had an exceptional opportunity of studying its agricultural needs, as also through my direct personal connection with farming interests.

In regard to the scope of a constitutional convention, which I favor, or to specific reforms in our legal procedure, I do not think as a business man I am competent to discuss these questions in detail. I would in such matters be governed by the judgement of progressive thinkers who, like yourself, have given particular attention to these problems.

I am convinced that, allowing for inevitable differences of temperament and experience, we are in substantial accord on constructive measures of legislative and administrative reform. I feel strongly that, if possible, the progressive forces of our state should be united. But any such union of forces must have behind it the enthusiastic endorsement of the rank and file, who designated us in our respective party primaries to make this fight.

Very truly yours,
Vance McCormick

———————

4. MCCORMICK'S PLEDGE TO THE PROGRESSIVES
(CAMPAIGN LITERATURE)

It is not necessary for me to tell you how deeply I appreciate the generous and patriotic action which your committee has taken to-day. Never in the history of Pennsylvania politics have we seen more unselfish devotion to ideals of public service than Dr. Lewis has exhibited in his voluntary and unconditional retirement from the Washington Party ticket in my favor.

As I have said in a letter which I wrote to Dr. Lewis in reply to a very courteous communication from him and which I am informed was read to you to-day, the objects which the Democratic and Progressive parties have in this campaign are essentially one. The issue in Pennsylvania is primarily Penrose and Penroseism. To the destruction of that form of government and party organization we Democrats and Progressives alike have dedicated our efforts, and I stand here to pledge to you that in accepting this nomination, which you have offered me, I will during my administration as Governor, be loyal to the pledges which both our party platforms have made.

I am convinced that Pennsylvania can never be free until we have torn out, root and branch, the corrupt system of government by graft intimidation, which has been going on here in Harrisburg for these many years past. With all the economic reforms which the Progressive party has so earnestly pressed for the last two years in Pennsylvania, I am in substantial and hearty agreement.

I recognize that in questions of national policies our parties are not united. But these national questions are not involved in our local fight in Pennsylvania. Here we are united and in closing these few remarks, I well realize that I am not alone the choice of the Democrats of Pennsylvania but also the choice of the progressive voters of the state, and, as such, I will endeavor to give an administration which will be representative of the common ideals which both parties are endeavoring to realize.

---

5. EDITORIAL, HARRISBURG *PATRIOT,* NOVEMBER 2, 1914,
   "NOW COMES THE VOTING"

No more momentous issues have been raised since Pennsylvania took a place among the states of the great republic. The really fundamental issue is whether Pennsylvania shall continue to be a standing reproach among the sisterhood of states, or whether here, in the state where was fought the battle of Gettysburg, and where Lincoln uttered his immortal address, there shall 'be a new birth of freedom,' freedom from boss domination and from the corrupting influence of the most disreputable political disorganization that ever cursed a state or nation.

For years the people of Pennsylvania have not ruled their commonwealth. Because of indifference, misunderstanding and misrepresentation they have been ruled by a coterie of cunning politicians who, to keep their hold on the state, pandered to the greed of the selfish privilege seekers and the depravity of the corrupt and corrupting liquor interests. . . .

The gang will have in its hands tomorrow the greatest corruption ever spent in the state in an attempt to buy the vote of confidence' that honest methods could not secure. Thousands of gang placeholders will make personal pleas on the grounds of personal friendship for support of the gang ticket. Unlimited promises of future favors have been and will be made for votes for the gang candidates. Fraudulent votes will be cast, though preventative measures already taken will materially reduce the total of such votes.

---

6. FRONT PAGE BOX, HARRISBURG *PATRIOT,* NOVEMBER 3, 1914,
"$50,000 REWARD"

The Palmer-McCormick Committee of One Hundred is authorized to offer the sum of $50,000 in rewards for the production of evidence leading to the arrest, conviction and imprisonment of any person who is guilty of ballot frauds at the election to be held Tuesday, Nov. 3, 1914.

———————

7. NEWSPAPER ARTICLE, HARRISBURG *PATRIOT,* NOVEMBER 4, 1914, "REPUBLICANS TAKE PENNSYLVANIA AND ELECT PENROSE AND BRUMBAUGH"

Unofficial results at 2:30 this morning [report McCormick with] 50 out of 67 counties . . . he went to Philadelphia with a majority of 50,000 over Dr. Martin G. Brumbaugh . . . but . . . the Republican majority there of 1,000,000 was too great to overcome.

———————

8. EDITORIAL, HARRISBURG *PATRIOT,* "THE FIGHTING TO CONTINUE"

The time will come when it will be recognized that such business depression as existed in the fall of 1914 was due to the war in Europe, and not to the tariff change, when public sentiment will so revolt against the debauchery of the electorate that elections cannot be purchased, and when indifference on the part of many really good citizens will give way to interest, and they will vote as they believe. The Patriot is enlisted for the war. It will stay on the fighting line until the war is ended and the people win.

McCormick's Management of Woodrow Wilson's 1916 Presidential Campaign

Political and Biographical Accounts

The political campaign that Vance McCormick could be proudest of was the one he managed for President Woodrow Wilson, running for re-election in 1916. As LeRoy W. Toddes describes in his master's paper and article, the president had doubts that McCormick would be "warhorse" enough as Democratic National Committee chairman and campaign chairman. Would McCormick be too highbrow and intolerant? But the Democrats went with him against the Republican opponent, Charles Evans Hughes. McCormick set up an effective structure of several departments, including one for publicity; he also established a campaign office in Chicago, to accompany the national headquarters in New York City. The contest was remarkably close. Wilson trailed in the vote count for two days after the November 7 election, but in the end, he was victorious.

McCormick's appointment as chairman of the campaign induced reporters to write biographical essays about him, which are among the most detailed, declamatory, and sometimes dubious statements we have of his political history and activities. Again, they relied on football metaphors. Those essays are included here, along with a congratulatory telegram from William G. McAdoo, President Wilson's son-in-law and secretary of the treasury, which documents again the kind of moralism Progressives brought to their politics.

---

1. NEWSPAPER ARTICLE, *PUBLIC LEDGER,* PHILADELPHIA, JUNE 25, 1916

VANCE C. MCCORMICK
A TYPICAL AMERICAN LIVE WIRE
President Wilson's Selection for Chairman of the Democratic
National Committee,
Whether as Political Reformer or Banker, Stock Raiser or Editor,
Spellbinder or Gridiron Star, Bucks the Hard Line
By Thomas F. Healey

To meet a man for the first time in a taxicab, when it was impossible to converse with him because of the bumps and jars of the dilapidated machine, to be suddenly thrown into the closest companionship with him, when he was worn and haggard and husky of voice because of the mental and physical strain of a political battle; to see him night after night in soiled linen and dusty clothes, now before an audience of miners in a Schuylkill county town, and again addressing a sleek, well-fed, well-dressed gathering of business men in a municipality—to meet a man under such trying circumstances and then sit down and write about him, his characteristics, his ability, his ambitions and his accomplishments, is an easy part of this trade. At least it would not be were he an ordinary man. We find they must be analyzed and assayed. We test them as by fire and still we sometimes doubt.

A Man Sure of Himself

But it was altogether different with Vance Criswell McCormick. The meeting was a happy one. It was under the best circumstances because it was in the midst of a fight, and McCormick was leading the fight. He was in fighting humor, in fighting clothes, and his handclasp of greeting was the hearty, honest grasp of the fighting man. His speech, crisp, short, whiplash sentences, every word to the point, every word carrying a definite, incontrovertible meaning, was the speech of a man who was sure of himself, positive in his motive and confident that the men who were with him— the ends, tackles, guards and halfbacks, let us say—knew that he was right and trusted him to carry the ball over the line. He was back in the fighting game, and thus it was not strange that, sitting in the taxicab opposite him, an imaginative man could easily understand why McCormick was a hero at Yale, a good student, a progressive Councilman and, as has been said, the man who as Mayor found Harrisburg a city of mud and transformed it into a well-paved, well-lighted, well-governed municipality. It was easily understood how and by what methods he was able to wrest control of the Democratic party in this State from the grip of the old-line bosses who for years had dictated what should be done and the manner of the performance. All this could be grasped in a moment, because coming upon McCormick in such circumstances one saw him as his teammates saw him on the gridiron—frantically happy in the zest and stress of battle, eager for the crush and fury of the fray, in the center of the scrimmage which was never too strenuous for him.

Stocky Veteran of Conflict

So, now, looking back to that first meeting and remembering subsequent and more peaceful meetings [word illegible] epoch in the life of the nation. It is not at all difficult to understand why Woodrow Wilson, who knows and has written much about men and is pretty generally known as a fighter himself, should pick this Pennsylvanian to direct his campaign against the Republican Organization as the Chairman of the Democratic National committee. Casting aside all motives which are ascribed for the President's selection—and they are not few, the political quarters of the town have buzzed with rumors since his name was first mentioned for the place—it may be said with some surety of accuracy that the President picked McCormick because he was certain that if any man could direct and manage such an all-important nation-wide contest as it should be directed, as the issue warrants, that man is the square-jawed stocky veteran of conflict who has done a great deal without making a noise about it.

It has been said that McCormick plays politics in much the same manner as he played football. It has been said that he is ruthless, overpowering, cruel at the game. The first statement is true. The second is not. During a long campaign, when he was personally assailed, when his motives were misconstrued and purposely so, when even his family affiliations were dragged into the contest, McCormick was the fairest-minded man on the stump; and, although others might inject personalities to befog the issue, he stuck to the issue and did effective work thereby.

Red Blood and Courage

To describe properly the new chairman of the national Democracy, it is imperative to start at the beginning of his career, because every stage of it is interesting. It is an unusual career. It is such a one as any man might carve out for himself, given the native ability [of] McCormick, even though fortune ever smiled upon him, for each of [his] accomplishments can be traced directly back to hard work. One would never suppose him to be possessor of [more] than $5,000,000 in his own name. [He] has nothing of appearance of a [man] who controls a trusteeship valued at several times that. He is altogether a very pleasant, hospitable gentleman, who lives a life with his mother and sister at Harrisburg, who has never married, or "played" society, but has played every sort of game which requires courage of a man.

McCormick was born in Harrisburg in 1872. His ancestors were among the early settlers of Central Pennsylvania and were prominent in agricultural pursuits and the industrial and professional life of that section of the State. He attended the schools in Harrisburg and private schools, where he prepared for Yale. The value of his mental and physical make-up first displayed itself when he entered the Harrisburg Academy, for he became a leader in the work and sports of the institution, and he remained a leader until he left the institution for Yale.

He entered Yale in 1890. He lived the usual student's life, working hard, playing hard, unspoiled by wealth, but using it to the best possible advantage. The nation heard nothing of him until one raw autumn day in 1893 [sic], when the sporting pages told how McCormick won the game for Yale against Princeton by booting the pigskin over the goal from the 40-yard line. He was captain of the team that year, playing fullback [sic] as it had never been played for Yale before, and as his old classmates say, putting life and fire into every man under him.

Mayor and Editor

Yale gave him his sheepskin along about June of 1893, and a few months later he was back in Harrisburg anxious to "get into" something worth while, but something that must be strenuous enough to give full play to his muscles and his brain. He found it. It was the condition of the Democracy of the State and he saw that his native city was in dire need of improvements, physical and moral. He became a Common Councilman and immediately became known throughout the State as the "Fighting Councilman." He fought persistently. He was from what was known at the time as the "silk-stocking" ward, the 4th, but his independence, his grasp of affairs and his recognition of what was needed to improve the municipality gained such weight with his independent colleagues that a demand swept the city for McCormick to run for the mayoralty.

He did so and he won. He was but 29 years old at the time, but he won a sweeping victory for the reform wing of the Democratic party, and now not even his most bitter enemies will deny that he was the best and most capable executive who ever occupied the mayoralty. It was at that time that he engaged in the newspaper field. He had been Mayor but a short time when he purchased the Harrisburg Patriot as a side arm to his fight for reform, and he has been using it for that purpose ever since. While occupying the office of Mayor he was handling the immense estate left by his father, Henry McCormick, and was engaged in a score of additional enterprises. He never sought [word illegible] and took upon himself such responsibilities as were placed before him. Thus, while directing the work of repaving the streets of Harrisburg, improving its lighting system, providing a pure water supply for the citizens, he was actively engaged in educational affairs. He became a trustee of State College, interested himself in the work of the Y.M.C.A., of which he is a member of the executive committee, kept up a keen interest in the affairs of Yale, while at the same time using his keen sense of righteousness in doing his best to direct the affairs of the Democratic party along the lines which he thought it should follow as the party of the [word illegible].

McCormick is next seen in the limelight under peculiar conditions in 1910. It was in that year that he openly refused to support the regular Democratic ticket in the gubernatorial fight because of allegations that the nominee, Webster Grim, had been placed in the running by a corrupt alliance of bi-partisan liquor interests in order to assure victory for the Republican party. Instead, after stating [his] position in his usual clearcut, terse fashion, McCormick threw his strength to the movement which supported William H. Berry, the present collector of this port. Then started a fight which tested all the strength of McCormick and A. Mitchell Palmer, and, as is the usual case with strong men who stick to the fight to the end, they accomplished an object which was possibly of more importance in their fight than gubernatorial success, the wresting of control from the Guffey crowd who had handled the party for years. McCormick and Palmer defeated Guffey and his stalwarts, reorganized the party and have been its dominant factors ever since. They have fought its battles ceaselessly, have won official recognition from Washington for what has become known as the "reorganization faction," and McCormick now bids fair to bring about the closest and most serene harmony. At any rate, political gossip has it he will bend all his efforts toward a reunion of the party and an end of factionalism.

The fight in 1910 was precipitated by the eleventh-hour withdrawal of C. LaRue Munson, of Williamsport. McCormick in 1909 had suggested Munson as a candidate for the Supreme Court and he made such a good showing that a year later McCormick again selected him as the man who could lead the gubernatorial fight and crush the machine.

Battle for Party Reform

The withdrawal of Munson, followed by the nomination of Webster Grim and the formation of the Keystone ticket, headed by Berry, resulted in the reorganization movement the following year. The idea of taking the party out of the hands of the bipartisans was McCormick's. It was he who, through A. Mitchell Palmer, called the congressional meeting of Pennsylvania members at Washington, who called a meeting of the State Committee, which made arrangements to reorganize the party. McCormick was named as chairman of the Reorganization Committee and traveled the State from end to end in his work of interesting the county leaders in a movement to rid the party of the men who had been trading with the Republicans.

This movement resulted in victory, for James Guffey, who had dominated the affairs of the party, and his followers were ousted and George W. Guthrie, now Ambassador to Japan, was made State chairman. A delegation almost solid for Wilson was sent to the Baltimore convention and Pennsylvania's steadfast stand for Wilson made his nomination possible. After the Baltimore convention McCormick and Palmer continued in control of the Democratic party, and when in 1914 candidates were chosen for United States Senator and Governor, they were naturally picked to lead the reorganization Democrats against the nominees of the old Guard.

Campaign for Governor

That fight of two years ago was the stiffest battle of his career. He and Palmer had already won high places in national politics as leaders of the Pennsylvania delegation to the Baltimore convention, and so they stood well in the State. McCormick was the Democratic nominee for Governor. His nomination caused the withdrawal of William Draper Lewis and he accordingly won Progressive indorsement and support. His opponent, Governor Brumbaugh, with the united support of [word illegible] stronghold of Republicanism, had as hard and grueling fight as any political candidate ever suffered, with McCormick as an opponent. He had learned his lesson well while Mayor of Harrisburg and he knew all the tricks of the trade. He knew the inside of affairs at Capitol Hill and he knew how to "put them over." He went the limit in the campaign. He fought with every ounce of strength and energy he possessed and he did not spare money. It has been estimated that his expenditures during the fight totaled $33,000. It is needless to rehearse the outcome. McCormick took his defeat as philosophically as when he had been battered about the football field by a stronger opponent. He was beaten, but he was not put out of the game.

Mr. McCormick is one of the principal bankers of Harrisburg, and a member of the board of trustees of Yale. He succeeded ex-President Taft in this latter capacity. He is the owner of some of the best coal lands in Dauphin County, is interested in electric, traction and other corporations and especially in farmlands. In Harrisburg his home is on the Susquehanna, but he has a beautiful country place which he calls Rosegarden, and there he raises pure-blooded stock.

Under Palmer's Lead

The primaries this year again saw the followers of McCormick and Palmer in the lead, and the national delegates sent to St. Louis, while not all former reorganization men, were solid for Wilson from the start of their campaigns and worked in harmony with the men there under Palmer's lead.

The only reason that McCormick was not a candidate for delegate to the convention this year was the fact that he was a member of the Federal Reserve Board of the Philadelphia district. He resigned this post as soon as he received notification from St. Louis of his election as national chairman.

As a trustee of the McCormick estate he helps control millions of dollars worth of property. Much of this is in realty in Harrisburg, and includes numerous buildings along Market street, the business centre of the city. The Commonwealth Hotel, one of the oldest of the city, is one of these. Some years ago, when the McCormicks took over this property, the bar that was connected with it moved across the street, and it has since been conducted as a temperance hotel.

Hundreds of acres of farm land in Cumberland County and mine land in Cambria County and in West Virginia are included in the McCormick holdings. Just what proportion of the McCormick wealth is personally that of the new national chairman is unknown.

Rosegarden is the centre of the McCormick farms, and there is located a stable where Mr. McCormick breeds pure-blood cattle and thoroughbred horses. His agricultural interests are large, but he is more interested in his live stock than in any other branch of his farm life. He has done more to advance interest in good horses in the Cumberland Valley through his imported Percherons than any other agency in that fertile section.

Serene Under Attacks

Because of his interest in the agricultural development of the valley he started the Hogestown Horse and Cattle Show twelve years ago. There were entered a week ago 650 exhibits, covering the entire field of agricultural activities. Most of the entries were those of horses and cattle. Experts from agricultural colleges were the judges and the lecturers.

As is to be expected, he has bitter enemies. He has been reviled, verbally crucified as an enemy of labor, denounced as a hypocrite, charged with corruption in politics and the instigation of political crimes and jugglery. Opposing speakers have delved into the history of his family and have as they said, "exploded mines" under him. But somehow or other McCormick has always been able to maintain his poise under such attacks. He has never retaliated in such fashion. He is a quiet man, an earnest man, a deep-thinking, conscientious man, and he has a habit of dismissing disconcerting abuse with a smile.

Once Favored by "T. R."

Two years ago McCormick won the support of the Progressives. More than that, the idol of the Progressives, the leader of the party, the Colonel himself, came into the State and did two things. He said something about a "woolly lamb" and he said a great many generous things about the new chairman of the Democratic National Committee. Is it far-fetched to say that Progressives looking for a leader and the sheltering arms of a party may not again turn in with McCormick?

---

2. ARTICLE, NEW YORK *EVENING POST SATURDAY MAGAZINE*, JULY 1, 1916

WOODROW WILSON'S CAMPAIGN MANAGER
A Sketch by William A. McGarry

The Pennsylvania country gentleman upon whom President Wilson is depending more than upon any other man for reelection is sometimes called an idealist in politics, but woe betide the G.O.P. if it banks too heavily upon his idealism. For by the time the dust settles next fall everybody, big and little, actively opposed to the movement which Vance Criswell McCormick is leading will know definitely that he has been in a fight.

Not that the Democratic campaign manager and chairman of the party's National Committee will talk about it. He is so quiet as a rule that were it not for his political record of unswerving fealty to the Democracy, he might get into the category of men whom Woodrow Wilson said recently he was afraid of. But the record stands the test. It stands the test for the Democrats, and more than that, it stands the tests for the Progressives in Pennsylvania; not the "Bill" Flinn type, but that of the real reformers who broke away from the Republicans during the little disagreement of 1912; men like Dr. William Draper Lewis, of the University of Pennsylvania. It was Lewis who withdrew as Progressive Gubernatorial candidate in Pennsylvania two years ago in favor of McCormick, the Democrat running for the same office.

It has been said that President Wilson chose Vance McCormick to lead his fight for reelection as a wily political move to lure into the Democratic camp some of the 440,000 voters who cast Progressive ballots in 1912. This may be quite true. But those who know the President feel certain that he took occasion to look up the record of this Pennsylvanian and appointed him chiefly because of a demonstrated ability to do things.

It was in the comparatively recent year 1893 that Vance McCormick first got into the limelight. He happened to be employed at that time as a fullback on the Yale football team, which was engaged with Princeton in one of the annual struggles. Vance won the game by kicking a goal from the forty-yard line, thereby earning undying fame in the annals of Old Eli and winding up his college career in a blaze of glory.

Nearly everything that Vance McCormick has done since has been marked by some of the elements of the unexpected that made that winning kick thrilling. Nobody ever boasts about a goal before it is kicked, and the Democratic campaign manager has applied the same caution to virtually all of his actions. He didn't threaten to clean up Harrisburg, the Pennsylvania State capital, when they elected him Mayor. He simply went to work without any noise, and before long the State woke up to the knowledge that the one-time wicked seat of its government had been cleaned up, and cleaned up thoroughly.

McCormick was born June 19, 1872, near Harrisburg. He celebrated his forty-fourth birthday by paying a visit to the President and inaugurating plans for the forthcoming campaign. His ancestors, hardy Scots, were among the early settlers of central Pennsylvania. Long before Vance saw the light of day the family was wealthy. His father amassed a fortune in coal mining and oil. The value of the estate of which Vance is executor, has been estimated at $20,000,000. In addition, McCormick is said to have about $5,000,000 in his own right, but no one could tell it from talking to him. He is probably more interested in the magnificent Percherons

he raises on his stock farm near Harrisburg than in any of the big business interests that help to keep his fortune intact.

McCormick prepared for Yale at the Harrisburg Academy. He is now
president of the board of that institution. He entered Yale in 1889, and got
his Ph.D. [sic] four years later. During his last two years he was captain
of the football team. Four years later his Alma Mater conferred upon him
the honorary degree of M.A. Still later he became a fellow of the Yale Corporation, succeeding no less a personage than William Howard Taft. And
to show that he is still a football player at heart, McCormick is a member
of the executive board of the athletic committee at Yale.

When young McCormick went back to his home town after graduating from Yale he found Harrisburg in a sad state. The water system was a
joke, the streets were unpaved and deep with mire, and the city depended
almost entirely upon the moon and the stars for street illumination. In
1900 the ex-fullback became a member of the Common Council. He
served there two years. Then the Independents began to boom him for
Mayor. In a city that was rather inclined to be tough and "low-brow,"
McCormick apparently was badly handicapped. He came from the Fourth
Ward, otherwise the "silk-stocking ward." He was something of a highbrow and he was known as a reformer.

But the ability he had been demonstrating in Councils to do things
without making a noise about them had marked him out. In a rock-
ribbed Republican city he was swept into office as Mayor on the Democratic ticket, the good citizens cutting their tickets to vote for him. And
in the next three years he justified the confidence placed in him by making Harrisburg almost a model city.

While in the Mayor's office McCormick began to inquire into the activities of one Colonel Guffey, who had been for more than a decade, up to
that time, Democratic boss of the State. After McCormick had completed
his term, his inquiries got more and more persistent, until finally he had
developed into a very active thorn in the side of the "Old Guard" Pennsylvania Democracy. For years it had been an open secret that the Republicans could get anything they wanted from the Democrats, C.O.D. But
when the Gubernatorial campaign of 1910 started McCormick, now
become a power in Democratic politics, declined to support the candidate
of the Old Guard, charging that he had made a deal with the Republicans
and the liquor interests.

Through the activities of McCormick, William H. Berry was induced
to run. He won the nomination, thus helping to establish the "Reorganiz-

ers" in the Democratic party. Berry had been State Treasurer. He is the man generally credited with having brought about the exposure and conviction of the Capitol grafters, the men who sold chandeliers at so much a pound and paint at so much or more per square inch in the erection of the Capitol building. Berry made a good fight, but was defeated.

The Old Guard may have thought that McCormick would soon disappear. If so, it was doomed to disappointment. For in 1912 Vance McCormick and A. Mitchell Palmer licked the Old Guard to a frazzle and went to Baltimore with a complete delegation for Woodrow Wilson. When the Democrats failed to get Secretary of Labor Wilson to become their candidate for Governor in 1914, the President endorsed McCormick, and his record was so clean and above board that Dean Lewis withdrew from the Progressive ticket in his favor. McCormick spent $33,000 in the fight but he was beaten.

He has a bigger fight on his hands this time, but he likes action and he will be heard from. For McCormick is that rare combination of the idealist and the practical politician. He has learned his politics in a hard school. What he does not know of the tricks of the trade is not worth knowing. At the same time he plays an open game. Apparently, he is in politics for the love of it.

Physically, Mr. McCormick is a little below average height. He has broad shoulders, as befits a fullback, and a nicely squared jaw. Even his enemies call him good-looking. He is genial, companionable, and a good mixer. As a public speaker he doesn't rank with the orators. He simply talks in a sane, level-headed way that because of his record and the look in his eyes carries conviction. This quality of level-headedness—the innate sense of the fitness of things in the man—is perhaps best reflected by his newspaper, the Harrisburg *Patriot*. With all the opportunity in the world to throw mud and be "yellow" in its attacks on the Old Guard within the last decade, the paper has gained strength and following by its dignity and reserve.

Mr. McCormick has always been a busy man. He is a bachelor, and his friends say he has always been too much occupied with business matters to get married. If he has a hobby, it is his prize live stock. He exhibits at all the county fairs, and frequently carries off prizes. His farm and summer home are near Harrisburg. The estate is known as "Rosegarden." Just to show that there is a strong touch of the idealist in the Democratic campaign manager, it may be mentioned that when McCormick bought this estate he found upon it the ruins of an old mill, the water-wheel broken and stuck in the mud. He cleaned out the stream running through the estate, repaired the mill-wheel, and there it is still turning to the music of the falling water.

---

3. WESTERN UNION TELEGRAM, 12:20 P.M., NOVEMBER 10, 1916

Hon. Vance C. McCormick, Biltmore Hotel, New York

I congratulate you with all my soul upon the splendid victory achieved for popular government by the President's reelection and upon the splendid work you have done. You have met every situation with courage and ability of the highest order and you have conducted a clean and creditable campaign in sharp contrast with the unscrupulous and sinister methods of the opposition. The victory is doubly valuable because it will have a purifying effect upon American politics and make it no longer possible for corruption to triumph through the purchase of coercion of any American state. Mrs. McAdoo joins me in affectionate regards.

(Sig) W G McAdoo

---

4. UNIDENTIFIED NEW YORK CITY NEWSPAPER ARTICLE

Vance C. McCormick, Winner, Hit Republican Line Hard
National Chairman for Democrats Didn't Forget His Football Training

"Keep your eye on the ball and hit the line hard."

This was the motto of Vance C. McCormick, chairman of the Democratic National Committee, when he was a famous football player at Yale back in the early nineties.

It was his guide in his conduct of the campaign for the re-election of President Wilson, from which he has emerged as perhaps the foremost figure in national politics, except the President himself.

There were murmurings of discontent among the leaders of the democratic party at St. Louis when the word came over the wire from Washington that President Wilson had selected Mr. McCormick to run his campaign. The members of the committee had practically decided to elevate Homer S. Cummings, of Connecticut, vice chairman of the committee. Few of them knew anything of Mr. McCormick, except that he lived in Pennsylvania and was believed to have progressive tendencies.

The "Old Guard" of the democratic party growled considerably before it accepted Mr. McCormick as chairman. It did accept him, for President Wilson was in complete control of the situation and there was nothing else to do.

Started Off with a Jump

Within less than a week after his selection Mr. McCormick opened the national headquarters in the Forty-second Street Building, in this city, and started things humming all along the line. With the assistance of Henry Morgenthau, chairman of the Finance Committee, he organized one of the most efficient publicity bureaus ever established in a national campaign. Under his guidance Wilber W. Marsh, the treasurer, started his "endless chain" system of collecting campaign contributions, comparatively small individually but large in the aggregate. National committeemen and State chairmen in States where the democrats were believed to have a chance were instructed to "get busy," and the democratic campaign was under full headway before the republican national organization, confident of victory, had come to a realization that it was necessary to make any particular effort.

If Mr. McCormick failed to see any opportunity during the campaign and neglected to take it to the advantage of the President, it was not apparent to the casual observer. Whenever a statement with a "punch" was needed he was there with the "punch." He obtained a lead of about three jumps ahead of the republican national organization and kept there.

Mr. McCormick was quoted as saying after election that the only mistake he was conscious of having made was that he had not realized that there was a chance of carrying New England. If this was a mistake—and there is doubt if the republicans would have lost any of these States if they knew that there was a serious fight against them—it was trivial compared to those made on the republican side, which Mr. McCormick in each case turned to good account.

Stuck to His Guns in Dark Hour

Mr. McCormick displayed his gameness in the face of the early returns which indicated the election of Charles E. Hughes. He never lost confidence for a moment. While many of his opponents had sought their bedrooms, certain that victory was theirs, Mr. McCormick sent dispatches to every democratic national committeeman, every State chairman and every county chairman in doubtful States, telling them that President Wilson had been re-elected and directing them to spare no effort or expense to insure a correct count of those election districts as yet unreported.

Mr. McCormick remained uninterruptedly at his post for nearly forty-eight hours. Private dispatches at that time convinced him that the President's re-election was certain a day before it was confirmed by returns received through the usual channels.

Mr. McCormick made his first serious essay into politics in 1902 when he was elected Mayor of Harrisburg, Pennsylvania, his home city. A member of a wealthy family, which is one of the largest land owners in Pennsylvania, he had devoted himself since his father's death in 1900 principally to the management of his father's large estate. He also is owner of the Harrisburg *Patriot,* the only democratic newspaper in Harrisburg, and has long been a generous contributor to democratic campaign funds.

In 1912 Mr. McCormick joined with Representative A. Mitchell Palmer to wrest control from James M. Guffey, of Pittsburgh, who had long been the democratic national committeeman from Pennsylvania. This was accomplished after a bitter fight and Mr. Guffey's defeat was accomplished by a majority of only one in the State committee.

Popular with Progressives

In 1914, Mr. McCormick was the democratic nominee for Governor of Pennsylvania, but was defeated. William Draper Lewis, dean of the University of Pennsylvania, the progressive nominee, withdrew in his favor, and Mr. McCormick spoke in many places for the progressive nominees for minor offices. His selection as national chairman was believed to be due in part to his popularity among the progressives, and was said to have been suggested by Mr. Palmer.

Whatever may have been the original reason for his selection, no democrat can be found to-day who will deny that the choice was a happy one. Clean cut, aggressive and in perfect condition physically and mentally, Mr. McCormick was a national chairman whose efficiency and alertness will long be remembered in political circles.

Known as one of the hardest football players who ever donned a blue jersey, Mr. McCormick was also one of the cleanest. No foul tackling, no taking any underhand advantage of an opponent went for him. He was a bright star in a brilliant constellation to the members of which the old Yale slogan, "Keep your eye on the ball and hit the line hard." [sic] Running the team from his position of quarter back, he was one of the best field generals who ever dug a cleated shoe into the gridiron.

Mr. McCormick played the political game in the same way. He never lost sight of the ball, which in this case was Wilson's re-election.

McCormick Mementoes
of the 1917 House Mission
to London and Paris

Vance McCormick collected mementoes of his notable work overseas in 1917. These included British newspaper clippings about the House Mission; his invitation to luncheon at Buckingham Palace, on which "Dress" was underlined; his lifeboat assignment card, which said he was to go to boat no. 11 on the call of "abandon ship"; and the seating chart for official meetings, which had Monsieur McCormick taking chair 3, next to Marshal Joffre. He placed these items in a scrapbook with "London and Paris 1917" stamped on the spine and "V. C. McC." on the front cover. Some of his souvenirs are presented here for what they reveal about the imposing rituals of diplomacy, as well as submarine warfare. The two newspaper articles are instructive for showing the official positions that McCormick and his fellow diplomats would represent as the United Staes joined the war. The other mementoes show that McCormick could behave like any ordinary American tourist who would bring back matchbooks and notepads with hotel logos.

More formal artifacts can also be found in the McCormick Papers at the Historical Society of Dauphin County. These include the medals he received from European governments for his service, such as the Legion of Honor from the president of France, and orders from the king of Italy and the king of Belgium. They can be viewed on the McCormick website.

1. UNIDENTIFIED BRITISH NEWSPAPER ARTICLE

COLONEL HOUSE AND HIS MISSION
America's Indomitable Spirit
THE TIME TO DO!
Lord Northcliffe's Return

Colonel House, the Special Ambassador to Great Britain, asked by Reuters' representative as to the objects of his mission, said,

"This is not the time to talk, but rather the time to do. That indeed is the reason why we are here. Our object is to establish the closest possible co-ordination between the Allies generally. Our first purpose is to attend the Allied Conference in Paris, which is not a conference on war aims, but on the conduct of the war. As to what the United States is doing and intends to do, everyone knows that already, and it is unnecessary to dwell upon it. It will be seen from the personnel of the Mission that it includes men who are experienced in every department connected with the prosecution of the war.

"Our visit at this time is the President's response to an invitation to the United States from the Allied Governments to attend the war council which is presently to be held. It was thought that a still better co-ordination could be brought about if the United States were represented in these deliberations."

America and the Issue

"We need not tell you of our resources, for they are known to you as well as they are to us, but we would like you to know that there is an indomitable spirit with all these resources to use them in every way possible in order to make the world a better place in which to live. Our people see the issue clearly. Notwithstanding the many races that make up our entity, there is an undivided purpose to fight until it becomes certain that no group of selfish men can again bring about such a disaster.

"One hundred and forty-one years ago the makers of our nation laid down the doctrine that Governments derive their just powers from the consent of the governed, and are instituted among men to give security to life, liberty and the pursuit of happiness. We intend to live and develop under this doctrine which is now at stake, and we feel that our being would not be justified if at this critical hour we failed the other democracies who share with us this lofty and just conception of the dignity of man."

The Personnel

Colonel House lunched yesterday with Mr. Balfour. In addition to the special Ambassador, the members of the Mission include Admiral W. S. Benson, Chief of Naval Operations; General T. R. Bliss, Chief of the Staff of the United States Army; Mr. Oscar Crosby, Assistant Secretary of the Treasury; Mr. Paul D. Cravath, Legal Adviser to Mr. Crosby; Mr. V. C. McCormick, Chairman of the War Board; Mr. B. Colby, representative of the United States Shipping Board; Dr. A. E. Taylor, representing the Food Controller; Mr. T. M. Perkins, of the War Industries Board; and Mr. Gordon Auchincloss, secretary of the Mission.

The headquarters of the Mission are at Chesterfield House, which has been lent to Colonel House.

---

2. NEWSPAPER ARTICLE, *MORNING ADVERTISER*

ALLIED WAR COUNCIL.
The American Mission.
Mr. Wilson's Statement.

Colonel House, head of the American Mission to the Allied War Council about to be held, met last night at Chesterfield House, South Audley Street, a number of Press representatives, to whom he made the following statement:

"Our visit at this time is the President's response to an invitation to the United States from the Allied Governments to attend the war council which is presently to be held. It was thought that a still better co-ordination could be brought about if the United States were represented in these deliberations.

"We need not tell you of our resources, for they are known to you as well as they are to us, but we would like you to know that there is an indomitable spirit with all these resources to use them in every way possible in order to make the world a better place in which to live.

"Our people see the issue clearly. Notwithstanding the many races that make up our entity, there is an undivided purpose to fight until it becomes certain that no group of selfish men can again bring about such a disaster.

"One hundred and forty-one years ago the makers of our nation laid down the doctrine that Governments derive their just powers from the consent of the governed, and are instituted among men to give security to life, liberty and the pursuit of happiness. We intend to live and develop under this doctrine which is now at stake, and we feel that our being would not be justified if at this critical hour we failed the other democracies who share with us this lofty and just conception of the dignity of man."

Questioned as to whether peace proposals would form any part of the discussion at the council, Colonel House said the objects of the mission were definitely stated by President Wilson in an announcement which he had issued that day, and which was as follows,

"The Government of the United States will participate in the approaching conference of the Powers waging war against the German Empire, and has sent as its representative Mr. Edward M. House, who is accompanied by Admiral W. E. Benson, Chief of Naval Operations; General Tasker H. Bliss, Chief of Staff, U.S.A.; Oscar T. Crosby, Assistant Secretary of the Treasury; Vance C. McCormick, chairman of the War Trade Board; Bainbridge Colby, United States Shipping Board; Dr. Alonzo E. Taylor, representing the Food Controller; Thomas Nelson Perkins, representing Priority Board; and Gordon Auchincloss as secretary.

"The conference is essentially a 'War Conference,' with the object of perfecting a more complete co-ordination of the activities of the various nations engaged in the conflict, and a more comprehensive understanding of their respective needs in order that the joint effort of the co-belligerents may attain the highest war efficiency.

"While a definite programme has not been adopted, it may be assumed that the subjects to be discussed will embrace not only those pertaining to military and naval operations, but also the financial, commercial, economic, and other phases of the present situation which are of vital importance to the successful prosecution of the war. There will undoubtedly be an effort to avoid any conflict of interests among the participants, and there is every reason to anticipate that the result will be a fuller co-operation, and more vigorous prosecution of the war.

"The United States, in the employment of its manpower and material resources, desires to use them to the greatest advantage against Germany. It has been no easy problem to determine how they can be used most effectively since the independent presentation of requirements by the Allied Governments have been more or less conflicting on account of each Government's appreciation of its own wants, which are naturally given greater importance than the wants of other Governments.

"By a general survey of the whole situation and a free discussion of the needs of all, the approaching conference will undoubtedly be able to give to the demands of the several Governments their true perspective and proper place in the general plan for the conduct of the war. Though the resources of this country are vast, and though there is every purpose to devote them all, if need be, to winning the war, they are not without limit. But even if they were greater they should be used to the highest advantage in attaining the supreme object for which we are fighting. This can only be done by a full and frank discussion of the plans and needs of the various belligerents.

"It is the earnest wish of this Government to employ its military and naval forces, and its resources and energies where they will give the greatest returns in advancing the common cause. The exchange of views which will take place at the conference, and the conclusions which will be reached [word illegible] biggest value [word illegible] energy and in bringing into harmony the activities of the nations which have been unavoidably, acting in a measure independently.

"In looking forward to the assembling of the conference it cannot be too strongly emphasized that it is a war conference and nothing else, devoted to devising ways and means to intensify the effort of the belligerents against Germany by complete co-operation under a general plan, and thus bring the conflict to a speedy and satisfactory conclusion."

In reply to a question as to whether the United States would come forward with any specific plan of better co-ordination, Colonel House said, "That will be worked out by the Allies. Of course we have ideas, just as the Allies have, and they will be mentioned at the conference to see how they fit in."

Answering further questions, Colonel House said the conference would sit for two or three days, but he did not think it would sit in London. Mr. Crosby, who also would represent America at the Inter-Allied Council would stay for an indefinite period in England, "but have my own plans," added the colonel.

3. INSTRUCTIONS FOR SHIP SECURITY ON MCCORMICK'S 1917 VOYAGE TO LONDON.

U.S.S. HUNTINGTON,
30 October 1917.

N O T I C E

After sunset all battle ports must be kept closed
or the ports fitted with light proof screens.

No smoking is allowed except in officers quarters,
between sunset and sunrise. No smoking on deck under
any circumstances between sunset and sunrise.

Battle ports and air ports will be closed before
sunset by a carpenters mate and will be opened by a
carpenters mate in the morning.

Every person on board is provided with a life preserver, these will be found in the state rooms and cabins.

At the call for "abandon ship" all passengers will
assemble on the port side of the quarter deck ready to
embark in the first whale boat. They must bring their
life preservers with them.

H. K. CAGE,
Commander, U.S.Navy,
Executive Officer.

4. SEATING PLAN FOR NOVEMBER 15, 1917, DINNER IN THE HARCOURT ROOM
OF THE HOUSE OF COMMONS.

PLAN OF TABLES.

—·❀·—

DINNER

—

HOUSE OF COMMONS,

HARCOURT ROOM.

—·❀·—

NOVEMBER 15th, 1917.

BAXTER & CO., PRINTERS, 7 FRITH ST. W. 1.

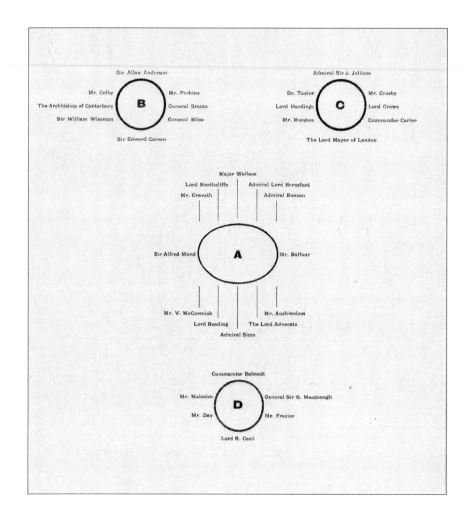

5. MENU FOR THE NOVEMBER 15, 1917, HOUSE OF COMMONS DINNER.

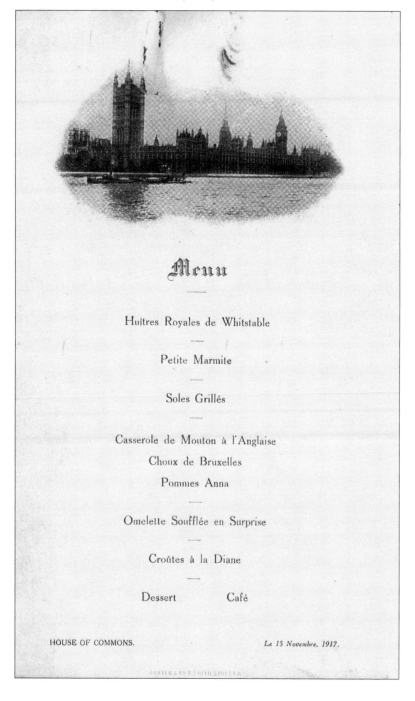

Menu

Huitres Royales de Whitstable

Petite Marmite

Soles Grillés

Casserole de Mouton à l'Anglaise
Choux de Bruxelles
Pommes Anna

Omelette Soufflée en Surprise

Croûtes à la Diane

Dessert   Café

HOUSE OF COMMONS.   *Le 15 Novembre, 1917.*

6. INVITATION TO LUNCH AT BUCKINGHAM PALACE, NOVEMBER 16, 1917.

The Lord Steward

has received Their Majesties' commands

to invite   Mr. Vance C. McCormick

to Luncheon at Buckingham Palace on

Friday   the 16th. November 1917 at   One   o'clock

The reply should be addressed
to the Master of the Household.   *Dress*

Buckingham Palace

7. SEATING CHART FOR NOVEMBER 20, 1917, MEETING IN THE CABINET ROOM
   AT 10 DOWNING STREET.

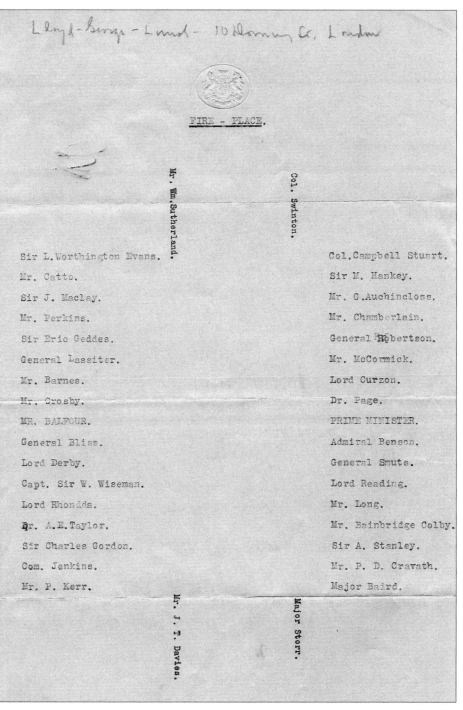

Lloyd-George — Lond — 10 Downing St, London

FIRE - PLACE.

Mr. Wm. Sutherland.

Col. Swinton.

Sir L. Worthington Evans.	Col. Campbell Stuart.
Mr. Catto.	Sir M. Hankey.
Sir J. Maclay.	Mr. G. Auchincloss.
Mr. Perkins.	Mr. Chamberlain.
Sir Eric Geddes.	General Robertson.
General Lassiter.	Mr. McCormick.
Mr. Barnes.	Lord Curzon.
Mr. Crosby.	Dr. Page.
MR. BALFOUR.	PRIME MINISTER.
General Bliss.	Admiral Benson.
Lord Derby.	General Smuts.
Capt. Sir W. Wiseman.	Lord Reading.
Lord Rhondda.	Mr. Long.
Mr. A. E. Taylor.	Mr. Bainbridge Colby.
Sir Charles Gordon.	Sir A. Stanley.
Com. Jenkins.	Mr. P. D. Cravath.
Mr. P. Kerr.	Major Baird.

Mr. J. T. Davies.

Major Storr.

8. FRONT AND BACK OF MCCORMICK'S PLACE CARD FOR THE
FRENCH DINNER ON NOVEMBER 24, 1917.

PRÉSIDENCE

DE LA RÉPUBLIQUE

Monsieur Vance C. Mc. Cormick

9. MENU CARD FOR THE NOVEMBER 24, 1917, FRENCH DINNER.

DÉJEUNER

du 24 Novembre 1917

Œufs Fedora

Homard Pompadour

Faisan rôti Cresson

Salade Rachel

Fonds d'artichauts Châtelaine

Bombe Florentine

Petits Gâteaux

10. THE USS *HUNTINGDON*, ON WHICH MCCORMICK SAILED IN 1917.

11. MCCORMICK (SECOND FROM RIGHT) AND OTHERS ABOARD SHIP EN ROUTE
     TO LONDON.

12. MCCORMICK SAVED HIS "ABANDON SHIP ASSIGNMENT" TICKET TELLING HIM WHICH BOAT TO TAKE IN CASE HIS SHIP TO LONDON IN 1917 WAS TORPEDOED.

ABANDON SHIP ASSIGNMENT

_Mr. Mc Cormack_____is assigned to
(name)

Boat
Raft } number_11_____for "Abandon Ship".

13. OFFICIAL PASS USED BY MCCORMICK FOR TRAVEL IN FRANCE.

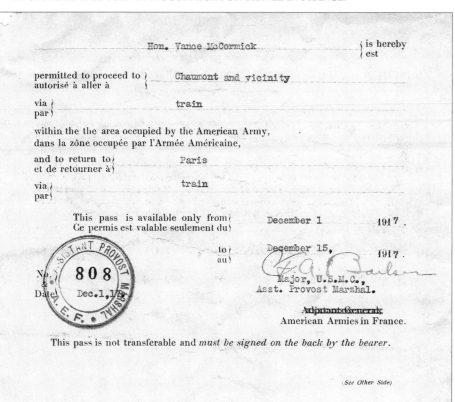

Hon. Vance McCormick _____ { is hereby
                                    { est

permitted to proceed to }   Chaumont and vicinity
autorisé à aller à   {

via {   train
par {

within the the area occupied by the American Army,
dans la zòne occupée par l'Armée Américaine,

and to return to {   Paris
et de retourner à {

via {   train
par {

This pass is available only from {   December 1   1917 .
Ce permis est valable seulement du {

                              to {   December 15,
                              au {   1917 .

No.   **808**   Major, U.S.M.C.,
&   Asst. Provost Marshal.
Date   Dec.1,1917

                                        Adjutant General
                                        American Armies in France.

This pass is not transferable and *must be signed on the back by the bearer.*

(See Other Side)

14. LIST OF GUIDELINES FOR BEARERS OF TRAVEL PASSES.

CONDITIONS AND RULES.

(1) The person to whom this Pass is issued, in accepting it, accepts responsibility for obeying all Routine and Standing Orders of the American Expeditionary Force.

(2) The holder of thiss Pass is specially warned that under no circumstances is a camera or any other photographic apparatus, instrument or accessory to be brought into the Zone of the Armies. If this order be disobeyed the camera, etc., will be confiscated, the Pass will be cancelled, and the individual who has broken this rule will be placed under arrest.

(3) This Pass merely confers upon the holder the right to travel over the route or within the area specified upon it, and does not confer any right to be transported either by road or by rail at the public expense, and must be shown when demanded.

(4) This Pass, when expired, will be handed to the American Military Authorities for transmission to Permit Office, G.H.Q.

Signature of bearer

15. INVITATION CARD FOR FRENCH LUNCHEON ON DECEMBER 1, 1917.

16. MENU CARD FOR THE DECEMBER 1, 1917, FRENCH LUNCHEON.

1ᴱᴿ DÉCEMBRE 1917

Huîtres de Marennes

Suprêmes de Soles Victoria

Poulardes à la Rossini

Haricots verts

Fromage — Fruits

Montrachet 1895

Haut-Brion 1891

Champagne Louis Rœderer

17. LIST OF ATTENDEES AT A MEETING OF THE ALLIES, NOVEMBER 29, 1917.

[This Document is the Property of His Britannic Majesty's Government.]

Printed for the War Cabinet. April 1918.

SECRET.

I.C.-35 (c).

CONFÉRENCE DES ALLIÉS.

LA Conférence des Alliés s'est réunie en séance plénière le 29 novembre, 1917, au Ministère des Affaires Étrangères, dans le grand salon de l'Horloge.

Assistaient à la Séance :

Pour la France :

M. Clemenceau, Président du Conseil, Ministre de la Guerre.
M. Stéphen Pichon, Ministre des Affaires Étrangères.
M. Georges Leygues, Ministre de la Marine.
M. Klotz, Ministre des Finances.
M. Clémentel, Ministre du Commerce.
M. Loucheur, Ministre de l'Armement.
M. Victor Boret, Ministre du Ravitaillement.
M. Lebrun, Ministre du Blocus.
M. Tardieu, Haut-Commissaire du Gouvernement français aux États-Unis.
M. Jules Cambon, Ambassadeur de France, Secrétaire général du Ministère des Affaires Étrangères.
M. de Margerie, Ministre plénipotentiaire, Directeur des Affaires politiques et commerciales au Ministère des Affaires Étrangères.
M. le Général Foch, Chef d'État-Major général de l'Armée.
M. l'Amiral de Bon, Chef d'État-Major général de la Marine.
M. le Général Weygrand, Représentant militaire français au Conseil supérieur de Guerre.
M. de Bearn, Secrétaire d'Ambassade.

Pour la Belgique :

Son Excellence le Baron de Brocqueville, Président du Conseil, Ministre des Affaires Étrangères.
Le Baron de Gaiffier-d'Hestroy, Ministre de Belgique à Paris.
M. le Général Rucquoy, Chef d'État-Major de l'Armée belge.

Pour le Brésil :

M. O. de Magalhães, Ministre du Brésil à Paris.

Pour la Chine :

M. Hoo Wei Teh, Ministre de Chine à Paris.
M. le Général Tang-Tsaï Li, Général de division de l'Armée chinoise.

Pour Cuba :

M. le Général Carlos Garcia Vélez, Ministre de Cuba à Londres.

Pour les États-Unis :

M. le Colonel House, Chef de Mission.
Son Excellence W. G. Sharp, Ambassadeur des États-Unis en France.
M. l'Amiral W. S. Benson.
M. le Général Tasker Bliss.
M. le Général Pershing, Commandant les Troupes américaines en France.
M. l'Amiral Sims.
M. O. T. Crosby, Secrétaire-Adjoint du Trésor.
M. Vance McCormick, Président de la Commission du Commerce et de Guerre.
M. Bainbridge Colby, Membre de la Commission du Fret.
M. Taylor, Secrétaire de la Commission du Commerce de Guerre, Représentant de la Direction de l'Alimentation.
M. T. N. Perkins, Représentant de la Commission des Munitions.
M. P. Cravath, Conseiller juridique.

[169—1]

B

A Correspondence Recovered, or the Popover Papers

J ust as our Citizen Extraordinaire *editorial project was nearing comple-*
tion, we received an e-mail from The Book Haven, *a book dealer in Lan-*
caster, Pennsylvania, informing us that they had some letters written to Vance
McCormick by Woodrow Wilson and Mrs. Edith Bolling Wilson. The dealer
had discovered through the McCormick website our interest in McCormick
documents and wanted to know if we might want to acquire them. How these
documents moved from McCormick to the book dealer, we are not sure, nor
is the dealer. In any case, we told the dealer how grateful we were to have
been notified at the last minute, and we purchased the documents for the His-
torical Society.

Reproduced here is one of the original handwritten documents recently
acquired from the dealer. Its contents were known to us through a typed copy
that had long been in the Historical Society's possession. LeRoy W. Toddes
referred to the Society's copy in his 1992 Cumberland County History *arti-*
cle about McCormick-Wilson correspondence. It begins with a message dated
January 14, 1920, from Edith Bolling Wilson to Vance McCormick, asking
him to come to the White House to discuss a matter of "great importance."
On the back of her letter McCormick has written his account of a meeting on
January 19, at which he told Mrs. Wilson that he could not accept the Presi-
dent's request that he take the post of Secretary of the Interior. The document

is important for showing the Wilsons' affection for McCormick, and also for demonstrating how Mrs. Wilson worked in her husband's stead during his convalescence from his stroke. It is now one of the very few handwritten documents of Vance McCormick that the Society possesses.

The White House
Washington

Jan. 14, 1920

My dear Mr. McCormick:

The President is very anxious for me to have a talk with you about a matter that is very dear to him and of great importance so I am wondering if you will be in Washington within the next few days? and if so if you will come in and see me at your earliest convenience. Come to lunch and have some "popovers" as in the good old fighting days.

A telegram or telephone message will find me ready.

With warm remembrances to you, your dear mother and sister, believe me

Faithfully,
Edith Bolling Wilson

Edith Bolling Wilson's original note to McCormick.

[handwritten memorandum — illegible cursive]

466.6.11.01   V. C. McC

McCormick's original memorandum.

[MEMORANDUM IN VANCE MCCORMICK'S HANDWRITING
ON THE BACK OF THE NOTE FROM MRS. WILSON]

On Monday Jan 19 I lunched with Mrs. Wilson at the White House and she told me of the President's great regret at my not accepting the appointment as Secretary of Commerce as the President wanted me in his official family as one of his advisers and that he now was insisting upon my accepting the position of Secretary of the Interior. I explained my desire to remain off the Cabinet and out of official life even as far back as 1913 when the Pa. delegation offered to back me and I still had that feeling and felt I could help the President more off than on because as soon as you were on the C., due to rank and official precedent under the Presidential system, I could only see him concerning my own department and I would lose freedom of action which now existed, and I added that a Western man should be appointed Secretary of Interior. Mrs. Wilson was delightful and most sympathetic and we discussed for a [sic] hour ways of helping the P. in his convalescing days. Mrs. W. is a remarkable woman, full of charm and great common sense.

V. C. McC.

Smashing the Home Front
The [Authorized] Story
of the War Trade Board

Dean Hoffman, the author of this published account of the activities of the War Trade Board, was an employee of Vance McCormick at the Harrisburg Patriot. We can surmise, therefore, that it had McCormick's approval as well as his cooperation and constitutes an authorized history. The writing is surprisingly vivid and efficient, given its subject, economics and management, which confirms that the author was a journalist and not an academic.

While Hoffman wrote a favorable account of the War Trade Board's role during the war, it was not simply a celebration of McCormick's leadership. In fact, McCormick's name is mentioned only once, when the board's members are introduced. Hoffman's history is, as its title says, the story of a successful organization. His emphasis is on the unprecedented size and effectiveness of its operations: Three thousand persons were employed, and each day up to $50 million worth of goods was affected. The board managed more than an embargo against Germany; in effect, they were the czar of world trade, managing commerce between Allies and neutrals at the same time that they were trying to undermine enemies. And the enemy they finally defeated turned out to be, as Hoffman explains, not German soldiers, but civilians.

The copy in the Historical Society's possession has a few grammatical changes penciled in; these have not been included here, as they were of no

*particular consequence to the text. On the cover page are printed the words
"January 1919 Revised December 1926," but these have been crossed out,
suggesting that another printing was planned.*

When the representatives of a vanquished Germany went to meet Marshal Foch in the little war-torn French town of Senlis, in November 1918, they knew exactly what had brought them there. They made a confession of defeat not only in action but in words.

Facing the great French warrior, their spokesman said:

> "Germany's army is at your mercy, Marshal. Our reserves of men and munitions are completely exhausted, making it impossible for us to continue the war."

With more than three million soldiers in the fighting line, amply fed and clothed and though beaten back resisting, why did Germany sign the armistice? All military critics agree that while Germany could not have escaped ultimate defeat, she could have staved off a military disaster for a time, so why did this arrogant, militaristic nation ingloriously surrender her fighting front when she did?

The answer is obvious. German's [sic] "home front" had collapsed. Her people were hungry. Her trade was paralyzed. Her munition factories were producing "duds." Her civilians were bubbling with revolution and no matter how staunchly her army stood, the case for her was hopeless.

And that situation was the triumph of the United States and its allies just as was President Wilson's masterly diplomacy and the memorable battles of the Marne, the Somme and the Meuse, for it revealed the economic defeat of Germany as clearly as the war maps disclosed her military failure. Germany was fought on the fields of economy as well as on the field of battle and she lost both places.

A Contest of Nations

Wars long since ceased to be fought with munitions alone. From the time that war became a contest of nations, rather than of armies, the forces of economics, food, subsistence, indeed all life-essentials joined with the military to wrest victory from the enemy. And so as this war was greatest in the employment of vast military resources, so it was greatest in the employment of trade devices to beat Germany into submission. Never before were the military and economic legions so closely coordinated, so effectively in cooperation.

When Uncle Sam went into the war it was with "both feet." Not only, he decided, should military campaigns be waged against the enemy, but economic warfare, too, and both with the same relentlessness, the same intelligence, the same vigor.

How splendidly the military triumphed is familiar to all. How successfully the economic campaigns ended is still to be told and best told through the work of a government organization, large in numbers, vital in function, wonderful in results and inconspicuous in print, the War Trade Board.

When German war factories lacked steel-hardening materials for shells; when German firms shut up shop in South America; when Pershing's men obtained saddles and mules from Spain; when we and our Allies received lumber from Switzerland and iron ore from Scandinavia; when "movies" spreading German propaganda were banished from the theaters of neutrals; when German trade with contiguous neutrals was virtually cut off; when hidden German-owned property was revealed in this country and its possessions; and when hundreds of thousands of ship tonnage were diverted to meet the requirements of the Yanks overseas, the trail of responsibility led directly to the War Trade Board.

Trade Board's Weapons

Constantly the Board's efforts were centered on weakening the enemy with economic weapons so that the armies, once they got into position, could deliver the knock-out blow. Had the war continued six months longer, Germany's "place in the sun" would have been in the class of economic minutiae.

Until the United States did get into the war, Germany's trade, while crippled, was still far from that complete paralysis certain Allied victory required. The very existence of the United States as a neutral made an effective blockade for the Allies difficult and rendered impossible perhaps the final welding of the iron ring about the Central Powers. It was only when America did enter the war that the noose about Germany's neck, until then, tied in a loose knot, began to tighten.

Prior to that time Holland was sending enough foodstuffs into Germany to feed the entire Boche army on the western front. Denmark was doing as much. Norway and Sweden, just across the Baltic, were exporting enormous quantities of minerals and other materials for German war factories.

Many of these neutrals, wholly within their rights under international law, were sending large quantities of food into Germany and then meeting their domestic needs by imports. The marked increase in food impor-tations by such neutrals showed what was being done. While the Allies detected this obvious advantage to Germany, they could control the situ-ation only in part.

German firms outside of Germany, notably in Spain, South America, Mexico, Central America and elsewhere, were piling up undisturbed for-tunes in business which they used to spread propaganda against the Allies or conserved for after-war purposes in re-establishing German credit and commercial power. In fact, Germany was so little hampered that the hope of starving her into submission had vanished.

Cooperation with Allies

America recognized these facts as she joined the Allies. It became evi-dent that sterner measures were required to win. It was patent that the essential war materials of the world must be conserved for ourselves and the Allies, that new policies toward neutrals must be established. From the first there was the heartiest kind of cooperation between America and the Allies.

There was nothing in our own experience to serve as guide, except our Allies' plans. There was no foundation upon which to build. So far as the United States was concerned, it was an unchartered sea. Whatever was done had to be created. By virtue of the Espionage Act of June 15, 1917, the Exports Council was created by Presidential proclamation to meet the conditions of that time. A month later there was issued the first list of restricted exports for which licenses must be obtained. August 27, 1917, the list was extended and an Exports Administrative Board was estab-lished. The trading with the Enemy Act was enacted October 6, 1917, which gave power over imports, as well, and October 12 the War Trade Board came into being. Three days later it issued its first order.

At once the Board declared intensive economic warfare on the enemy, determined to prevent Germany from obtaining a single commodity it needed in war making and resolved that Germany's trade with neutral nations must be restricted as far as legal limits permitted. All essential war materials here or abroad must be conserved for ourselves and our Allies. All imports must be controlled to conserve ships for the business of the war. If the United States was to supply the Allied and neutral world with food stuffs, a rationing system must be adopted. Through the control of exports and imports, ships must be diverted from normal trade to war routes. Sugar must be brought from Cuba; wool from the Argentine; nitrates from Chile. These were war necessities and tonnage must be switched from other to trans-Atlantic routes to meet the necessities of war.

Biggest Business Interest

These were the broad policies of the War Trade Board. It resolved itself into the biggest export and import business in the history of the world. It put virtually the world's shipping into its own hands. It meant that every export and every import touching this country and its war associates and, by virtue of bunker licensing, every neutral country required a permit to be moved. It involved daily transactions running from $40,000,000 to $50,000,000. It required the service of 3000 employees, mostly in Washington, but also in every importing trading post in the world. It stood as the clearing house of world trade and the "contact" for the State, Treasury, War, Navy, Shipping, War Industries, Food and other government agencies. It was the focal point of trade agencies of the earth. Branches of Allied embassies had their offices in the Board's building. Ambassadors, ministers, consuls, high commissions of neutrals were its frequent conferees and visitors. The world trade dreams of Kultur were but nightmares compared with this necessary war-period actuality.

To prevent supplies from reaching Germany was an obvious necessity and little less so the crippling of what trade she had. Through the splendid blockade of the British and Allied navies, virtually no supplies reached Germany directly from overseas. What entered Germany came from contiguous and the so-called northern neutrals across the Baltic, whose waters were safe from Allied patrol. Yet this undisturbed flow of supplies was too vital to neglect, even though difficult to regulate.

Regard for Humanity

Humanity dictated that America provide the neutrals with the absolute essentials of life. To the neutrals America said "we will ascertain exactly just what your living needs are and we will provide those things insofar as we are able. We will not do it if Germany is to profit directly or indirectly. We will not give you oil for your factories to make war supplies for Germany. We will not send you oil cakes to feed your cattle to make butter and milk and cheese for our enemy. In return we ask that you put at our disposal such shipping as is now lying idle or engaged in non-essential trade and provide us with what commodities you can spare."

What the United States and its allies really did was to offer these neutrals a better proposition than Germany could. It was a system of bargaining and the neutrals accepted the better offer.

As a consequence the War Trade Board negotiated agreements with Denmark, Switzerland, Sweden and Norway, made progress with Holland, whom Germany had by the throat, and consummated a commercial bond with Spain. The result was that these neutrals cut off Germany completely in some materials and in all others cut down their former exports.

The agreement with Switzerland was made December 5, 1917, to run from October 1, that year, to September 30, 1918. Agreements made at various times during 1917 with Norway, Sweden and Denmark ran for the duration of the war. As illustrating the effect on Germany of just one of these agreements, the following table is illuminating:

Control of Exports

Swiss exports to Central Powers in pounds for the first three months of

	1917	1918
Oatmeal	187,391	0
Flour	63,933	0
Dried Fruit	127,866	0
Raw hides	725,313	0
Leather shoes	396,828	0
Cotton cloth	1,183,870	68,342

Switzerland agreed further to send no milk, edible fats or poultry to Germany. Norway cut its normal fish exports of hundreds of thousands of tons to 48,000 and exported no fish oil or other foodstuffs. Sweden's trade with Germany in foodstuffs was limited to cranberries. Denmark, solely dependent on Germany for coal, held its exports of butter, bacon, cheese and eggs to only a fraction of the amounts sent previous to the War Trade Board's agreement, and for every pound of foodstuffs Denmark sent Germany she sent a like amount to England. Germany did not receive a pound of cotton from these sources.

The agreements worked out the same way in respect to other foodstuffs. Scandinavia and Switzerland ordinarily sent large quantities of metals and minerals to Germany for munitions. These stopped. In some cases not a single pound was shipped. Norway agreed to send Germany 200 tons of copper annually but Germany had to return a like amount in manufactured articles. Of such essential war materials as bismuth, nickel, chrome and manganese, Norway sent no more to Germany.

Enemy's Double Loss

Germany not only lost these prized war commodities for herself but she lost them to the Allies, for when the neutrals ceased to market them with Germany they sent them to Germany's enemies because Germany's enemies were keeping them alive. And so not only were Germans tightening their belts for lack of food but their war industries were beginning to starve.

An agreement along similar lines was in process of negotiations with Holland when the armistice was signed. That it was not signed along with the other neutrals was due to the pistol which Germany held at Holland's head, and the threat of invasion. Holland was too close to Belgium to risk that.

In rationing neutrals the Board took safeguards to prevent our supplies from leaking through neutral nations to the enemy. This was accomplished by the organization of distributing agencies and under inter-allied committee supervision. Violation, of course, meant rupture with America and the Allies. In Denmark, the Danish Merchants' Guild; in Holland, the Netherlands Overseas Trust and in Switzerland the Societe Suisse de Surveillance Economique were scrupulous in sealing their frontiers tightly.

Another very advantageous arrangement was made by the Board with Spain by which General Pershing's legions and our Allied armies received supplies. Spain needed our oils and other commodities. Our soldiers needed military supplies. The bargainers of the War Trade Board and the American Expeditionary Forces got busy and Spain provided under an agreement of March 7, 1918, about 500,000 army blankets, 50,000 mules, 240,000 yards of canvas, 20,000 saddles and bridles, 100,000 pounds of harness leather and other supplies.

Rationing the Ships

Scarcity of tonnage required a strict rationing of ships both of neutrals, the Allies and ourselves. Our war needs called for nitrate and wool from South America. South America needed our coal. Priorities and allocations for these were essential.

One of the most effective weapons designed to dominate the situation was the control of all bunker fuel through license for every ship touching American ports, continental or insular. Every ship of neutral or allied ownership had to be licensed if it wanted bunkers. As a consequence, the Board could govern both voyage and cargo. If, in the Board's opinion, the length of voyage or the character of cargo was detrimental to the winning of the war, it simply refused ship fuel, until the skipper or owner agreed to those things which did help us win the war. The United States possessed these bunkers, coal, oils, etc., and it was plain efficiency that it should parcel them out in its own, rather than in the enemy's, interest.

The Board's policy was to urge ships asking bunkers to return directly. This enabled the Board to confine them to war trade instead of allowing them to wander all over the Seven Seas. At the same time it enabled the Board to check profiteering in ocean freight rates.

Guerno Hermanos, of Mazatlan, Mexico, was suspected of pro-German activities. He bought a racing yacht and took it to Los Angeles to be fitted with new machinery. When he went to clear port, he was refused fuel unless he agreed to return to Los Angeles. He refused and the racing yacht was left rusting in Los Angeles and Germany commerce raiders did not profit thereby.

Starving the Submarines

Similar methods kept in port a flotilla of small vessels operating off Florida and strongly suspected of supplying enemy submarines with gasoline and other supplies.

Relentless as was the Board's effort to keep supplies from reaching Germany, just as relentless was the campaign to cripple her trade, to smash her foreign business and to prevent her from recouping abroad her losses at home. This vital work was intrusted to the War Trade Intelligence best known as "W.T.I." and directed by Paul Fuller, of New York, a distinguished lawyer.

If enemy trade was to be stopped, the Board had to know the identity of foreign traders, their affiliations and their "cloaks," throughout the world. If a cargo of agricultural implements was to be licensed for export, the character of both consignor and consignee must be known. If either had German origin or connection, the license was refused. It was the business of "W.T.I." to "get the goods" and determine the enemy or non-enemy character of the parties to an export or import transaction, a process in which our Allies played a substantial part.

In December of 1917, the Board, just getting under way really, had information on 8% of the persons named in the license applications. Later the percentage grew to 80%. There were on file about 360,000 information cards bearing on 165,000 firms and individuals throughout the world. To obtain this information 67,000 special reports were made by agents of the

Board scattered all over the globe and working in harmony with agents of other departments and other governments.

The "Eyes" of the Board

The size of the job facing the Intelligence Bureau is indicated by the fact that from January 1, 1918, to the signing of the armistice, it passed upon more than 2,000,000 trade applications, ranging from 7,000 to 10,000 a day and with an average valuation of $3,500. In August, 1918, alone there were 127,846 applications.

All enemy traders were placed on one of three "black" lists. A place on any one of these was a trade death warrant. Neither neutral nor ally would deal with the branded name. One list, the enemy trading list, was public and included all whose enemy standing was patent. Another, the confidential suspect list, explains itself, and a third, the "cloaks' list" included those "straw men" who acted for enemy traders.

South America, Mexico and Central America at once offered a fertile field for enemy trade list recruiting stations. All the disguises of old Castillian names and Spanish accent and mannerisms which the crafty German adopted were penetrated by "W.T.I." and "to let" and "for sale" signs soon hung all over the one-time German establishments.

The German house of Hasenclever, the big distributor of agricultural machinery on the east coast of South America, was put out of business. Hasenclever, once on the black list, was a commercial outcast. He could deal with none. None dealt with him. In Chile the nitrate interests were in German hands. The United States, through its control of fuel oil ousted the Germans. In Peru, the great Gildemeister sugar interests soon ceased to be Gildemeister. Put on the enemy trading list they became traders without trade and had to renounce their control. With the consent of America and to protect the 10,000 employees, the Peruvian government took over the German concern.

Crippling Enemy Trade

The Casa Grande Sugar Company of Peru, the largest electric power company in Brazil, and three great banks in that section, all dominated by Germans, closed up. The "blacklist" branded them.

That sort of German trade suppression took place all over the world, because of the sleepless vigil of "W.T.I." Even the German movies in neutral nations did not escape the farflung arm. This was accomplished again through the control of exports. South American "movie" managers, wanting American and Italian films, were told they could not obtain license for export if their theaters showed German pictures, all of them, of course, propaganda films. The "movie" theaters had to have our own and other pictures because even the congenital pro-German could not spend evening after evening looking at just German pictures. The "movie" men saw the point and banned the German moving picture propaganda. This was true not only in South American countries, but in Germany's near-neighbor, Norway.

When not turning up enemy traders, War Trade Intelligence was revealing enemy owned property to the Alien Property Custodian. A letter from an Austrian in an Austrian officers' training camp to a friend in this country was intercepted. It asked for $15,000 for spending money. That was the clue. It led to the uncovering of $400,000 worth of Austrian property in this country which was turned over to the Alien Property Custodian.

Undoubtedly the War Trade Board was a real trouble-maker for Germany. When it was not cutting off trade in one direction, it was in another. It not only put German firms out of business abroad, but injured their business at home with nearby neutrals.

Establishing New Markets

If America could supply neutrals with supplies formerly received from Germany, why not, even if America needed the money less than it needed to fight Germany with every available weapon. So licenses were issued for adding machines, bicycles, carpets, clocks, cutlery, dyes and other things for Holland, Denmark and other neutrals, cutting down German business just that much.

But while Germany must be prevented from getting war supplies, and while her trade must be crippled, the United States and the Allies must conserve their own raw materials for war-making. Thus conservation was another function of the War Trade Board. Here was a problem requiring the most intimate cooperation between units of our own government as well as of the Allies. What these war essentials were was left to the War Industries Board and Food Administration to determine chiefly.

Not only our country, but all the world had to be combed for these essentials, and none of them dare reach the enemy at all or even private hands before the war machines were supplied. Commodities must be controlled to prevent speculation, to maintain a proper rate of foreign exchange, to check profiteering and to guarantee a correct and equitable distribution.

Through the War Trade Board, American manufacturers were enabled to obtain their supplies from abroad, the distribution here being left to trade associations and a rationing plan. This was particularly true of wool, rubber, cocoa beans, hides and skins.

Speculation Restrained

By this same control speculation was prevented, for no importer was permitted to have a second consignment until the first had been distributed. In this same way prices were maintained, a saving of $50,000,000 on wool alone being accomplished.

Perhaps no function of the Board was more vital or richer in results than its diversion of ship tonnage to meet war needs. The submarine had cut deeply into world shipping by millions of tons. We had started our shipbuilding program, but still the need for more bottoms was urgent if we were to send our soldiers abroad and maintain them. It was necessary to control our own and allied tonnage but the war crisis demanded still more ships. The neutrals had some of them. They must be obtained by bargaining or diversion. It was up to the War Trade Board again.

In September and October alone, due to control of imports and exports, the Board was able to divert from trade to war purposes 1,200,000 tons of shipping in addition to smaller quantities obtained in similar fashion before that.

Much neutral tonnage was either idle or engaged in trade not essential to war. Carrying cargoes of bric-a-brac may be a very desirable business in times of peace, but when Uncle Sam and his allies need those ships to transport armies and supplies to France or bring sugar from Cuba or manganese from Brazil, it was irritating and ridiculous, particularly if the ships were using our fuel.

The Control of Bunkers

By the control of bunkers it was easy for the Board to persuade neutrals that if they wanted coal, they could get it by engaging in some useful maritime pursuit. An equally fascinating offer was to place, as before mentioned, certain much-needed commodities at the disposal of the neutrals if they would put ship tonnage at our disposal. And so again the bargain was struck.

In this fashion the War Trade Board obtained from Norway 154 vessels of 607,544 tons; from Sweden 67 vessels of 200,000 tons; from Denmark 53 vessels for 265,000 tons. Holland, under an upraised German club, hesitated. She was offered wheat if she would come for it. Still the German threat persisted, so 484,053 tons of shipping lying idle in American ports were acquired under international law by executive order under pledge of fair compensation and full return.

Japan also had considerable tonnage and shipbuilding facilities, too. She needed steel ship plates badly. America had the steel ship plates, but steel was a war essential and had to be conserved. But the United States could afford to export the plates of ships, if Japan turned over and contracted 522,903 tons. And Japan did.

This process added more than two million tons to our shipping resources, making possible an uninterrupted flow of war supplies to the fighting line and of war materials to the munition factories in our own and allied lands.

Only the Essentials

But the result could not have been achieved by barter alone. Even after we had the tonnage, it had to be conserved and devoted to the most urgent needs of the war. For months there had been coming into this country large quantities of non-essential goods. Some of these commodities were trivial. Either they were not needed in wartimes or their substitutes could be found here. So certain imports were banned entirely and others restricted. One list issued April 14, 1918, restricted 82 commodities. Later the list was extended.

For years America had been getting all its manganese from Brazil. When the pinch came, prospectors found enough manganese deposits in this country to spare 100,000 tons of shipping from the Brazil trade. Tapioca flour, used both for glue-making and puddings, and imported from the Dutch East Indies, was banned entirely and the ships engaged in that traffic diverted to war purposes. The economy amounted to 50,000 tons. This form of conservation meant the creation of many hundred thousand tons of shipping for the American Expeditionary Forces and the Allies.

While these restrictions forced radical changes in private business, it is the ready statement of members of the Board that American trade promptly approved the policies and submitted patriotically to the sacrifices.

The Board's Personnel

To direct the vast and far-reaching policies of the War Trade Board called for men of vision and capacity. Vance C. McCormick was made chairman. He had been directing chief of both the Exports Council and the Exports Administrative Board and brought to the larger task the experience and guidance that his training in business gave him.

Thomas L. Chadbourne, Jr., like Mr. McCormick, represented the State Department and acted as counselor. Theirs was the diplomatic phase of the Board's work. Mr. Chadbourne was intrusted with the delicate and difficult task of formulating trade agreements with neutrals.

Dr. Alonzo E. Taylor represented the Agriculture Department. He is a chemist and food specialist of the first order, it being said of him that he could train food calories to skip rope or roll hoop. In civilian life he was a member of the faculty of the University of Pennsylvania, and before joining the Trade Board was attached to the American Embassy in Berlin with particular assignment to safeguard the food interests of British prisoners of war.

Clarence M. Woolley represented the Department of Commerce and War Industries Board. He was president of the American Radiator Company, one of the nation's prominent businessmen. He reached the top of the company from the bottom. His work with the Board was largely with imports, to which he contributed valuable knowledge, obtained through the international character of his business.

Representing Food Supply

Beaver White, who was the Food Administration's member, is a man of wide experience in engineering and finance. He is a Pennsylvanian, born at Milroy and Governor Beaver was his uncle. He had spent much of his time abroad in electrical enterprises and when the war broke in August, 1914, he was a resident in England, a member of the world-known firm of J. G. White & Co. He quickly enrolled with the American Committee for the Relief of Belgium. Later he was made London director of the Commission and when America entered the war he came to this country and became associated with Food Administrator Hoover.

Edwin F. Gay spoke for the Shipping Board. He was previously dean of Harvard Graduate School of Business Administration, a thorough scholar, a student of economic affairs and a master statistician. It was largely through his commanding mastery of facts and figures and their correlation that the Board was enabled to economize so much in the matter of ship tonnage.

Frank C. Munson, president of the Munson Line of Steamships, was a Shipping Board representative also. He had wide experience in shipping matters which qualified him to handle the problem of obtaining ship tonnage from neutrals and the Allies.

Albert Strauss was the Board member, representing the Treasury Department. He was a prominent New York banker and was named by President Wilson to succeed Paul Warburg on the Federal Reserve Board.

Headquarters' Camp

So day after day this clearing house met to formulate the policies winning the war required. To execute its orders, called for a vast organization, which soon outgrew the dozen buildings it occupied in its youth and later was centered in a mammoth two-story building all its own and covering an entire Washington block, 400x415 feet.

In this building were one and one-half miles of hallways, 300,000 square feet of floor space, 300 separate offices. Distances were so great that a corps of twenty-five boys used roller skates to deliver messages and make 1800 calls daily. It had its own mail service which handled 4000 to 5000 communications a day with a delivery and collection every twenty minutes.

There were 372 main telephones and 161 extensions. To provide the buzzer system required 250 miles of wire. There were 500 electric fans, 1000 typewriters, a print shop with 3,000,000 impressions a month. A mailing list to exporters, importers, newspapers and others numbered 20,000.

The welfare of the employees was not neglected. A fire drill could empty the building in less than two minutes. A cafeteria in the building could feed 1300 persons very palatable meals. Three times a day meals were served. A basketball court was provided between wings of the building and girls' and boys' athletic teams developed friendly rivalry. Men of the organization contributed $3000 with which to establish a clubhouse for girl employees.

Keeping the Staff Healthy

A hospital and rest room were in the building with nurses and doctors in attendance. During the "flu" epidemic the Board established its own hospital and from the ranks of employees recruited sixty-five trained nurses. There were 350 victims at one time. The morale of the organization was reflected in the athletic contests and in being the first in Washington to celebrate the armistice with a procession.

Eighty per cent of the employees were women. Some of the work was very tedious. To meet this condition recess periods of three and five-minute duration were established during which everybody left the building. The beneficial results were so obvious that the recess idea was adopted by the War, Navy and other government departments. There was never a shortage of stenographers. A school of stenography with free instruction was conducted within the building.

Naturally an army of employees was required. The Board's immediate predecessor, the Exports Administrative Board, had 186 employees, August 27, 1917. There were 1721 on January 31, 1918, and they increased until they numbered in mid-November 3000, of whom 450 were in branches of the Board. To acquaint all these workfolks with the business of the Board, two daily newspapers as well as monthly publications were issued.

The Economic Army

This was the Economic Army and these its weapons in the war on the Central Powers. Every day the shrapnel of trade, embargo and blockade devices fell over a constantly increasing area of the enemy whose raw materials were shrinking and its food supplies dwindling. The noose the War Trade Board and its allied associates had slipped around the German neck was tightening.

German munition factories were so hard pressed for copper, cotton and other raw materials for shell making in the later days of the war that church bells, door knobs, even the guns of their inactive navy, were being melted down to make munitions for the hard-pressed German military machine. The embargo and the blockade and the agreements engineered by the War Trade Board with neutrals were getting in their fine work. The proportion of "duds," dead shells on the battlefield, was increasing.

Germany Feels the Pinch

When the embargo cut off fodder supplies to Germany, and restricted feedstuffs to neutrals, it was felt shortly in the horse transport service of the enemy. Germany had done wonders with motors, but when America cut off its supplies of rubber, these noiseless tires gave way to clanging iron bands. Consequently motor trucks, thus equipped, carrying supplies, had to withdraw from front line service and horses substituted. But the horses, scantily fed, lacked pulling power and shells and food for the fighters began arriving later.

Nor was this the only way the War Trade Board attacked the German army from the rear. The enemy was getting ammunition in reduced quantity and quality. Not only had the Board prevented steel hardening materials from getting into Germany but the food supplies for the munition worker were getting so shabby that they failed to produce the energy which would produce the munitions in former quantities. The workers' rations were just about enough to sustain life, with nothing left for the generation of energy.

By ruthless effort the German government seemed able to supply its army with food, but it was at the expense of the people back home, who constituted the "home front." It is one of the ironies of the war that no matter how much wheat-growing territory Germany conquered, her grain supplies kept decreasing. Economic warfare was again hitting the mark. It prevented fertilizer from getting into Germany so completely that the soil became impoverished and in the hands of equally impoverished agriculturists, simply refused to yield. All the invaded lands of Russia, Belgium, northern France, Serbia and Rumania failed to provide Germany with her required grain supplies.

The Menu Changes

When the United States entered the war, the German civilian was getting 250 grammes (about a half pound) of meat every week. This did not include liver, game, poultry. The Berliner was not painfully short of meat. It was easy to obtain in any café.

Those happy meat days did not linger long after the United States took a hand at the war game. Due to restricted imports, Germany soon cut the meat ration by including fifty grammes of bone in the 250 allotment. Later the bone ration was increased to a fourth and still later fifty more grammes of the hungry German's meat ration had to be "sawdust" sausage or similar substitutes.

There was no easing of the pressure by the War Trade Board. Germany was getting less and less meat. Eventually meatless weeks were instituted, at first only one a month; later four weeks in ten.

Butter, fats and oils began to disappear. Neutrals, which formerly supplied them, were pleased with their agreement with America not to feed Germany, and refused food to the Central Powers. The bread, wretched as it was, must now be eaten without butter, a dry, choking morsel. Fruits obtained from Switzerland, made marmalade and jellies which made the bread a trifle more palatable, but now the fruit supply was cut. Even the German was deprived of his morning coffee and chicory. He was beginning to fret.

All cotton supplies were exhausted and could not be renewed from outside. That reduced the natives to paper clothing and forced them indoors in wet weather There was irritation on every side.

Enemy Grows Desperate

The wheat supply was going fast. The war lords decided on a desperate gamble. Vice-Chancellor Helferrich months and months before, warned the military masters that ruthless submarine warfare on the United States would bring the country into the war and the economic consequences would defeat the Fatherland. Finally the militarists had their day. Unrestricted submarine attacks followed. America was forced into the war and now in the early spring of 1918 the price Germany had to pay was becoming apparent.

Ordinarily wheat harvests are left untouched for several months after they are gathered. The 1917 harvests of Germany ordinarily would not have been drawn upon until October of that year. But the grain supply was so low that the 1917 harvest was distributed in August instead of October. Naturally that meant exhaustion of the crops two months earlier the following spring. And so it came about that in the spring of 1918, Germany's wheat supply had about vanished and if Germany was to win at all, it must be by a single and desperate throw.

The gamble was agreed upon. The great offensive started. A great rush and then a pause. Another great rush and another pause. And so on, always a pause between attacks. And there was a reason. It was not to rest tired fighting men. Famished munition workers back home could not keep up the stream of military supplies and so the army rested until its munitions were replenished. Every new attack exhausted the supplies still more until the invading armies reached the Marne, threatening Paris and sending chills along Allied spines.

The Army Delivers

Then at Chateau-Thierry, American marines and doughboys turned on the invaders and brushed them back. Germany's munitions were failing. Her starved horses could not deliver rapidly enough what supplies they had. "Duds" instead of "live ones" were sent across No Man's Land.

Back home in Germany, the people were without those foods which produce energy—butter, meat, fats, oils. At this time the German civilian received per week the same weight of fat that a three-cent postage stamp could carry in America. His coffee was gone. His bread was vanishing. Meat was a memory. Of fruit there was none. About all he had left were small quantities of rice, sago, home-grown vegetables and an unending list of the famous German food substitutes. These might sustain life, but not energy.

Enemy Collapse Begins

The War Trade Board with its Allied associates was accomplishing what it set out to do. The German was becoming demoralized, dispirited. That wonderful loyalty and devotion to the German war machine was disintegrating. This epidemic spread to the army. The fighting forces here and there became affected. Wealthy Germans who had spent lifetimes building up business abroad saw it crumbling before the attacks of America's trading with the enemy lists. A great wave of depression spread over the whilom granite empire.

President Wilson's candid appeals to the German people to conduct their own government were circulating and making converts. German hearts were becoming faint. The seed of revolution fell on fertile soil. American legions were pouring overseas. The German army was slowly if doggedly retreating. The food situation was hopeless. Winter was just around the corner. The promises of victory held out by the military masters were vain. Here and there the home front began to sway and crumble and shortly with a crash collapsed in a dismal heap, leaving the army machine nothing to do but sign the armistice.

The War Trade Board with economic warfare had attained its goal.

Vance McCormick and the Municipal League, 1939

This informative pamphlet about the Municipal League, printed around 1939, shows the civic spirit of Harrisburg's leaders, who wanted to advertise their accomplishments and motivate the citizenry. The Municipal League had been a force behind Harrisburg's "City Beautiful" movement and figured prominently in McCormick's 1902 mayoral campaign. Along with his co-reformer, J. Horace McFarland, he was still active in the organization almost forty years later, as chairman of its Regional Planning Committee, which showed his continuing commitment to a progressive political agenda at the local level.

WHAT'S BEEN DONE
for Harrisburg IN ONLY ONE YEAR by
the Municipal League's
REGIONAL PLANNING COMMITTEE

Brought to the city a resident planner, Malcolm H. Dill, whose full time is given to the Committee, and who acts as a coordinator in planning activities of state, county, city and community officials, as well as private agencies, within the Harrisburg Area.

351

Engaged the services of Earle S. Draper, nationally known planning consultant, who outlined the work being done by Mr. Dill.

Studied and checked, with expert advice, and thereafter supported the program for bringing pure soft mountain water to Harrisburg.

Furnished consultant service to the six official planning commissions on both sides of the Susquehanna, looking toward unified action.

Prepared map of all properties taken over by Harrisburg in tax sales, and cooperated in planning for use and disposition of these properties.

Engineered extension of the Real Property Inventory, as a WPA project, to include communities adjoining Harrisburg on both sides of the river, as a basis for study of planning within this important metropolitan area.

Made studies for extension of Capitol Park to Forster Street between Third Street and the railroad, suggesting sites for public buildings, and working with public agencies instrumental in having provided three eminent consultants employed for study of the Extension Area—Paul P. Cret, William H. Gehron, and Thomas W. Sears.

Initiated negotiations which led to acquisition by gifts from Harrisburg Railways and County Commissioners of old Paxtang Park for recreational and by-pass purposes, and similarly to the donation of 25 acres for park purposes to the borough of West Fairview by the James McCormick heirs.

Gave assistance to Lemoyne and other West Shore communities in connection with establishing needed parks.

Prepared a plan to improve bus routes and stops in congested sections, also a map indicating present and available sites for parking lots.

After exhaustive study, drafted a map of the city and its suburbs, to accompany a report covering existing and proposed highways in the interest of facilitating traffic through and around Harrisburg by means of by-passes, radial highways, elevated highways, "short cuts" and bridges. Final recommendations for highway routes and bridge sites await a traffic count by the State Highway Department to ascertain origins and destinations of traffic. (This count was instigated by the Regional Planning Committee.)

Obtained agreement of Pennsylvania Railroad to eliminate billboards on its property near the Lemoyne Bottleneck and improve by planting this "gateway" to Harrisburg and the West Shore.

Mr. Dill, as consultant landscape architect, coöperated with Federal and local housing authorities in location and landscape planning of two housing projects.

Stimulated interest and cooperated with West Shore Planning Federation, which embraces many borough and district units.

WHAT'S YET TO BE DONE
for Harrisburg with the help of the
REGIONAL PLANNING COMMITTEE

Develop a Land Use report, and a MASTER PLAN for the orderly growth not only of Harrisburg proper but of an area many miles outside of the city, to provide a basis for a system of highways, and appropriate land-uses for recreational, industrial, commercial and residential purposes (avoiding the creation of potential slums) thus providing a chart for as many as 25 years of growth.

Continue watchful care to see that all the projects continue to develop in the public interest.

WHAT NEXT?

No city can remain stationary . . . it either improves or deteriorates.

Competition among cities, as in industry, is keen. Just as industrial products have been streamlined for both beauty and greater efficiency so does the planned, efficient, livable city have the advantage over one which is allowed to just grow, like Topsy.

Even if a city does not have a rapidly increasing population, there are always new public works needed—streets, bridges, playgrounds, parks, public buildings to be replaced. These need planning consideration.

No city can afford to spend money on poorly planned, ill-advised or unnecessary public works. Only a well-planned and coordinated program can show which improvements are really needed and which should come first.

Harrisburg is a central city, and it and its suburbs must face the future together. Physical planning must cover the whole metropolitan area, over-stepping borough, township, and county lines.

Harrisburg, like all other cities today, finds people moving to the suburbs, leaving blighted-area problems in the older parts of the city. The result is a weakened tax base and increasingly higher taxes. With such protective tools as zoning and wise planning, we can prevent or retard real estate depreciation, and can plan wisely for rehabilitation.

Planning CAN and MUST prevent new suburbs from making the same mistakes which blight the older city—narrow lots, inadequate street systems, lack of playgrounds and open spaces. We have some horrible examples!

How long would an industry last today which did not carefully plan for future activities, expansion, replacements? Which did not carefully correlate the work of its various departments?

About 75 agencies, local, state, Federal and private, in the Harrisburg Area, are concerned with planning problems and projects. Only a Regional Planning Commission can keep in touch with and interrelate all their varied activities. Otherwise, overlapping efforts and expenditures result.

Who Should Be Interested In Planning?

Banks and Insurance Companies:
Because Regional Planning protects and preserves values of real estate loans on old and new properties.

Retail Stores and Markets:
Because Regional Planning helps solve traffic and parking problems, thus preserving shopping districts. It makes the city a better place for all our citizens to live and shop in.

Oil Companies, Automobile Dealers, Transportation Companies:
Because the products of these concerns can move only when traffic moves, and Regional Planning aims to keep traffic moving in the right places and directions.

Manufacturers:
Because Regional Planning guards against excessive taxes due to depreciated land values and ill-advised expenditures for public works, and makes better living conditions for all their employees.

Dairies and Farm Land Owners:
Because Regional Planning can take steps to assure permanence of agricultural land-use near suburbs, where that use is appropriate.

EVERYBODY

Because Regional Planning is concerned with well-balanced growth, prevention of errors in laying out streets, highways, and use of land, all to the end of making the region a better place in which to reside, to do business and to enjoy life.

Regional Planning Committee
of the Municipal League of Harrisburg
OFFICERS
Vance C. McCormick, Chairman
J. Horace McFarland, Secretary

Thomas B. Schmidt, Treasurer
Malcolm H. Dill, Regional Planner

EXECUTIVE COMMITTEE

Robert Hall Craig   Sterling G. McNees
Ross A. Hickok   John E. Myers
Joseph N. Hobart   Frank A. Robbins, Jr.

WHAT'S BEEN DONE
In the Past Thirty-eight Years for Harrisburg
with the help of
THE MUNICIPAL LEAGUE

Paved streets increased from 4 miles in 1901 to 121 miles today.

Safe water supply provided, with a reduction in typhoid deaths from 422 per 100,000 to virtually zero.

Comprehensive sewer system built, removing stench from river front.

Mulberry Street viaduct constructed, joining two important sections of the city.

River Park salvaged from a public dump, to now charm residents and visitors.

Park system expanded from 45 acres in 1901 to 1,100 acres today.

A National consultant provided in connection with the school-building program, resulting in construction of two high schools, conveniently situated, with ample athletic facilities.

The Island converted into a public park and recreation center.

River dam constructed, providing low-water protection and a basin for water sports.

Unique river-front promenade created, incidental to protection of the intercepting sewer.

Grade crossings eliminated from Second and Paxton streets.

Satisfactory rate adjustments secured with utilities.

Market Street subway widened.

All these improvements have made Harrisburg not only a better place in which to live, but have given the city a high national standing for civic enterprise.

McCormick,
the Country Gentleman

Two articles here tell a side of Vance McCormick's life that does not usually receive our full attention. Besides being an urban mayor and an international diplomat, he was also a resident of the countryside and was deeply involved in all aspects of farming. If he had never been involved in politics, he might have had a reputation as an agribusinessman or champion developer of livestock.

The first article, from a popular magazine, was written soon after McCormick had successfully managed Wilson's 1916 reelection campaign. The writer treats him as a friendly baron, a man who owns thirty farms but has fellowship with his farmers.

The second article, "The McCormicks in Upper Allen Township," was a speech given by McCormick's step-grandson, Spencer G. Nauman Jr., to members of the Upper Allen Township Heritage Committee in September, 1980. His subject was the farming achievements and rural life of Col. Henry McCormick and Vance McCormick. We are grateful that Mr. Nauman has given his consent to republish the speech in this volume, so that we can give permanency to his research and his memory of the McCormicks.

On the matter of the McCormick properties outside Harrisburg, we also recommend several recent articles in the Yellow Breeches Gazette by Paul A. Miller, who, along with his father Raymond, was an employee of the McCormicks.

1. MAGAZINE ARTICLE, *COUNTRYSIDE*, JANUARY 1917

Vance C. Mccormick, Country Gentleman
The Man Who Elected Wilson and the Place He Lives In
By Charles G. Miller

Vance C. McCormick, chairman of the Democratic National Committee, who has just made possible the reelection of President Wilson, and who had a big part in the original selection of Mr. Wilson by the Baltimore convention in 1912, does not spend all his time in politics. Six months of most years he is a farmer.

During the summer months, he deserts his wisteria-covered residence, at Harrisburg, Pennsylvania, for life at Rosegarden, his country home, twelve miles away along the Yellow Breeches Creek in the fertile Cumberland Valley. This summer place is just near enough to Harrisburg to permit him to spend part of each day at his office, where, as trustee of the McCormick estate, he looks after the large realty holdings of his family.

It was at this country place and at this office that he evolved the plan of wiping out the bi-partisan machine that at election time always meant that the Democratic party in Pennsylvania became the annex of the Republican party. His fight sent a delegation to Baltimore that stood for Wilson so long that the tide was turned and he became the nominee even after Speaker Clark had a majority of the votes.

Mr. McCormick lives with his mother and his sister at Harrisburg, just a few doors from the Governor's mansion, and all three move to Rosegarden with the first signs of spring. Their summer place is ideally located in a maple grove at the side of the winding Yellow Breeches, which, dammed up at that point, flows over an artificial falls and turns a water-wheel, whose splashings are heard all day long from the broad porches of the house. This place, commodious but unpretentious, is in the center of the McCormick farms, which hold records for their crops and stocks in a state that ranks high in the agricultural world.

The house at Rosegarden has held more prominent men as guests in the last dozen years than any other in central Pennsylvania, and has played its part in the strenuous political work Mr. McCormick has done. His life there gives him the punch that he exerts so effectively during the months of political strain, and, which incidentally, he conserves by neither smoking nor drinking.

Picturesque planting of trees and shrubbery makes Rosegarden one of the most beautiful farms in Central Pennsylvania. Mr. McCormick is a trustee of the McCormick estate, which owns some thirty farms in this vicinity. The managers of these farms aim to point the way to greater success to the tenant farmers of the community, and do so through various sorts of organizations and cooperation, including a strong Farmers' Club. Mr. McCormick not only desires to raise more crops per acre on this particular farm than crop averages show to be normal, but tries to produce pure blood stock that will serve as an example. His hobby is to breed Percherons and cattle that will take blue ribbons at exhibits. In order that his efforts might prove of benefit to the farmers of the valley, twelve years ago he started the Hogestown Cattle Show at which the stock of the entire district is shown. Annually this exhibition attracts not only the people of the nearby farms but the experts from the agricultural colleges of the country.

Mr. McCormick's idea of a day off is to spend twelve hours at actual work on the farm, ending in a plunge in the dam pool at the side of the cottage.

---

2. SPEECH TO UPPER ALLEN TOWNSHIP HERITAGE COMMITTEE, SEPTEMBER 1980

The McCormicks in Upper Allen Township,
by Spencer G. Nauman, Jr., Esq.

When I was researching my subject, I asked a neighbor of mine, who had studied local history, a question. He could not give me an answer but said, "Why not make it up? They won't know the difference." Trusting that you will assume I did not take his advice, this is the story of the McCormicks in Upper Allen Township.

Just over one hundred years ago, in early 1880, Col. Henry McCormick purchased Rosegarden from the heirs of Eleanor Roseborayh (Rosebery). This was his first purchase in Upper Allen Township and the first purchase of the family there. The McCormicks owned land in Cumberland County at the time in Hamden and Silver Spring Townships, as well as East Pennsboro Township. The Gery House on Arcona Road in Upper Allen Township, mentioned in the Upper Allen Township Heritage book on early architecture in the Township, was originally on the McCormick land in East Pennsboro Township. The Home Farm east of Hogestown still is maintained by a trust for the Chicago branch of the family and was lived on by the Colonel's grandfather, William McCormick, as early as 1797, having come into the family in 1765. . . .

Rosegarden was bought as a working farm as well as a summer residence. It was always very fertile, level land, and the care the McCormicks gave it made it even more productive over the years. When first purchased by the Colonel, it contained 201 acres and 100 perches [square rods]. It was about the same size when it passed to Henry McCormick's second son, Vance, on the Colonel's death in 1900. In 1901, Vance added 14 acres by a purchase from Ella Logan. When he transferred Rosegarden to his sister, Anne, in 1925, it was recorded as having 212 acres. Rosegarden is located in the extreme southwestern corner of the township along the Yellow Breeches Creek and is actually partially in Monroe Township. . . .

The house is a farmhouse enlarged over the years to meet the needs of the family. The architecture of the additions with their Mansard roofs identifies these as from the late Victorian era. As a summer home, it remained a very comfortable farmhouse, without the addition of tennis courts and swimming pools. Still, the banks of the sluiceway on the creek behind the house were landscaped and planted with flowers. Also, bridges were built to make access to the garden and trout fishing easier.

On the property was a carriage house, barn, combination corncrib and tenant house, corncrib and vehicle shed, another machinery shed, and a tenant farmhouse in which Vance McCormick had an office before he married and moved. This is where George Weber lived with his family for 38 years.

The farming operation to me, and, indeed, Rosegarden in many respects, was George Weber. George came to Rosegarden in 1926. According to Mrs. Weber, he had been farming on the land of Anne McCormick's cousin, Mary Cameron. However, when the price of milk dropped in 1925, he decided it was not worth it and sold out his quite extensive herd. Anne McCormick came to see him on the advice of her cousin. After a lengthy interview, she hired him as the farmer at Rosegarden.

This may seem unusual in the years before women's liberation. However, the role of the two maiden ladies was not that much different from other women in Upper Allen and Cumberland County. As can be seen from the names of the persons from whom the McCormicks bought land, women acquired farms either by operation of law as widows of a farm owner, by inheritance as a daughter or other relative, or by purchase. Besides doing the chores, women actually worked the farms. Some women even did the tedious and back-breaking job of plowing behind a team. Many women had charge of the cattle. Most women helped at harvest time. I remember Mrs. Weber and her daughter driving the tractors pulling the wagon and bailer at Rosegarden when George was pressing to get the hay in.

My father would consult George on a regular basis and take me along. He farmed Rosegarden for 40 years altogether. He worked for two years for General Gross after the death of Anne McCormick in 1964.

The barn was the center of the farm operation. It is one of the largest of the bank barns in the township and was extremely well suited to its use at the time. Presently the practice is not to confine large animals as much during the winter, and so open shelters are more common now on working farms.

On the right as you face the barn were the cow stalls. Rosegarden usually had a herd of 10 or 12 cows, which is much smaller than is standard today but was common in earlier times. They were Guernseys, and for years led the Country Dairy Herd Improvement Association in testing for a combination of butterfat and milk production. This preeminence began to be lost with the coming of the Canadian Holsteins in the late 1940s. However, this herd remained one of the best Guernsey herds until they were dispersed after the death of Anne McCormick.

In the middle of the barn was the steer pen. There were always about 20 or 30 steers, usually Herefords, being fattened over the winter at Rosegarden. In my memory, George Weber would usually select them at the Lancaster Stockyard and send them there for sale when they reached 1500 pounds—somewhat larger than steers are now sold. The McCormicks always maintained that the manure generated by the steers would benefit the farm whether or not money was actually made from selling them. However, George Weber was always very shrewd. In the years he was there, over a ten-year average, the steers made money.

At the left end of the barn as you face it were the horse stalls. Here, in the years before the First World War, were kept the prize Percherons, usually 10 or 12. Vance McCormick would go to France to purchase purebred stallions which he would make available to his neighbors for breeding purposes. There were usually two stallions—one for older mares and one for younger ones. I am told that stud fees were $10, or $30 for a guaranteed foal.

Besides pulling the machinery, the Percherons were shown at such expositions as the annual Hogestown Horse and Cattle Show. This annual gathering was held for two days the first full week in June from 1905 to 1922, at the Big Head Farm in Silver Spring Township, which was also a McCormick farm.

When George Weber came to Rosegarden, there were only four farm horses. He preferred mules for their agility and comparatively faster walking speed. After some objection from Anne McCormick but with the intercession of Vance McCormick, he sold the horses and purchased several teams of mules. These were augmented by tractors in the late 1930s, and finally, after being relegated to mowing, disappeared from the farm operation.

Vance McCormick also used to purchase Guernsey bulls, sometimes before they were born, to be bred to the Rosegarden herd, his herd at Cedar Cliff, and my father's herd at Chilton. These were kept across Route 15 at the Mill Property. Only the houses and mill remain. . . .

Two years after purchasing Rosegarden, in 1882, Col. Henry McCormick purchased the Allen Grange Farm from Jacob Grissinger. This farm, along McCormick Road and on the southern edge of the Township, contained 152 acres and 89 perches, of which 102 were in Upper Allen Township. The rest was a woods lot across the Yellow Breeches Creek in Monaghan Township, York County. This farm, like all the McCormick farms except Rosegarden, was farmed on the shares by tenant farmers.

The McCormick share arrangement was basically 50-50. Thus, the farmer shared in half the proceeds from the sale of crops and cattle, paid half the taxes and for half the seed. The landlord kept the buildings in repair and the tenant furnished the machinery and horses. The McCormicks wished to encourage the fattening of cattle, so they would advance the price of the cattle to be purchased. They preferred to have corn and hay used for feed, and so the farmer could be limited in his cash sales to wheat. To stimulate the raising of potatoes, a cash crop, the McCormicks took only one-third of the proceeds from their crop in later years.

The McCormicks and their cousins, the Camerons, held extensive farm holdings in Cumberland, Dauphin, Lancaster, and Perry counties. In 1880, the farmers farming their land joined together to form the McCormick-Cameron Farmers Club, which lasted until 1930. There were at one time over thirty farmers involved. Their wives formed a wives' club in 1892. The organization met usually as a group of 20 or 30 people to discuss various farm subjects as the farmhouses of the tenants. The landlord contributed $10 toward dinner. Sometimes, including guests, there were 150 people in attendance at the larger picnic gatherings. At many meetings there were visitors from the Agricultural School at Penn State. County agents were always invited. At one meeting, at least in 1930, the State Secretary of Agriculture attended. . . .

In February 1902, Henry B. McCormick, known as Harry, the eldest son of Col. Henry McCormick, made his first purchase in Upper Allen Township. This was the two acres on which the McCormick Mill is located. This property was purchased from William Lantz. . . . This land had on it the mill and the miller's house. Later, the chauffeur's house was added with the garage for the cars.

The mill tract was purchased with a larger tract of 111 acres across the white bridge in Monaghan Township, York County. On this property, Harry McCormick built "Cona" [named for the McCormick family vacation home in Nova Scotia]. His ideas for a summer home differed from those of his father. Instead of having his house next to the barn on a farm, he set it off in the woods and built it on a somewhat more expansive scale. To the property he added certain special use buildings and areas not seen at Rosegarden. These included a boathouse and camp meeting ground. Further, he designed a driveway which was not merely utilitarian but somewhat consciously part of the landscape. . . .

In 1905, Mary Boyd McCormick, the wife of Harry McCormick, began buying land in Upper Allen Township. Her first purchase was the property known to the McCormicks as the Fruit Farm. It contained two plots totaling 9 acres and is located on McCormick Road along the Yellow Breeches Creek, west of the Cona Farm. . . .

At one point, the McCormicks owned 582 acres in Upper Allen Township. Harry McCormick died in 1941 and Vance McCormick died in 1946. Anne McCormick died in 1964. None of them left children. Mrs. Harry McCormick is still living but does not reside in the township. All the buildings have been sold now. However, their memory lives on. In talking to Mrs. George Weber, Mrs. Miller Hobaugh, Karl Achenbach, and Mark Bashore, you would think they had been at Rosegarden or at Cona only yesterday. Besides the handsome physical remembrances which they have left, to be remembered as vividly as these people are is to know that it was all worthwhile. . . .

Obituaries of Vance Criswell McCormick, 1946

The most complete account of Vance McCormick's accomplishments is found in his obituaries, written in June 1946. Such records are typically laudatory writings that do not draw attention to the controversies of the person's career, but historians are grateful for the authoritative information they do provide.

McCormick's obituaries also show the respect he commanded nationwide. Comments from other publishers were consistent in praising both his political teamwork and his independence. They agreed on his high-mindedness and his enormous civic spirit. He was both a fighter and a constructive critic. "He had a hand in shaping the destiny of the world," said one editor. "Such men are always too young to die," said another. Most mentioned that he had been Yale's quarterback.

---

1. HARRISBURG *PATRIOT,* JUNE 17, 1946

VANCE C. MCCORMICK DIES; NEWSPAPER PUBLISHER AND FORMER HARRISBURG MAYOR.

One of President Wilson's Advisers at Peace Parley
Served as Chairman of War Trade Board in First World War

Vance C. McCormick, publisher of *The Patriot* and *The Evening News,* died yesterday at his country home, Cedar Cliff Farms, near New Cumberland.

A former Mayor of Harrisburg, once chairman of the Democratic National Committee, and one of President Wilson's advisers at the Versailles peace conference, Mr. McCormick would have been 74 years old next Wednesday.

Death followed a brief illness, which confined him to his home since Thursday. His condition became serious early Saturday.

He is survived by his wife, Mrs. Gertrude Howard McCormick, and a sister, Miss Anne McCormick. Funeral announcement will be made later.

His public career, to which he devoted the greater part of his life, was begun at the age of 28, when he was elected to Harrisburg's city council. Two years later he was elected Mayor, at the age of 30.

In 1912, as delegate-at-large to the Democratic National Convention at Baltimore, he supported Woodrow Wilson for nomination for the Presidency. From then on until Mr. Wilson's death, their personal and public relationship was close.

He was Mr. Wilson's choice for chairman of the Democratic National Committee in the successful campaign for his re-election to the Presidency. During the First World War, Mr. McCormick served as chairman of the War Trade Board, and the President took him to the Versailles conference as one of his advisers on economic phases of the peace treaty.

Following the war, Mr. McCormick returned to Harrisburg where his interests have since been centered on civic improvements and public welfare.

Vance Criswell McCormick was born in Silver Spring Township, a son of Col. Henry McCormick. Vance McCormick's mother was Annie Criswell, daughter of John Vance Criswell and Hannah Dull and he was one of six children. Isabel and Hugh died in infancy; Mary died at 9; Henry B. died in 1939 and Miss Anne survives.

His School Career

As a youth, Mr. McCormick attended Harrisburg Academy where his football and baseball career began. At Phillips Andover Academy he captained both the football and baseball teams. When he entered Yale in the Sheffield school he was made captain of the Freshmen football and baseball teams. In Mr. McCormick's second year at Yale, 1891, he qualified for fullback on the varsity team. It was the season that Yale won all its games without being scored on. In Mr. McCormick's senior year, 1892, he was captain and quarterback of the Yale team which was the only Eastern college eleven with a perfect record of all victories and no defeats. Yale had rolled up 435 points on 13 opponents who got zero, including Penn, Harvard and Princeton teams played on successive Saturdays. Walter Camp included Captain McCormick on his all-American football team that year.

In College YMCA

In addition to his football and baseball activities at Yale, he served as Deacon of his class. He was a vice-president of the college YMCA.

He was at Yale when he registered [for the] first time as a Democrat and he was chosen vice-president of the Cleveland-Stevenson Club of the University. For some years after his graduation, he was advisory coach at Yale and he attended most of Yale's football games until recent years. Through a long time he was on the Board of Control of the University Athletic Association and though he declined many offers to coach college and prep school football teams, he did coach the famous Carlisle Indian school eleven for a time.

His interest in politics began expanding on leaving Yale, when he was associated with his father in the management of iron and other business interests. He was elected to represent the Fourth Ward in Common Council in 1900 when he was 28 years old.

In 1902 he ran for mayor and though a Democrat in a normally Republican city, he won by a majority of 2566.

He Buys The Patriot

Purchase of *The Patriot*, August 1, 1902, gave him another medium to keep the tax payers informed on municipal matters. He turned on the spotlight in the interest of a better city and whenever it seemed likely to benefit the taxpayer, especially the small home owner.

On leaving the Mayor's office at the end of his term, Mr. McCormick maintained his interest in civic and municipal affairs, at the same time remaining active, independently, in the Democratic party.

In 1912 he was elected as delegate-at-large to the Democratic National Convention at Baltimore and with his delegation participated in 46 ballots until Woodrow Wilson was chosen as the party's standard bearer for President.

Wilson's election brought Mr. McCormick several offers to take an ambassadorship but each he declined, preferring to remain in Harrisburg. In 1914, his party drafted him to run for Governor and nation-wide attention was attracted by the fall campaign in which the late Theodore Roosevelt made speeches on behalf of the Democratic nominee and his running mate. He lost this election to Martin G. Brumbaugh.

Made National Chairman

In 1916, President Wilson named Mr. McCormick Democratic National chairman, with the responsibilities of conducting the presidential campaign.

Germany's submarine attacks and the declaration of World War I followed soon after President Wilson was inaugurated for his second term. Mr. McCormick offered his services and promptly was made a member of the American War Mission to the Inter-Allied Conferences in London and Paris. He also was made chairman of the Export Administrative Board, subsequently changed to the War Trade Board, to control exports to allies and neutral countries.

This Board, with a staff of 3000 and handling 40 to 50 million dollars in merchandise daily was concerned with imposing a blockade on the enemy. Marshal Foch was quoted after the war as having said "the blockade to which the War Trade Board had contributed so much, had hastened the day of the Armistice."

Mr. McCormick gave up his post with the quick liquidation of the War Trade Board and in 1919 he went to the Versailles Peace Conference. Meanwhile he had resigned as Democratic National chairman. His next national activity was as a member of the League to Enforce Peace in which, with others, vain efforts were made to have the Senate ratify the Versailles Peace Treaty.

The publisher was a delegate to the Democratic National Convention in San Francisco in 1920 and again four years later, in Madison Square Garden, New York.

On State College Board

His interest in farming brought the publisher recognition in 1908 from the agricultural group of the State who were empowered to elect a representative to the Board of Trustees of Pennsylvania State College and they elected him to the College Board. Latterly he served as vice-president of the Board.

His interest in education as a patron covered a broad field. He was for many years president of the Trustees' Board of the old Harrisburg Academy and he also had served one term as president of the Andover Academy Alumni. His alma mater, Yale, conferred upon him the degree of Master of Arts in 1907 and then in June, 1913, he succeeded former President William Howard Taft as a member of the Yale Corporation and served continuously until his retirement on age in 1936.

The publisher's interest in the Harrisburg Hospital goes back many years. His father was one of its founders and his brother, the late Henry B. McCormick, was its president a number of years. Equally so, he strongly supported the Associated Aid Societies, sometimes called the forerunner of the Community Chest and its predecessor, the Welfare Federation.

His Church Activities

He was a member of Pine Street Presbyterian Church and for many years served as president of its board of trustees. When the family was at the country home, it was their custom to attend services in Silver Spring Church, near Mechanicsburg, and when it was decided, a decade or so ago, to restore that old church to as nearly possible its colonial day appearance, he financed the undertaking.

Mr. McCormick had served through many years as a director of the State YMCA and in the First World War was a member of the War Work Council of the International Committee of the "Y". He was a member of the Yale Foreign Missionary Society and on the university's Council on Religious Life.

During the Second World War he served as a regional director of the United War Fund Campaign.

His experience with *The Patriot* instilled a desire to issue an evening newspaper also. Accordingly, *The Evening News* began publication February 15, 1925.

His Organizations

In addition to other organizations, Mr. McCormick was a member of the University, Yale and St. Anthony Clubs of New York; Graduates Club, New Haven; Philadelphia Club, Philadelphia; Metropolitan and National Press Clubs, Washington; the Oakland Club, St. Stephens, South Carolina; University Club, State College; Country Club of Harrisburg; Yeomen's Hall, Charleston, S.C., and Farmington Club, Charlottesville, Va.

He was a member also of the Engineers Society of Pennsylvania; Harrisburg Chamber of Commerce; American Civic Association; Harrisburg Story Tellers League; Central YMCA; the Wednesday Club; Sons of the American Revolution; Advisory Committee of the Woodrow Wilson Birthday Memorial and the Woodrow Wilson Foundation; China Society of America; American Geographic Society of America; Sons of Veterans and the Society of Colonial Wars in Pennsylvania.

Others include: American Academy of Political and Social Science; National Economic League; American Society of the French Legion of Honor, Inc.; Council of Foreign Relations; Pennsylvania Parks Association; National Parks Association; Historical Society of Pennsylvania, and of Dauphin County; Harrisburg Civic Club; National Institute of Social Sciences; League of Nations Association and the Golf Club of Northeast Harbor, Maine. He was identified with the American Institute of Mining and Metallurgical Engineers, Yale Engineering Association, Harrisburg Natural History Society, Pennsylvania Scotch Irish Society, Connecticut Academy of Arts and Sciences and the Northeast Harbor Fleet Maine.

Honored Abroad

He held the decoration of the Commander Legion d'honneur of France and was made a Grand Officer de l'Order de la Couronne of Belgium in 1919 for his services in World War I. In 1920 Italy gave him decorations of a Grand Officer of the Royal Order of the Crown. Back in 1916 he was elected a director of the Federal Reserve Bank, Philadelphia but resigned in that same year when he became Democratic National Chairman. In 1921 he was a member of the Advisory Board Citizens Military Training Camps for Pennsylvania and he was a member of the Greater Pennsylvania Council in the 1931–32 term. Through that same period he was treasurer of the Fifth Realization corporation and appointed its Private Banker for handling problems of closed banks. He was made chairman of the Dauphin County Emergency Relief Board in 1933 and two years later became chairman of the Disaster Relief Committee of the Red Cross in Harrisburg.

Aside from the management of his father's and grandfather's estates, Mr. McCormick had other business interests. He was president of *The Patriot* and *The Evening News;* he was a director of the Dauphin Deposit Trust Company and was chairman of the Board of the Central Iron and Steel Company until the recent purchase of his interests in the company by Barium Steel. He was a director of the Wilmore Sonman Coal Company, the Harrisburg Bridge Company, Elk-River Coal & Lumber Company and Buffalo Creel and Gauley Railroad Company.

2. HARRISBURG *PATRIOT,* JUNE 18, 1946

MESSAGES TELL GRIEF
AT DEATH OF PUBLISHER
Mr. McCormick's Colleagues in Public Affairs Wire Sympathy
FUNERAL WEDNESDAY AT PINE ST. CHURCH
City Hall Flag at Half Staff in Tribute to Former Mayor

Funeral arrangements for Vance C. McCormick, publisher of *The Patriot* and *The Evening News,* who died Sunday afternoon after a brief illness, were completed yesterday as tributes were expressed by his former associates and friends.

Funeral services will be held at 2 o'clock tomorrow afternoon in the Pine Street Presbyterian Church. The Rev. C. Ralston Smith, pastor of the church, will officiate, assisted by the Rev. Edward J. Ardis, pastor of the Silver Spring Presbyterian Church. Burial will be in the Harrisburg Cemetery.

Edith Bolling Wilson, widow of President Wilson under whom Mr. McCormick served as chairman of the War Trade Board during the first World War and later accompanied to Europe as economic advisor during peace negotiations, expressed "a deep sense of personal loss of a dear and loyal friend."

From Former Associates

Bernard M. Baruch, Presidential advisor and statesman, who also was a member of the Wilson peace delegation to Europe, said "I am deeply grieved," and termed Mr. McCormick a "patriotic defender of our America," and an "outstanding citizen."

Josephus Daniels, publisher of the *News and Observer* at Raleigh, N.C., and a member of Wilson's Cabinet as Secretary of the Navy, said: "We were comrades through the years from 1912. President Wilson loved him and leaned on him."

Gov. Edward Martin termed Mr. McCormick as "one of the very outstanding men in Pennsylvania. He was a man whose friendship I enjoyed over a good many years. His services in this period of national emergency will be greatly missed," the State's Chief Executive said.

Tribute to Former Mayor

Mayor Howard E. Milliken announced that the City Hall flag was ordered at half-staff yesterday and that his office would be closed during the hour of the funeral of the former Mayor. "Harrisburg has lost a good and upright citizen in the passing of Mr. Vance McCormick," Mayor Milliken said.

Among other tributes received yesterday were:

Elisha Hanson, chief counsel of the American Newspaper Publishers' Association, Washington: "I am terribly shocked to hear of Mr. McCormick's death. Our Country has lost one of its finest, most courageous men. His contributions to our way of life have not been exceeded by those of any other."

From Penn State College

Dr. Ralph D. Hetzel, president of Pennsylvania State College: "In the death of Mr. Vance C. McCormick the Pennsylvania State College has suffered a great loss. Mr. McCormick was a member of its board of trustees for 38 years. . . . Mr. McCormick was a wise counsellor and gave most generously of his time and genius. He was a business man of broad experience. At no time did he ever permit any private interest to qualify his loyalty or duty as a trustee."

Ramsey S. Black, Pennsylvania State Treasurer: "As Mayor of Harrisburg, Mr. McCormick was the spearhead of the civic improvement program which changed Harrisburg from an old muddy town to a well-ordered city."

William N. Hardy, manager of the Pennsylvania Newspaper Publishers' Association: "He contributed a great deal to journalism by printing a nonsensational newspaper which met the needs of his community. He was a citizen of the world and a leading citizen of Pennsylvania."

Cranston Williams, manager of the American Newspaper Publishers' Association, New York, expressed "deepest sympathy to the family and associates of Mr. Vance C. McCormick."

Message From Cruisers

E. W. Schleisner, president of the Harrisburg Chamber of Commerce, on cruise with the Chamber members at Quebec, said: "Cruisers shocked at news of sudden passing of Vance McCormick, lifelong leader in civic and philanthropic endeavors."

Mr. McCormick led a "noble life," said Dr. and Mrs. Henry Sloane Coffin, of Ladeville, Conn. Doctor Coffin, a clergyman and author, is president of the Union Theological Seminary, and is a former moderator of the Presbyterian General Assembly.

Dr. J. Horace McFarland, [of] Harrisburg, said: "I am keenly conscious that right up to the very last week, Vance C. McCormick was carrying on for Harrisburg. He was not only serving Harrisburg, but he was serving

Pennsylvania with the same vigor, ability and spirit manifested in Washington when he was head of the War Trade Board." Doctor McFarland termed Mr. McCormick a "man who made his citizenship in Harrisburg count, regardless of political difficulties and deterrents all through his life."

From Fellow Publisher

Fellow publishers also joined in the tribute to Mr. McCormick.

Frank Gannett, head of the Gannett Newspapers, Rochester, N.Y., said: "I feel a deep personal loss in the passing of Vance C. McCormick. He was a great American and played an important role in the re-election of Woodrow Wilson as President. He was outstanding in the field of journalism. He was courageous and always fought for his honest convictions and high ideals."

J. L. Stackhouse, business manager of the *Easton Express,* said, "your community, the Nation and the newspaper industry will miss this great character of fine principles for which he was willing to risk all in upholding."

Edward H. Butler, editor and publisher of the *Buffalo Evening News,* termed Mr. McCormick "an outstanding figure Nationally, and an exemplar of the finest traditions of journalism. A staunch supporter of the finer things in civic and National life, he will be greatly missed by the citizens of Harrisburg and by his colleagues."

From Dauphin Co. Court

Speaking for the Dauphin County Court, President Judge William M. Hargest, said: "In the passing of Mr. McCormick, this community has lost one of its foremost citizens, one who from his young manhood was devoted to the best interests of the city, and was actively engaged in promoting its welfare. His activities comprehended artistic endeavors, civic improvement, planning, zoning, government and religious influence. To accomplish these objectives he gave unselfishly of his time and talent. His efforts in these fields brought him distinction and reflected credit upon the community."

---

3. EDITORIAL, HARRISBURG *PATRIOT,* JUNE 18, 1946

The difficulties facing one attempting to write a tribute to the life and character of Vance C. McCormick in these columns which he guided and inspired for more than 40 years need not be emphasized to be apparent.

It would be far easier, and more in sympathy with his desires, to devote this space to a furtherance of policies which he sponsored and ideals which he upheld, or to attack practices which he condemned.

Readers doubtless will prefer to remember him through the ideals as expressed in these columns, for they do proclaim the man. There is a personal background to ideals, however, which may add something to the understanding of them.

In the first place there was the will, the determination, the persistency which characterized his efforts in behalf of whatever he sensed was of benefit to the community, State or Nation. He had that something which athletes call a "follow through," which carries a punch to a successful conclusion.

He had the courage to hold on for a principle he knew was right. He had the tenacity to refuse to concede defeat while there was hope to winning, as in the campaign which he directed in 1916 which retained Woodrow Wilson in the White House.

His energy was boundless, and also contagious. Those who worked with him could justly wonder how he did it, and at the same time take satisfaction in the hope that they could follow him. At the age when many men retire, he was his busiest. Only a week ago he was deeply considering a plan which appealed to him as promising community benefit, although he knew the plan could not possibly be consummated for another 20 years.

He had that vision that sees beyond time's horizons, and the knack of imparting it to others. It gave him supreme delight in recent years when young men and women took hold of public affairs with zealous interest. He was continually seeking recruits for the campaigns which he helped inaugurate and which he hoped to see continued.

He was also consistent. Where principle was concerned, he knew no such word as expediency. Nor would he take refuge in silence or inaction, if he had the slightest suspicion that silence would be interpreted as approval.

He was patient with everything except breach of trust, evasion of effort or dereliction of duty. He was considerate of those who tried, even if they failed. He was loyal to his newspaper staff even when we blundered.

It is needless to note in these columns that his home community was his primary interest. It was to Harrisburg that he invariably returned after successes elsewhere which would have tempted many to seek wider fields of endeavor. He came home after a collegiate career which brought him athletic laurels and chose public service in his own city. He returned again 20 years later after an interlude of National honors earned through opportunities of service under President Wilson, whom he revered and for whose ideals he fought.

Harrisburg was home to him, and his love for his home city was an impelling force behind his planning for its present and future welfare. His activities, his interests and his efforts were too numerous and varied to be enumerated here. He had many irons in the fire and he kept them all in use.

A dated tablet on his desk, on which he kept a list of meetings and conferences to which he gave time and attention would read like a directory of agencies and organizations devoted to school, church, welfare and kindred service.

He was continually planning, planning, planning. He conscientiously sought the best advisors he could find to search out facts to give his plans a sound basis. As soon as he was convinced of their soundness, their practicability, their promise of beneficial results, he would go the limit to promote them.

Much of this attempt to review his efforts on behalf of his community could be done better by others of his colleagues in the varied enterprises which claimed his interest. It has been better expressed by many who have sent messages of sympathetic recognition of this newspaper's loss.

If these lines stumble, if these words appear inadequate, readers will understand. But if they will bear with some of his recruits, perhaps the spark that inspires, the advice that guides, and the patience that encourages will continue to leave his mark on his newspapers and his community.

---

4. HARRISBURG *PATRIOT,* JUNE 19, 1946

PIONEER POLICE ADD TRIBUTES
Council Also passes Resolution on Death
of Former Mayor McCormick

Harrisburg City Council yesterday adopted a resolution in tribute to the memory of Vance C. McCormick, and City Hall flags were at half-staff as expressions of sympathy from associates in public affairs continued to arrive.

Funeral services will be held in Pine Street Presbyterian Church at 2 o'clock this afternoon. The Rev. C. Ralston Smith, pastor, assisted by the

Rev. Edward J. Ardis pastor of Silver Spring Presbyterian Church, will officiate.

From Former Policemen

Yesterday's messages included [an] expression of sympathy from the Pioneers of 1902, an organization of men who were members of the City Police force when Mr. McCormick was Harrisburg's Mayor, and who have joined him in annual reunions.

C. O. Backenstoss, secretary of the Pioneers of 1902, said: "In the death of Mr. McCormick the Nation has lost a most useful, active and honored citizen, and Harrisburg, a great benefactor. However, to each and every member of our organization, his death means a personal loss when we recall our 44 years of intimate acquaintance with him. His memory, I am sure, will linger with us to the last surviving member."

Council Resolutions

In adopting a resolution in Mr. McCormick's memory, City Council referred to his long membership in the Pine Street Presbyterian Church, his interest in civic matters, and said "the community has lost a good and upright citizen."

The resolution further stated "that in honor of the memory of Vance C. McCormick, all City offices be closed on Wednesday, June 19, 1946, from 12 o'clock noon."

Offices of the Community Chest will close at noon in respect to Mr. McCormick, who was its treasurer and those closely associated with the Chest organization will meet at Second and South streets at 1:30 P.M. to go to the funeral.

In a letter to this newspaper, Andrew S. Taylor, Stamford, Conn., said, "I knew Vance C. McCormick, both in Phillips Andover, and in Yale. In both seats of learning he was outstanding for strong character which was beautifully enriched by a wonderfully fine disposition. There never was any doubt about the courage of Vance McCormick. If certain facts pointed to a certain conclusion, he was not the man to try temporary political expediency, but he acted on a categorical imperative. To know Vance McCormick was to love him for his many fine qualities of both mind and heart."

From President of Yale

Dr. Charles Seymour, president of Yale, Mr. McCormick's alma mater, said, "All Yale joins me in sending our expression of profound sympathy. We were always mindful of the devoted service Vance gave. His death creates a gap in our alumni ranks that no one else can fill." Mr. McCormick was a member of the Yale Corporation from 1913 until he reached the retirement age in 1936.

David Lawrence, Washington newspaper columnist, in a message of sympathy, referred to Mr. McCormick as "a wonderful person and a great servant of the public welfare."

George C. Biggers, general manager of the *Atlanta Journal*, Atlanta, Ga., said, "the newspaper business loses a great publisher" in the passing of Mr. McCormick.

D. A. Elias, vice-president of the Harrisburg division of the Pennsylvania Power & Light Company, said the loss of Mr. McCormick is "felt by the citizens and enterprises of the community, all of which have benefitted from the results of his long life of untiring activity devoted to the interest of his fellow men."

From News Services

Officials of news-gathering organizations joined in the tribute to the publisher. Hugh Baillie, president of the United Press, said: "We were deeply grieved to learn of the passing of Vance McCormick. Both as a great public figure and as the publisher of a great newspaper, he will be sorely missed."

Basil A. Caparell, of the International News Service, in extending sympathies, said: "In my book, Vance McCormick stood for everything that was fine in journalism. . . . The newspaper fraternity as a whole will feel his loss."

---

5. HARRISBURG *PATRIOT,* JUNE 20, 1946

SERVICES HELD AT PINE ST
FOR MR. McCORMICK
Many From Out of City Join In Mark of Respect to Former Mayor
PASTOR REFERS TO LIFE AS CHURCHMAN
Associates in Welfare and Other Activities Among Those Attending

Funeral services for Vance C. McCormick were held yesterday afternoon in Pine Street Presbyterian Church, in charge of his pastor, the Rev. C. Ralston Smith, assisted by the Rev. C. Edward J. Ardis, pastor of Silver Spring Presbyterian Church. Many friends, relatives and associates from out of the city joined those from Harrisburg in the mark of respect to the newspaper publisher and former mayor of the city.

The services were deeply spiritual. The Rev. Mr. Ardis read several passages from the Scriptures. The Pine Street choir led the congregation in a hymn, "Dear Lord and Father of Mankind," the poem of John Greenleaf Whittier. The pastor introduced the hymn with the explanation that "Mr. McCormick liked to sing."

In a brief tribute, the Rev. Mr. Smith referred to Mr. McCormick's life as a Christian and churchman from the time in early manhood when he became affiliated with Pine Street. On vital issues, the pastor said, there was never any doubt on which side Mr. McCormick would be found.

Prayer for Leaders

Following an eloquent prayer that God would provide leaders to take Mr. McCormick's place in the church and the community, the Rev. Mr. Smith announced as the final hymn "Rock of Ages," which choir and congregation sang. The services closed with the benediction. Burial services in Harrisburg Cemetery were attended by the family only.

Prior to the services at the church, Frank A. McCarrell, Pine Street organist, played excerpts from familiar hymns. Beautiful floral tributes were placed throughout the sanctuary.

Mr. McCormick's associates in many endeavors occupied pews reserved for them. They included officers and official boards of Pine Street Church; members of the staffs of the Community Chest, Associated Aid, Girl Scouts and other Welfare organizations; employees of his two newspapers, *The Patriot* and *The Evening News;* of the Dauphin Deposit Trust Company, of which he was a director; of Central Iron and Steel Company; members of the Harrisburg Regional Planning Committee and representatives of the Harrisburg Bridge Company.

Among those from out of the city who came here for the services are: Mrs. James D. Cameron Bradley, with her son and daughter-in-law, Mr. and Mrs. James D. Cameron Bradley, Jr., of Southboro, Mass.; Mrs. Chandler Hale and her daughter, Mrs. Howland Chase, both of Washington; Mr. Preston Bliss and Mr. Robert Bliss of Wilmington, Del., sons of the late Laurence Bliss, who was captain of a Yale football team on which Mr. McCormick played; Gen. and Mrs. Frank R. McCoy, of Washington; Miss Margaretta McCoy and Miss Hannah McCoy, of Lewistown; Judge and Mrs. W. W. Uttley, of Lewistown; Dr. Ralph D. Hetzel, president of Pennsylvania State College.

Also Miss Jeannie Howard, sister of Mrs. McCormick, and her cousin, Mrs. J. R. A. Hobson, of Richmond; Mr. and Mrs. Robert Broughton, of

Bryn Mawr; Mr. and Mrs. Henry Cushing Olmsted and son Richard, and Mrs. Olmsted Houghton, of New York City; Mr. and Mrs. Conway Howard Olmsted, of Lake Forrest, Ill.; Mr. and Mrs James Logan Starr, of Germantown; Mrs Charles S. Wurts, Sr., and Mr. Charles Stewart Wurts, Jr., and Mr. John Wurts, of Philadelphia; Mrs. Edward B. Meigs, of Washington.

Also Jackson Herr Boyd, of Hot Springs, Va.; Mr. and Mrs. Frederick H. Brooke, of Washington; Mr. Nicholas Roosevelt, of Philadelphia; Mr. Leander McCormick-Goodhart, of Washington; Miss Mary Linn, of Bellefonte; Mrs. William Rutherford, of Bethlehem; Mr. and Mrs. William B. Wright, of Baltimore; Miss Gertrude Ely, of Bryn Mawr.

Representing the Pennsylvania Newspaper Publishers Association were: Col. J. Hale Steinman, Lancaster Newspapers, Inc.; J. L. Stackhouse, *Easton Express*; Allan D. Thompson, *Carlisle Sentinel*; Dr. F. J. Schropp, *Lebanon News-Times*; and William N. Hardy, PNPA manager. Among others who attended the services were Frank W. Miller and James E. Mullin, of Kelly Smith Company, New York, National newspaper representatives.

More Expressions of Sympathy Are Received

Tributes to the late Vance C. McCormick continued to be received yesterday.

Among these, Kent Cooper, general manager of the Associated Press, wrote: "I feel a deep personal loss in the passing of Mr. McCormick. He was a mighty fortress. Wherever there was a need for community service, there was this great editor and true citizen. He leaves many monuments in his fine newspaper, his city that is better for his having lived, and his incalculable contributions to the State and Nation."

"The passing of Vance McCormick is a sad blow to American Journalism," said Col. Henry M. Shoemaker, publisher of the *Altoona Tribune*. "In him the ethics of the profession reached their highest point of development. In a part-time sojourn in Harrisburg of over 25 years, I have seen his newspapers promptly assume the policies which stood for betterment of world, State and Nation. The McCormick newspapers have never missed leadership in all that is forward thinking and sound Americanism. I had seen Mr. McCormick only a few days before his illness and, as usual, found him alert to all the needs of the post-war world, keen, incisive, but always friendly, genial and human. His is a great loss to the newspaper fraternity, not only as a great publisher, but as a man and friend. The *Altoona Tribune* sympathizes for your great loss more than words can express."

6. HARRISBURG *PATRIOT,* JUNE 24, 1946

EDITORIAL TRIBUTES TO
VANCE C. McCORMICK

Editorial tributes to Vance C. McCormick, publisher of *The Patriot* and *The Evening News,* which have appeared since his death on June 16, include the following:

From Valley Daily News, Tarentum, Pa.

Pennsylvania lost one of its finest and most valuable citizens when Vance C. McCormick died in his Harrisburg home the other day. His services to his community, state and nation encompassed a wide range of activities. Once national chairman of the Democratic party, he was a close friend and adviser of the late President Woodrow Wilson and held several important federal offices during the period of the first World War.

In recent years Mr. McCormick devoted most of his time and effort to his two newspaper properties, the Harrisburg *Patriot* and the Harrisburg *News.* Their editorial policy has ever been a reflection of his own sturdy character and high idealism. His papers are clean and vigorous and possess great influence. They have fought hard for good government and for civic morality not alone in the state capital, but in the state and nation as well. They have always vigorously attacked every form of error and wrong.

Mr. McCormick broke with the New Deal on the third term issue and no newspapers were louder in their denunciation of some Rooseveltian policies than the *Patriot* and *News.*

Mr. McCormick always placed the common welfare above selfish interest. He possessed a high degree of independence and he always welcomed a hard fight in a good cause, even though he knew that failure was almost inevitable.

Perhaps the highest tribute that can be paid to Mr. McCormick is to say that America needs more citizens of his kind.

From Youngstown, Ohio, Vindicator

In the death of Vance C. McCormick, publisher of the Harrisburg *Patriot* and the Harrisburg *Evening News,* Pennsylvania loses one of its most high-minded men. Mr. McCormick was not trained for newspaper publishing. The son of a wealthy iron manufacturer, he attended Yale University, and soon after returning to his home in Harrisburg entered politics in an effort to clean up bad state and local conditions. He bought the *Patriot* to make sure that the people understood his program of reform.

He was mayor of his city from 1902 to 1905. He backed Woodrow Wilson for President, as the aims and ideals of the two men were much the same, and in 1917 was Wilson's personal choice for chairman of the Democratic National Committee.

Mr. McCormick was in close touch with the government's activities during the First World War. He headed the War Trade Board and went to Europe in 1917 as a member of the American War Commission. He accompanied President Wilson to the Peace Conference, where he was chairman of several commissions and a member of the Supreme Economic Council.

Mr. McCormick's own independence of character appeared in 1918 when he urged Wilson not to make his appeal for a Democratic Congress. Although he supported Franklin D. Roosevelt in 1932 and '36, he declined to do so later holding that no President should serve more than two terms. Like Browning's hero, he was "always a fighter," and throughout his long career he used his wealth and power for the good of his city, state and country. He was a most human sort of man, a lover of nature and country life, and a delightful friend and companion.

From Pittsburgh Post-Gazette

Pennsylvania has lost one of its most distinguished citizens in the death of Vance C. McCormick. Thirty years ago he was one of the best known figures on the national political scene. A great friend and admirer of Woodrow Wilson, he played an influential role in the campaigns of 1912 and 1916. In the latter year, he served as national chairman of the Democratic party and ranked among President Wilson's closest advisers. He was given varied and important assignments during World War I and following the armistice served as an economic adviser at the Peace Conference and as a member of the Supreme Economic and Reparations Councils.

Early in his career, Mr. McCormick served as Mayor of his home city of Harrisburg, and in 1914 he ran for Governor of Pennsylvania. He carried most of the counties but the G.O.P. machines of Philadelphia and Allegheny counties were well-oiled and running smoothly in that day and he was defeated in a close race.

In recent years Mr. McCormick confined himself largely to the direction of his newspaper properties, the Harrisburg "Patriot" and "Evening News." It was at the editorial desk that he found the greatest satisfaction and his personality was strongly reflected in his publications. His papers were clean, vigorous and influential. He was a life-long Democrat but he broke with the New Deal and opposed the third term. His strong personal feelings and convictions always assured a marked degree of independence. He liked a good fight—even when he did not expect to win it.

There could never be any question of his unselfish devotion to what he deemed the public interest. That was reflected in both his political and his journalistic careers.

From Scranton Times

Vance C. McCormick, publisher of The Harrisburg *Patriot* and *The Evening News,* who died yesterday had a career which ranged from Democratic national committeeman. He was described as "a rugged independent in politics" and, it might be added an unashamed and militant prohibitionist.

Although he had directed President Woodrow Wilson's second campaign in 1916, when Al Smith was nominated, in 1940 and again in 1944 Mr. McCormick jumped the party traces, refusing to support President Roosevelt for a third and fourth term.

Mr. McCormick came into prominence as a potential state and national leader in the decade 1900–1910. Of an old Dauphin County family, active in financial and community affairs, he served in Harrisburg Council, was elected mayor in a city then, as now, strongly republican. He helped in reorganizing the Democratic State Committee in 1912, was the party's candidate for governor in 1914.

Mr. McCormick's appointment as national chairman in 1916 was a great surprise. Later Mr. McCormick broke with Democratic leaders. Invariably when the wet and dry issue was injected into a campaign he and his newspapers supported the dry candidates and cause. Had he been willing to compromise on the question of principle Mr. McCormick might have gone far in a political way. He preferred, however, to hold to his convictions.

From New York Herald-Tribune

The Democratic party has changed so greatly in character and policy in the last two generations that already the term "Wilson Democrat" has become a political anachronism. There are only a few of them left. Vance C. McCormick, who died in Pennsylvania the other day at the age of seventy-three, was one of the best examples of that earlier Democratic leadership which gave the party its character a quarter of a century ago and is now practically extinct.

Mr. McCormick came out of his Harrisburg newspaper office in 1916 to lead President Wilson's campaign for a second term. But the fact of his service as National Chairman did not turn him into a party wheel horse or deprive him of independence of action. In 1928, when Alfred E. Smith's stand against the Prohibition Amendment modified the Democratic platform adopted at Houston, Mr. McCormick denounced this Democratic strategy and supported Herbert Hoover. Again, in 1940, when the Democrats violated the third-term tradition, Mr. McCormick bolted his party and vigorously campaigned for Wendell L. Willkie. His was a vital, free spirit, completely independent which served the Democratic party loyally when he believed it right, and which had courage to follow its own conscience when he believed it wrong.

---

7. HARRISBURG *PATRIOT,* JUNE 25, 1946

CHARITIES LEFT TRUST FUND
BY Mr. McCORMICK
Income of $100,000 to Be Applied to Needs of Agencies Here
YALE UNIVERSITY TO GET $250,000 BEQUEST
Pine St., Silver Spring Churches Remembered
Along With Employees

Bequests to Harrisburg charities are made in the will of Vance C. McCormick, publisher and former mayor, which was probated yesterday at the Dauphin County Courthouse.

Mr. McCormick, whose death occurred on June 16, left $100,000 in trust, the income from which is to be applied to charities in the city and vicinity as his widow, Mrs. Gertrude Howard McCormick, shall direct.

The sum of $20,000 is left in trust, the income from which is to be used by trustees of Pine Street Presbyterian Church for work among women and girls. This fund is a memorial to Mr. McCormick's mother "in recognition of the great interest taken by her during her lifetime in the work of the Mothers' Meeting" of the church.

A trust fund of $5,000 is left for Silver Spring Church in Cumberland County.

$5000 for State College

Pennsylvania State College, of which Mr. McCormick was a trustee is left $5000, the income from which is to help needy and meritorious students obtain an education.

Yale University is to receive $250,000 after Mrs. McCormick's death, the fund to be used to establish a professorship as a memorial to his father, Henry B. McCormick, of the class of 1852.

There are other bequests to members of his family, to employees of The Patriot and The Evening News with many years of service, and to other employees.

After the death of Mrs. McCormick and his sister, Miss Anne McCormick, the remaining estate is to be held in trust "for such local charitable purposes as certain designated members of the family shall from time to time direct, and after their death as directed by the Dauphin Deposit Trust Company."

Summary of Will

The trust company, one of the executors and trustees, made the following summary of the will and its bequests:

"The will of Vance C. McCormick was today offered for probate in the Office of the Register of Wills of Dauphin County. Under the will, Gertrude Howard McCormick (Mrs. Vance C. McCormick), Conway H. Olmsted and Dauphin Deposit Trust Company are named executors and trustees. Mr. McCormick leaves various farms and other pieces of real estate, the contents of his homes and similar articles to Mrs. McCormick. She is also named to receive the income from the residuary estate for life.

"Miss Anne McCormick is to receive Mr. McCormick's undivided interest in property 301 North Front Street and the contents, and the sum of $25,000. Miss McCormick is also to receive the income from the residuary estate if she shall survive Mrs. McCormick.

Bequest to Relatives

"The following bequests are given to other relatives: Henry M. Gross, cousin, $20,000; John Campbell, Jr., and Edward G. Campbell, sons of Hannah Gross Campbell, deceased cousin, each the sum of $10,000. Mrs. Spencer G. Nauman, Mrs. Olmsted Houghton, Conway H. Olmsted and Henry C. Olmsted each the sum of $10,000. Each of the children of the above four of whom there are eight, is to receive the sum of $5,000.

"The following employees of the Patriot Company are given the amount set opposite their respective names 'in appreciation of the long and faithful service rendered by the following employees of The Patriot Company, the average length of employment which is in excess of twenty years.'

"Charles H. Morrison, $10,000; Homer Mover, $8,000; Dean Hoffman, $6,000; V. Hummel Berghaus and Carl Sprout each $5,000; Charles G.

Miller, A. S. Hamman, L. C. Lightner, David Fair, E. A. Doepke, Jr., Benj. F. Lantz, John L. Fetterhoff, Lewis H. Zarker, John W. Troup, Lewis B. Neidhammer and W. Henry Wilson, each $1,000; C. William Britsch, $750; Mrs. Jean D. Miller, $500; James A. Titzes, $500.

"To Hazel S. Snyder and Karl F. Achenbach the sum of $100 for each year they have been in Mr. McCormick's employ.

Servants Given Bequest

"To each chauffeur, the head gardener and each household servant who has been in the employ of Mr. McCormick for 10 years or more, the sum of $1,000, and to each other household servant who has been employed for less than that period lesser amounts.

"The remainder of the estate is left for charitable purposes:

"Five thousand dollars to Pennsylvania State College 'to use and apply the net income therefrom in assisting needy and meritorious students to obtain an education at said college.'

"One hundred thousand dollars in trust with Dauphin Deposit Trust Company to apply the income to 'charities located within the said City of Harrisburg and/or administered for charitable purposes in said city and vicinity' as Mrs. McCormick may from time to time direct, and after her death as Miss Anne McCormick shall direct, and after her death as the trustees shall deem proper.

Bequest to Pine Street

"Twenty thousand dollars in trust with Dauphin Deposit Trust Company, to pay the net income to the Trustees of the Presbyterian Church of Harrisburg (Pine Street Presbyterian Church) for work among women and girls. This is given as a memorial to Mr. McCormick's mother, Annie C. McCormick 'in recognition of the great interest taken by her during her lifetime in the work of the Mothers' Meeting of said Church.'

"Five thousand dollars in trust with Dauphin Deposit Trust Company to pay the net income therefrom [to] the Trustees of the Silver Spring Church of Cumberland County, Pennsylvania.'

"Two thousand dollars in trust with Dauphin Deposit Trust Company to be used for maintenance of cemetery lots in Harrisburg Cemetery to the extent necessary, and otherwise for general charitable purposes.

Yale Scholarship Fund

"Two hundred and fifty thousand dollars is given to Yale University after Mrs. McCormick's death to establish a professorship as a memorial to Mr. McCormick's father, Henry McCormick, of the Class of 1852.

"After the death of both Mrs. McCormick and Miss Anne McCormick, the remaining estate is to be held in trust for such local charitable purposes as certain designated members of the family shall from time to time direct, and after their death as directed by Dauphin Deposit Trust Company."

---

8. HARRISBURG *PATRIOT,* JUNE 27, 1946

EDITORIAL TRIBUTES TO
VANCE C. McCORMICK

Additional editorial tributes to Vance C. McCormick which have appeared in Pennsylvania newspapers since his death on June 16 follow:

From Somerset American

In Yale, where he took his college course, Vance McCormick took an active part in athletics and rose to stardom on the grid-iron.

Returning to Harrisburg, where there was an opportunity for leadership in civic improvement, he stepped to the fore and began the movement which lifted Harrisburg out of the mud into the model city class with beautiful paved streets

Mr. McCormick was a conscientious churchman. He was abstemious in his habits. He encouraged similar habits in others.

When church people complained about the barroom of an important hotel, Mr. McCormick quietly purchased the hotel and closed the barroom. There was no publicity given his deed. He wanted no notoriety, but words of appreciation were passed from lips to ears until the whole city knew the story.

Genial, democratic, keenly alive, he was a brilliant conversationalist and a courteous listener.

The world is better because Vance McCormick lived in it. He set an example worthy of emulation to the generations which have followed him. He was too young to die, only 74. Such men are always too young to die.

From Oil City Derrick

In the death of Vance Criswell McCormick the state of Pennsylvania has lost a solid citizen. Mr. McCormick was publisher of the Harrisburg *Patriot* and the *Evening News.* He was born in that city 74 years ago and was a graduate of Yale and Dickinson.

Politically Vance McCormick had a splendid career. He was chairman of the Democratic National Committee in 1916 when Woodrow Wilson was elected for a second term. He served one term as mayor of Harrisburg and ran for governor of Pennsylvania in 1914. He was chairman of the War Trade Board from 1917 to 1919, and a member of the war mission to Britain and France. He was an adviser to President Wilson in the peace negotiations. He served as a director of the Federal Reserve Bank, was a member of the Yale corporation, was a trustee of Pennsylvania State College and president of the Board of Harrisburg Academy.

Early in the Roosevelt administration Vance McCormick saw the dangers which were being created and his interest in the Democratic party diminished. He was valued in the state capital because of his leadership in church and civic affairs. He was one of the constructive figures in both of the Wilson administrations, and he and the late A. Mitchell Palmer, who served for a time as U.S. attorney general, did much for Pennsylvania when they were politically capable of doing so.

Vance McCormick's newspapers are reflexes of his character. They are clean, well-edited and constructive. His death is a distinct loss to the Pennsylvania newspaper industry.

From Altoona Tribune

Vance C. McCormick, Harrisburg newspaper publisher who died the other day, was one of Pennsylvania's most brilliant sons.

Mr. McCormick played a vital role in American history during and after World War I. He was a confidante of President Woodrow Wilson. He served as chairman of the World War I war trade board, and he represented the President at the inter-Allied blockade commission and later as a member of the supreme economic council and the reparations commission.

He had a great career that started early, when he was named all-America fullback while captain of the Yale football team in 1892.

Mr. McCormick started his political career on the Harrisburg common council, and later served as the city's mayor. At about the same time, he bought the Harrisburg Morning Patriot to support his continuous fight against vice and political corruption.

As a newspaper publisher, he was constantly aware of the vital part his papers, the Patriot and Evening News, played in the life of the community and he made of them great public servants.

His influence will be greatly missed.

From Allentown Call

The death in Harrisburg of Vance McCormick removes one of the leading newspaper publishers not alone of this State but of the United States. For decades the name McCormick has associated favorably with journalism in Pennsylvania. Allentown for years had a daily published by a kinsman and Reading later enjoyed the lively and intelligent approach to news which has been characteristic of the members of this family.

But Harrisburg for the longest time has felt the McCormick influence which in turn has radiated to so many points in the State and nation. That influence has been pronounced in politics and in matters designed to promote the public welfare.

Pennsylvania has lost a splendid citizen and newspaperdom a great publisher.

From Wilkes-Barre Times-Leader-Evening News

As publisher of the Harrisburg Patriot, Vance McCormick wielded no little influence in the State capital and throughout the Commonwealth. A flair for politics made him a powerful figure on the national scene as well.

Mr. McCormick became interested in public affairs early in life. He was not content to be a mere observer; he was an active participant, both as an office holder and as a leader of his party. As chairman of the Democratic National Committee, he was credited largely with the triumph of Woodrow Wilson in the latter's second campaign. Thus, Mr. McCormick had a hand in shaping the destiny of the world.

While an ambition to be Governor of Pennsylvania was not realized, Mr. McCormick was numbered among the State's first citizens by virtue of the role he played. His death at 74 writes finis to a career of great distinction.

From Williamsport Sun

In the death of Vance C. McCormick, publisher of The Harrisburg Patriot and The Evening News, Pennsylvania loses one of its useful citizens.

Mr. McCormick exemplified the best in civic spirit and in political interest. He made of his newspapers strongly influential instruments for the betterment of his community. The circumstance that his publications originate in the state capital has made them valuable as observers of the state government in action. Because they have differed from the state administration in political preference during all but four of the years of Mr. McCormick's ownership, his newspapers have had a special value in this respect.

It is a measure of Mr. McCormick's fine appreciation of the proper extent to which political sympathies should be served that he did not allow partisanship to run rampant. When he directed criticism, it was of a constructive sort, backed by a full sense of responsibility. He aimed it with equal vigor and impartiality at his own party, in which he was nationally prominent, as well as at the opposition.

From Carlisle Sentinel

Vance C. McCormick won fame early in life through his championship football playing at Yale, but his first leadership in politics and in civic affairs came when he was elected mayor of Harrisburg in 1902. This marked the beginning of Harrisburg as a modern city, making it worthy of being the Capital of the State. His newspaper publishing interest grew out of his desire to publicize and win support for his reform measures in Harrisburg. * * * He had a wide variety of interests—religious, social, political, industrial and agricultural—so that he had a great many acquaintances and most of these were his friends. Because of his high personal character, his wide public service and his great business success he stood as one of the foremost citizens of Pennsylvania.

BIBLIOGRAPHY

Books

Ambrosius, Lloyd E. *Woodrow Wilson and the American Diplomatic Tradition: The Treaty Fight in Perspective.* Cambridge: Cambridge University Press, 1987.

————. *Wilsonianism: Woodrow Wilson and His Legacy in American Foreign Relations.* New York: Palgrave, 2002.

Bane, Suda Lorena, and Ralph Haswell Lutz, eds. *The Blockade of Germany after the Armistice, 1918–1919: Selected Documents of the Supreme Economic Council, American Relief Administrations, and Other Wartime Organizations.* New York: Howard Fertig, 1972.

Barton, Michael. *Life by the Moving Road: An Illustrated History of Greater Harrisburg.* Woodland Hills, CA: Windsor Publications, 1983. Second revised edition published as *An Illustrated History of Greater Harrisburg: Life by the Moving Road.* Sun Valley, CA: American Historical Press, 1998.

Baruch, Bernard M. *The Making of the Reparation and Economic Sections of the Treaty.* New York: Harper & Brothers, 1920.

Beers, Paul B. *Profiles from the Susquehanna Valley.* Harrisburg, PA: Stackpole Books, 1973.

Boyd's Directory of Harrisburg and Steelton. Harrisburg: W. H. Boyd, 1917.

Caroli, Betty Boyd. *The Roosevelt Women.* New York: Basic Books, 1998.

Coit, Margaret L. *Mr. Baruch.* Boston: Houghton Mifflin, 1957.

Crist, Robert Grant, ed. *The First Century: A History of the 28th Infantry Division.* Harrisburg, PA: Stackpole Books, 1979.

Crowell, Benedict, and Robert Forrest Wilson. *The Road to France.* Vol. 2, *The Transportation of Troops and Military Supplies, 1917–1918.* New Haven, CT: Yale University Press, 1921.

Daniels, Josephus. *The Wilson Era: Years of War and After, 1917–1923.* Chapel Hill: University of North Carolina Press, 1946.

DeConde, Alexander, ed. *Encyclopedia of American Foreign Policy: Studies of the Principal Movements and Ideas,* vol. 3. New York: Scribner, 1978.

Desmond, Adrian, and James Moore. *Darwin.* New York: Warner Books, 1991.

391

Desmond, Robert W. *Windows on the World: The Information Process in a Changing Society, 1900–1920.* Iowa City: University of Iowa Press, 1980.

Eggert, Gerald G. *Harrisburg Industrializes: The Coming of Factories to an American Community.* University Park, PA: Penn State Press, 1993.

Farrar, Marjorie Milbank. *Conflict and Compromise: The Strategy, Politics and Diplomacy of the French Blockade, 1914–1918.* The Hague: Martinus Nikhoff, 1974.

Findling, John E. *Dictionary of American Diplomatic History.* 2nd ed. New York: Greenwood Press, 1989.

Flanders, Stephen A., and Carl N. Flanders. *Dictionary of American Foreign Affairs.* New York: MacMillan, 1993.

Fleming, Peter. *The Fate of Admiral Kolchak.* London: Rupert Hart-Davis, 1963.

Foreign Relations of the United States: Paris Peace Conference 1919, vol. 3. Washington, D.C.: Department of State, 1958.

Gavin, Lettie. *American Women in World War I: They Also Served.* Niwotz, CO: University of Colorado Press, 1997.

Godcharles, Frederic. *Pennsylvania: Political, Government, Military and Civil.* New York: American Historical Society, n.d.

Gatzke, Hans W. *European Diplomacy between Two Wars, 1919–1939.* Chicago: Quadrangle Books, 1972.

Haskins, Charles H., and Robert H. Lord. *Some Problems of the Peace Conference.* Boston: Harvard University Press, 1920.

Hoffman, Dean. *Smashing the Homefront.* N.p.: January 1917. Revised December 1926.

Hoover, Herbert. *The Memoirs of Herbert Hoover: Years of Adventure, 1874–1920.* New York: MacMillan Company, 1951.

House, Edward M. *The Intimate Papers of Colonel House.* Boston: Houghton Mifflin Company, 1926.

House, Edward Mandell, and Charles Seymour, ed. *What Really Happened at the Paris: The Peace Conference.* New York: Charles Scribner's Sons, 1921.

Hurley, Edward Nash. *Bridge to France.* Philadelphia: J. B. Lippincott, 1927.

Johnson, Owen. *Stover at Yale.* Boston: Little and Brown, 1911.

———. *Stover at Yale.* Introd. by Kingman Brewster, Jr. New York: Collier Books, 1968 (orig. ed. 1911).

Johnson, Paul. *A History of the American People.* New York: Harper-Collins, 1997.

Keegan, John. *The First World War.* New York: Alfred Knopf, 1998.

Kelker, Luther Reily. *History of Dauphin County.* 3 vols. New York: Lewis Publishing Co., 1907.

Kennan, George F. *Russia Leaves the War.* Princeton: Princeton University Press, 1956.

Keylor, William R., ed. *The Legacy of the Great War: Peacemaking, 1919.* Boston: Houghton Mifflin, 1998.

Lamont, Thomas William. "Reparations." In *What Really Happened at Paris: The Story of the Peace Conference, 1918–1919,* edited by Edward Mandell House and Charles Seymour. New York: Charles Scribner's Sons, 1921.

Lansing, Robert. *The Peace Negotiations: A Personal Narrative.* New York: Houghton Mifflin Co., 1921.

Lederer, Ivo J., ed. *The Versailles Settlement: Was It Foredoomed to Failure?* Lexington, MA: D. C. Heath and Co., 1960.

Link, Arthur S., ed. *The Deliberations of the Council of Four, March 24–June 28, 1919: Notes of the Official Interpreter.* Princeton, NJ: Princeton University Press, 1992.

MacMillan, Margaret. *Paris 1919: Six Months That Changed the World.* New York: Random House, 2001.

Mayer, Arno J. *Politics and Diplomacy of Peacemaking: Containment and Counterrevolution at Versailles, 1918–1919.* New York: Alfred A. Knopf, 1967.

McCormick, Vance. *Diary of Vance C. McCormick: Adviser to President Wilson at Peace Conference in Paris.* Privately printed, n.d.

Meehan, Susan. *The New Way: Greeks Come to Carlisle, Pennsylvania.* Carlisle, PA: Cumberland County Historical Society, 2003.

New York Times Current History: The European War, vol. 18. New York: New York Times, 1919.

Noble, George Gernard. *Policies and Opinions at Paris, 1919: Wilsonian Diplomacy, the Versailles Peace, and French Public Opinion.* New York: Howard Fertig, 1968.

O'Brien, Francis William, ed. *Two Peacemakers in Paris: The Hoover-Wilson Post-Armistice Letters, 1918–1920.* College Station: Texas A&M University Press, 1978.

Palmer, Frederick. *Bliss, Peacemaker: The Life and Letters of General Tasker Howard Bliss.* New York: Dodd, Mead, 1934.

Seymour, Charles. *Intimate Papers of Colonel House.* 4 vols. Boston: Houghton Miflin Company, 1926.

———. *Letters from the Paris Peace Conference.* New Haven, CT: Yale University Press, 1965.

Standish, Burt L. (*pseud.*) *Frank Merriwell at Yale, or Playing a Square Game.* New York: Street and Smith, 1897.

Standish, Burt L. (*pseud.*) *Frank Merriwell at Yale Again; or Battling for the Blue.* New York: Street and Smith, 1899.

Tang, Peter S. H. *Russian and Soviet Policy in Manchuria and Outer Mongolia, 1911–1931.* Durham, NC: Duke University Press, 1959.

Thompson, John M. *Russia, Bolshevism and the Versailles Peace.* Princeton, NJ: Princeton University Press, 1966.

Tucker, Spencer C., ed. *The European Powers in the First World War: An Encyclopedia.* New York: Garland, 1996.

Venzon, Anne Cipriano, ed. *The United States in the First World War: An Encyclopedia.* New York: Garland, 1995.

Walworth, Arthur. *Wilson and His Peacemakers: American Diplomacy at the Paris Peace Conference, 1919.* New York: W. W. Norton & Company, 1986.

Wheatley, Henry B. *London Past and Present: A History of Its History, Associations and Traditions.* London: John Murray, 1891. Reprint. Detroit: Singing Tree Press, 1968.

Wilson, Edith Bolling. *My Memoir.* Indianapolis: Bobbs-Merrill, 1938.

Wilson, Woodrow. *The Papers of Woodrow Wilson,* vol. 60. Princeton, NJ: Princeton University Press, 1989.

Journal Articles

Branch, Mark Alden. "The Ten Greatest Yalies Who Never Were." *Yale Alumni Magazine,* February, 2003, online at http://www.yalealumnimagazine.com/issues/03_02/fictional.html

Clark, Thomas. "Cleaning Up Harrisburg: The Good Government Reforms of Mayor Vance C. McCormick, 1902–1903." *Susquehanna Heritage* 1 (Summer 2003): 8–40.

DeAngelis, Margaret. "William McCormick, Friend of Youth." *Historical Review of Berks County* 61 (Summer 1996): 114–16, 135.

Murphy, Emily. "'I Am Raising Boys . . . Not Grass': The McCormick Homes in Central Pennsylvania." *Susquehanna Heritage* 1 (Summer 2003): 97–108.

Shirk, Willis. "William McCormick's Estate Papers, 1805." *Cumberland County History* 12 (Summer 1995): 36–56.

Steel, Ronald. "The Missionary." *New York Review of Books* (November 20, 2003): 26–28, 35.

Titzel, Art. "The Ablest Navigator: The Rise of Vance McCormick in the Wilson Years." *Susquehanna Heritage* 1 (Summer 2003): 41–76.

Toddes, LeRoy W. "Vance McCormick's Relationship with Woodrow Wilson: A View through Their Correspondence." *Cumberland County History* 9 (Winter 1992): 69–91.

Tuma, Gary. "William McCormick's Work with Working Boys." *Susquehanna Heritage* 1 (Summer 2003): 77–96.

Newspapers

"Clemenceau Picks Radical Cabinet." *New York Times.* November 17, 1917, 1+.

Harrisburg Patriot, January–March, 1919.

"Hoover Picks Aid in London." *New York Times.* September 1, 1917, 16.

"Jonnart Returns for Conference." *New York Times.* July 10, 1917, 3.

"L. McCormick-Goodheart, 81, British Embassy Counselor." *New York Times.* December 18, 1965, 30.

"The Saving Grace." *London Times.* October 11, 1917, 11E.

Websites

Americans Living in Paris.
http://library.thinkquest.org/25909/html/content/notable_american_volunteers.html.

Captain Evans and the Battle of Dover Straits.
http://www.naval-history.net/NAVAL1914-18.htm.

McCormick Family Papers website:
http://www.hbg.psu.edu/hum/McCormick/index2.htm.

Reparations Committee.
http://www.lib.byu.edu/~rdh/wwi/versa/versa7.html.

Versailles Treaty.
http://history.acusd.edu/gen/text/versaillestreaty/vercontents.html, and
http://www.nv.cc.va.us/home/cevans/Versailles.

War Trade Board.
http://www.nara.gov/guide/rg182.html.

World War I.
http://www.spartacus.schoolnet.co.uk/,
http://www.worldwar1.com/dbc/ct_vaux/htm, and
http://www.ku.edu/~libsite/wwi-www/Rodd/Rodd12.htm.

INDEX